The Richard Hanny Collection

Volume II

The Three Hostages
The Island of Sheep

By

John Buchan

British Library Cataloguing-in-Publication Data
A catalogue record for this book is available from the
British Library

John Buchan

John Buchan, first Baron Tweedsmuir of Elsfield, was born in Perth, Scotland in 1875. In his youth, his father immersed him in the history, legends and myths of Scotland, and he was an avid reader, stating some years later that John Bunyan's *The Pilgrim's Progress* was a "constant companion" to him. Buchan's education was uneven, but at the age of seventeen he obtained a scholarship to study classics at Glasgow University, where he began to write poetry. His first work, *The Essays and Apothegms of Francis Lord Bacon*, was published in 1894, and a year later he enrolled at Oxford University to study law.

In 1900, Buchan moved to London, and two years later accepted a civil service post in South Africa. In the years leading up to World War I, he worked at a publishers, and also wrote *Prester John* (1910) – which later became a school reader, translated into many languages – as well as a number of biographies. In 1915, Buchan become a war correspondent for *The Times*, and published his most well-known book, the thriller *The Thirty-Nine Steps.* After the war he became a director of the news agency Reuters.

Over the course of his life, Buchan would eventually publish some one hundred books, forty or so of which were novels, mostly wartime thrillers. In the latter part of his life he worked in politics, serving as Conservative MP for the Scottish universities and Lord High Commissioner of the Church of Scotland (1933-34). In 1935, Buchan moved to Canada, where he became the thirty-fifth Governor General of Canada. He died in 1940, aged 64.

Contents

The Three Hostages

The Island of Sheep

PART I. Fosse

PART II. Laverlaw

PART III. The Island of Sheep

The Three Hostages

By

John Buchan

DEDICATION

To a Young Gentleman of Eton College

HONOURED SIR,

On your last birthday a well-meaning godfather presented you with a volume of mine, since you had been heard on occasion to express approval of my works. The book dealt with a somewhat arid branch of historical research, and it did not please you. You wrote to me, I remember, complaining that I had "let you down," and summoning me, as I valued your respect, to "pull myself together." In particular you demanded to hear more of the doings of Richard Hannay, a gentleman for whom you professed a liking. I, too, have a liking for Sir Richard, and when I met him the other day (he is now a country neighbour) I observed that his left hand had been considerably mauled, an injury which I knew had not been due to the War. He was so good as to tell me the tale of an unpleasant business in which he had recently been engaged, and to give me permission to retell it for your benefit. Sir Richard took a modest pride in the affair, because from first to last it had been a pure contest of wits, without recourse to those more obvious methods of strife with which he is familiar. So I herewith present it to you, in the hope that in the eyes of you and your friends it may atone for certain other writings of mine with which you have been afflicted by those in authority.

J.B.

June, 1924.

CHAPTER I

DOCTOR GREENSLADE THEORISES

That evening, I remember, as I came up through the Mill Meadow, I was feeling peculiarly happy and contented. It was still mid- March, one of those spring days when noon is like May, and only the cold pearly haze at sunset warns a man that he is not done with winter. The season was absurdly early, for the blackthorn was in flower and the hedge roots were full of primroses. The partridges were paired, the rooks were well on with their nests, and the meadows were full of shimmering grey flocks of fieldfares on their way north. I put up half a dozen snipe on the boggy edge of the stream, and in the bracken in Sturn Wood I thought I saw a woodcock, and hoped that the birds might nest with us this year, as they used to do long ago. It was jolly to see the world coming to life again, and to remember that this patch of England was my own, and all these wild things, so to speak, members of my little household.

As I say, I was in a very contented mood, for I had found something I had longed for all my days. I had bought Fosse Manor just after the War as a wedding present for Mary, and for two and a half years we had been settled there. My son, Peter John, was rising fifteen months, a thoughtful infant, as healthy as a young colt and as comic as a terrier puppy. Even Mary's anxious eye could scarcely detect in him any symptoms of decline.

But the place wanted a lot of looking to, for it had run wild during the War, and the woods had to be thinned, gates and fences repaired, new drains laid, a ram put in to supplement the wells, a heap of thatching to be done, and the garden borders to be brought back to cultivation. I had got through the worst of it, and as I came out of the Home Wood on to the lower lawns and saw the old stone gables that the monks had built, I felt that I was anchored at last in the pleasantest kind of harbour.

There was a pile of letters on the table in the hall, but I let them be, for I was not in the mood for any communication with the outer world. As I was having a hot bath Mary kept giving me the news through her bedroom door. Peter John had been raising Cain over a first tooth; the new shorthorn cow was drying off; old George Whaddon had got his granddaughter back from service; there was a new brood of runner-ducks; there was a missel-thrush building in the box hedge by the lake. A chronicle of small beer, you will say, but I was by a long chalk more interested in it than in what might be happening in Parliament or Russia or the Hindu Kush. The fact is I was becoming such a mossback that I had almost stopped reading the papers. Many a day The Times would remain unopened, for Mary never looked at anything but the first page to see who was dead or married. Not that I didn't read a lot, for I used to spend my evenings digging into county history, and learning all I could about the old fellows who had been my predecessors. I liked to think that I lived in a place that had been continuously inhabited for a thousand years. Cavalier and Roundhead had fought over the countryside, and I was becoming a considerable authority on their tiny battles. That was about the only interest I had left in soldiering.

As we went downstairs, I remember we stopped to look out of the long staircase window which showed a segment of lawn, a corner of the lake, and through a gap in the woods a vista of green downland. Mary squeezed my arm. "What a blessed country," she said. "Dick, did you ever dream of such peace? We're lucky, lucky people."

Then suddenly her face changed in that way she has and grew very grave. I felt a little shiver run along her arm.

"It's too good and beloved to last," she whispered. "Sometimes I am afraid."

"Nonsense," I laughed. "What's going to upset it? I don't believe in being afraid of happiness." I knew very well, of course, that Mary couldn't be afraid of anything.

She laughed too. "All the same I've got what the Greek called aidos. You don't know what that means, you old savage. It means that you feel you must walk humbly and delicately to propitiate the Fates. I wish I knew how."

She walked too delicately, for she missed the last step and our descent ended in an undignified shuffle right into the arms of Dr. Greenslade.

Paddock--I had got Paddock back after the War and he was now my butler--was helping the doctor out of his ulster, and I saw by the satisfied look on the latter's face that he was through with his day's work and meant to stay to dinner. Here I had better introduce Tom Greenslade, for of all my recent acquaintances he was the one I had most taken to. He was a long lean fellow with a stoop in his back from bending over the handles of motor-bicycles, with reddish hair, and the greeny-blue eyes and freckled skin that often accompany that kind of hair. From his high cheek bones and his colouring you would have set him down as a Scotsman, but as a matter of fact he came from Devonshire--Exmoor, I think, though he had been so much about the world that he had almost forgotten where he was raised. I have travelled a bit, but nothing to Greenslade. He had started as a doctor in a whaling ship. Then he had been in the South African War and afterwards a temporary magistrate up Lydenburg way. He soon tired of that, and was for a long spell in Uganda and German East, where he became rather a swell on tropical diseases, and nearly perished through experimenting on himself with fancy inoculations. Then he was in South America, where he had a good practice in Valparaiso, and then in the Malay States, where he made a bit of money in the rubber boom. There was a gap of three years after that when he was wandering about Central Asia, partly with a fellow called Duckett exploring Northern Mongolia, and partly in Chinese Tibet hunting for new flowers, for he was mad about botany. He came home in the summer of 1914, meaning to do some laboratory research work, but the War swept him up and he went to France as M.O. of a territorial battalion. He got wounded of course, and after a spell in hospital went out to Mesopotamia, where he stayed till the Christmas of 1918, sweating hard at his job but managing to tumble into a lot of varied adventures, for he was at Baku with Dunsterville and got as far as Tashkend, where the Bolsheviks shut him up for a fortnight in a bath-house. During the War he had every kind of sickness, for he missed no experience, but nothing seemed to damage permanently his whipcord physique. He told me that his heart and lungs and blood pressure were as good as a lad's of twenty-one, though by this time he was on the wrong side of forty.

But when the War was over he hankered for a quiet life, so he bought a practice in the deepest and greenest corner of England. He said his motive was the same as that which in the rackety Middle Ages made men retire into monasteries; he wanted quiet and leisure to consider his soul. Quiet he may have found, but uncommon little leisure, for I never heard of a country doctor that toiled at his job as he did. He would pay three visits a day to a panel patient, which shows the kind of fellow he was; and he would be out in the small hours at the birth of a gipsy child under a hedge. He was a first-class man in his profession, and kept abreast of it, but doctoring was only one of a thousand interests. I never met a chap with such an insatiable curiosity about everything in heaven and earth. He lived in two rooms in a farmhouse some four miles from us, and I dare say he had several thousand books about him. All day, and often half the night, he would scour the country in his little run-about car, and yet, when he would drop in to see me and have a drink after maybe twenty visits, he was as full of beans as if he had just got out of bed. Nothing came amiss to him in talk-- birds, beasts, flowers, books, politics, religion--everything in the world except himself. He was the best sort of company, for behind all his quickness and cleverness, you felt that he was solid bar-gold. But for him I should have taken root in the soil and put out shoots, for I have a fine natural talent for vegetating. Mary strongly approved of him and Peter John adored him.

He was in tremendous spirits that evening, and for once in a way gave us reminiscences of his past. He told us about the people he badly wanted to see again; an Irish Spaniard up in the north of the Argentine who had for cattle-men a most murderous brand of native from the mountains, whom he used to keep in good humour by arranging fights every Sunday, he himself taking on the survivor with his fists and always knocking him out; a Scots trader from Hankow who had turned Buddhist priest and intoned his prayers with a strong Glasgow accent; and most of all a Malay pirate, who, he said, was a sort of St. Francis with beasts, though a perfect Nero with his fellow-men. That took him to Central Asia, and he observed that if ever he left England again he would make for those parts, since they were the refuge of all the superior rascality of creation. He had a notion that something very odd might happen there in the long run. "Think of it!" he cried. "All the places with names like spells--Bokhara, Samarkand--run by seedy little gangs of communist Jews. It won't go on for ever. Some day a new Genghis Khan or a Timour will be thrown up out of the maelstrom. Europe is confused enough, but Asia is ancient Chaos."

After dinner we sat round the fire in the library, which I had modelled on Sir Walter Bullivant's room in his place on the Kennet, as I had promised myself seven years ago. I had meant it for my own room where I could write and read and smoke, but Mary would not allow it. She had a jolly panelled sitting-room of her own upstairs, which she rarely entered; but though I chased her away, she was like a hen in a garden and always came back, so that presently she had staked out a claim on the other side of my writing-table. I have the old hunter's notion of order, but it was useless to strive with Mary, so now my desk was littered with her letters and needlework, and Peter John's toys and picture-books were stacked in the cabinet where I kept my fly-books, and Peter John himself used to make a kraal every morning inside an upturned stool on the hearth-rug.

It was a cold night and very pleasant by the fireside, where some scented logs from an old pear-tree were burning. The doctor picked up a detective novel I had been reading, and glanced at the title- page.

"I can read most things," he said, "but it beats me how you waste time over such stuff. These shockers are too easy, Dick. You could invent better ones for yourself."

"Not I. I call that a dashed ingenious yarn. I can't think how the fellow does it."

"Quite simple. The author writes the story inductively, and the reader follows it deductively. Do you see what I mean?"

"Not a bit," I replied.

"Look here. I want to write a shocker, so I begin by fixing on one or two facts which have no sort of obvious connection."

"For example?"

"Well, imagine anything you like. Let us take three things a long way apart--" He paused for a second to consider--"say, an old blind woman spinning in the Western Highlands, a barn in a Norwegian saeter, and a little curiosity shop in North London kept by a Jew with a dyed beard. Not much connection between the three? You invent a connection--simple enough if you have any imagination, and you weave all three into the yarn. The reader, who knows nothing about the three at the start, is puzzled and intrigued and, if the story is well arranged, finally satisfied. He is pleased with the ingenuity of the solution, for he doesn't realise that the author fixed upon the solution first, and then invented a problem to suit it."

"I see," I said. "You've gone and taken the gilt off my favourite light reading. I won't be able any more to marvel at the writer's cleverness."

"I've another objection to the stuff--it's not ingenious enough, or rather it doesn't take account of the infernal complexity of life. It might have been all right twenty years ago, when most people argued and behaved fairly logically. But they don't nowadays. Have you ever realised, Dick, the amount of stark craziness that the War has left in the world?"

Mary, who was sitting sewing under a lamp, raised her head and laughed.

Greenslade's face had become serious. "I can speak about it frankly here, for you two are almost the only completely sane people I know. Well, as a pathologist, I'm fairly staggered. I hardly meet a soul who hasn't got some slight kink in his brain as a consequence of the last seven years. With most people it's rather a pleasant kink--they're less settled in their grooves, and they see the comic side of things quicker, and are readier for adventure. But with some it's pukka madness, and that means crime. Now, how are you going to write detective stories about that kind of world on the old lines? You can take nothing for granted, as you once could, and your argus-eyed, lightning-brained expert has nothing solid with which to build his foundations."

I observed that the poor old War seemed to be getting blamed for a good deal that I was taught in my childhood was due to original sin.

"Oh, I'm not questioning your Calvinism. Original sin is always there, but the meaning of civilisation was that we had got it battened down under hatches, whereas now it's getting its head up. But it isn't only sin. It's a dislocation of the mechanism of human reasoning, a general loosening of screws. Oddly enough, in spite of parrot-talk about shell-shock, the men who fought suffer less from it on the whole than other people. The classes that shirked the War are the worst--you see it in Ireland. Every doctor nowadays has got to be a bit of a mental pathologist. As I say, you can hardly take anything for granted, and if you want detective stories that are not childish fantasy you'll have to invent a new kind. Better try your hand, Dick."

"Not I. I'm a lover of sober facts."

"But, hang it, man, the facts are no longer sober. I could tell you--" He paused and I was expecting a yarn, but he changed his mind.

"Take all this chatter about psycho-analysis. There's nothing very new in the doctrine, but people are beginning to work it out into details, and making considerable asses of themselves in the process. It's an awful thing when a scientific truth becomes the quarry of the half-baked. But as I say, the fact of the subconscious self is as certain as the existence of lungs and arteries."

"I don't believe that Dick has any subconscious self," said Mary.

"Oh yes, he has. Only, people who have led his kind of life have their ordinary self so well managed and disciplined--their wits so much about them, as the phrase goes--that the subconscious rarely gets a show. But I bet if Dick took to thinking about his soul, which he never does, he would find some queer corners. Take my own case." He turned towards me so that I had a full view of his candid eyes and hungry cheek-bones which looked prodigious in the firelight. "I belong more or less to the same totem as you, but I've long been aware that I possessed a most curious kind of subconsciousness. I've a good memory and fair powers of observation, but they're nothing to those of my subconscious self. Take any daily incident. I see and hear, say, about a twentieth part of the details and remember about a hundredth part--that is, assuming that there is nothing special to stimulate my interest. But my subconscious self sees and hears practically everything, and remembers most of it. Only I can't use the memory, for I don't know that I've got it, and can't call it into being when I wish. But every now and then something happens to turn on the tap of the subconscious, and a thin trickle comes through. I find myself sometimes remembering names I was never aware of having heard, and little incidents and details I had never consciously noticed. Imagination, you will say; but it isn't, for everything that that inner memory provides is exactly true. I've tested it. If I could only find some way of tapping it at will, I should be an uncommonly efficient fellow. Incidentally I should become the first scientist of the age, for the trouble with investigation and experiment is that the ordinary brain does not observe sufficiently keenly or remember the data sufficiently accurately."

"That's interesting," I said. "I'm not at all certain I haven't noticed the same thing in myself. But what has that to do with the madness that you say is infecting the world?"

"Simply this. The barriers between the conscious and the subconscious have always been pretty stiff in the average man. But now with the general loosening of screws they are growing shaky and the two worlds are getting mixed. It is like two separate tanks of fluid, where the containing wall has worn into holes, and one is percolating into the other. The result is confusion, and, if the fluids are of a certain character, explosions. That is why I say that you can't any longer take the clear psychology of most civilised human beings for granted. Something is welling up from primeval deeps to muddy it."

"I don't object to that," I said. "We've overdone civilisation, and personally I'm all for a little barbarism. I want a simpler world."

"Then you won't get it," said Greenslade. He had become very serious now, and was looking towards Mary as he talked. "The civilised is far simpler than the primeval. All history has been an effort to make definitions, clear rules of thought, clear rules of conduct, solid sanctions, by which we can conduct our life. These are the work of the conscious self. The subconscious is an elementary and lawless thing. If it intrudes on life two results must follow. There will be a weakening of the power of reasoning, which after all is the thing that brings men nearest to the Almighty. And there will be a failure of nerve."

I got up to get a light, for I was beginning to feel depressed by the doctor's diagnosis of our times. I don't know whether he was altogether serious, for he presently started on fishing, which was one of his many hobbies. There was very fair dry-fly fishing to be had in our little river, but I had taken a deer-forest with Archie Roylance for the season, and Greenslade was coming up with me to try his hand at salmon. There had been no sea-trout the year before in the West Highlands, and we fell to discussing the cause. He was ready with a dozen theories, and we forgot about the psychology of mankind in investigating the uncanny psychology of fish. After that Mary sang to us, for I considered any evening a failure without that, and at half-past ten the doctor got into his old ulster and departed.

As I smoked my last pipe I found my thoughts going over Greenslade's talk. I had found a snug harbour, but how yeasty the waters seemed to be outside the bar and how erratic the tides! I wondered if it wasn't shirking to be so comfortable in a comfortless world. Then I reflected that I was owed a little peace, for I had had a roughish life. But Mary's words kept coming back to me about "walking delicately." I considered that my present conduct filled that bill, for I was mighty thankful for my mercies and in no way inclined to tempt Providence by complacency.

Going up to bed, I noticed my neglected letters on the hall table. I turned them over and saw that they were mostly bills and receipts or tradesmen's circulars. But there was one addressed in a handwriting that I knew, and as I looked at it I experienced a sudden sinking of the heart. It was from Lord Artinswell--Sir Walter Bullivant, as was--who had now retired from the Foreign Office, and was living at his place on the Kennet. He and I occasionally corresponded about farming and fishing, but I had a premonition that this was something different. I waited for a second or two before I opened it.

"MY DEAR DICK,

"This note is in the nature of a warning. In the next day or two you will be asked, nay pressed, to undertake a troublesome piece of business. I am not responsible for the request, but I know of it. If you consent, it will mean the end for a time of your happy vegetable life. I don't want to influence you one way or another; I only give you notice of what is coming in order that you may adjust your mind and not be taken by surprise. My love to Mary and the son.

"Yours ever,

"A."

That was all. I had lost my trepidation and felt very angry. Why couldn't the fools let me alone? As I went upstairs I vowed that not all the cajolery in the world would make me budge an inch from the path I had set myself. I had done enough for the public service and other people's interests, and it was jolly well time that I should be allowed to attend to my own.

CHAPTER II

I HEAR OF THE THREE HOSTAGES

There is an odour about a country-house which I love better than any scent in the world. Mary used to say it was a mixture of lamp and dog and wood-smoke, but at Fosse, where there was electric light and no dogs indoors, I fancy it was wood-smoke, tobacco, the old walls, and wafts of the country coming in at the windows. I liked it best in the morning, when there was a touch in it of breakfast cooking, and I used to stand at the top of the staircase and sniff it as I went to my bath. But on the morning I write of I could take no pleasure in it; indeed it seemed to tantalise me with a vision of country peace which had somehow got broken. I couldn't get that confounded letter out of my head. When I read it I had torn it up in disgust, but I found myself going down in my dressing-gown, to the surprise of a housemaid, piecing together the fragments from the waste-paper basket, and reading it again. This time I flung the bits into the new-kindled fire.

I was perfectly resolved that I would have nothing to do with Bullivant or any of his designs, but all the same I could not recapture the serenity which yesterday had clothed me like a garment. I was down to breakfast before Mary, and had finished before she appeared. Then I lit my pipe and started on my usual tour of my domain, but nothing seemed quite the same. It was a soft fresh morning with no frost, and the scillas along the edge of the lake were like bits of summer sky. The moorhens were building, and the first daffodils were out in the rough grass below the clump of Scots firs, and old George Whaddon was nailing up rabbit wire and whistling through his two remaining teeth, and generally the world was as clear and jolly as spring could make it. But I didn't feel any more that it was really mine, only that I was looking on at a pretty picture. Something had happened to jar the harmony between it and my mind, and I cursed Bullivant and his intrusions.

I returned by the front of the house, and there at the door to my surprise stood a big touring Rolls-Royce. Paddock met me in the hall and handed me a card, on which I read the name of Mr. Julius Victor.

I knew it, of course, for the name of one of the richest men in the world, the American banker who had done a lot of Britain's financial business in the War, and was in Europe now at some international conference. I remembered that Blenkiron, who didn't like his race, had once described him to me as "the whitest Jew since the Apostle Paul."

In the library I found a tall man standing by the window looking out at our view. He turned as I entered, and I saw a thin face with a neatly trimmed grey beard, and the most worried eyes I have ever seen in a human countenance. Everything about him was spruce and dapper--his beautifully-cut grey suit, his black tie and pink pearl pin, his blue-and-white linen, his exquisitely polished shoes. But the eyes were so wild and anxious that he looked dishevelled.

"General," he said, and took a step towards me.

We shook hands and I made him sit down.

"I have dropped the 'General,' if you don't mind," I said. "What I want to know is, have you had breakfast?"

He shook his head. "I had a cup of coffee on the road. I do not eat in the morning."

"Where have you come from, sir?" I asked.

"From London."

Well, London is seventy-six miles from us, so he must have started early. I looked curiously at him, and he got out of his chair and began to stride about.

"Sir Richard," he said, in a low pleasant voice which I could imagine convincing any man he tried it on, "you are a soldier and a man of the world and will pardon my unconventionality. My business is too urgent to waste time on apologies. I have heard of you from common friends as a man of exceptional resource and courage. I have been told in confidence something of your record. I have come to implore your help in a desperate emergency."

I passed him a box of cigars, and he took one and lit it carefully. I could see his long slim fingers trembling as he held the match.

"You may have heard of me," he went on. "I am a very rich man, and my wealth has given me power, so that Governments honour me with their confidence. I am concerned in various important affairs, and it would be false modesty to deny that my word is weightier than that of many Prime Ministers. I am labouring, Sir Richard, to secure peace in the world, and consequently I have enemies, all those who would perpetuate anarchy and war. My life has been more than once attempted, but that is nothing. I am well guarded. I am not, I think, more of a coward than other men, and I am prepared to take my chance. But now I have been attacked by a subtler weapon, and I confess I have no defence. I had a son, who died ten years ago at college. My only other child is my daughter, Adela, a girl of nineteen. She came to Europe just before Christmas, for she was to be married in Paris in April. A fortnight ago she was hunting with friends in Northamptonshire--the place is called Rushford Court. On the morning of the 8th of March she went for a walk to Rushford village to send a telegram, and was last seen passing through the lodge gates at twenty-minutes past eleven. She has not been seen since."

"Good God!" I exclaimed, and rose from my chair. Mr. Victor was looking out of the window, so I walked to the other end of the room and fiddled with the books on a shelf. There was silence for a second or two, till I broke it.

"Do you suppose it is loss of memory?" I asked.

"No," he said. "It is not loss of memory. I know--we have proof-- that she has been kidnapped by those whom I call my enemies. She is being held as a hostage."

"You know she is alive?"

He nodded, for his voice was choking again. "There is evidence which points to a very deep and devilish plot. It may be revenge, but I think it more likely to be policy. Her captors hold her as security for their own fate."

"Has Scotland Yard done nothing?"

"Everything that man could do, but the darkness only grows thicker."

"Surely it has not been in the papers. I don't read them carefully but I could scarcely miss a thing like that."

"It has been kept out of the papers--for a reason which you will be told."

"Mr. Victor," I said, "I'm most deeply sorry for you. Like you, I've just the one child, and if anything of that kind happened to him I should go mad. But I shouldn't take too gloomy a view. Miss Adela will turn up all right, and none the worse, though you may have to pay through the nose for it. I expect it's ordinary blackmail and ransom."

"No," he said very quietly. "It is not blackmail, and if it were, I would not pay the ransom demanded. Believe me, Sir Richard, it is a very desperate affair. More, far more is involved than the fate of one young girl. I am not going to touch on that side, for the full story will be told you later by one better equipped to tell it. But the hostage is my daughter, my only child. I have come to beg your assistance in the search for her."

"But I'm no good at looking for things," I stammered. "I'm most awfully sorry for you, but I don't see how I can help. If Scotland Yard is at a loss, it's not likely that an utter novice like me would succeed."

"But you have a different kind of imagination and a rarer kind of courage. I know what you have done before, Sir Richard. I tell you you are my last hope."

I sat down heavily and groaned. "I can't begin to explain to you the bottomless futility of your idea. It is quite truc that in thc War I had somc queer jobs and was lucky enough to bring some of them off. But, don't you see, I was a soldier then, under orders, and it didn't greatly signify whether I lost my life from a crump in the trenches or from a private bullet on the backstairs. I was in the mood for any risk, and my wits were strung up and unnaturally keen. But that's all done with. I'm in a different mood now and my mind is weedy and grass-grown. I've settled so deep into the country that I'm just an ordinary hayseed farmer. If I took a hand--which I certainly won't--I'd only spoil the game."

Mr. Victor stood looking at me intently. I thought for a moment he was going to offer me money, and rather hoped he would, for that would have stiffened me like a ramrod, though it would have spoiled the good notion I had of him. The thought may have crossed his mind, but he was clever enough to reject it.

"I don't agree with a word you say about yourself, and I'm accustomed to size up men. I appeal to you as a Christian gentleman to help me to recover my child. I am not going to press that appeal, for I have already taken up enough of your time. My London address is on my card. Good-bye, Sir Richard, and believe me, I am very grateful to you for receiving me so kindly."

In five minutes he and his Rolls-Royce had gone, and I was left in a miserable mood of shame-faced exasperation. I realised how Mr. Julius Victor had made his fame. He knew how to handle men, for if he had gone on pleading he would only have riled me, whereas he had somehow managed to leave it all to my honour, and thoroughly unsettle my mind.

I went for a short walk, cursing the world at large, sometimes feeling horribly sorry for that unfortunate father, sometimes getting angry because he had tried to mix me up in his affairs. Of course I would not touch the thing; I couldn't; it was manifestly impossible; I had neither the capacity nor the inclination. I was not a professional rescuer of distressed ladies whom I did not know from Eve.

A man, I told myself, must confine his duties to his own circle of friends, except when his country has need of him. I was over forty, and had a wife and a young son to think of; besides, I had chosen a retired life, and had the right to have my choice respected. But I can't pretend that I was comfortable. A hideous muddy wave from the outer world had come to disturb my little sheltered pool. I found Mary and Peter John feeding the swans, and couldn't bear to stop and play with them. The gardeners were digging in sulphates about the fig trees on the south wall, and wanted directions about the young chestnuts in the nursery; the keeper was lying in wait for me in the stable-yard for instructions about a new batch of pheasants' eggs, and the groom wanted me to look at the hocks of Mary's cob. But I simply couldn't talk to any of them. These were the things I loved, but for a moment the gilt was off them, and I would let them wait till I felt better. In a very bad temper I returned to the library.

I hadn't been there two minutes when I heard the sound of a car on the gravel. "Let 'em all come," I groaned, and I wasn't surprised when Paddock entered, followed by the spare figure and smooth keen face of Macgillivray.

I don't think I offered to shake hands. We were pretty good friends, but at that moment there was no one in the world I wanted less to see.

"Well, you old nuisance," I cried, "you're the second visitor from town I've had this morning. There'll be a shortage of petrol soon."

"Have you had a letter from Lord Artinswell?" he asked.

"I have, worse luck," I said.

"Then you know what I've come about. But that can keep till after luncheon. Hurry it up, Dick, like a good fellow, for I'm as hungry as a famished kestrel."

He looked rather like one, with his sharp nose and lean head. It was impossible to be cross for long with Macgillivray, so we went out to look for Mary. "I may as well tell you," I told him, "that you've come on a fool's errand. I'm not going to be jockeyed by you or anyone into making an ass of myself. Anyhow, don't mention the thing to Mary. I don't want her to be worried by your nonsense."

So at luncheon we talked about Fosse and the Cotswolds, and about the deer-forest I had taken--

Machray they called it--and about Sir Archibald Roylance, my co-tenant, who had just had another try at breaking his neck in a steeplechase. Macgillivray was by way of being a great stalker and could tell me a lot about Machray. The crab of the place was its neighbours, it seemed; for Haripol on the south was too steep for the lessee, a middle-aged manufacturer, to do justice to it, and the huge forest of Glenaicill on the east was too big for any single tenant to shoot, and the Machray end of it was nearly thirty miles by road from the lodge. The result was, said Macgillivray, that Machray was surrounded by unauthorised sanctuaries, which made the deer easy to shift. He said the best time was early in the season when the stags were on the upper ground, for it seemed that Machray had uncommonly fine high pastures. . . . Mary was in good spirits, for somebody had been complimentary about Peter John, and she was satisfied for the moment that he wasn't going to be cut off by an early consumption. She was full of housekeeping questions about Machray, and revealed such spacious plans that Macgillivray said that he thought he would pay us a visit, for it looked as if he wouldn't be poisoned, as he usually was in Scotch shooting-lodges. It was a talk I should have enjoyed if there had not been that uneasy morning behind me and that interview I had still to get over.

There was a shower after luncheon, so he and I settled ourselves in the library. "I must leave at three-thirty," he said, "so I have got just a little more than an hour to tell you my business in."

"Is it worth while starting?" I asked. "I want to make it quite plain that under no circumstances am I open to any offer to take on any business of any kind. I'm having a rest and a holiday. I stay here for the summer and then I go to Machray."

"There's nothing to prevent your going to Machray in August," he said, opening his eyes. "The work I am going to suggest to you must be finished long before then."

I suppose that surprised me, for I did not stop him as I had meant to. I let him go on, and before I knew I found myself getting interested. I have a boy's weakness for a yarn, and Macgillivray knew this and played on it.

He began by saying very much what Dr. Greenslade had said the night before. A large part of the world had gone mad, and that involved the growth of inexplicable and unpredictable crime. All the old sanctities had become weakened, and men had grown too well accustomed to death and pain. This meant that the criminal had far greater resources at his command, and, if he were an able man, could mobilise a vast amount of utter recklessness and depraved ingenuity. The moral imbecile, he said, had been more or less a sport before the War; now he was a terribly common product, and throve in batches and battalions. Cruel, humourless, hard, utterly wanting in sense of proportion, but often full of a perverted poetry and drunk with rhetoric--a hideous, untamable breed had been engendered. You found it among the young Bolshevik Jews, among the young gentry of the wilder Communist sects, and very notably among the sullen murderous hobbledehoys in Ireland.

"Poor devils," Macgillivray repeated. "It is for their Maker to judge them, but we who are trying to patch up civilisation have to see that they are cleared out of the world. Don't imagine that they are devotees of any movement, good or bad. They are what I have called them, moral imbeciles, who can be swept into any movement by those who understand them. They are the neophytes and hierophants of crime, and it is as criminals that I have to do with them. Well, all this desperate degenerate stuff is being used by a few clever men who are not degenerates or anything of the sort, but only evil. There has never been such a chance for a rogue since the world began."

Then he told me certain facts, which must remain unpublished, at any rate during our life-times. The main point was that there were sinister brains at work to organise for their own purposes the perilous stuff lying about. All the contemporary anarchisms, he said, were interconnected, and out of the misery of decent folks and the agony of the wretched tools certain smug entrepreneurs were profiting. He and his men, and indeed the whole police force of civilisation--he mentioned especially the Americans--had been on the trail of one of the worst of these combines and by a series of fortunate chances had got their hand on it. Now at any moment they could stretch out that hand and gather it in.

But there was one difficulty. I learned from him that this particular combine was not aware of the danger in which it stood, but that it realised that it must stand in some danger, so it had taken precautions. Since Christmas it had acquired hostages.

Here I interrupted, for I felt rather incredulous about the whole business. "I think since the War we're all too ready to jump at grandiose explanations of simple things. I'll want a good deal of convincing before I believe in your international clearing-house for crime."

"I guarantee the convincing," he said gravely. "You shall see all our evidence, and, unless you have changed since I first knew you, your conclusion won't differ from mine. But let us come to the hostages."

"One I know about," I put in. "I had Mr. Julius Victor here after breakfast."

Macgillivray exclaimed. "Poor soul! What did you say to him?"

"Deepest sympathy, but nothing doing."

"And he took that answer?"

"I won't say he took it. But he went away. What about the others?"

"There are two more. One is a young man, the heir to a considerable estate, who was last seen by his friends in Oxford on the 17th day of February, just before dinner. He was an undergraduate of Christ Church, and was living out of college in rooms in the High. He had tea at the Gridiron and went to his rooms to dress, for he was dining that night with the Halcyon Club. A servant passed him on the stairs of his lodgings, going up to his bedroom. He apparently did not come down, and since that day has not been seen. You may have heard his name--Lord Mercot."

I started. I had indeed heard the name, and knew the boy a little, having met him occasionally at our local steeplechases. He was the grandson and heir of the old Duke of Alcester, the most respected of the older statesmen of England.

"They have picked their bag carefully," I said. "What is the third case?"

"The cruellest of all. You know Sir Arthur Warcliff. He is a widower--lost his wife just before the War, and he has an only child, a little boy about ten years old. The child--David is his name--was the apple of his eye, and was at a preparatory school near Rye. The father took a house in the neighbourhood to be near him, and the boy used to be allowed to come home for luncheon every

Sunday. One Sunday he came to luncheon as usual, and started back in the pony-trap. The boy was very keen about birds, and used to leave the trap and walk the last half-mile by a short cut across the marshes. Well, he left the groom at the usual gate, and, like Miss Victor and Lord Mercot, walked into black mystery."

This story really did horrify me. I remembered Sir Arthur Warcliff--the kind, worn face of the great soldier and administrator, and I could imagine his grief and anxiety. I knew what I should have felt if it had been Peter John. A much-travelled young woman and an athletic young man were defenceful creatures compared to a poor little round-headed boy of ten. But I still felt the whole affair too fantastic for real tragedy.

"But what right have you to connect the three cases?" I asked. "Three people disappear within a few weeks of each other in widely separated parts of England. Miss Victor may have been kidnapped for ransom, Lord Mercot may have lost his memory, and David Warcliff may have been stolen by tramps. Why should they be all part of one scheme? Why, for that matter, should any one of them have been the work of your criminal combine? Have you any evidence for the hostage theory?"

"Yes." Macgillivray took a moment or two to answer. "There is first the general probability. If a band of rascals wanted three hostages they could hardly find three better--the daughter of the richest man in the world, the heir of our greatest dukedom, the only child of a national hero. There is also direct evidence." Again he hesitated.

"Do you mean to say that Scotland Yard has not a single clue to any one of these cases?"

"We have followed up a hundred clues, but they have all ended in dead walls. Every detail, I assure you, has been gone through with a fine comb. No, my dear Dick, the trouble is not that we're specially stupid on this side, but that there is some superlative cunning on the other. That is why I want YOU. You have a kind of knack of stumbling on truths which no amount of ordinary reasoning can get at. I have fifty men working day and night, and we have mercifully kept all the cases out of the papers, so that we are not hampered by the amateur. But so far it's a blank. Are you going to help?"

"No, I'm not. But, supposing I were, I don't see that you've a scrap of proof that the three cases are connected, or that any one of them is due to the criminal gang that you say you've got your hand on. You've only given me presumptions, and precious thin at that. Where's your direct evidence?"

Macgillivray looked a little embarrassed. "I've started you at the wrong end," he said. "I should have made you understand how big and desperate the thing is that we're out against, and then you'd have been in a more receptive mood for the rest of the story. You know as well as I do that cold blood is not always the most useful accompaniment in assessing evidence. I said I had direct evidence of connection, and so I have, and the proof to my mind is certain."

"Well, let's see it."

"It's a poem. On Wednesday of last week, two days after David Warcliff disappeared, Mr. Julius Victor, the Duke of Alcester, and Sir Arthur Warcliff received copies of it by the first post. They were typed on bits of flimsy paper, the envelopes had the addresses typed, and they had been posted in the West Central district of London the afternoon before."

He handed me a copy, and this was what I read:

"Seek where under midnight's sun Laggard crops are hardly won;-- Where the sower casts his seed in Furrows of the fields of Eden;-- Where beside the sacred tree Spins the seer who cannot see."

I burst out laughing, for I could not help it--the whole thing was too preposterous. These six lines of indifferent doggerel seemed to me to put the coping-stone of nonsense on the business. But I checked myself when I saw Macgillivray's face. There was a slight flush of annoyance on his cheek, but for the rest it was grave, composed, and in deadly earnest. Now Macgillivray was not a fool, and I was bound to respect his beliefs. So I pulled myself together and tried to take things seriously.

"That's proof that the three cases are linked together," I said. "So much I grant you. But where's the proof that they are the work of the great criminal combine that you say you have got your hand on?"

Macgillivray rose and walked restlessly about the room. "The evidence is mainly presumptive, but to my mind it is certain presumption. You know as well as I do, Dick, that a case may be final and yet very difficult to set out as a series of facts. My view on the matter is made up of a large number of tiny indications and cross-bearings, and I am prepared to bet that if you put your mind honestly to the business you will take the same view. But I'll give you this much by way of direct proof--in hunting the big show we had several communications of the same nature as this doggerel, and utterly unlike anything else I ever struck in criminology. There's one of the miscreants who amuses himself with sending useless clues to his adversaries. It shows how secure the gang thinks itself."

"Well, you've got that gang anyhow. I don't quite see why the hostages should trouble you. You'll gather them in when you gather in the malefactors."

"I wonder. Remember we are dealing with moral imbeciles. When they find themselves cornered they won't play for safety. They'll use their hostages, and when we refuse to bargain they'll take their last revenge on them."

I suppose I stared unbelievingly, for he went on: "Yes. They'll murder them in cold blood--three innocent people--and then swing themselves with a lighter mind. I know the type. They've done it before." He mentioned one or two recent instances.

"Good God!" I cried. "It's a horrible thought! The only thing for you is to go canny, and not strike till you have got the victims out of their clutches."

"We can't," he said solemnly. "That is precisely the tragedy of the business. We must strike early in June. I won't trouble you with the reasons, but believe me, they are final. There is just a chance of a settlement in Ireland, and there are certain events of the first importance impending in Italy and America, and all depend upon the activities of the gang being at an end by midsummer. Do you grasp that? By midsummer we must stretch out our hand. By midsummer, unless they are released, the three hostages will be doomed. It is a ghastly dilemma, but in the public interest there is only one way out. I ought to say that Victor and the Duke and Warcliff are aware of this fact, and accept the situation. They are big men, and will do their duty even if it breaks their hearts."

There was silence for a minute or two, for I did not know what to say. The whole story seemed to me incredible, and yet I could not doubt a syllable of it when I looked at Macgillivray's earnest face. I felt the horror of the business none the less because it seemed also partly unreal; it had the fantastic grimness of a nightmare. But most of all I realised that I was utterly incompetent to help, and as I understood that I could honestly base my refusal on incapacity and not on disinclination I began to feel more comfortable.

"Well," said Macgillivray, after a pause, "are you going to help us?"

"There's nothing doing with that Sunday-paper anagram you showed me. That's the sort of riddle that's not meant to be guessed. I suppose you are going to try to work up from the information you have about the combine towards a clue to the hostages."

He nodded.

"Now, look here," I said; "you've got fifty of the quickest brains in Britain working at the job. They've found out enough to put a lasso round the enemy which you can draw tight whenever you like. They're trained to the work and I'm not. What on earth would be the use of an amateur like me butting in? I wouldn't be half as good as any one of the fifty. I'm not an expert, I'm not quick- witted, I'm a slow patient fellow, and this job, as you admit, is one that has to be done against time. If you think it over, you'll see that it's sheer nonsense, my dear chap."

"You've succeeded before with worse material."

"That was pure luck, and it was in the War when, as I tell you, my mind was morbidly active. Besides, anything I did then I did in the field, and what you want me to do now is office-work. You know I'm no good at office-work--Blenkiron always said so, and Bullivant never used me on it. It isn't because I don't want to help, but because I can't."

"I believe you can. And the thing is so grave that I daren't leave any chance unexplored. Won't you come?"

"No. Because I could do nothing."

"Because you haven't a mind for it."

"Because I haven't the right kind of mind for it."

He looked at his watch and got up, smiling rather ruefully.

"I've had my say, and now you know what I want of you. I'm not going to take your answer as final. Think over what I've said, and let me hear from you within the next day or two."

But I had lost all my doubts, for it was very clear to me that on every ground I was doing the right thing.

"Don't delude yourself with thinking that I'll change my mind," I said, as I saw him into his car. "Honestly, old fellow, if I could be an atom of use I'd join you, but for your own sake you've got to count me out this time."

Then I went for a walk, feeling pretty cheerful. I settled the question of the pheasants' eggs with the keeper, and went down to the stream to see if there was any hatch of fly. It had cleared up to a fine evening, and I thanked my stars that I was out of a troublesome business with an easy conscience, and could enjoy my peaceful life again. I say "with an easy conscience," for though there were little dregs of disquiet still lurking about the bottom of my mind, I had only to review the facts squarely to approve my decision. I put the whole thing out of my thoughts and came back with a fine appetite for tea.

There was a stranger in the drawing-room with Mary, a slim oldish man, very straight and erect, with one of those faces on which life has written so much that to look at them is like reading a good book. At first I didn't recognise him when he rose to greet me, but the smile that wrinkled the corners of his eyes and the slow deep voice brought back the two occasions in the past when I had run across Sir Arthur Warcliff. . . . My heart sank as I shook hands, the more as I saw how solemn was Mary's face. She had been hearing the story which I hoped she would never hear.

I thought it best to be very frank with him. "I can guess your errand, Sir Arthur," I said, "and I'm extremely sorry that you should have come this long journey to no purpose." Then I told him of the visits of Mr. Julius Victor and Macgillivray, and what they had said, and what had been my answer. I think I made it as clear as day that I could do nothing, and he seemed to assent. Mary, I remember, never lifted her eyes.

Sir Arthur had also looked at the ground while I was speaking, and now he turned his wise old face to me, and I saw what ravages his new anxiety had made in it. He could not have been much over sixty and he looked a hundred.

"I do not dispute your decision, Sir Richard," he said. "I know that you would have helped me if it had been possible. But I confess I am sorely disappointed, for you were my last hope. You see--you see--I had nothing left in the world but Davie. If he had died I think I could have borne it, but to know nothing about him and to imagine terrible things is almost too much for my fortitude."

I have never been through a more painful experience. To hear a voice falter that had been used to command, to see tears in the steadfastest eyes that ever looked on the world, made me want to howl like a dog. I would have given a thousand pounds to be able to bolt into the library and lock the door.

Mary appeared to me to be behaving very oddly. She seemed to have the deliberate purpose of probing the wound, for she encouraged Sir Arthur to speak of his boy. He showed us a miniature he carried with him--an extraordinarily handsome child with wide grey eyes and his head most nobly set upon his shoulders. A grave little boy, with the look of utter trust which belongs to children who have never in their lives been unfairly treated. Mary said something about the gentleness of the face.

"Yes, Davie was very gentle," his father said. "I think he was the gentlest thing I have ever known. That little boy was the very flower of courtesy. But he was curiously stoical, too. When he was distressed, he only shut his lips tight, and never cried. I used often to feel rebuked by him."

And then he told us about Davie's performances at school, where he was not distinguished, except as showing a certain talent for cricket. "I am very much afraid of precocity," Sir Arthur said with the ghost of a smile. "But he was always educating himself in the right way, learning to observe and think." It seemed that the boy was a desperately keen naturalist and would be out at all hours watching wild things. He was a great fisherman, too, and had killed a lot of trout with the fly on hill burns in Galloway. And as the father spoke I suddenly began to realise the little chap, and to think that he was just the kind of boy I wanted Peter John to be. I liked the stories of his love of nature and trout streams. It came on me like a thunderclap that if I were in his father's place I should certainly go mad, and I was amazed at the old man's courage.

"I think he had a kind of genius for animals," Sir Arthur said. "He knew the habits of birds by instinct, and used to talk of them as other people talk of their friends. He and I were great cronies, and he would tell me long stories in his little quiet voice of birds and beasts he had seen on his walks. He had odd names for them too. . . ."

The thing was almost too pitiful to endure. I felt as if I had known the child all my life. I could see him playing, I could hear his voice, and as for Mary she was unashamedly weeping.

Sir Arthur's eyes were dry now, and there was no catch in his voice as he spoke. But suddenly a sharper flash of realisation came on him and his words became a strained cry: "Where is he now? What are they doing to him? Oh, God! My beloved little man--my gentle little Davie!"

That fairly finished me. Mary's arm was round the old man's neck, and I saw that he was trying to pull himself together, but I didn't see anything clearly. I only know that I was marching about the room, scarcely noticing that our guest was leaving. I remember shaking hands with him, and hearing him say that it had done him good to talk to us. It was Mary who escorted him to the car, and when she returned it was to find me blaspheming like a Turk at the window. I had flung the thing open, for I felt suffocated, though the evening was cool. The mixture of anger and disgust and pity in my heart nearly choked me.

"Why the devil can't I be left alone?" I cried. "I don't ask for much--only a little peace. Why in Heaven's name should I be dragged into other people's business? Why on earth--"

Mary was standing at my elbow, her face rather white and tear- stained.

"Of course you are going to help," she said.

Her words made clear to me the decision which I must have taken a quarter of an hour before, and all the passion went out of me like wind out of a pricked bladder.

"Of course," I answered. "By the way, I had better telegraph to Macgillivray. And Warcliff too. What's his address?"

"You needn't bother about Sir Arthur," said Mary. "Before you came in--when he told me the story--I said he could count on you. Oh, Dick, think if it had been Peter John!"

CHAPTER III

RESEARCHES IN THE SUBCONSCIOUS

I went to bed in the perfect certainty that I wouldn't sleep. That happened to me about once a year, when my mind was excited or angry, and I knew no way of dodging it. There was a fine moon, and the windows were sheets of opal cut by the dark jade limbs of trees; light winds were stirring the creepers; owls hooted like sentries exchanging passwords, and sometimes a rook would talk in its dreams; the little odd squeaks and rumbles of wild life came faintly from the woods; while I lay staring at the ceiling with my thoughts running round about in a futile circus. Mary's even breathing tantalised me, for I never knew anyone with her perfect gift for slumber. I used to say that if her pedigree could be properly traced it would be found that she descended direct from one of the Seven Sleepers of Ephesus who married one of the Foolish Virgins.

What kept me wakeful was principally the thought of that poor little boy, David Warcliff. I was sorry for Miss Victor and Lord Mercot, and desperately sorry for the parents of all three, but what I could not stand was the notion of the innocent little chap, who loved birds and fishing and the open air, hidden away in some stuffy den by the worst kind of blackguards. The thing preyed on me till I got to think it had happened to us and that Peter John was missing. I rose and prowled about the windows, looking out at the quiet night, and wondering how the same world could contain so much trouble and so much peace.

I laved my face with cold water and lay down again. It was no good letting my thoughts race, so I tried to fix them on one point in the hope that I would get drowsy. I endeavoured to recapitulate the evidence which Macgillivray had recited, but only made foolishness of it, for I simply could not concentrate. I saw always the face of a small boy, who bit his lips to keep himself from tears, and another perfectly hideous face that kept turning into one of the lead figures in the rose garden. A ridiculous rhyme too ran in my head--something thing about the "midnight sun" and the "fields of Eden." By and by I got it straightened out into the anagram business Macgillivray had mentioned. I have a fly- paper memory for verse when there is no reason why I should remember it, and I found I could repeat the six lines of the doggerel.

After that I found the lines mixing themselves up, and suggesting all kinds of odd pictures to my brain. I took to paraphrasing them--"Under the midnight sun, where harvests are poor"--that was Scandinavia anyhow, or maybc Iceland or Greenland or Labrador. Who on earth was the sower who sowed in the fields of Eden? Adam, perhaps, or Abel, who was the first farmer? Or an angel in heaven? More like an angel, I thought, for the line sounded like a hymn. Anyhow it was infernal nonsense.

The last two lines took to escaping me, and that made me force my mind out of the irritable confusion in which it was bogged. Ah! I had them again:

"Where beside the sacred tree Spins the seer who cannot see."

The sacred tree was probably Yggdrasil and the spinner one of the Norns. I had once taken an interest in Norse mythology, but I couldn't remember whether one of the Norns was blind. A blind woman spinning. Now where had I heard something like that? Heard it quite recently, too?

The discomfort of wakefulness is that you are not fully awake. But now I was suddenly in full possession of my senses, and worrying at that balderdash like a dog at a bone. I had been quite convinced that there was a clue in it, but that it would be impossible to hit on the clue. But now I had a ray of hope, for I seemed to feel a very faint and vague flavour of reminiscence.

Scandinavian harvests, the fields of Eden, the blind spinner--oh, it was maddening, for every time I repeated them the sense of having recently met with something similar grew stronger. The North--Norway--surely I had it there! Norway--what was there about Norway?--Salmon, elk, reindeer, midnight sun, saeters--the last cried out to me. And the blind old woman that spun!

I had it. These were two of the three facts which Dr. Greenslade had suggested the night before as a foundation for his imaginary "shocker." What was the third? A curiosity shop in North London kept by a Jew with a dyed beard. That had no obvious connection with a sower in the fields of Eden. But at any rate he had got two of them identical with the doggerel. . . . It was a clue. It must be a clue. Greenslade had somewhere and somehow heard the jingle or the substance of it, and it had sunk into the subconscious memory he had spoken of, without his being aware of it. Well, I had got to dig it out. If I could discover where and how he had heard the thing, I had struck a trail.

When I had reached this conclusion, I felt curiously easier in my mind, and almost at once fell asleep. I awoke to a gorgeous spring morning, and ran down to the lake for my bath. I felt that I wanted all the freshening and screwing up I could get, and when I dressed after an icy plunge I was ready for all comers.

Mary was down in time for breakfast, and busy with her letters. She spoke little, and seemed to be waiting for me to begin; but I didn't want to raise the matter which was uppermost in our minds till I saw my way clearer, so I said I was going to take two days to think things over. It was Wednesday, so I wired to Macgillivray to expect me in London on Friday morning, and I scribbled a line to Mr. Julius Victor. By half-past nine I was on the road making for Greenslade's lodgings.

I caught him in the act of starting on his rounds, and made him sit down and listen to me. I had to give him the gist of Macgillivray's story, with extracts from those of Victor and Sir Arthur. Before I was half-way through he had flung off his overcoat, and before I had finished he had lit a pipe, which was a breach of his ritual not to smoke before the evening. When I stopped he had that wildish look in his light eyes which you see in a cairn terrier's when he is digging out a badger.

"You've taken on this job?" he asked brusquely.

I nodded.

"Well, I shouldn't have had much respect for you if you had refused. How can I help? Count on me, if I'm any use. Good God! I never heard a more damnable story."

"Have you got hold of the rhyme?" I repeated it, and he said it after me.

"Now, you remember the talk we had after dinner the night before last. You showed me how a 'shocker' was written, and you took at random three facts as the foundation. They were, you remember, a blind old woman spinning in the Western Highlands, a saeter in Norway, and a curiosity shop in North London, kept by a Jew with a dyed beard. Well, two of your facts are in that six-line jingle I have quoted to you."

"That is an odd coincidence. But is it anything more?"

"I believe that it is. I don't hold with coincidences. There's generally some explanations which we're not clever enough to get at. Your inventions were so odd that I can't think they were mere inventions. You must have heard them somehow and somewhere. You know what you said about your subconscious memory. They're somewhere in it, and, if you can remember just how they got there, you'll give me the clue I want. That six-line rhyme was sent in by people who were so confident that they didn't mind giving their enemies a clue--only it was a clue which they knew could never be discovered. Macgillivray and his fellows can make nothing of it--never will. But if I can start from the other end I'll get in on their rear. Do you see what I mean? I'm going to make you somehow or other dig it out."

He shook his head. "It can't be done, Dick. Admitting your premise--that I heard the nonsense and didn't invent it--the subconscious can't be handled like a business proposition. I remember unconsciously and I can't recall consciously. . . . But I don't admit your premise. I think the whole thing is common coincidence."

"I don't," I said stubbornly, "and even if I did I'm bound to assume the contrary, for it's the only card I possess. You've got to sit down, old chap, and do your damnedest to remember. You've been in every kind of odd show, and my belief is that you HEARD that nonsense. Dig it out of your memory and we've a chance to win. Otherwise, I see nothing but tragedy."

He got up and put on his overcoat. "I've got a long round of visits which will take me all day. Of course I'll try, but I warn you that I haven't the ghost of a hope. These things don't come by care and searching. I'd better sleep at the Manor to-night. How long can you give me?"

"Two days--I go up to town on Friday morning. Yes, you must take up your quarters with us. Mary insists on it."

There was a crying of young lambs from the meadow, and through the open window came the sound of the farm-carts jolting from the stackyard into the lane. Greenslade screwed up his face and laughed.

"A nasty breach in your country peace, Dick. You know I'm with you if there's any trouble going. Let's get the thing clear, for there's a lot of researching ahead of me. My three were an old blind woman spinning in the Western Highlands--Western Highlands, was it?--a saeter barn, and a Jew curiosity shop. The other three were a blind spinner under a sacred tree, a saeter of sorts, and a sower in the fields of Eden--Lord, such rot! Two pairs seem to coincide, the other pair looks hopeless. Well, here goes for fortune! I'm going to break my rule and take my pipe with me, for this business demands tobacco."

I spent a busy day writing letters and making arrangements about the Manor, for it looked as if I might be little at home for the next month. Oddly enough, I felt no restlessness or any particular anxiety. That would come later; for the moment I seemed to be waiting on Providence in the person of Tom Greenslade. I was trusting my instinct which told me that in those random words of his there was more than coincidence, and that with luck I might get from them a line on our problem.

Greenslade turned up about seven in the evening, rather glum and preoccupied. At dinner he ate nothing, and when we sat afterwards in the library he seemed to be chiefly interested in reading the advertisements in The Times. When I asked "What luck?" he turned on me a disconsolate face.

"It is the most futile job I ever took on," he groaned. "So far it's an absolute blank, and anyhow I've been taking the wrong line. I've been trying to THINK myself into recollection, and, as I said, this thing comes not by searching, nor yet by prayer and fasting. It occurred to me that I might get at something by following up the differences between the three pairs. It's a familiar method in inductive logic, for differences are often more suggestive than resemblances. So I worried away at the 'sacred tree' as contrasted with the 'Western Highlands' and the 'fields of Eden' as set against the curiosity shop. No earthly good. I gave myself a headache and I dare say I've poisoned half my patients. It's no use, Dick, but I'll peg away for the rest of the prescribed two days. I'm letting my mind lie fallow now and trusting to inspiration. I've got two faint glimmerings of notions. First, I don't believe I said 'Western Highlands.'"

"I'm positive those were your words. What did you say, then?"

"Hanged if I know, but I'm pretty certain it wasn't that. I can't explain properly, but you get an atmosphere about certain things in your mind and that phrase somehow jars with the atmosphere. Different key. Wrong tone. Second, I've got a hazy intuition that the thing, if it is really in my memory, is somehow mixed up with a hymn tune. I don't know what tune, and the whole impression is as vague as smoke, but I tell it you for what it is worth. If I could get the right tune, I might remember something."

"You've stopped thinking?"

"Utterly. I'm an Aeolian harp to be played on by any wandering wind. You see, if I did hear these three things there is no conscious rational clue to it. They were never part of my workaday mind. The only chance is that some material phenomenon may come along and link itself with them and so rebuild the scene where I heard them. A scent would be best, but a tune might do. Our one hope--and it's about as strong as a single thread of gossamer on the grass--is that that tune may drift into my head. You see the point, Dick? Thought won't do, for the problem doesn't concern the mind, but some tiny physical sensation of nose, ear, or eye might press the button. Now, it may be hallucination, but I've a feeling that the three facts I thought I invented were in some infinitely recondite way connected with a hymn tune."

He went to bed early, while I sat up till nearly midnight writing letters. As I went upstairs, I had a strong sense of futility and discouragement. It seemed the merest trifling to be groping among these spectral unrealities, while tragedy, as big and indisputable as a mountain, was overhanging us. I had to remind myself how often the trivial was the vital before I got rid of the prick in my conscience. I was tired and sleepy, and as I forced myself to think of the immediate problem, the six lines of the jingle were all blurred. While I undressed I tried to repeat them, but could not get the fourth to scan. It came out as "fields of Erin," and after that "the green fields of Erin." Then it became "the green fields of Eden."

I found myself humming a tune.

It was an old hymn which the Salvation Army used to play in the Cape Town streets when I was a schoolboy. I hadn't heard it or thought of it for thirty years. But I remembered the tune very clearly, a pretty, catchy thing like an early Victorian drawing- room ballad, and I remembered the words of the chorus--

"On the other side of Jordan In the green fields of Eden, Where the Tree of Life is blooming, There is rest for you."

I marched off to Greenslade's room and found him lying wide awake staring at the ceiling, with the lamp by his bedside lit. I must have broken in on some train of thought, for he looked at me crossly.

"I've got your tune," I said, and I whistled it, and then quoted what words I remembered.

"Tune be blowed," he said. "I never heard it before." But he hummed it after me, and made me repeat the words several times.

"No good, I'm afraid. It doesn't seem to hank on to anything. Lord, this is a fool's game. I'm off to sleep."

But three minutes later came a knock at my dressing-room door, and Greenslade entered. I saw by his eyes that he was excited.

"It's the tune all right. I can't explain why, but those three blessed facts of mine fit into it like prawns in an aspic. I'm feeling my way towards the light now. I thought I'd just tell you, for you may sleep better for hearing it."

I slept like a log, and went down to breakfast feeling more cheerful than I had felt for several days. But the doctor seemed to have had a poor night. His eyes looked gummy and heavy, and he had ruffled his hair out of all hope of order. I knew that trick of his; when his hair began to stick up at the back he was out of sorts either in mind or body. I noticed that he had got himself up in knickerbockers and thick shoes.

After breakfast he showed no inclination to smoke. "I feel as if I were going to be beaten on the post," he groaned. "I'm a complete convert to your view, Dick. I HEARD my three facts and didn't invent them. What's more, my three are definitely linked with the three in those miscreants' doggerel. That tune proves it, for it talks about the 'fields of Eden' and yet is identified in my memory with my three which didn't mention Eden. That's a tremendous point and proves we're on the right road. But I'm hanged if I can get a step farther. Wherever I heard the facts I heard the tune, but I'm no nearer finding out that place. I've got one bearing, and I need a second to give me the point of intersection I want, and how the deuce I'm to get it I don't know."

Greenslade was now keener even than I was on the chase, and indeed his lean anxious face was uncommonly like an old hound's. I asked him what he was going to do.

"At ten o'clock precisely I start on a walk--right round the head of the Windrush and home by the

Forest. It's going to be a thirty- mile stride at a steady four and a half miles an hour, which, with half an hour for lunch, will get me back here before six. I'm going to drug my body and mind into apathy by hard exercise. Then I shall have a hot bath and a good dinner, and after that, when I'm properly fallow, I may get the revelation. The mistake I made yesterday was in trying to THINK."

It was a gleamy blustering March morning, the very weather for a walk, and I would have liked to accompany him. As it was I watched his long legs striding up the field we call Big Pasture, and then gave up the day to the job of putting Loch Leven fry into one of the ponds--a task so supremely muddy and wet that I had very little leisure to think of other things. In the afternoon I rode over to the market-town to see my builder, and got back only just before dinner to learn that Greenslade had returned. He was now wallowing in a hot bath, according to his programme.

At dinner he seemed to be in better spirits. The wind had heightened his colour, and given him a ferocious appetite, and the 1906 Clicquot, which I regard as the proper drink after a hard day, gave him the stimulus he needed. He talked as he had talked three nights ago, before this business got us in its clutches. Mary disappeared after dinner, and we sat ourselves in big chairs before the library fire, like two drowsy men who have had a busy day in the open air. I thought I had better say nothing till he chose to speak.

He was silent for a long time, and then he laughed not very mirthfully.

"I'm as far off it as ever. All day I've been letting my mind wander and measuring off miles with my two legs like a pair of compasses. But nothing has come to me. No word yet of that confounded cross-bearing I need. I might have heard that tune in any one of a thousand parts of the globe. You see, my rackety life is a disadvantage--I've had too many different sorts of experience. If I'd been a curate all my days in one village it would have been easier."

I waited, and he went on, speaking not to me but to the fire: "I've got an impression so strong that it amounts to certainty that I never heard the words 'Western Highlands.' It was something like it, but not that."

"Western Islands," I suggested.

"What could they be?"

"I think I've heard the phrase used about the islands off the west coast of Ireland. Does that help you?"

He shook his head. "No good. I've never been in Ireland."

After that he was silent again, staring at the fire, while I smoked opposite him, feeling pretty blank and dispirited. I realised that I had banked more than I knew on this line of inquiry which seemed to be coming to nothing. . . .

Then suddenly there happened one of those trivial things which look like accidents but I believe are part of the reasoned government of the universe.

I leaned forward to knock out the ashes of my pipe against the stone edge of the hearth. I hammered harder than I intended, and the pipe, which was an old one, broke off at the bowl. I exclaimed irritably, for I hate to lose an old pipe, and then pulled up sharp at the sight of Greenslade.

He was staring open-mouthed at the fragments in my hand, and his eyes were those of a man whose thoughts are far away. He held up one hand, while I froze into silence. Then the tension relaxed, and he dropped back into his chair with a sigh.

"The cross-bearing!" he said. "I've got it. . . . Medina."

Then he laughed at my puzzled face.

"I'm not mad, Dick. I once talked to a man, and as we talked he broke the bowl of his pipe as you have just done. He was the man who hummed the hymn tune, and though I haven't the remotest recollection of what he said, I am as certain as that I am alive that he gave me the three facts which sunk into the abyss of my subconscious memory. Wait a minute. Yes. I see it as plain as I see you. He broke his pipe just as you have done, and some time or other he hummed that tune."

"Who was he?" I asked, but Greenslade disregarded the question. He was telling his story in his own way, with his eyes still abstracted as if he were looking down a long corridor of memory.

"I was staying at the Bull at Hanham--shooting wild-fowl on the sea marshes. I had the place to myself, for it wasn't weather for a country pub, but late one night a car broke down outside, and the owner and his chauffeur had to put up at the Bull. Oddly enough I knew the man. He had been at one of the big shoots at Rousham Thorpe and was on his way back to London. We had a lot to say to each other and sat up into the small hours. We talked about sport, and the upper glens of the Yarkand river, where I first met him. I remember quite a lot of our talk, but not the three facts or the tune, which made no appeal to my conscious memory. Only of course they must have been there."

"When did this happen?"

"Early last December, the time we had the black frost. You remember, Dick, how I took a week's holiday and went down to Norfolk after duck."

"You haven't told me the man's name."

"I have. Medina."

"Who on earth is Medina?"

"Oh Lord! Dick. You're overdoing the rustic. You've heard of Dominick Medina."

I had, of course, when he mentioned the Christian name. You couldn't open a paper without seeing something about Dominick Medina, but whether he was a poet or a politician or an actor- manager I hadn't troubled to inquire. There was a pile of picture- papers on a side-table, and I fetched them and began to turn them over. Very soon I found what I wanted. It was a photograph of a group at a country-house party for some steeplechase, the usual "reading-from-left-to-right" business, and there between a Duchess and a foreign Princess was Mr. Dominick Medina. The poverty of the photograph could not conceal the extraordinary good looks of the man. He had the kind of head I fancy Byron had, and I seemed to discern, too, a fine, clean, athletic figure.

"If you had happened to look at that rag you might have short- circuited your inquiry."

He shook his head. "No. It doesn't happen that way. I had to get your broken pipe and the tune or I would have been stuck."

"Then I suppose I have to get in touch with this chap and find where he picked up the three facts and the tune. But how if he turns out to be like you, another babbler from the subconscious?"

"That is the risk you run, of course. He may be able to help you, or more likely he may prove only another dead wall."

I felt suddenly an acute sense of the difficulty of the job I had taken on, and something very near hopelessness.

"Tell me about this Medina. Is he a decent fellow?"

"I suppose so. Yes, I should think so. But he moves in higher circles than I'm accustomed to, so I can't judge. But I'll tell you what he is beyond doubt--he's rather a great man. Hang it, Dick, you must have heard of him. He's one of the finest shots living, and he's done some tall things in the exploration way, and he was the devil of a fellow as a partisan leader in South Russia. Also--though it may not interest you--he's an uncommon fine poet."

"I suppose he's some sort of a Dago."

"Not a bit of it. Old Spanish family settled here for three centuries. One of them rode with Rupert. Hold on! I rather believe I've heard that his people live in Ireland, or did live, till life there became impossible."

"What age?"

"Youngish. Not more than thirty-five. Oh, and the handsomest thing in mankind since the Greeks."

"I'm not a flapper," I said impatiently. "Good looks in a man are no sort of recommendation to me. I shall probably take a dislike to his face."

"You won't. From what I know of him and you you'll fall under his charm at first sight. I never heard of a man that didn't. He has a curious musical voice and eyes that warm you--glow like sunlight. Not that I know him well, but I own I found him extraordinarily attractive. And you see from the papers what the world thinks of him."

"All the same I'm not much nearer my goal. I've got to find out where he heard those three blessed facts and that idiotic tune. He'll probably send me to blazes, and, even if he's civil, he'll very likely be helpless."

"Your chance is that he's a really clever man, not an old blunderer like me. You'll get the help of a first-class mind, and that means a lot. Shall I write you a line of introduction?"

He sat down at my desk and wrote. "I'm saying nothing about your errand--simply that I'd like you to know each other--common interest in sport and travel--

that sort of thing. You're going to be in London, so I had better give your address as your club."

Next morning Greenslade went back to his duties and I caught the early train to town. I was not very happy about Mr. Dominick Medina, for I didn't seem able to get hold of him. Who's Who only gave his age, his residence--Hill Street, his club, and the fact that he was M.P. for a South London division. Mary had never met him, for he had appeared in London after she had stopped going about, but she remembered that her Wymondham aunts raved about him, and she had read somewhere an article on his poetry. As I sat in the express, I tried to reconstruct what kind of fellow he must be-- a mixture of Byron and Sir Richard Burton and the young political highbrow. The picture wouldn't compose, for I saw only a figure like a waxwork, with a cooing voice and a shop-walker's suavity. Also his name kept confusing me, for I mixed him up with an old ruffian of a Portugee I once knew at Beira.

I was walking down St. James's Street on my way to Whitehall, pretty much occupied with my own thoughts, when I was brought up by a hand placed flat on my chest, and lo! and behold! it was Sandy Arbuthnot.

CHAPTER IV

I MAKE THE ACQUAINTANCE OF A POPULAR MAN

You may imagine how glad I was to see old Sandy again, for I had not set eyes on him since 1916. He had been an Intelligence Officer with Maude, and then something at Simla, and after the War had had an administrative job in Mesopotamia, or, as they call it nowadays, Iraq. He had written to me from all kinds of queer places, but he never appeared to be coming home, and, what with my marriage and my settling in the country, we seemed to be fixed in ruts that were not likely to intersect. I had seen his elder brother's death in the papers, so he was now Master of Clanroyden and heir to the family estates, but I didn't imagine that that would make a Scotch laird of him. I never saw a fellow less changed by five years of toil and travel. He was desperately slight and tanned--he had always been that, but the contours of his face were still soft like a girl's, and his brown eyes were merry as ever.

We stood and stared at each other.

"Dick, old man," he cried, "I'm home for good. Yes--honour bright. For months and months, if not years and years. I've got so much to say to you I don't know where to begin. But I can't wait now. I'm off to Scotland to see my father. He's my chief concern now, for he's getting very frail. But I'll be back in three days. Let's dine together on Tuesday."

We were standing at the door of a club--his and mine--and a porter was stowing his baggage into a taxi. Before I could properly realise that it was Sandy, he was waving his hand from the taxi window and disappearing up the street.

The sight of him cheered me immensely and I went on along Pall Mall in a good temper. To have Sandy back in England and at call made me feel somehow more substantial, like a commander who knows his reserves are near. When I entered Macgillivray's room I was smiling, and the sight of me woke an answering smile on his anxious face. "Good man!" he said. "You look like business. You're to put yourself at my disposal while I give you your bearings."

He got out his papers and expounded the whole affair. It was a very queer story, yet the more I looked into it the thinner my scepticism grew. I am not going to write it all down, for it is not yet time; it would give away certain methods which have not yet exhausted their usefulness; but before I had gone very far, I took off my hat to these same methods, for they showed amazing patience and ingenuity. It was an odd set of links that made up the chain. There was an importer of Barcelona nuts with a modest office near Tower Hill. There was a copper company, purporting to operate in Spain, whose shares were not quoted on the Stock Exchange, but which had a fine office in London Wall, where you could get the best luncheon in the City. There was a respectable accountant in Glasgow, and a French count, who was also some kind of Highland laird and a great supporter of the White Rose League. There was a country gentleman living in Shropshire, who had bought his place after the War and was a keen rider to hounds and a very popular figure in the county. There was a little office not far from Fleet Street, which professed to be the English agency of an American religious magazine; and there was a certain publicist, who was always appealing in the newspapers for help for the distressed populations of Central Europe. I remembered his appeals well, for I had myself twice sent him small subscriptions. The way Macgillivray had worked out the connection between these gentry filled me with awe.

Then he showed me specimens of their work. It was sheer unmitigated crime, a sort of selling a bear on a huge scale in a sinking world. The aim of the gang was money, and already they had made scandalous profits. Partly their business was mere conscienceless profiteering well inside the bounds of the law, such as gambling in falling exchanges and using every kind of brazen and subtle trick to make their gamble a certainty. Partly it was common fraud of the largest size. But there were darker sides-- murder when the victim ran athwart their schemes, strikes engineered when a wrecked industry somewhere or other in the world showed symptoms of reviving, shoddy little outbursts in shoddy little countries which increased the tangle. These fellows were wreckers on the grand scale, merchants of pessimism, giving society another kick downhill whenever it had a chance of finding its balance, and then pocketing their profits.

Their motive, as I have said, was gain but that was not the motive of the people they worked through. Their cleverness lay in the fact that they used the fanatics, the moral imbeciles as Macgillivray called them, whose key was a wild hatred of something or other, or a reasoned belief in anarchy. Behind the smug exploiters lay the whole dreary wastes of half-baked craziness. Macgillivray gave me examples of how they used these tools, the fellows who had no thought of profit, and were ready to sacrifice everything, including their lives, for a mad ideal. It was a masterpiece of cold-blooded, devilish ingenuity. Hideous, and yet comic too; for the spectacle of these feverish cranks toiling to create a new heaven and a new earth and thinking themselves the leaders of mankind, when they were dancing like puppets at the will of a few scoundrels engaged in the most ancient of pursuits, was an irony to make the gods laugh.

I asked who was their leader.

Macgillivray said he wasn't certain. No one of the gang seemed to have more authority than the others, and their activities were beautifully specialised. But he agreed that there was probably one master mind, and said grimly that he would know more about that when they were rounded up. "The dock will settle that question."

"How much do they suspect?" I asked.

"Not much. A little, or they would not have taken hostages. But not much, for we have been very careful to make no sign. Only, since we became cognisant of the affair, we have managed very quietly to put a spoke in the wheels of some of their worst enterprises, though I am positive they have no suspicion of it. Also we have put the brake on their propaganda side. They are masters of propaganda, you know. Dick, have you ever considered what a diabolical weapon that can be--using all the channels of modern publicity to poison and warp men's minds? It is the most dangerous thing on earth. You can use it cleanly--as I think on the whole we did in the War--but you can also use it to establish the most damnable lies. Happily in the long run it defeats itself, but only after it has sown the world with mischief. Look at the Irish! They are the cleverest propagandists extant, and managed to persuade most people that they were a brave, generous, humorous, talented, warm-hearted race, cruelly yoked to a dull mercantile England, when God knows they were exactly the opposite."

Macgillivray, I may remark, is an Ulsterman, and has his prejudices.

"About the gang--I suppose they're all pretty respectable to outward view?"

"Highly respectable," he said. "I met one of them at dinner the other night at ----'s"--he mentioned the name of a member of the Government. "Before Christmas I was at a cover shoot in Suffolk, and one of the worst had the stand next me--an uncommonly agreeable fellow."

Then we sat down to business. Macgillivray's idea was that I should study the details of the thing and then get alongside some of the people. He thought I might begin with the Shropshire squire. He fancied that I might stumble on something which would give me a line on the hostages, for he stuck to his absurd notion that I had a special flair which the amateur sometimes possessed and the professional lacked. I agreed that that was the best plan, and arranged to spend Sunday in his room going over the secret dossiers. I was beginning to get keen about the thing, for Macgillivray had a knack of making whatever he handled as interesting as a game.

I had meant to tell him about my experiments with Greenslade; but after what he had shown me I felt that that story was absurdly thin and unpromising. But as I was leaving, I asked him casually if he knew Mr. Dominick Medina.

He smiled. "Why do you ask? He's scarcely your line of country."

"I don't know. I've heard a lot about him and I thought I would rather like to meet him."

"I barely know him, but I must confess that the few times I've met him I was enormously attracted. He's the handsomest being alive."

"So I'm told, and it's the only thing that puts me off."

"It wouldn't if you saw him. He's not in the least the ordinary matinée idol. He is the only fellow I ever heard of who was adored by women and also liked by men. He's a first-class sportsman and said to be the best shot in England after His Majesty. He's a coming man in politics, too, and a most finished speaker. I once heard him, and, though I take very little stock in oratory, he almost had me on my feet. He has knocked a bit about the world, and he is also a very pretty poet, though that wouldn't interest you."

"I don't know why you say that," I protested. "I'm getting rather good at poetry."

"Oh, I know. Scott and Macaulay and Tennyson. But that is not Medina's line. He is a deity of les jeunes and a hardy innovator. Jolly good, too. The man's a fine classical scholar."

"Well, I hope to meet him soon, and I'll let you know my impression."

I had posted my letter to Medina, enclosing Greenslade's introduction, on my way from the station, and next morning I found a very civil reply from him at my club. Greenslade had talked of our common interest in big-game shooting, and he professed to know all about me, and to be anxious to make my acquaintance. He was out of town unfortunately for the week-end, he said, but he suggested that I should lunch with him on the Monday. He named a club, a small, select, old-fashioned one of which most of the members were hunting squires.

I looked forward to meeting him with a quite inexplicable interest and on Sunday, when I was worrying through papers in Macgillivray's room, I had him at the back of my mind. I had made a picture of something between a Ouida guardsman and the Apollo Belvedere and rigged it out in the smartest clothes. But when I gave my name to the porter at the club door, and a young man who was warming his hands at the hall fire came forward to meet me, I had to wipe that picture clean off my mind.

He was about my own height, just under six feet, and at first sight rather slightly built, but a hefty enough fellow to eyes which knew where to look for the points of a man's strength. Still he appeared slim, and therefore young, and you could see from the way he stood and walked that he was as light on his feet as a rope- dancer. There is a horrible word in the newspapers, "well-groomed," applied to men by lady journalists, which always makes me think of a glossy horse on which a stable-boy has been busy with the brush and currycomb.

I had thought of him as "well-groomed," but there was nothing glossy about his appearance. He wore a rather old well-cut brown tweed suit, with a soft shirt and collar, and a russet tie that matched his complexion. His get-up was exactly that of a country squire who has come up to town for a day at Tattersalls'.

I find it difficult to describe my first impression of his face, for my memory is all overlaid with other impressions acquired when I looked at it in very different circumstances. But my chief feeling, I remember, was that it was singularly pleasant. It was very English, and yet not quite English; the colouring was a little warmer than sun or weather would give, and there was a kind of silken graciousness about it not commonly found in our countrymen. It was beautifully cut, every feature regular, and yet there was a touch of ruggedness that saved it from conventionality. I was puzzled about this, till I saw that it came from two things, the hair and the eyes. The hair was a dark brown, brushed in a wave above the forehead, so that the face with its strong fine chin made an almost perfect square. But the eyes were the thing. They were of a startling blue, not the pale blue which is common enough and belongs to our Norse ancestry, but a deep dark blue, like the colour of a sapphire. Indeed if you think of a sapphire with the brilliance of a diamond, you get a pretty fair notion of those eyes. They would have made a plain-headed woman lovely, and in a man's face, which had not a touch of the feminine, they were startling. Startling--I stick to that word--but also entrancing.

He greeted me as if he had been living for this hour, and also with a touch of the deference due to a stranger.

"This is delightful, Sir Richard. It was very good of you to come. We've got a table to ourselves by the fire. I hope you're hungry. I've had a devilish cold journey this morning and I want my luncheon."

I was hungry enough and I never ate a better meal. He gave me Burgundy on account of the bite in the weather, and afterwards I had a glass of the Bristol Cream for which the club was famous; but he drank water himself. There were four other people in the room, all of whom he appeared to call by their Christian names, and these lantern-jawed hunting fellows seemed to cheer up at the sight of him. But they didn't come and stand beside him and talk, which is apt to happen to your popular man. There was that about Medina which was at once friendly and aloof, the air of a simple but tremendous distinction.

I remember we began by talking about rifles. I had done a good deal of shikar in my time, and I could see that this man had had a wide experience and had the love of the thing in his bones. He never bragged, but by little dropped remarks showed what a swell he was. We talked of a new .240 bore which had remarkable stopping power, and I said I had never used it on anything more formidable than a Scotch stag. "It would have been a godsend to me in the old days on the

Pungwe where I had to lug about a .500 express that broke my back."

He grinned ruefully. "The old days!" he said. "We've all had 'em, and we're all sick to get 'em back. Sometimes I'm tempted to kick over the traces and be off to the wilds again. I'm too young to settle down. And you, Sir Richard--you must feel the same. Do you never regret that that beastly old War is over?"

"I can't say I do. I'm a middle-aged man now and soon I'll be stiff in the joints. I've settled down in the Cotswolds, and though I hope to get a lot of sport before I die I'm not looking for any more wars. I'm positive the Almighty meant me for a farmer."

He laughed. "I wish I knew what He meant me for. It looks like some sort of politician."

"Oh, you!" I said. "You're the fellow with twenty talents. I've only got the one, and I'm jolly well going to bury it in the soil."

I kept wondering how much help I would get out of him. I liked him enormously, but somehow I didn't yet see his cleverness. He was just an ordinary good fellow of my own totem--just such another as Tom Greenslade. It was a dark day, and the firelight silhouetted his profile, and as I stole glances at it I was struck by the shape of his head. The way he brushed his hair front and back made it look square, but I saw that it was really round, the roundest head I have ever seen except in a Kaffir. He was evidently conscious of it and didn't like it, so took some pains to conceal it.

All through luncheon I was watching him covertly, and I could see that he was also taking stock of me. Very friendly these blue eyes were, but very shrewd. He suddenly looked me straight in the face.

"You won't vegetate," he said. "You needn't deceive yourself. You haven't got the kind of mouth for a rustic. What is it to be? Politics? Business? Travel? You're well off?"

"Yes. For my simple tastes I'm rather rich. But I haven't the ambition of a maggot."

"No. You haven't." He looked at me steadily. "If you don't mind my saying it, you have too little vanity. Oh, I'm quick at detecting vanity, and anyhow it's a thing that defies concealment. But I imagine--indeed I know--that you can work like a beaver, and that your loyalty is not the kind that cracks. You won't be able to help yourself, Sir Richard. You'll be caught up in some machine. Look at me. I swore two years ago never to have a groove, and I'm in a deep one already. England is made up of grooves, and the only plan is to select a good one."

"I suppose yours is politics," I said.

"I suppose it is. A dingy game as it's played at present, but there are possibilities. There is a mighty Tory revival in sight, and it will want leading. The newly enfranchised classes, especially the women, will bring it about. The suffragists didn't know what a tremendous force of conservatism they were releasing when they won the vote for their sex. I should like to talk to you about these things some day."

In the smoking-room we got back to sport and he told me the story of how he met Greenslade in Central Asia. I was beginning to realise that the man's reputation was justified, for there was a curious mastery about his talk, a careless power as if everything came easily to him and was just taken in his stride. I had meant to open up the business which had made me seek his acquaintance, but I did not feel the atmosphere quite right for it. I did not know him well enough yet, and I felt that if I once started on those ridiculous three facts, which were all I had, I must make a clean breast of the whole thing and take him fully into my confidence. I thought the time was scarcely ripe for that, especially as we would meet again.

"Are you by any chance free on Thursday?" he asked as we parted. "I would like to take you to dine at the Thursday Club. You're sure to know some of the fellows, and it's a pleasant way of spending an evening. That's capital! Eight o'clock on Thursday. Short coat and black tie."

As I walked away, I made up my mind that I had found the right kind of man to help me. I liked him, and the more I thought of him the more the impression deepened of a big reservoir of power behind his easy grace. I was completely fascinated, and the proof of it was that I went off to the nearest bookseller's and bought his two slim volumes of poems. I cared far more about poetry than Macgillivray imagined--Mary had done a lot to educate me--but I hadn't been very fortunate in my experiments with the new people. But I understood Medina's verses well enough. They were very simple, with a delicious subtle tune in them, and they were desperately sad. Again and again came the note of regret and transcience and disillusioned fortitude. As I read them that evening I wondered how a man, who had apparently such zest for life and got so much out of the world, should be so lonely at heart. It might be a pose, but there was nothing of the conventional despair of the callow poet. This was the work of one as wise as Ulysses and as far-wandering. I didn't see how he could want to write anything but the truth. A pose is a consequence of vanity, and I was pretty clear that Medina was not vain.

Next morning I found his cadences still running in my head and I could not keep my thoughts off him. He fascinated me as a man is fascinated by a pretty woman. I was glad to think that he had taken a liking for me, for he had done far more than Greenslade's casual introduction demanded. He had made a plan for us to meet again, and he had spoken not as an acquaintance but as a friend. Very soon I decided that I would get

Macgillivray's permission and take him wholly into our confidence. It was no good keeping a man like that at arm's length and asking him to solve puzzles presented as meaninglessly as an acrostic in a newspaper. He must be told all or nothing, and I was certain that if he were told all he would be a very tower of strength to me. The more I thought of him the more I was convinced of his exceptional brains.

I lunched with Mr. Julius Victor in Carlton House Terrace. He was carrying on his ordinary life, and when he greeted me he never referred to the business which had linked us together. Or rather he only said one word. "I knew I could count on you," he said. "I think I told you that my daughter was engaged to be married this spring. Well, her fiancé has come over from France and will be staying for an indefinite time with me. He can probably do nothing to assist you, but he is here at your call if you want him. He is the Marquis de la Tour du Pin."

I didn't quite catch the name, and, as it was a biggish party, we had sat down to luncheon before I realised who the desolated lover was. It was my ancient friend Turpin, who had been liaison officer with my old division. I had known that he was some kind of grandee, but as everybody went by nicknames I had become used to think of him as Turpin, a version of his title invented, I think, by Archie Roylance. There he was, sitting opposite me, a very handsome pallid young man, dressed with that excessive correctness found only among

Frenchmen who get their clothes in England. He had been a tremendous swashbuckler when he was with the division, unbridled in speech, volcanic in action, but always with a sad gentleness in his air. He raised his heavy-lidded eyes and looked at me, and then, with a word of apology to his host, marched round the table and embraced me.

I felt every kind of a fool, but I was mighty glad all the same to see Turpin. He had been a good pal of mine, and the fact that he had been going to marry Miss Victor seemed to bring my new job in line with other parts of my life. But I had no further speech with him, for I had conversational women on both sides of me, and in the few minutes while the men were left alone at table I fell into talk with an elderly man on my right, who proved to be a member of the Cabinet. I found that out by a lucky accident, for I was lamentably ill-informed about the government of our country.

I asked him about Medina and he brightened up at once.

"Can you place him?" he asked. "I can't. I like to classify my fellow-men, but he is a new specimen. He is as exotic as the young Disraeli and as English as the late Duke of Devonshire. The point is, has he a policy, something he wants to achieve, and has he the power of attaching a party to him? If he has these two things, there is no doubt about his future. Honestly, I'm not quite certain. He has very great talents, and I believe if he wanted he would be in the front rank as a public speaker. He has the ear of the House, too, though he doesn't often address it. But I am never sure how much he cares about the whole business, and England, you know, demands wholeheartedness in her public men. She will follow blindly the second-rate, if he is in earnest, and reject the first- rate if he is not."

I said something about Medina's view of a great Tory revival, based upon the women. My neighbour grinned.

"I dare say he's right, and I dare say he could whistle women any way he pleased. It's extraordinary the charm he has for them. That handsome face of his and that melodious voice would enslave anything female from a charwoman to a Cambridge intellectual. Half his power of course comes from the fact that they have no charm for HIM. He's as aloof as Sir Galahad from any interest in the sex. Did you ever hear his name coupled with a young woman's? He goes everywhere and they would give their heads for him, and all the while he is as insensitive as a nice Eton boy whose only thought is of getting into the Eleven. You know him?"

I told him, very slightly.

"Same with me. I've only a nodding acquaintance, but one can't help feeling the man everywhere and being acutely interested. It's lucky he's a sound fellow. If he were a rogue he could play the devil with our easy-going society."

That night Sandy and I dined together. He had come back from Scotland in good spirits, for his father's health was improving, and when Sandy was in good spirits it was like being on the Downs in a south-west wind. We had so much to tell each other that we let our food grow cold. He had to hear all about Mary and Peter John, and what I knew of Blenkiron and a dozen other old comrades, and I had to get a sketch--the merest sketch--of his doings since the Armistice in the East. Sandy for some reason was at the moment disinclined to speak of his past, but he was as ready as an undergraduate to talk of his future. He meant to stay at home now, for a long spell at any rate; and the question was how he should fill up his time. "Country life's no good," he said. "I must find a profession or I'll get into trouble."

I suggested politics, and he rather liked the notion.

"I might be bored in Parliament," he reflected, "but I should love the rough-and-tumble of an election. I only once took part in one, and I discovered surprising gifts as a demagogue and made a speech in our little town which is still talked about. The chief row was about Irish Home Rule, and I thought I'd better have a whack at the Pope. Has it ever struck you, Dick, that ecclesiastical language has a most sinister sound? I knew some of the words, though not their meaning, but I knew that my audience would be just as ignorant. So I had a magnificent peroration. 'Will you men of Kilclavers,' I asked, 'endure to see a chasuble set up in your market-place? Will you have your daughters sold into simony? Will you have celibacy practised in the public streets?' Gad, I had them all on their feet bellowing 'Never!'"

He also rather fancied business. He had a notion of taking up civil aviation, and running a special service for transporting pilgrims from all over the Moslem world to Mecca. He reckoned the present average cost to the pilgrim at not less than £30, and believed that he could do it for an average of £15 and show a handsome profit. Blenkiron, he thought, might be interested in the scheme and put up some of the capital.

But later, in a corner of the upstairs smoking-room, Sandy was serious enough when I began to tell him the job I was on, for I didn't need Macgillivray's permission to make a confidant of him. He listened in silence while I gave him the main lines of the business that I had gathered from Macgillivray's papers, and he made no comment when I came to the story of the three hostages. But, when I explained my disinclination to stir out of my country rut, he began to laugh.

"It's a queer thing how people like us get a sudden passion for cosiness. I feel it myself coming over me. What stirred you up in the end? The little boy?"

Then very lamely and shyly I began on the rhymes and Greenslade's memory. That interested him acutely. "Just the sort of sensible- nonsensical notion you'd have, Dick. Go on. I'm thrilled."

But when I came to Medina he exclaimed sharply.

"You've met him?"

"Yesterday at luncheon."

"You haven't told him anything?"

"No. But I'm going to."

Sandy had been deep in an arm-chair with his legs over the side, but now he got up and stood with his arms on the mantelpiece looking into the fire.

"I'm going to take him into my full confidence," I said, "when I've spoken to Macgillivray."

"Macgillivray will no doubt agree?"

"And you? Have you ever met him?"

"Never. But of course I've heard of him. Indeed I don't mind telling you that one of my chief reasons for coming home was a wish to see Medina."

"You'll like him tremendously. I never met such a man."

"So everyone says." He turned his face and I could see that it had fallen into that portentous gravity which was one of Sandy's moods, the complement to his ordinary insouciance. "When are you going to see him again?"

"I'm dining with him the day after to-morrow at a thing called the Thursday Club."

"Oh, he belongs to that, does he? So do I. I think I'll give myself the pleasure of dining also."

I asked about the Club, and he told me that it had been started after the War by some of the people who had had queer jobs and wanted to keep together. It was very small, only twenty members. There were Collatt, one of the Q-boat V.C.'s, and Pugh of the Indian Secret Service, and the Duke of Burminster, and Sir Arthur Warcliff, and several soldiers all more or less well-known. "They elected me in 1919," said Sandy, "but of course I've never been to a dinner. I say, Dick, Medina must have a pretty strong pull here to be a member of the Thursday. Though I says it as shouldn't, it's a show most people would give their right hand to be in."

He sat down again and appeared to reflect, with his chin on his hand.

"You're under the spell, I suppose," he said.

"Utterly. I'll tell you how he strikes me. Your ordinary very clever man is apt to be a bit bloodless and priggish, while your ordinary sportsman and good fellow is inclined to be a bit narrow. Medina seems to me to combine all the virtues and none of the faults of both kinds. Anybody can see he's a sportsman, and you've only to ask the swells to discover how high they put his brains."

"He sounds rather too good to be true." I seemed to detect a touch of acidity in his voice. "Dick," he said, looking very serious, "I want you to promise to go slow in this business--I mean about telling Medina."

"Why?" I asked. "Have you anything against him?"

"No--o--o," he said. "I haven't anything against him. But he's just a little incredible, and I would like to know more about him. I had a friend who knew him. I've no right to say this, and I haven't any evidence, but I've a sort of feeling that Medina didn't do him any good."

"What was his name?" I asked, and was told "Lavater"; and when I inquired what had become of him Sandy didn't know. He had lost sight of him for two years.

At that I laughed heartily, for I could see what was the matter. Sandy was jealous of this man who was putting a spell on everybody. He wanted his old friends to himself. When I taxed him with it he grinned and didn't deny it.

CHAPTER V

THE THURSDAY CLUB

We met in a room on the second floor of a little restaurant in Mervyn Street, a pleasant room, panelled in white, with big fires burning at each end. The Club had its own cook and butler, and I swear a better dinner was never produced in London, starting with preposterously early plovers' eggs and finishing with fruit from Burminster's houses. There were a dozen present including myself, and of these, besides my host, I knew only Burminster and Sandy. Collatt was there, and Pugh, and a wizened little man who had just returned from bird-hunting at the mouth of the Mackenzie. There was Pallister-Yeates, the banker, who didn't look thirty, and Fulleylove, the Arabian traveller, who was really thirty and looked fifty. I was specially interested in Nightingale, a slim peering fellow with double glasses, who had gone back to Greek manuscripts and his Cambridge fellowship after captaining a Bedouin tribe. Leithen was there, too, the Attorney-General, who had been a private in the Guards at the start of the War, and had finished up a G.S.O.I., a toughly built man, with a pale face and very keen quizzical eyes. I should think there must have been more varied and solid brains in that dozen than you would find in an average Parliament.

Sandy was the last to arrive, and was greeted with a roar of joy. Everybody seemed to want to wring his hand and beat him on the back. He knew them all except Medina, and I was curious to see their meeting. Burminster did the introducing, and Sandy for a moment looked shy. "I've been looking forward to this for years," Medina said, and Sandy, after one glance at him, grinned sheepishly and stammered something polite.

Burminster was chairman for the evening, a plump, jolly little man, who had been a pal of Archie Roylance in the Air Force. The talk to begin with was nothing out of the common. It started with horses and the spring handicaps, and then got on to spring salmon- fishing, for one man had been on the Helmsdale, another on the Naver, and two on the Tay. The fashion of the Club was to have the conversation general, and there was very little talking in groups. I was next to Medina, between him and the Duke, and Sandy was at the other end of the oval table. He had not much to say, and more than once I caught his eyes watching Medina.

Then by and by, as was bound to happen, reminiscences began. Collatt made me laugh with a story of how the Admiralty had a notion that sea-lions might be useful to detect submarines. A number were collected, and trained to swim after submarines to which fish were attached as bait, the idea being that they would come to associate the smell of submarines with food, and go after a stranger. The thing shipwrecked on the artistic temperament. The beasts all came from the music-halls and had names like Flossie and Cissie, so they couldn't be got to realise that there was a war on, and were always going ashore without leave.

That story started the ball rolling, and by the time we had reached the port the talk was like what you used to find in the smoking- room of an East African coastal steamer, only a million times better. Everybody present had done and seen amazing things, and, moreover, they had the brains and knowledge to orientate their experiences. It was no question of a string of yarns, but rather of the best kind of give-and-take conversation, when a man would buttress an argument by an apt recollection. I especially admired Medina. He talked little, but he made others talk, and his keen interest seemed to wake the best in everybody. I noticed that, as at our luncheon three days before, he drank only water.

We talked, I remember, about the people who had gone missing, and whether any were likely still to turn up. Sandy told us about three British officers who had been in prison in Turkestan since the summer of '18 and had only just started home. He had met one of them at Marseilles, and thought there might be others tucked away in those parts. Then someone spoke of how it was possible to drop off the globe for a bit and miss all that was happening. I said I had met an old prospector in Barberton in 1920 who had come down from Portuguese territory and when I asked him what he had been doing in the War, he said "What war?" Pugh said a fellow had just turned up in Hong Kong, who had been a captive of Chinese pirates for eight years and had never heard a word of our four years' struggle, till he said something about the Kaiser to the skipper of the boat that picked him up.

Then Sandy, as the new-comer, wanted news about Europe. I remember that Leithen gave him his views on the malaise that France was suffering from, and that Palliser-Yeates, who looked exactly like a Rugby three-quarter back, enlightened him--and incidentally myself--on the matter of German reparations. Sandy was furious about the muddle in the Near East and the mishandling of Turkey. His view was that we were doing our best to hammer a much-divided Orient into a hostile unanimity.

"Lord!" he cried, "how I loathe our new manners in foreign policy. The old English way was to regard all foreigners as slightly childish and rather idiotic and ourselves as the only grown-ups in a kindergarten world. That meant that we had a cool detached view and did even-handed unsympathetic justice. But now we have got into the nursery ourselves and are bear-fighting on the floor. We take violent sides, and make pets, and of course if you are -phil something or other you have got to be -phobe something else. It is all wrong. We are becoming Balkanised."

We would have drifted into politics, if Pugh had not asked him his opinion of Gandhi. That led him into an exposition of the meaning of the fanatic, a subject on which he was well qualified to speak, for he had consorted with most varieties.

"He is always in the technical sense mad--that is, his mind is tilted from its balance, and since we live by balance he is a wrecker, a crowbar in the machinery. His power comes from the appeal he makes to the imperfectly balanced, and as these are never the majority his appeal is limited. But there is one kind of fanatic whose strength comes from balance, from a lunatic balance. You cannot say that there is any one thing abnormal about him, for he is all abnormal. He is as balanced as you or me, but, so to speak, in a fourth-dimensional world. That kind of man has no logical gaps in his creed. Within his insane postulates he is brilliantly sane. Take Lenin for instance. That's the kind of fanatic I'm afraid of."

Leithen asked how such a man got his influence. "You say that there is no crazy spot in him which appeals to a crazy spot in other people."

"He appeals to the normal," said Sandy solemnly, "to the perfectly sane. He offers reason, not visions--in any case his visions are reasonable. In ordinary times he will not be heard, because, as I say, his world is not our world. But let there come a time of great suffering or discontent, when the mind of the ordinary man is in desperation, and the rational fanatic will come by his own. When he appeals to the sane and the sane respond, revolutions begin."

Pugh nodded his head, as if he agreed. "Your fanatic of course must be a man of genius."

"Of course. And genius of that kind is happily rare. When it exists, its possessor is the modern wizard. The old necromancer fiddled away with cabalistic signs and crude chemicals and got nowhere; the true wizard is the man who works by spirit on spirit. We are only beginning to realise the strange crannies of the human soul. The real magician, if he turned up to-day, wouldn't bother about drugs and dopes. He would dabble in far more deadly methods, the compulsion of a fiery nature over the limp things that men call their minds."

He turned to Pugh. "You remember the man we used to call Ram Dass in the War--I never knew his right name?"

"Rather," said Pugh. "The fellow who worked for us in San Francisco. He used to get big sums from the agitators and pay them in to the British Exchequer, less his commission of ten per cent."

"Stout fellow!" Burminster exclaimed approvingly. "Well, Ram Dass used to discourse to me on this subject. He was as wise as a serpent and as loyal as a dog, and he saw a lot of things coming that we are just beginning to realise. He said that the great offensives of the future would be psychological, and he thought the Governments should get busy about it and prepare their defence. What a jolly sight it would be--all the high officials sitting down to little primers! But there was sense in what he said. He considered that the most deadly weapon in the world was the power of mass-persuasion, and he wanted to meet it at the source, by getting at the mass-persuader. His view was that every spell- binder had got something like Samson's hair which was the key of his strength, and that if this were tampered with he could be made innocuous. He would have had us make pets of the prophets and invite them to Government House. You remember the winter of 1917 when the Bolsheviks were making trouble in Afghanistan and their stuff was filtering through into India. Well, Ram Dass claimed the credit of stopping that game by his psychological dodges."

He looked across suddenly at Medina. "You know the Frontier. Did you ever come across the guru that lived at the foot of the Shansi pass as you go over to Kaikand?"

Medina shook his head. "I never travelled that way. Why?"

Sandy seemed disappointed. "Ram Dass used to speak of him. I hoped you might have met him."

The club madeira was being passed round, and there was a little silence while we sipped it. It was certainly a marvellous wine, and I noticed with pain Medina's abstinence.

"You really are missing a lot, you know," Burminster boomed in his jolly voice, and for a second all the company looked Medina's way.

He smiled and lifted his glass of water.

"Sit vini abstemius qui hermeneuma tentat aut hominum petit dominatum," he said.

Nightingale translated. "Meaning that you must be pussyfoot if you would be a big man."

There was a chorus of protests, and Medina again lifted his glass.

"I'm only joking. I haven't a scrap of policy or principle in the matter. I don't happen to like the stuff--that's all."

I fancy that the only two scholars among us were Nightingale and Sandy. I looked at the latter and was surprised by the change in his face. It had awakened to the most eager interest. His eyes, which had been staring at Medina, suddenly met mine, and I read in them not only interest but disquiet.

Burminster was delivering a spirited defence of Bacchus, and the rest joined in, but Sandy took the other side.

"There's a good deal in that Latin tag," he said. "There are places in the world where total abstinence is reckoned a privilege. Did you ever come across the Ulai tribe up the Karakoram way?" He was addressing Medina. "No? Well, the next time you meet a man in the Guides ask him about them, for they're a curiosity. They're Mahommedan and so should by rights be abstainers, but they're a drunken set of sweeps, and the most priest-ridden community on earth. Drinking is not only a habit among them, it's an obligation, and their weekly tamasha would make Falstaff take the pledge. But their priests--they're a kind of theocracy--are strict teetotal. It is their privilege and the secret of their power. When one of them has to be degraded he is filled compulsorily full of wine. That's your--how does the thing go?--your 'hominum dominatus.'"

From that moment I found the evening go less pleasantly. Medina was as genial as ever, but something seemed to have affected Sandy's temper and he became positively grumpy. Now and then he contradicted a man too sharply for good manners, but for the most part he was silent, smoking his pipe and answering his neighbours in monosyllables. About eleven I began to feel it was time to leave, and Medina was of the same opinion. He asked me to walk with him, and I gladly accepted, for I did not feel inclined to go to bed.

As I was putting on my coat, Sandy came up. "Come to the Club, Dick," he said. "I want to talk to you." His manner was so peremptory that I opened my eyes.

"Sorry," I said. "I've promised to walk home with Medina."

"Oh, damn Medina!" he said. "Do as I ask or you'll be sorry for it."

I wasn't feeling very pleased with Sandy, especially as Medina was near enough to hear what he said. So I told him rather coldly that I didn't intend to go back on my arrangement. He turned and marched out, cannoning at the doorway into Burminster, to whom he did not apologise. That nobleman rubbed his shoulder ruefully. "Old Sandy hasn't got used to his corn yet," he laughed. "Looks as if the madeira had touched up his liver."

It was a fine still March night with a good moon, and as we walked along Piccadilly I was feeling cheerful. The good dinner I had eaten and the good wine I had drunk played their part in this mood, and there was also the satisfaction of having dined with good fellows and having been admitted into pretty select company. I felt my liking for Medina enormously increase, and I had the unworthy sense of superiority which a man gets from seeing an old friend whom he greatly admires behave rather badly. I was considering what had ailed Sandy when Medina raised the subject.

"A wonderful fellow Arbuthbot," he said. "I have wanted to meet him for years, and he is certainly up to my expectations. But he has been quite long enough abroad. A mind as keen as his, if it doesn't have the company of its equals, is in danger of getting viewy. What he said to-night was amazingly interesting, but I thought it a little fantastic."

I agreed, but the hint of criticism was enough to revive my loyalty. "All the same there's usually something in his most extravagant theories. I've seen him right when all the sober knowledgeable people were wrong."

"That I can well believe," he said. "You know him well?"

"Pretty well. We've been in some queer places together."

The memory of those queer places came back to me as we walked across Berkeley Square. The West End of London at night always affected me with a sense of the immense solidity of our civilisation. These great houses, lit and shuttered and secure, seemed the extreme opposite of the world of half-lights and perils in which I had sometimes journeyed. I thought of them as I thought of Fosse Manor, as sanctuaries of peace. But to-night I felt differently towards them. I wondered what was going on at the back of those heavy doors. Might not terror and mystery lurk behind that barricade as well as in tent and slum? I suddenly had a picture of a plump face all screwed up with fright muffled beneath the bed-clothes.

I had imagined that Medina lived in chambers or a flat, but we stopped before a substantial house in Hill Street.

"You're coming in? The night's young and there's time for a pipe."

I had no wish to go to bed, so I followed him as he opened the front door with a latch-key. He switched on a light, which lit the first landing of the staircase but left the hall in dusk. It seemed to be a fine place full of cabinets, the gilding of which flickered dimly. We ascended thickly-carpeted stairs, and on the landing he switched off the first light and switched on another which lit a further flight. I had the sensation of mounting to a great height in a queer shadowy world.

"This is a big house for a bachelor," I observed.

"I've a lot of stuff, books and pictures and things, and I like it round me."

He opened a door and ushered me into an enormous room, which must have occupied the whole space on that floor. It was oblong, with deep bays at each end, and it was lined from floor to ceiling with books. Books, too, were piled on the tables, and sprawled on a big flat couch which was drawn up before the fire. It wasn't an ordinary gentleman's library, provided by the bookseller at so much a yard. It was the working collection of a scholar, and the books had that used look which makes them the finest tapestry for a room. The place was lit with lights on small tables, and on a big desk under a reading lamp were masses of papers and various volumes with paper slips in them. It was workshop as well as library.

A servant entered, unsummoned, and put a tray of drinks on a side table. He was dressed like an ordinary butler, but I guessed that he had not spent much of his life in service. The heavy jowl, the small eyes, the hair cut straight round the nape of the neck, the swollen muscles about the shoulder and upper arm told me the profession he had once followed. The man had been in the ring, and not so very long ago. I wondered at Medina's choice, for a pug is not the kind of servant I would choose myself.

"Nothing more, Odell," said Medina. "You can go to bed. I will let Sir Richard out."

He placed me in a long arm-chair, and held the syphon while I mixed myself a very weak whisky-and-soda. Then he sat opposite me across the hearth-rug in a tall old-fashioned chair which he pulled forward from his writing-table. The servant in leaving had turned out all the lights except one at his right hand, which vividly lit up his face, and which, since the fire had burned low, made the only bright patch in the room. I stretched my legs comfortably and puffed at my pipe, wondering how I would have the energy to get up and go home. The long dim shelves, where creamy vellum and morocco ran out of the dusk into darkness, had an odd effect on me. I was visited again by the fancies which had occupied me coming through Berkeley Square. I was inside one of those massive sheltered houses, and lo and behold! it was as mysterious as the aisles of a forest. Books--books--old books full of forgotten knowledge! I was certain that if I had the scholarship to search the grave rows I would find out wonderful things.

I was thirsty, so I drank off my whisky-and-soda, and was just adding a little more soda-water from the syphon at my elbow, when I looked towards Medina. There was that in his appearance which made me move my glass so that a thin stream of liquid fell on my sleeve. The patch was still damp next morning.

His face, brilliantly lit up by the lamp, seemed to be also lit from within. It was not his eyes or any one feature that enthralled me, for I did not notice any details. Only the odd lighting seemed to detach his head from its environment so that it hung in the air like a planet in the sky, full of intense brilliance and power.

It is not very easy to write down what happened. For twelve hours afterwards I remembered nothing--only that I had been very sleepy, and must have been poor company and had soon got up to go. . . . But that was not the real story: it was what the man had willed that I should remember, and because my own will was not really mastered I remembered other things in spite of him; remembered them hazily, like a drunkard's dream.

The head seemed to swim in the centre of pale converging lines. These must have been the book-shelves, which in that part of the room were full of works bound in old vellum. My eyes were held by two violet pin-points of light which were so bright that they hurt me. I tried to shift my gaze, but I could only do that by screwing round my head towards the dying fire. The movement demanded a great effort, for every muscle in my body seemed drugged with lethargy.

As soon as I looked away from the light I regained some possession of my wits. I felt that I must be in for some sickness, and had a moment of bad fright. It seemed to be my business to keep my eyes on the shadows in the hearth, for where darkness was there I found some comfort. I was as afraid of the light before me as a child of a bogy. I thought that if I said something I should feel better, but I didn't seem to have the energy to get a word out. Curiously enough I felt no fear of Medina; he didn't seem to be in the business; it was that disembodied light that scared me.

Then I heard a voice speaking, but still I didn't think of Medina.

"Hannay," it said. "You are Richard Hannay?"

Against my will I slewed my eyes round, and there hung that intolerable light burning into my eyeballs and my soul. I found my voice now, for it seemed to be screwed out of me, and I said "Yes" like an automaton.

I felt my wits and my sense slipping away under that glare. But my main discomfort was physical, the flaming control of the floating brightness--not face, or eyes, but a dreadful overmastering aura. I thought--if at that moment you could call any process of my mind thought--that if I could only link it on to some material thing I should find relief. With a desperate effort I seemed to make out the line of a man's shoulder and the back of a chair. Let me repeat that I never thought of Medina, for he had been wiped clean out of my world.

"You are Richard Hannay," said the voice. "Repeat, 'I am Richard Hannay.'"

The words came out of my mouth involuntarily. I was concentrating all my wits on the comforting outline of the chair-back, which was beginning to be less hazy.

The voice spoke again.

"But till this moment you have been nothing. There was no Richard Hannay before. Now, when I bid you, you begin your life. You remember nothing. You have no past."

"I remember nothing," said my voice, but as I spoke I knew I lied, and that knowledge was my salvation.

I have been told more than once by doctors who dabbled in the business that I was the most hopeless subject for hypnotism that they ever struck. One of them once said that I was about as unsympathetic as Table Mountain. I must suppose that the intractable bedrock of commonplaceness in me now met the something which was striving to master me and repelled it. I felt abominably helpless, my voice was not my own, my eyes were tortured and aching, but I had recovered my mind.

I seemed to be repeating a lesson at someone's dictation. I said I was Richard Hannay, who had just come from South Africa on his first visit to England. I knew no one in London and had no friends. Had I heard of a Colonel Arbuthnot? I had not. Or the Thursday Club? I had not. Or the War? Yes, but I had been in Angola most of the time and had never fought. I had money? Yes, a fair amount, which was in such-and-such a bank and such-and-such investments. . . . I went on repeating the stuff as glibly as a parrot, but all the while I knew I lied. Something deep down in me was insisting that I was Sir Richard Hannay, K.C.B., who had commanded a division in France, and was the squire of Fosse Manor, the husband of Mary, and the father of Peter John.

Then the voice seemed to give orders. I was to do this and that, and I repeated them docilely. I was no longer in the least scared. Someone or something was trying to play monkey-tricks with my mind, but I was master of that, though my voice seemed to belong to an alien gramophone, and my limbs were stupidly weak. I wanted above all things to be allowed to sleep. . . .

I think I must have slept for a little, for my last recollection of that queer sederunt is that the unbearable light had gone, and the ordinary lamps of the room were switched on. Medina was standing by the dead fire, and another man beside him--a slim man with a bent back and a lean grey face. The second man was only there for a moment, but he looked at me closely and I thought Medina spoke to him and laughed. . . . Then I was being helped by Medina into my coat, and conducted downstairs. There were two bright lights in the street which made me want to lie down on the kerb and sleep. . . .

* * * * *

I woke about ten o'clock next morning in my bedroom at the Club, feeling like nothing on earth. I had a bad headache, my eyes seemed to be backed with white fire, and my legs were full of weak pains as if I had influenza. It took me several minutes to realise where I was, and when I wondered what had brought me to such a state I could remember nothing. Only a preposterous litany ran in my brain--the name "Dr. Newhover," and an address in Wimpole Street. I concluded glumly that

that for a man in my condition was a useful recollection, but where I had got it I hadn't an idea.

The events of the night before were perfectly clear. I recalled every detail of the Thursday Club dinner, Sandy's brusqueness, my walk back with Medina, my admiration of his great library. I remembered that I had been drowsy there and thought that I had probably bored him. But I was utterly at a loss to account for my wretched condition. It could not have been the dinner; or the wine, for I had not drunk much, and in any case I have a head like cast iron; or the weak whisky-and-soda in Medina's house. I staggered to my feet and looked at my tongue in the glass. It was all right, so there could be nothing the matter with my digestion.

You are to understand that the account I have just written was pieced together as events came back to me, and that at 10 a.m. the next morning I remembered nothing of it--nothing but the incidents up to my sitting down in Medina's library, and the name and address of a doctor I had never heard of. I concluded that I must have got some infernal germ, probably botulism, and was in for a bad illness. I wondered dismally what kind of fool I had made of myself before Medina, and still more dismally what was going to happen to me. I decided to wire for Mary when I had seen a doctor, and to get as soon as possible into a nursing home. I had never had an illness in my life, except malaria, and I was as nervous as a cat.

But after I had had a cup of tea I felt a little better, and inclined to get up. A cold bath relieved my headache, and I was able to shave and dress. It was while I was shaving that I observed the first thing which made me puzzle about the events of the previous evening. The valet who attended to me had put out the contents of my pockets on the dressing-table--my keys, watch, loose silver, notecase, and my pipe and pouch. Now I carry my pipe in a little leather case, and, being very punctilious in my habits, I invariably put it back in the case when it is empty. But the case was not there, though I remembered laying it on the table beside me in Medina's room, and, moreover, the pipe was still half full of unsmoked tobacco. I rang for the man, and learned that he had found the pipe in the pocket of my dinner jacket, but no case. He was positive, for he knew my ways and had been surprised to find my pipe so untidily pocketed.

I had a light breakfast in the coffee-room, and as I ate it I kept wondering as to what exactly I had been doing the night before. Odd little details were coming back to me; in particular, a recollection of some great effort which had taken all the strength out of me. Could I have been drugged? Not the Thursday Club madeira. Medina's whisky-and-soda?

The idea was nonsense; in any case a drugged man does not have a clean tongue the next morning.

I interviewed the night porter, for I thought he might have something to tell me.

"Did you notice what hour I came home last night?" I asked.

"It was this morning, Sir Richard," the man replied, with the suspicion of a grin. "About half-past three, it would be, or twenty minutes to four."

"God bless my soul!" I exclaimed. "I had no notion it was so late. I sat up talking with a friend."

"You must have been asleep in the car, Sir Richard, for the chauffeur had to wake you, and you were that drowsy I thought I'd better take you upstairs myself. The bedrooms on the top floor is not that easy found."

"I didn't drop a pipe case?" I asked.

"No, sir." The man's discreet face revealed that he thought I had been dining too well but was not inclined to blame me for it.

By luncheon-time I had decided that I was not going to be ill, for there was no longer anything the matter with my body except a certain stiffness in the joints and the ghost of a headache behind my eyes. But my mind was in a precious confusion. I had stayed in Medina's room till after three, and had not been conscious of anything that happened there after, say, half-past eleven. I had left finally in such a state that I had forgotten my pipe-case, and had arrived at the Club in somebody's car--probably Medina's--so sleepy that I had to be escorted upstairs, and had awoke so ill that I thought I had botulism. What in Heaven's name had happened?

I fancy that the fact that I had resisted the influence brought to bear on me with my MIND, though tongue and limbs had been helpless, enabled me to remember what the wielder of the influence had meant to be forgotten. At any rate bits of that strange scene began to come back. I remembered the uncanny brightness--remembered it not with fear but with acute indignation. I vaguely recalled that I had repeated nonsense to somebody's dictation, but what it was I could not yet remember. The more I thought of it the angrier I grew. Medina must have been responsible, though to connect him with it seemed ridiculous when I thought of what I had seen of him. Had he been making me the subject of some scientific experiment? If so, it was infernal impertinence. Anyhow it had failed--that was a salve to my pride--for I had kept my head through it. The doctor had been right who had compared me with Table Mountain.

I had got thus far in my reflections, when I recollected that which put a different complexion on the business. Suddenly I remembered the circumstances in which I had made Medina's acquaintance. From him Tom Greenslade had heard the three facts which fitted in with the jingle which was the key to the mystery that I was sworn to unravel. Hitherto I had never thought of this dazzling figure except as an ally. Was it possible that he might be an enemy? The turn-about was too violent for my mind to achieve it in one movement. I swore to myself that Medina was straight, that it was sheer mania to believe that a gentleman and a sportsman could ever come within hailing distance of the hideous underworld which Macgillivray had revealed to me. . . . But Sandy had not quite taken to him. . . . I thanked my stars that anyhow I had said nothing to him about my job. I did not really believe that there was any doubt about him, but I realised that I must walk very carefully.

And then another idea came to me. Hypnotism had been tried on me, and it had failed. But those who tried it must believe from my behaviour that it had succeeded. If so, somehow and somewhere they would act on that belief. It was my business to encourage it. I was sure enough of myself to think that, now I was forewarned, no further hypnotic experiments could seriously affect me. But let them show their game, let me pretend to be helpless wax in their hands. Who "they" were I had still to find out.

I had a great desire to get hold of Sandy and talk it over, but though I rung up several of his lairs I could not find him. Then I decided to see Dr. Newhover, for I was certain that that name had come to me out of the medley of last night. So I telephoned and made an appointment with him for that afternoon, and four o'clock saw me starting out to walk to Wimpole Street.

CHAPTER VI

THE HOUSE IN GOSPEL OAK

It was a dry March afternoon, with one of those fantastic winds which seem to change their direction hourly, and contrive to be in a man's face at every street corner. The dust was swirling in the gutters, and the scent of hyacinth and narcissus from the flower- shops was mingled with that bleak sandy smell which is London's foretaste of spring. As I crossed Oxford Street I remember thinking what an odd pointless business I had drifted into. I saw nothing for it but to continue drifting and see what happened. I was on my way to visit a doctor of whom I knew nothing, about some ailment which I was not conscious of possessing. I didn't even trouble to make a plan, being content to let chance have the guiding of me.

The house was one of those solid dreary erections which have usually the names of half a dozen doctors on their front doors. But in this case there was only one-- Dr. M. Newhover. The parlourmaid took me into the usual drab waiting-room furnished with Royal Academy engravings, fumed oak, and an assortment of belated picture-papers, and almost at once she returned and ushered me into the consulting-room. This again was of the most ordinary kind-- glazed bookcases, wash-hand basin in a corner, roll-top desk, a table with a medical journal or two and some leather cases. And Dr.

Newhover at first sight seemed nothing out of the common. He was a youngish man, with high cheek-bones, a high forehead, and a quantity of blond hair brushed straight back from it. He wore a pince-nez, and when he removed it showed pale prominent blue eyes. From his look I should have said that his father had called himself Neuhofer.

He greeted me with a manner which seemed to me to be at once patronising and dictatorial. I wondered if he was some tremendous swell in his profession, of whom I ought to have heard. "Well, Mr. Hannay, what can I do for you?" he said. I noticed that he called me "Mr.," though I had given "Sir Richard" both on the telephone and to the parlourmaid. It occurred to me that someone had already been speaking of me to him, and that he had got the name wrong in his memory.

I thought I had better expound the alarming symptoms with which I had awakened that morning.

"I don't know what's gone wrong with me," I said. "I've a pain behind my eyeballs, and my whole head seems muddled up. I feel drowsy and slack, and I've got a weakness in my legs and back like a man who has just had 'flu."

He made me sit down and proceeded to catechise me about my health. I said it had been good enough, but I mentioned my old malaria and several concussions, and I pretended to be pretty nervous about my condition.

Then he went through the whole bag of tricks--sounding me with a stethoscope, testing my blood pressure, and hitting me hard below the knee to see if I reacted. I had to play up to my part, but upon my soul I came near reacting too vigorously to some of his questions and boxing his ears. Always he kept up that odd, intimate, domineering, rather offensive manner.

He made me lie down on a couch while he fingered the muscles of my neck and shoulder and seemed to be shampooing my head with his long chilly hands. I was by this time feeling rather extra well, but I managed to invent little tendernesses here and there and a lot of alarming mental aberrations. I wondered if he were not getting suspicious, for he asked abruptly: "Have you had these symptoms long?" so I thought it better to return to the truth, and told him "only since this morning."

At last he bade me get up, took off the tortoise-shell spectacles he had been wearing and resumed his pince-nez, and while I was buttoning my collar seemed to be sunk in reflection. He made me sit in the patient's chair, and stood up and looked down on me with a magisterial air that made me want to laugh.

"You are suffering," he said, "from a somewhat abnormal form of a common enough complaint. Just as the effects of a concussion are often manifest only some days after the blow, so the results of nervous strain may take a long time to develop. I have no doubt that in spite of your good health you have during recent years been working your mind and body at an undue pressure, and now this morning quite suddenly you reap the fruits. I don't want to frighten you, Mr. Hannay, but neurosis is so mysterious a disease in its working that we must take it seriously, especially at its first manifestations. There are one or two points in your case which I am not happy about. There is, for example, a certain congestion--or what seems to me a congestion--in the nerve centres of the neck and head. That may be induced by the accidents-- concussion and the like--which you have told me of, or it may not. The true cure must, of course, take time, and rest and change of scene are obligatory. You are fond of sport? A fisherman?"

I told him I was.

"Well, a little later I may prescribe a salmon river in Norway. The remoteness of the life from ordinary existence and the contemplation of swift running water have had wonderful results with some of my patients. But Norway is not possible till May, and in the meantime I am going to order you specific treatment. Yes. I mean massage, but by no means ordinary massage. That science is still in its infancy, and its practitioners are only fumbling at the doorway. But now and then we find a person, man or woman, with a kind of extra sense for disentangling and smoothing out muscular and nervous abnormalities. I am going to send you to such an one. The address may surprise you, but you are man of the world enough to know that medical skill is not confined to the area between Oxford Street and the Marylebone Road." He took off his glasses, and smiled.

Then he wrote something on a slip of paper and handed it to me. I read "Madame Breda, 4 Palmyra Square, N.W."

"Right!" I said. "Much obliged to you. I hope Madame Breda will cure this infernal headache. When can I see her?"

"I can promise you she will cure the headache. She is a Swedish lady who has lived in London since the War, and is so much an enthusiast in her art that she will only now and then take a private patient. For the most part she gives her skill free to the children's hospitals. But she will not refuse me. As for beginning, I should lose no time for the sake of your own comfort. What about to-morrow morning?"

"Why not to-night? I have nothing to do, and I want to be quit of my headache before bedtime. Why shouldn't I go on there now?"

"No reason in the world. But I must make an appointment. Madame is on the telephone. Excuse me a moment."

He left the room and returned in a few minutes to say that he had made an appointment for seven o'clock. "It is an outlandish place to get to, but most taxi-drivers know it. If your man doesn't, tell him to drive to Gospel Oak, and then any policeman will direct you."

I had my cheque-book with me, but he didn't want his fee, saying that he was not done with me. I was to come back in a week and report progress. As I left I had a strong impression of a hand as cold as a snake, pale bulging eyes, and cheekbones like a caricature of a Scotchman. An odd but rather impressive figure was Dr. Newhover. He didn't look a fool, and if I hadn't known the uncommon toughness of my constitution I might have been unsettled by his forebodings.

I walked down to Oxford Street and had tea in a tea-shop. As I sat among the chattering typists and shopboys I kept wondering whether I was not wasting my time and behaving like a jackass. Here was I, as fit as a hunter, consulting specialists and visiting unknown masseuses in North London, and all with no clear purpose. In less than twenty-four hours I had tumbled into a perfectly crazy world, and for a second I had a horrid doubt whether the craziness was not inside my mind. Had something given in my brain last night in Medina's room, so that now I was what people call "wanting"? I went over the sequence of events again, and was reassured by remembering that in it all I had kept my head. I had not got to the stage of making theories; I was still only waiting on developments, and I couldn't see any other way before me. I must, of course, get hold of Sandy, but first let me see what this massage business meant. It might all be perfectly square; I might have remembered Dr. Newhover's name by a queer trick of memory-- heard it, perhaps, from some friend--and that remarkable practitioner might be quite honest. But then I remembered the man's manner--I was quite clear that he knew something of me, that someone had told him to expect me. Then it occurred to me that I might be doing a rash thing in going off to an unknown house in a seedy suburb. So I went into a public telephone-booth, rang up the Club, and told the porter that if Colonel Arbuthnot called, I was at 4 Palmyra Square, N.W.--I made him write down the address--and would be back before ten o'clock.

I was rather short of exercise, so I decided to walk, since I had plenty of time. Strangely enough, the road was pretty much that which I had taken on that June day of 1914 when I had been waiting on Bulivant and the Black Stone gentry, and had walked clean out of London to pass the time. Then, I remembered, I had been thrilling with wild anticipation, but now I was an older and much wiser man, and though I was sufficiently puzzled I could curb my restlessness with philosophy. I went up Portland Place, past the Regent's Park, till I left the houses of the well-to-do behind me, and got into that belt of mean streets which is the glacis of the northern heights. Various policemen directed me, and I enjoyed the walk as if I had been exploring, for London is always to me an undiscovered country. I passed yards which not so long ago had been patches of market-garden, and terraces, sometime pretentious, and now sinking into slums; for London is like the tropical bush--

if you don't exercise constant care the jungle, in the shape of the slums, will break in. The streets were full of clerks and shop-girls waiting for buses, and workmen from the St. Pancras and Clerkenwell factories going home. The wind was rising, and in the untidy alleys was stirring up a noisome dust; but as the ground rose it blew cleaner and seemed to bring from Kentish fields and the Channel the tonic freshness of spring. I stopped for a little and watched behind me the plain of lights, which was London, quivering in the dark-blue windy dusk.

It was almost dark when at last, after several false casts, I came into Palmyra Square. It was a square only in name, for one side was filled with a warehouse of sorts, and another straggled away in nests of small brick houses. One side was a terrace of artisans' dwellings, quite new, each with a tiny bow-window and names like "Chatsworth" and "Kitchener Villa." The fourth side, facing south, had once had a certain dignity, and the builder who had designed the place seventy years ago had thought, no doubt, that he was creating a desirable residential quarter. There the houses stood apart, each in a patch of garden, which may at one time have had lawns and flowers. Now these gardens were mere dusty yards, the refuge of tin cans and bits of paper, and only a blackened elm, an ill-grown privet hedge, and some stunted lilacs told of the more cheerful past. On one house was the brass plate of a doctor, on another that of a teacher of music; several advertised lodgings to let; the steps were untidy, the gates askew on their hinges, and over everything was written the dreary legend of a shabby gentility on the very brink of squalor.

Number 4 was smarter than the others, and its front door had been newly painted a vivid green. I rang the bell, which was an electric one, and the door was opened by a maid who looked sufficiently respectable. When I entered I saw that the house was on a more generous scale than I had thought, and had once, no doubt, been the home of some comfortable citizen. The hall was not the tank-like thing of the small London dwelling, and the room into which I was ushered, though small, was well furnished and had an electric fire in the grate. It seemed to be a kind of business room, for there was a telephone, a big safe, and on the shelves a line of lettered boxes for papers. I began to think that Madame Breda, whoever she might be, must be running a pretty prosperous show on ordinary business lines.

I was presently led by the maid to a room on the other side of the hall, where I was greeted by a smiling lady. Madame was a plump person in the early forties, with dark hair and a high colour, who spoke English almost without an accent. "Dr. Newhover has sent you. So? He has told me. Will you please go in there and take off your coat and waistcoat? Your collar, too, please."

I did as I was bid, and in a little curtained cubicle divested myself of these garments and returned in my shirt-sleeves. The room was a very pleasant one, with folding doors at one end, furnished like an ordinary drawing-room, with flowers in pots and books, and what looked like good eighteenth-century prints. Any suspicion I may have had of the bona fides of the concern received a rude shock. Madame had slipped over her black dress a white linen overall, such as surgeons wear, and she had as her attendant a small thin odd-looking girl, who also wore an overall, and whose short hair was crowned with a small white cap.

"This is Gerda," Madame said. "Gerda helps me. She is very clever." She smiled on Gerda, and Gerda smiled back, a limp little contortion of a perfectly expressionless face.

Madame made me lie down on a couch. "You have a headache?"

I mendaciously said that I had.

"That I can soon cure. But there are other troubles? So? These I must explore. But first I will take away the pain."

"I felt her light firm fingers playing about my temples and the base of my skull and my neck muscles. A very pleasant sensation it was, and I am certain that if I had been suffering from the worst headache in the world it would have been spirited away. As it was, being in excellent health, I felt soothed and freshened.

"So," she said, beaming down on me. "You are better? You are so beeg that it is not easy to be well all over at once. Now, I must look into more difficult things. You are not happy in your nerves-- not altogether. Ah! these nerves! We do not quite know what they are, except that they are what you call the devil. You are very wakeful now. Is it not so? Well I must put you to sleep. That is necessary, if you are willing."

"Right-o," I answered; but inwardly I said to myself, "No, my woman, I bet you don't." I was curious to see if, now that I was forewarned, I could resist any hypnotic business, as I believed I could.

I imagined that she would try to master me with her eyes, which were certainly remarkable orbs. But her procedure was the very opposite, for the small girl brought some things on a tray, and I saw that they were bandages. First of all, with a fine cambric handkerchief, she swathed my eyes, and then tied above it another of some heavy opaque material. They were loosely bound, so that I scarcely felt them, but I was left in the thickest darkness. I noticed that she took special pains so to adjust them that they should not cover my ears.

"You are not wakeful," I heard her voice say, "I think you are sleepy. You will sleep now."

I felt her fingers stray over my face, and the sensation was different, for whereas, when she had treated my headache, they had set up a delicious cool tingling of the skin, now they seemed to induce wave upon wave of an equally pleasant langour. She pressed my forehead, and my senses seemed to be focused there and to be lulled by that pressure. All the while she was cooing to me in a voice which was like the drowsy swell of the sea. If I had wanted to go to sleep I could have dropped off easily, but, as I didn't want to, I had no difficulty in resisting the gentle coercion. That, I fancy, is my position about hypnotism. I am no kind of use under compulsion, and for the thing to affect me it has to have the backing of my own will. Anyhow, I could appreciate the pleasantness of it and yet disregard it. But it was my business to be a good subject, so I pretended to drift away into slumber. I made my breath come slowly and softly, and let my body relax into impassivity.

Presently she appeared to be satisfied. She said a word to the child, whose feet I could hear cross the room. There was a sound of opening doors--my ears, remember, were free of the bandages and my hearing is acute--and then it seemed to me that the couch on which I lay began slowly to move. I had a moment of alarm and nearly gave away the show by jerking up my head. The couch seemed to travel very smoothly on rails, and I was conscious that I had passed through the folding doors and was now in another room. Then the movement stopped, and I realised that I was in an entirely different atmosphere. I realised, too, that a new figure had come on the scene.

There was no word spoken, but I had the queer inexplicable consciousness of human presences which is independent of sight and hearing. I have said that the atmosphere of the place had changed. There was a scent in the air which anywhere else I would have sworn was due to peat smoke, and mixed with it another intangible savour which I could not put a name to, but which did not seem to belong to London at all, or to any dwelling, but to some wild out-of- doors. . . . And then I was aware of noiseless fingers pressing my temples.

They were not the plump capable hands of Madame Breda. Nay, they were as fine and tenuous as a wandering wind, but behind their airy lightness was a hint of steel, as if they could choke as well as caress. I lay supine, trying to keep my breathing regular, since I was supposed to be asleep, but I felt an odd excitement rising in my heart. And then it quieted for the fingers seemed to be smoothing it away. . . . A voice was speaking in a tongue of which I knew not a word, not speaking to me, but repeating, as it were, a private incantation. And the touch and voice combined to bring me nearer to losing my wits than even on the night before, nearer than I have ever been in all my days.

The experience was so novel and overpowering that I find it hard to give even a rough impression of it. Let me put it this way. A man at my time of life sees old age not so very far distant, and the nearer he draws to the end of his journey the more ardently he longs for his receding youth. I do not mean that, if some fairy granted him the gift, he would go back to boyhood; few of us would choose such a return; but he clothes all his youth in a happy radiance and aches to recapture the freshness and wonder with which he then looked on life. He treasures, like a mooning girl, stray sounds and scents and corners of landscape, which for a moment push the door ajar. . . . As I lay blindfolded on that couch I felt mysterious hands and voices plucking on my behalf at the barrier of the years and breaking it down. I was escaping into a delectable country, the Country of the Young, and I welcomed the escape. Had I been hypnotised, I should beyond doubt have moved like a sheep whithersoever this shepherd willed.

But I was awake, and, though on the very edge of surrender, I managed to struggle above the tides. Perhaps to my waking self the compulsion was too obvious and aroused a faint antagonism. Anyhow I had already begun a conscious resistance when the crooning voice spoke in English.

"You are Richard Hannay," it said. "You have been asleep, but I have wakened you. You are happy in the world in which you have wakened?"

My freedom was now complete, for I had begun to laugh, silently, far down at the bottom of my heart. I remembered last night, and the performance in Medina's house which had all day been growing clearer in my memory. I saw it as farce, and this as farce, and at the coming of humour the spell died. But it was up to me to make some kind of an answer, if I wanted to keep up the hoax, so I did my best to screw out an eerie sleep-walker's voice.

"I am happy," I said, and my pipe sounded like the twittering of sheeted ghosts.

"You wish to wake often in this world?"

I signified by a croak that I did.

"But to wake you must first sleep, and I alone can make you sleep and wake. I exact a price, Richard Hannay. Will you pay my price?"

I was puzzled about the voice. It had not the rich foreign tones of Madame Breda, but it had a very notable accent, which I could not place. At one moment it seemed to have the lilt which you find in Western Ross, but there were cadences in it which were not Highland. Also, its timbre was curious--very light and thin like a child's. Was it possible that the queer little girl I had seen was the sibyl? No, I decided; the hands had not been a child's hands.

"I will pay any price," I said, which seemed to be the answer required of me.

"Then you are my servant when I summon you. Now, sleep again."

I had never felt less like being anyone's servant. The hands fluttered again around my temples, but they had no more effect on me than the buzzing of flies. I had an insane desire to laugh, which I repressed by thinking of the idiotic pointlessness of my recent doings. . . . I felt my couch slide backwards, and heard the folding doors open again and close. Then I felt my bandages being deftly undone, and I lay with the light on my closed eyelids, trying to look like a sleeping warrior on a tomb. Someone was pressing below my left ear and I recognised the old hunter's method of bringing a man back gently from sleep to consciousness, so I set about the job of making a workmanlike awaking. I hope I succeeded. Anyhow I must have looked dazed enough, for the lamps hurt my eyes after the muffled darkness.

I was back in the first room, with only Madame beside me. She beamed on me with the friendliest eyes, and helped me on with my coat and collar. "I have had you under close observation," she said, "for sleep often reveals where the ragged ends of the nerves lie. I have made certain deductions, which I will report to Dr. Newhover. . . . No, there is no fee. Dr. Newhover will make arrangements." She bade me good-bye in the best professional manner, and I descended the steps into Palmyra Square as if I had been spending a commonplace hour having my back massaged for lumbago.

Once in the open air I felt abominably tired and very hungry. By good luck I hadn't gone far when I picked up a taxi and told it to drive to the Club. I looked at my watch and saw that it was later than I thought--close on ten o'clock. I had been several hours in the house, and small wonder I was weary.

I found Sandy wandering restlessly about the hall. "Thank God!" he said when he saw me. "Where the devil have you been, Dick? The porter gave me a crazy address in North London. You look as if you wanted a drink."

"I feel as if I wanted food," I said. "I have a lot to tell you, but I must eat first. I've had no dinner."

Sandy sat opposite me while I fed, and forbore to ask questions.

"What put you in such a bad humour last night?" I asked.

He looked very solemn. "Lord knows. No, that's not true, I know well enough. I didn't take to Medina."

"Now I wonder why?"

"I wonder too. But I'm just like a dog: I take a dislike to certain people at first sight, and the queer thing is that my instinct isn't often wrong."

"Well, you're pretty well alone in your opinion. What sets you against him? He is well-mannered, modest, a good sportsman, and you can see he's as clever as they make."

"Maybe. But I've got a notion that the man is one vast lie. However, let's put it that I reserve my opinion. I have various inquiries to make."

We found the little back smoking-room on the first floor empty, and when I had lit my pipe and got well into an armchair, Sandy drew up another at my elbow. "Now, Dick," he said.

"First," I said, "it may interest you to learn that Medina dabbles in hypnotism."

"I knew that," he said, "from his talk last night."

"How on earth--?"

"Oh, from a casual quotation he used. It's a longish story, which I'll tell you later. Go on."

I began from the break-up of the Thursday Club dinner and told him all I could remember of my hours in Medina's house. As a story it met with an immense success. Sandy was so interested that he couldn't sit in his chair, but must get up and stand on the hearth- rug before me. I told him that I had wakened up feeling uncommonly ill, with a blank mind except for the address of a doctorman in Wimpole Street, and how during the day recollection had gradually come back to me. He questioned me like a cross-examining counsel.

"Bright light--ordinary hypnotic property. Face, which seemed detached--that's a common enough thing in Indian magic. You say you must have been asleep, but were also in a sense awake and could hear and answer questions, and that you felt a kind of antagonism all the time which kept your will alive. You're probably about the toughest hypnotic proposition in the world, Dick, and you can thank God for that. Now, what were the questions? A summons to forget your past and begin as a new creature, subject to the authority of a master. You assented, making private reservations of which the hypnotist knew nothing. If you had not kept your head and made those reservations, you would have remembered nothing at all of last night, but there would have been a subconscious bond over your will. As it is, you're perfectly free: only the man who tried to monkey with you doesn't know that. Therefore you begin by being one up on the game. You know where you are and he doesn't know where he is."

"What do you suppose Medina meant by it? It was infernal impertinence anyhow. But was it Medina? I seem to remember another man in the room before I left."

"Describe him."

"I've only a vague picture--a sad grey-faced fellow."

"Well, assume for the present that the experimenter was Medina. There's such a thing, remember, as spiriting away a man's recollection of his past, and starting him out as a waif in a new world. I've heard in the East of such performances, and of course it means that the memory-less being is at the mercy of the man who has stolen his memory. That is probably not the intention in your case. They wanted only to establish a subconscious control. But it couldn't be done at once with a fellow of your antecedents, so they organised a process. They suggested to you in your trance a doctor's name, and the next stage was his business. You woke feeling very seedy and remembering a doctor's address, and they argued that you would think that you had been advised about the fellow and make a bee-line for him. Remember, they would assume that you had no recollection of anything else from the night's doings. Now go ahead and tell me about the chirurgeon. Did you go to see him?"

I continued my story, and at the Wimpole Street episode Sandy laughed long and loud.

"Another point up in the game. You say you think the leech had been advised of your coming and not by you? By the way, he seems to have talked fairly good sense, but I'd as soon set a hippopotamus for nerves as you." He wrote down Dr. Newhover's address in his pocket book. "Continuez. You then proceeded, I take it, to 4 Palmyra Square."

At the next stage in my narrative he did not laugh. I dare say I told it better than I have written it down here, for I was fresh from the experience, and I could see that he was a good deal impressed.

"A Swedish masseuse and an odd-looking little girl. She puts you to sleep, or thinks she has, and then, when your eyes are bandaged, someone else nearly charms the soul out of you. That sounds big magic. I see the general lines of it, but it is big magic, and I didn't know that it was practised on these shores. Dick, this is getting horribly interesting. You kept wide awake--you are an old buffalo, you know--but you gave the impression of absolute surrender. Good for you--you are now three points ahead in the game."

"Well, but what is the game? I'm hopelessly puzzled."

"So am I, but we must work on assumptions. Let us suppose Medina is responsible. He may only be trying to find out the extent of his powers, and selects you as the most difficult subject to be found. You may be sure he knows all about your record. He may be only a vain man experimenting."

"In which case," I said, "I propose to punch his head."

"In which case, as you justly observe, you will give yourself the pleasure of punching his head. But suppose that he has got a far deeper purpose, something really dark and damnable. If by his hypnotic power he could make a tool of you, consider what an asset he would have found. A man of your ability and force. I have always said, you remember, that you had a fine natural talent for crime."

"I tell you, Sandy, that's nonsense. It's impossible that there's anything wrong--badly wrong--with Medina."

"Improbable, but not impossible. We're taking no chances. And if he were a scoundrel, think what a power he might be with all his talents and charm and popularity."

Sandy flung himself into a chair and appeared to be meditating. Once or twice he broke silence.

"I wonder what Dr. Newhover meant by talking of a salmon river in Norway. Why not golf at North Berwick?"

And again:

"You say there was a scent like peat in the room? Peat! You are certain?"

Finally he got up. "To-morrow," he said, "I think I will have a look round the house in Gospel Oak. Gospel Oak, by the way, is a funny name, isn't it? You say it has electric light. I will visit it as a man from the corporation to see about the meter. Oh, that can easily be managed. Macgillivray will pass the word for me."

The mention of Macgillivray brought me to attention. "Look here," I said, "I'm simply wasting my time. I got in touch with Medina in order to ask his help, and now I've been landed in a set of preposterous experiences which have nothing to do with my job. I must see Macgillivray to-morrow about getting alongside his Shropshire squire. For the present there can be nothing doing with Medina."

"Shropshire squire be hanged! You're an old ass, Dick. For the present there's everything doing with Medina. You wanted his help. Why? Because he was the next stage in the clue to that nonsensical rhyme. Well, you've discovered that there may be odd things about him. You can't get his help, but you may get something more. You may get the secret itself. Instead of having to burrow into his memory, as you did with Greenslade, you may find it sticking out of his life."

"Do you really believe that?" I asked in some bewilderment.

"I believe nothing as yet. But it is far the most promising line. He thinks that from what happened last night PLUS what happened two hours ago you are under his influence, an acolyte, possibly a tool. It may be all quite straight, or it may be most damnably crooked. You have got to find out. You must keep close to him, and foster his illusions, and play up to him for all you're worth. He is bound to show his hand. You needn't take any steps on your own account. He'll give you the lead all right."

I can't say I liked the prospect, for I have no love for playacting, but I am bound to admit that Sandy talked sense. I asked him about himself, for I counted on his backing more than I could say.

"I propose to resume my travels," he said. "I wish to pursue my studies in the Bibliothèque Nationale of France."

"But I thought you were with me in this show."

"So I am. I go abroad on your business, as I shall explain to you some day. Also I want to see the man whom we used to call Ram Dass. I believe him to be in Munich at this moment. The day after to-morrow you will read in The Times that Colonel the Master of Clanroyden has gone abroad for an indefinite time on private business."

"How long will you be away?" I groaned.

"A week perhaps, or a fortnight--or more. And when I come back it may not be as Sandy Arbuthnot."

CHAPTER VII

SOME EXPERIENCES OF A DISCIPLE

I didn't see Sandy again, for he took the night train for Paris next evening, and I had to go down to Oxford that day to appear as a witness in a running-down case. But I found a note for me at the Club when I got back the following morning. It contained nothing except these words: "Coverts drawn blank, no third person in house." I had not really hoped for anything from Sandy's expedition to Palmyra Square, and thought no more about it.

He didn't return in a week, nor yet in a fortnight, and, realising that I had only a little more than two months to do my job in, I grew very impatient. But my time was pretty well filled with Medina, as you shall hear.

While I was reading Sandy's note Turpin turned up, and begged me to come for a drive in his new Delage and talk to him. The Marquis de la Tour du Pin was, if possible, more pallid than before, his eyelids heavier, and his gentleness more silken. He drove me miles into the country, away through Windsor Forest, and as we raced at sixty miles an hour he uncovered his soul. He was going mad, it seemed; was, indeed, already mad, and only a slender and doubtless ill-founded confidence in me prevented him shooting himself. He was convinced that Adela Victor was dead, and that no trace of her would ever be found. "These policemen of yours--bah!" he moaned. "Only in England can people vanish." He concluded, however, that he would stay alive till he had avenged her, for he believed that a good God would some day deliver her murderer into his hands. I was desperately sorry for him, for behind his light gasconading manner there were marks of acute suffering, and indeed in his case I think I should have gone crazy. He asked me for hope, and I gave him it, and told him what I did not believe--that I saw light in the business, and had every confidence that we would restore him his sweetheart safe and sound. At that he cheered up and wanted to embrace me, thereby jolly nearly sending the Delage into a ditch and us both into eternity. He was burning for something to do, and wanted me to promise that as soon as possible I would inspan him into my team. That made me feel guilty, for I knew I had no team, and nothing you could call a clue; so I talked hastily about Miss Victor, lest he should ask me more.

I had her portrait drawn for me in lyric prose. She was slight, it seemed, middling tall, could ride like Diana and dance like the nymphs. Her colouring and hair were those of a brunette, but her eyes were a deep grey, and she had the soft voice which commonly goes with such eyes. Turpin, of course, put all this more poetically, relapsing frequently into French. He told me all kinds of things about her--how she was crazy about dogs, and didn't fear anything in the world, and walked with a throw-out, and lisped delightfully when she was excited.

Altogether at the end of it I felt I had a pretty good notion of Miss Victor, especially as I had studied about fifty photographs of her in Macgillivray's room.

As we were nearing home again it occurred to me to ask him if he knew Medina. He said no, but that he was dining at the Victors' that evening--a small dinner party, mostly political. "He is wonderful, that Mr. Victor. He will not change his life, and his friends think Adela is in New York for a farewell visit. He is like the Spartan boy with the fox."

"Tell Mr. Victor, with my compliments," I said, "that I would like to dine there to-night. I have a standing invitation. Eight- fifteen, isn't it?"

It turned out to be a very small and select party--the Foreign Secretary, Medina, Palliser-Yeates, the Duke of Alcester, Lord Sunningdale, the ex-Lord Chancellor, Levasseur the French Minister, besides Turpin and myself. There were no women present. The behaviour of the Duke and Mr. Victor was a lesson in fortitude, and you would never have guessed that these two men were living with a nightmare. It was not a talkative assembly, though Sunningdale had a good deal to say to the table about a new book that a German had written on the mathematical conception of infinity, a subject which even his brilliant exposition could not make clear to my thick wits. The Foreign Secretary and Levasseur had a tête-à-tête, with Turpin as a hanger-on, and the rest of us would have been as dull as sticks if it had not been for

Medina. I had a good chance of observing his quality, and I must say I was astonished at his skill. It was he who by the right kind of question turned Sunningdale's discourse on infinity, which would otherwise have been a pedantic monologue, into good conversation. We got on to politics afterwards, and Medina, who had just come from the House, was asked what was happening.

"They had just finished the usual plat du jour, the suspension of a couple of Labour mountebanks," he said.

This roused Sunningdale, who rather affected the Labour Party, and I was amused to see how Medina handled the ex-Chancellor. He held him in good-humoured argument, never forsaking his own position, but shedding about the whole subject an atmosphere of witty and tolerant understanding. I felt that he knew more about the business than Sunningdale, that he knew so much he could afford to give his adversary rope. Moreover, he never forgot that he was at a dinner-table, the pitch and key of his talk were exactly right, and he managed to bring everyone into it.

To me he was extraordinarily kind. Indeed he treated me like a very ancient friend, bantering and affectionate and yet respectful, and he forced me to take a full share in the conversation. Under his stimulus, I became quite intelligent, and amazed Turpin, who had never credited me with any talents except for fighting. But I had not forgotten what I was there for, and if I had been inclined to, there were the figures of Victor and the

Duke to remind me. I watched the two, the one thin, grey-bearded, rather like an admiral with his vigilant dark eyes, the other heavy-jowled, rubicund, crowned with fine silver hair; in both I saw shadows of pain stealing back to the corners of lip and eye, whenever the face was in repose. And Medina--the very beau ideal of a courteous, kindly, open-air Englishman. I noted how in his clothes he avoided any touch of overdressing, no fancifully-cut waistcoat or too-smartly- tied tie. In manner and presence he was the perfection of unselfconscious good breeding. It was my business to play up to him, and I let my devotion be pretty evident. The old Duke, whom I now met for the first time, patted my shoulder as we left the dining-room. "I am glad to see that you and Medina are friends, Sir Richard. Thank God that we have a man like him among the young entry. They ought to give him office at once, you know, get him inside the shafts of the coach. Otherwise he'll find something more interesting to do than politics."

By tacit consent we left the house together, and I walked the streets by his side, as I had done three nights before. What a change, I reflected, in my point of view! Then I had been blind, now I was acutely watchful. He slipped an arm into mine as we entered Pall Mall, but its pressure did not seem so much friendly as possessive.

"You are staying at your Club?" he said. "Why not take up your quarters with me while you are in town? There's ample room in Hill Street."

The suggestion put me into a fright. To stay with him at present would wreck all my schemes; but, supposing he insisted, could I refuse, if it was my role to appear to be under his domination? Happily he did not insist. I made a lot of excuses--plans unsettled, constantly running down to the country, and so on.

"All right. But some day I may make the offer again and then I'll take no refusal."

They were just the kind of words a friend might have used, but somehow, though the tone was all right, they slightly grated on me.

"How are you?" he asked. "Most people who have led your life find the English spring trying. You don't look quite as fit as when I first saw you."

"No. I've been rather seedy this past week--headachy, loss of memory, stuffed-up brain and that sort of thing. I expect it's the spring fret. I've seen a doctor and he doesn't worry about it."

"Who's your man?"

"A chap Newhover in Wimpole Street."

He nodded. "I've heard of him. They tell me he's good."

"He has ordered me massage," I said boldly. "That cures the headaches anyway."

"I'm glad to hear it."

Then he suddenly released my arm.

"I see Arbuthnot has gone abroad."

There was a coldness in his voice to which I hastened to respond.

"So I saw in the papers," I said carelessly. "He's a hopeless fellow. A pity, for he's able enough; but he won't stay put, and that makes him pretty well useless."

"Do you care much for Arbuthnot?"

"I used to," I replied shamelessly. "But till the other day I hadn't seen him for years, and I must say he has grown very queer. Didn't you think he behaved oddly at the Thursday dinner?"

He shrugged his shoulders. "I wasn't much taken by him. He's too infernally un-English. I don't know how he got it, but there seems to be a touch of the shrill Levantine in him. Compare him with those fellows to-night. Even the Frenchmen--even Victor, though he's an American and a Jew--are more our own way of thinking."

We were at the Club door, and as I stopped he looked me full in the face.

"If I were you I wouldn't have much to do with Arbuthnot," he said, and his tone was a command. I grinned sheepishly, but my fingers itched for his ears.

I went to bed fuming. This new possessory attitude, this hint of nigger-driving, had suddenly made me hate Medina. I had been unable to set down the hypnotist business clearly to his account, and, even if I had been certain, I was inclined to think it only the impertinent liberty of a faddist--a thing which I hotly resented but which did not arouse my serious dislike. But now--to feel that he claimed me as his man, because he thought, no doubt, that he had established some unholy power over me--that fairly broke my temper. And his abuse of Sandy put the lid on it--abuse to which I had been shamefully compelled to assent. Levantine, by gad! I swore that Sandy and I would make him swallow that word before he was very much older. I couldn't sleep for thinking about it. By this time I was perfectly willing to believe that Medina was up to any infamy, and I was resolved that in him and him alone lay the key to the riddle of the three hostages. But all the time I was miserably conscious that if I suggested such an idea to anyone except Sandy I should be set down as a lunatic. I could see that the man's repute was as solidly planted as the British Constitution.

Next morning I went to see Macgillivray. I explained that I had not been idle, that I had been pursuing lines of my own, which I thought more hopeful than his suggestion of getting alongside the Shropshire squire. I said I had nothing as yet to report, and that I didn't propose to give him the faintest notion of what I was after till I had secured some results. But I wanted his help, and I wanted his very best men.

"Glad to see you've got busy, Dick," he said. "I await your commands."

"I want a house watched. No. 4 Palmyra Square, up in North London. So far as I know it is occupied by a woman, who purports to be a Swedish masseuse and calls herself Madame Breda, one or more maids, and an odd-looking little girl. I want you to have a close record kept of the people who go there, and I want especially to know who exactly are the inmates of the house and who are the frequent visitors. It must be done very cautiously, for the people must have no suspicion that they are being spied on."

He wrote down the details.

"Also I want you to find out the antecedents of Medina's butler."

He whistled. "Medina. Dominick Medina, you mean?"

"Yes. Oh, I'm not suspecting HIM." We both laughed, as if at a good joke. "But I should like to hear something about his butler, for reasons which I'm not yet prepared to give you. He answers to the name of Odell, and has the appearance of an inferior prize-fighter. Find out all you can about his past, and it mightn't be a bad plan to have him shadowed. You know Medina's house in Hill Street. But for Heaven's sake, let it be done tactfully."

"I'll see to that for my own sake. I don't want head-lines in the evening papers--'House of Member of Parliament Watched. Another Police Muddle.'"

"Also, could you put together all you can get about Medina? It might give me a line on Odell."

"Dick," he said solemnly, "are you growing fantastic?"

"Not a bit of it. You don't imagine I'm ass enough to think there's anything shady about Medina. He and I have become bosom friends and I like him enormously. Everybody swears by him, and so do I. But I have my doubts about Mr. Odell, and I would like to know just how and where Medina picked him up. He's not the ordinary stamp of butler." It seemed to me very important to let no one but Sandy into the Medina business at present, for our chance lay in his complete confidence that all men thought well of him.

"Right," said Macgillivray. "It shall be done. Go your own way, Dick. I won't attempt to dictate to you. But remember that the thing is desperately serious, and that the days are slipping past. We're in April now, and you have only till midsummer to save three innocent lives."

I left his office feeling very solemn, for I had suddenly a consciousness of the shortness of time and the magnitude of the job which I had not yet properly begun. I cudgelled my brains to think of my next step. In a few days I should again visit Dr. Newhover, but there was not likely to be much assistance there. He might send me back to Palmyra Square, or I might try to make an appointment with Madame Breda myself, inventing some new ailment; but I would only find the same old business, which would get me no further forward. As I viewed it, the Newhover and Palmyra Square episodes had been used only to test my submission to Medina's influence, and it was to Medina that I must look for further light. It was a maddening job to sit and wait and tick off the precious days on the calendar, and I longed to consult with Sandy. I took to going down to Fosse for the day, for the sight of Mary and Peter John somehow quieted my mind and fixed my resolution. It was a positive relief when at the end of the week Medina rang me up and asked me to luncheon.

We lunched at his house, which, seen on a bright April day, was a wonderful treasury of beautiful things. It was not the kind of house I fancied myself, being too full of museum pieces, and all the furniture strictly correct according to period. I like rooms in which there is a pleasant jumble of things, and which look as if homely people had lived in them for generations. The dining-room was panelled in white, with a Vandyck above the mantelpiece and a set of gorgeous eighteenth-century prints on the walls. At the excellent meal Medina as usual drank water, while I obediently sampled an old hock, an older port, and a most prehistoric brandy. Odell was in attendance, and I had a good look at him--his oddly- shaped head, his flat sallow face, the bunches of black eyebrow above his beady eyes. I calculated that if I saw him again I would not fail to recognise him. We never went near the library on the upper floor, but sat after luncheon in a little smoking-room at the back of the hall, which held my host's rods and guns in glass cabinets, and one or two fine heads of deer and ibex.

I had made up my mind, as I walked to Hill Street, that I was going to convince Medina once and for all of the abjectness of my surrender. He should have proof that I was clay in his hands, for only that way would he fully reveal himself. I detested the job, and as I walked through the pleasant crisp noontide I reflected with bitterness that I might have been fishing for salmon in Scotland, or, better still, cantering with Mary over the Cotswold downs.

All through luncheon I kept my eyes fixed on him like a dog's on his master. Several times I wondered if I were not overdoing it, but he seemed to accept my homage as quite natural. I had thought when I first met him that the man had no vanity; now I saw that he had mountains of it, that he was all vanity, and that his public modesty was only a cloak to set off his immense private conceit. He unbent himself, his whole mind was in undress, and behind the veneer of good-fellowship I seemed to see a very cold arrogant soul. Nothing worse, though that was bad enough. He was too proud to boast in words, but his whole attitude was one long brag. He was cynical about everything, except, as I suspected, his private self-worship. The thing would have been monstrously indecent, if it had not been done with such consummate skill. Indeed I found my part easy to play, for I was deeply impressed and had no difficulty in showing it.

The odd thing was that he talked a good deal about myself. He seemed to take pains to rout out the codes and standards, the points of honour and points of conduct, which somebody like me was likely to revere, and to break them down with his cynicism. I felt that I was looking on at an attempt, which the devil is believed to specialise in, to make evil good and good evil. . . . Of course I assented gladly. Never had master a more ready disciple. . . . He broke down, too, my modest ambitions. A country life, a wife and family--he showed that they were too trivial for more than a passing thought. He flattered me grossly, and I drank it all in with a silly face. I was fit for bigger things, to which he would show me the way. He sketched some of the things--very flattering they were and quite respectable, but somehow they seemed out of the picture when compared to his previous talk. He was clearly initiating me step by step into something for which I was not yet fully ready. . . . I wished Sandy could have seen me sitting in Medina's arm-chair, smoking one of his cigars, and agreeing to everything he said like a schoolgirl who wants to keep on the good side of her schoolmistress. And yet I didn't find it difficult, for the man's talk was masterly and in its way convincing, and, while my mind repudiated it, it was easy for my tongue to assent. He was in a prodigious good-humour, and he was kindly, as a keeper is kind to a well-broken dog.

On the doorstep I stammered my thanks. "I wish I could tell you what knowing you means to me. It's--it's far the biggest thing in my life. What I mean to say is--" the familiar patois of the tongue-tied British soldier.

He looked at me with those amazing eyes of his, no kindness in them, only patronage and proprietorship. I think he was satisfied that he had got someone who would serve him body and soul.

I, too, was satisfied, and walked away feeling more cheerful than I had done for days. Surely things would begin to move now, I thought. At the Club, too, I got encouragement in the shape of a letter from Sandy. It bore a French postmark which I could not decipher, and it was the merest scribble, but it greatly heartened me.

"I have made progress," it ran, "but I have still a lot to do and we can't talk to each other yet awhile. But I shall have to send you letters occasionally, which you must burn on receipt. I shall sign them with some letter of the Greek alphabet--no, you wouldn't recognise that--with the names of recent Derby winners. Keep our affair secret as the grave--don't let in a soul, not even Mac. And for God's sake stick close to M. and serve him like a slave."

There wasn't much in it, but it was hopeful, though the old ruffian didn't seem in a hurry to come home. I wondered what on earth he had found out--something solid, I judged, for he didn't talk lightly of making progress.

That evening I had nothing to do, and after dinner I felt too restless to sit down to a pipe and book. There was no one in the Club I wanted to talk to, so I sallied forth to another pot-house to which I belonged, where there was a chance of finding some of the younger and cheerier generation. Sure enough the first man I saw there was Archie Roylance, who greeted me with a whoop and announced that he was in town for a couple of days to see his doctor. He had had a bad fall steeplechasing earlier in the year, when he had all but broken his neck, but he declared that he was perfectly fit again except for some stiffness in his shoulder muscles. He was as lame as a duck from his flying smash just before the Armistice, but all the same he got about at a surprising pace. Indeed, out of cussedness he walked more than he used to do in the old days, and had taken to deer-stalking with enthusiasm. I think I have mentioned that he was my partner in the tenancy of Machray forest.

I proposed that we should go to a music-hall or cut into the second act of some play, but Archie had another idea. One of his fads was to be an amateur of dancing, though he had never been a great performer before his smash and would never dance again. He said he wanted to see the latest fashions and suggested that we should go for an hour to a small (and he added, select) club somewhere in Marylebone, of which he believed he was a member. It bore an evil reputation, he said, for there was a good deal of high play, and the licensing laws were not regarded, but it was a place to see the best dancing. I made no objection, so we strolled up Regent Street in that season of comparative peace when busy people have gone home and the idle are still shut up in theatres and restaurants.

It was a divine April night, and I observed that I wished I were in a better place to enjoy spring weather. "I've just come from a Scotch moor," said Archie. "Lord! the curlews are makin' a joyful noise. That is the bird for my money. Come back with me, Dick, on Friday and I'll teach you a lot of things. You're a wise man, but you might be a better naturalist."

I thought how much I would have given to be able to accept, as the light wind blew down Langham Place.

Then I wished that this job would take me out of town into fresh air, where I could get some exercise. The result was that I was in a baddish temper when we reached our destination, which was in one of the streets near Fitzroy Square. The place proved to be about as hard to get into as the Vatican. It took a long harangue and a tip from Archie to persuade the door-keeper that we were of the right brand of disreputability to be admitted. Finally we found ourselves in a room with sham Chinese decorations, very garishly lit, with about twenty couples, dancing and about twenty more sitting drinking at little tables.

We paid five shillings apiece for a liqueur, found a table and took notice of the show. It seemed to me a wholly rotten and funereal business. A nigger band, looking like monkeys in uniform, pounded out some kind of barbarous jingle, and sad-faced marionettes moved to it. There was no gaiety or devil in that dancing, only a kind of bored perfection. Thin young men with rabbit heads and hair brushed straight back from their brows, who I suppose were professional dancing partners, held close to their breasts women of every shape and age, but all alike in having dead eyes and masks for faces, and the macabre procession moved like automata to the niggers' rhythm. I dare say it was all very wonderful, but I was not built by Providence to appreciate it.

"I can't stand much more of this," I told Archie.

"It's no great shakes. But there are one or two high-class performers. Look at that girl dancing with the young Jew--the one in green."

I looked and saw a slim girl, very young apparently, who might have been pretty but for the way her face was loaded with paint and the preposterous style in which her hair was dressed. Little though I know of dancing, I could see that she was a mistress of the art, for every motion was a delight to watch, and she made poetry out of that hideous ragtime. But her face shocked me. It was BLIND, if you understand me, as expressionless as a mummy, a kind of awful death-in-life. I wondered what kind of experience that poor soul had gone through to give her the stare of a sleep-walker.

As my eyes passed from her they fell on another figure that seemed familiar. I saw that it was Odell the butler, splendidly got up for his night out in dress clothes, white waistcoat, and diamond studs. There was no mistaking the pugilistic air of the fellow, now I saw him out of service; I had seen a dozen such behind the bars of sporting public-houses. He could not see me, but I had a fair view of him, and I observed that he also was watching the girl in green.

"Do you know who she is?" I asked.

"Some professional. Gad, she can dance, but the poor child looks as if she found it a hard life. I'd rather like to talk to her."

But the music had stopped, and I could see that Odell had made a sign to the dancer. She came up to him as obediently as a dog, he said something to another man with him, a man with a black beard, and the three passed out at the further door. A moment later I caught a glimpse of her with a cloak round her shoulders passing the door by which we had entered.

Archie laughed. "That big brute is probably her husband. I bet she earns the living of both by dancing at these places, and gets beaten every night. I would say my prayers before taking on that fellow in a scrap."

CHAPTER VIII

THE BLIND SPINNER

I look back upon those days of waiting as among the beastliest of my life. I had the clearest conviction now that Medina was the key of the whole puzzle, but as yet I had found out nothing worth mentioning, and I had to wait like the sick folk by the pool of Bethesda till something troubled the waters. The only thing that comforted me was the fine old-fashioned dislike to the man which now possessed me. I couldn't pretend to understand more than a fragment of him, but what I understood I detested. I had been annexed by him as a slave, and every drop of free blood in my veins was in revolt; but I was also resolved to be the most docile slave that ever kissed the ground before a tyrant. Some day my revenge would come and I promised myself that it would be complete. Meantime I thanked Heaven that he had that blind spot of vanity, which would prevent him seeing the cracks in my camouflage.

For the better part of a week we were very little separate. I lunched with him two days out of three, and we motored more than once down to Brighton for fresh air. He took me to a dinner he gave at the House of Commons to a Canadian statesman who was over on a visit, and he made me accompany him to a very smart dance at Lady Amysfort's, and he got me invited to a week-end party at Wirlesdon because he was going there.

I went through the whole programme dutifully and not unpleasurably. I must say he treated me admirably in the presence of other people--with a jolly affectionate friendliness, constantly asking for my opinion, and deferring to me and making me talk, so that the few people I met whom I had known before wondered what had come over me. Mary had a letter from a cousin of hers, who reported that I seemed to have got into society and to be making a big success of it--a letter she forwarded to me with a pencilled note of congratulation at the end. On these occasions I didn't find my task difficult, for I fell unconsciously under the man's spell and could easily play up to him. . . . But when we were alone his manner changed. Iron crept into his voice, and, though he was pleasant enough, he took a devil of a lot for granted, and the note of authority grew more habitual. After such occasions I used to go home grinding my teeth. I never had a worse job than to submit voluntarily to that insolent protection.

Repeatedly in my bedroom at the Club I tried to put together the meagre handful of ascertained facts, but they were like a lot of remnants of different jig-saw puzzles and nothing fitted in to anything else. Macgillivray reported that so far he had drawn a blank in the case of Odell; and that the watchers at Palmyra Square had noted very few visitors except tradesmen and organ-grinders. Nothing resembling a gentleman had been seen to enter or leave, so it appeared that my estimate of Madame Breda's flourishing business was wrong. A woman frequently went out and returned, never walking but always in a taxi or a motor-car--probably the same woman, but so hooded and wrapped up as to make details difficult to be clear about. There were a host of little notes--coal or firewood had been delivered one day, twice the wrapped-up lady had gone out in the evening, to come back in a couple of hours, but mostly she made her visits abroad in daylight, the household woke late and retired to bed early, once or twice a sound like weeping had been heard but it might have been the cat. Altogether it was a poor report, and I concluded that I was either barking up the wrong tree, or that Macgillivray's agents were a pretty useless crowd.

For the rest, what had I? A clear and well-founded suspicion of Medina. But of what? Only that he was behaving towards me in a way that I resented, that he dabbled in an ugly brand of hypnotism, and that the more I saw of him the less I liked him. I knew that his public repute was false, but I had no worse crime to accuse him of than vanity. He had a butler who had been a prize-fighter, and who had a taste for night clubs. I remember I wrote all this down, and sat staring blankly at it, feeling how trivial it was. Then I wrote down the six-line jingle and stared at that too, and I thought of the girl, and the young man, and the small boy who liked birds and fishing. I hadn't a scrap of evidence to link up Medina with that business, except that Tom Greenslade believed that he had got from him the three facts which ran more or less in the rhyme; but Tom might be mistaken, or Medina might have learned them in some perfectly innocent way. I hadn't enough evidence to swing a cat on. But yet--the more I thought of Medina the more dark and subtle his figure loomed in my mind. I had a conviction, on which I would have staked my life, that if I stuck to him I would worry out some vital and damning truth; so, with no very lively or cheerful hope, but with complete certainty, I resolved for the hundredth time to let logic go and back my fancy.

As in duty bound I paid another visit to Dr. Newhover. He received me casually, and appeared to have forgotten about my case till he looked up his diary.

"Ah yes, you saw Madame Breda," he said. "I have her report. Your headaches are cured but you are still a little shaky? Yes, please. Take off your coat and waistcoat."

He vetted me very thoroughly, and then sat down in his desk-chair and tapped his eye-glasses on his knee.

"You are better, much better, but you are not cured. That will take time and care, and lies, of course, in your own hands. You are leading a quiet life? Half town, half country--it is probably the best plan. Well, I don't think you can improve on that."

"You said something about fishing in Norway when I was here last."

"No, on the whole I don't recommend it. Your case is slightly different from what I at first supposed."

"You are a fisherman yourself?" I said.

He admitted that he was, and for a minute or two spoke more like a human being. He always used a two-piece Castle-Connell rod, though he granted it was a cumbrous thing to travel with. For flies he swore by Harlows--certainly the best people for Norwegian flies. He thought that there was a great difference between Norwegian rivers than most people imagined, and Harlows understood that.

He concluded by giving me some simple instructions about diet and exercise.

"If my headaches return, shall I go back to Madame Breda?" I asked.

He shook his head. "Your headaches won't return."

I paid him his fee, and, as I was leaving, I asked if he wanted to see me again.

"I don't think it necessary. At any rate not till the autumn. I may have to be out of London myself a good deal this summer. Of course if you should find the malaise recurring, which I do not anticipate, you must come and see me. If I am out of town, you can see my colleague." He scribbled a name and address on a sheet of paper.

I left the house feeling considerably puzzled. Dr. Newhover, who on my first visit had made a great to-do about my health, seemed now to want to be quit of me. His manner was exactly that of a busy doctor dealing with a malade imaginaire. The odd thing was that I was really beginning to feel rather seedy, a punishment for my former pretence. It may have been the reaction of my mental worry, but I had the sort of indefinite out-of-sorts feeling which I believe precedes an attack of influenza. Only I had hitherto been immune from influenza.

That night I had another of Sandy's communications, a typed half- sheet with a Paris postmark.

"Keep close to M.," it ran. "Do everything he wants. Make it clear that you have broken for ever with me. This is desperately important."

It was signed "Buchan," a horse which Sandy seemed to think had been a Derby winner. He knew no more about racing than I knew of Chinese.

Next morning I woke with a bad taste in my mouth and a feeling that I had probably a bout of malaria due me. Now I had had no malaria since the autumn of '17, and I didn't like the prospect of the revisitation. However, as the day wore on, I felt better, and by midday I concluded I was not going to be ill. But all the same I was as jumpy as a cat in a thunderstorm. I had the odd sense of anticipation, which I used to have before a battle, a lurking excitement by no means pleasant--not exactly apprehension, but first cousin to it. It made me want to see Medina, as if there was something between him and me that I ought to get over.

All afternoon this dentist-anteroom atmosphere hung about me, and I was almost relieved when about five o'clock I got a telephone message from Hill Street asking me to come there at six. I went round to the Bath Club and had a swim and a shampoo, and then started for the house. On the way there I had those tremors in my legs and coldness in the pit of the stomach which brought back my childish toothaches. Yes, that was it. I felt exactly like a small boy setting off with dreadful anticipations to have a tooth drawn, and not all my self-contempt could cure me of my funk. The house when I reached it seemed larger and lonelier than ever, and the April evening had darkened down to a scurry of chill dusty winds under a sky full of cloud.

Odell opened the door to me, and took me to the back of the hall, where I found a lift which I had not known existed. We went up to the top of the house, and I realised that I was about to enter again the library where before I had so strangely spent the midnight hours.

The curtains were drawn, shutting out the bleak spring twilight, and the room was warmed by, and had for its only light, a great fire of logs. I smelt more than wood smoke; there was peat burning among the oak billets. The scent recalled, not the hundred times when I had sniffed peat-reek in happy places, but the flavour of the room in Palmyra Square when I had lain with bandaged eyes and felt light fingers touch my face. I had suddenly a sense that I had taken a long stride forward, that something fateful was about to happen, and my nervousness dropped from me like a cloak.

Medina was standing before the hearth, but his was not the figure that took my eyes. There was another person in the room, a woman. She sat in the high-backed chair which he had used on the former night, and she sat in it as if it were a throne. The firelight lit her face, and I saw that it was very old, waxen with age, though the glow made the wax rosy. Her dress was straight and black like a gaberdine, and she had thick folds of lace at her wrists and neck. Wonderful hair, masses of it, was piled on her head, and it was snow-white and fine as silk. Her hands were laid on the arms of the chair, and hands more delicate and shapely I have never seen, though they had also the suggestion of a furious power, like the talons of a bird of prey.

But it was the face that took away my breath. I have always been a great admirer of the beauty of old age, especially in women, but this was a beauty of which I had never dreamed. It was a long face, and the features were large, though exquisitely cut and perfectly proportioned. Usually in an old face there is a certain loosening of muscles or blurring of contours, which detracts from sheer beauty but gives another kind of charm. But in this face there was no blurring or loosening; the mouth was as firm, the curve of the chin as rounded, the arch of the eyes as triumphant as in some proud young girl.

And then I saw that the eyes which were looking at the fire were the most remarkable things of all. Even in that half-light I could see that they were brightly, vividly blue. There was no film or blearing to mar their glory. But I saw also that they were sightless. How I knew it I do not know, for there was no physical sign of it, but my conviction was instantaneous and complete. These starlike things were turned inward. In most blind people the eyes are like marbles, dead windows in an empty house; but--how shall I describe it?--these were blinds drawn in a room which was full of light and movement, stage curtains behind which some great drama was always set. Blind though they were, they seemed to radiate an ardent vitality, to glow and flash like the soul within.

I realised that it was the most wonderful face of a woman I had ever looked on. And I realised in the same moment that I hated it, that the beauty of it was devilish, and the soul within was on fire with all the hatred of Hell.

"Hannay," I heard Medina's voice, "I have brought you here because I wish to present you to my mother."

I behaved just like somebody in a play. I advanced to her chair, lifted one of the hands, and put it to my lips. That seemed to me the right thing to do. The face turned towards me, and broke into a smile, the kind of smile you may see on the marble of a Greek goddess.

The woman spoke to Medina in a tongue which was strange to me, and he replied. There seemed to be many questions and answers, but I did not trouble to try to catch a word I knew. I was occupied with the voice. I recognised in it those soft tones which had crooned over me as I lay in the room in Palmyra Square. I had discovered who had been the third person in that scene.

Then it spoke to me in English, with that odd lilting accent I had tried in vain to trace.

"You are a friend of Dominick, and I am glad to meet you, Sir Richard Hannay. My son has told me about you. Will you bring a chair and sit close to me?"

I pulled up a long low arm-chair, so long and low that the sitter was compelled almost to recline. My head was on a level with the hand which lay on the arm of her chair. Suddenly I felt that hand laid on my head, and I recognised her now by touch as well as voice.

"I am blind, Sir Richard," she said, "so I cannot see my son's friends. But I long to know how they look, and I have but one sense which can instruct me. Will you permit me to pass my hands over your face?"

"You may do what you please, Madame," I said. "I would to God I could give you eyes."

"That is a pretty speech," she said. "You might be one of my own people." And I felt the light fingers straying over my brow.

I was so placed that I was looking into the red heart of the fire, the one patch of bright light in the curtained room. I knew what I was in for, and, remembering past experience, I averted my eyes to the dark folios on the lowest shelves beyond the hearth. The fingers seemed to play a gentle tattoo on my temples, and then drew long soft strokes across my eyebrows. I felt a pleasant languor beginning to creep down my neck and spine, but I was fully prepared, and without much trouble resisted it. Indeed my mind was briskly busy, for I was planning how best to play my game. I let my head recline more and more upon the cushioned back of my chair, and I let my eyelids droop.

The gentle fingers were very thorough, and I had let myself sink back beyond their reach before they ceased.

"You are asleep," the voice said. "Now wake."

I was puzzled to know how to stage-manage that wakening, but she saved me the trouble. Her voice suddenly hissed like a snake's. "Stand up!" it said. "Quick--on your life."

I scrambled to my feet with extreme energy, and stood staring at the fire, wondering what to do next.

"Look at your master," came the voice again, peremptory as a drill- sergeant's.

That gave me my cue. I knew where Medina was standing, and, in the words of the Bible, my eyes regarded him as a handmaiden regards her master. I stood before him, dumb and dazed and obedient.

"Down," he cried. "Down, on all-fours."

I did as I was bid, thankful that my job was proving so easy.

"Go to the door--no, on all-fours, open it twice, shut it twice, and bring me the paper-knife from the far table in your mouth."

I obeyed, and a queer sight I must have presented prancing across the room, a perfectly sane man behaving like a lunatic.

I brought the paper-knife, and remained dog-wise. "Get up," he said, and I got up.

I heard the woman's voice say triumphantly: "He is well broken," and Medina laughed.

"There is yet the last test," he said. "I may as well put him through it now. If it fails, it means only that he needs more schooling. He cannot remember, for his mind is now in my keeping. There is no danger."

He walked up to me, and gave me a smart slap in the face.

I accepted it with Christian meekness. I wasn't even angry. In fact I would have turned the other cheek in the Scriptural fashion, if it hadn't occurred to me that it might be overacting.

Then he spat in my face.

That, I admit, tried me pretty high. It was such a filthy Kaffir trick that I had some trouble in taking it resignedly. But I managed it. I kept my eyes on the ground, and didn't even get out my handkerchief to wipe my cheek till he had turned away.

"Well broken to heel," I heard him say. "It is strange how easily these flat tough English natures succumb to the stronger spirit. I have got a useful weapon in him, mother mine."

They paid no more attention to me than if I had been a piece of furniture, which, indeed, in their eyes I was. I was asleep, or rather awake in a phantasmal world, and I could not return to my normal life till they bade me. I could know nothing--so they thought--and remember nothing, except what they willed. Medina sat in my chair, and the woman had her hand on his head, and they talked as if they were alone in the desert. And all the while I was standing sheepishly on the rug, not daring to move, scarcely to breathe, lest I should give the show away.

They made a pretty picture--"The Prodigal's Return" or "The Old Folks at Hone," by Simpkins, R.A., Royal Academy, 1887. No, by Heaven, there was no suggestion of that. It was a marvellous and tragic scene that I regarded. The fitful light of the fire showed figures of an antique beauty and dignity. The regal profile of the woman, her superb pose, and the soft eerie music of her voice were a world removed from vulgarity, and so was the lithe vigour and the proud face of the man. They were more like a king and queen in exile, decreeing the sea of blood which was to wash them back again. I realised for the first time that Medina might be damnable, but was also great. Yes, the man who had spat on me like a stable-boy had also something of the prince. I realised another thing. The woman's touch had flattened down the hair above his forehead, which he brushed square, and his head, outlined in the firelight against the white cushion, was as round as a football. I had suspected this when I first saw him, and now I was certain. What did a head like that portend? I had a vague remembrance that I had heard somewhere that it meant madness--at any rate degeneracy.

They talked rapidly and unceasingly, but the confounded thing was that I could hear very little of it. They spoke in low tones, and I was three yards off and daren't for my life move an inch nearer. Also they spoke for the most part in a language of which I did not know a word--it may have been Choctaw, but was probably Erse. If I had only comprehended that tongue I might there and then have learned all I wanted to know. But sometimes Medina talked English, though it seemed to me that the woman always tried to bring him back to the other speech. All I heard were broken sentences that horribly tantalised me.

My brain was cool and very busy. This woman was the Blind Spinner of the rhymes. No doubt of it. I could see her spinning beside a peat fire, nursing ancient hate and madness, and crooning forgotten poetry. "Beside the Sacred Tree." Yggdrasil be hanged! I had it, it was Gospel Oak. Lord, what a fool I had been not to guess it before! The satisfaction of having got one of the three conundrums dead right made me want to shout. These two harpies held the key to the whole riddle, and I had only to keep up my present character to solve it. They thought they were dealing with a hypnotised fool, and instead they had a peculiarly wide-awake if rather slow and elderly Englishman. I wished to Heaven I knew what they were saying. Sluicing out malice about my country, no doubt, or planning the ruin of our civilisation for the sake of a neurotic dream.

Medina said something impatiently about "danger," as if his purpose were to reassure. Then I caught nothing for several minutes, till he laughed and repeated the word "secundus." Now I was looking for three people, and if there was a "secundus" there must have been a "primus," and possibly a "tertius."

"He is the least easy to handle," he said. "And it is quite necessary that Jason should come home. I have decided that the doctor must go out. It won't be for long--only till midsummer."

The date interested me actuely. So did what followed, for he went on:

"By midsummer they liquidate and disband. There is no fear that it won't succeed. We have the whip hand, remember. Trust me, all will go smoothly, and then we begin a new life. . . ."

I thought she sighed, and for the first time she spoke in English:

"I fear sometimes that you are forgetting your own land, Dominick."

He put up an arm and drew her head to his.

"Never, mother mine. It is our strength that we can seem to forget and still remember."

I was finding my stand on that hearth-rug extraordinarily trying. You see I had to keep perfectly rigid, for every now and then Medina would look towards me, and I knew that the woman had an ear like a hound. But my knees were beginning to shake with fatigue and my head to grow giddy, and I feared that, like the soldiers who stand guard round a royal bier, I might suddenly collapse. I did my best to struggle against the growing weakness, and hoped to forget it by concentrating all my attention on the fragments of talk.

"I have news for you," Medina was saying. "Kharáma is in Europe and proposes to come to England."

"You will see him?" I thought her voice had a trace of alarm in it.

"Most certainly. I would rather see him than any living man."

"Dominick, be careful. I would rather you confined yourself to your old knowledge. I fear these new things from the East."

He laughed. "They are as old as ours--older. And all knowledge is one. I have already drunk of his learning and I must have the whole cup."

That was the last I heard, for at that moment I made my exit from the scene in a way which I could not have bettered by much cogitation. My legs suddenly gave under me, the room swam round, and I collapsed on the floor in a dead faint. I must have fallen heavily, for I knocked a leg off one of the little tables.

When I came to--which I suppose was a minute or two later--Odell was bathing my face, and Medina with a grave and concerned air was standing by with a brandy decanter.

"My dear fellow, you gave me a bad fright," he said, and his manner was that of the considerate friend. "You're not feeling ill?"

"I haven't been quite fit all day, and I suppose the hot room knocked me out. I say, I'm most awfully sorry for playing the fool like this. I've damaged your furniture, I'm afraid. I hope I didn't scare the lady."

"What lady?"

"Your mother."

He looked at me with a perfectly blank face, and I saw I had made a mistake.

"I beg your pardon--I'm still giddy. I've been dreaming."

He gave me a glass of brandy and tucked me into a taxi. Long before I got to the Club I was feeling all right, but my mind was in a fine turmoil. I had stumbled at last upon not one clue but many, and though they were confused enough, I hoped with luck to follow them out. I could hardly eat any dinner that night, and my brain was too unsettled to do any serious thinking. So I took a taxi up to Gospel Oak, and, bidding it wait for me, had another look at Palmyra Square. The place seemed to have been dead and decaying for centuries, seen in that windy moonless dark, and No. 4 was a shuttered tomb. I opened the gate and, after making sure that the coast was clear, stole round to the back-door where tradesmen called. There were some dilapidated outhouses, and the back garden, with rank grasses and obscene clothes-posts, looked like nothing so much as a neglected grave-yard. In that house was the terrible blind Fate that span. As I listened I heard from somewhere inside the sound of slow heartbroken sobs. I wondered if they came from the queer-looking little girl.

CHAPTER IX

I AM INTRODUCED TO STRONG MAGIC

The first thing I did when I got up next morning was to pay a visit to Harlows, the fishing-tackle people. They knew me well enough, for I used to buy my rods there, and one of the assistants had been down to Fosse to teach Mary how to use a light split-cane. With him I embarked on a long talk about Norwegian rivers and their peculiarities, and very soon got his views on the best flies. I asked which river was considered to be the earliest, and was told in an ordinary season the Nirdal and the Skarso. Then I asked if he knew my friend Dr. Newhover. "He was in here yesterday afternoon," I was told. "He is going to the Skarso this year, and hopes to be on the water in the last week of April. Rather too soon in my opinion, though salmon have been caught in it as early as April 17th. By the end of the first week of May it should be all right." I asked a good deal more about the Skarso, and was told that it was best fished from Merdal at the head of the Merdalfjord. There were only about three miles of fishable water before the big foss, but every yard of it was good. I told him I had hoped to get a beat on the Leardal for June, but had had to give up the notion this year and intended to confine myself to Scotland. I bought a new reel, a quantity of sea-trout flies, and a little book about Norwegian fishing.

Then I went on to see Macgillivray, with whom I had made an appointment by telephone.

"I've come to ask your help," I told him. "I'm beginning to get a move on, but it's a ticklish business, and I must walk very warily. First of all, I want you to find out the movements of a certain Dr. Newhover of Wimpole Street. He is going to Norway some time in the next fortnight, to the Skarso to fish, and his jumping-off place will be Stavanger. Find out by which boat he takes a passage, and book me a berth in it also. I'd better have my old name, Cornelius Brand."

"You're not thinking of leaving England just now?" he asked reproachfully.

"I don't know. I may have to go or I may not, but in any case I won't be long away. Anyhow, find out about Dr. Newhover. Now for the more serious business. Just about when have you settled to round up the gang?"

"For the reasons I gave you it must be before midsummer. It is an infernally complicated job and we must work to a time-table. I had fixed provisionally the 20th of June."

"I think you'd better choose an earlier date."

"Why?"

"Because the gang are planning themselves to liquidate by midsummer, and, if you don't hurry, you may draw the net tight and find nothing in it."

"Now how on earth did you find that out?" he asked, and his usually impassive face was vivid with excitement.

"I can't tell you. I found it out in the process of hunting for the hostages, and I give you my word it's correct."

"But you must tell me more. If you have fresh lines on what you call my 'gang,' it may be desperately important for me to know."

"I haven't. I've just the one fact, which I have given you. Honestly, old man, I can't tell you anything more till I tell you everything. Believe me, I'm working hard."

I had thought the thing out, and had resolved to keep the Medina business to myself and Sandy. Our one chance with him was that he should be utterly unsuspecting, and even so wary a fellow as Macgillivray might, if he were told, create just that faint breath of suspicion that would ruin all. He grunted, as if he were not satisfied. "I suppose you must have it your own way. Very well, we'll fix the 10th of June for Der Tag. You realise, of course, that the round-up of all must be simultaneous--that's why it takes such a lot of bandobast. By the way, you've got the same problem with the hostages. You can't release one without the others, or the show is given away--not your show only but mine. You realise that?"

"I do," I said, "and I realise that the moving forward of your date narrows my time down to less than two months. If I succeed, I must wait till the very eve of your move. Not earlier, I suppose, than June 9th? Assume I only find one of the three? I wait till June 9th before getting him out of their clutches. Then you strike, and what happens to the other two?"

He shrugged his shoulders. "The worst, I fear. You see, Dick, the gang I mean to crush and the people who hold the hostages are allied, but I take it they are different sets. I may land every member of my gang, and yet not come within speaking distance of the other lot. I don't know, but I'm pretty certain that even if we found the second lot we'd never be able to prove complicity between the two. The first are devilish deep fellows, but the second are great artists."

"All the same," I said, "I'm in hopes of finding at least one of the hostages, and that means some knowledge of the kidnappers."

"I must not ask, but I'd give my head to know how and where you're working. More power to you! But I wonder if you'll ever get near the real prime fountain of iniquity."

"I wonder," I said, and took my leave.

I had been playing with sickness, and now it looked as if I was going to be punished by getting the real thing. For all the rest of that day I felt cheap, and in the evening I was positive I had a temperature. I thought I might have 'flu, so I went round after dinner to see a doctor whom I had known in France. He refused to admit the temperature. "What sort of life have you been leading these last weeks?" he asked, and when I told him that I had been hanging round London waiting on some tiresome business developments, he said that that was the whole trouble. "You're accustomed to an active life in fresh air and you've been stuffing in town, feeding too well and getting no exercise. Go home to-morrow and you'll be as right as a trivet."

"It rather would suit me to be sick for a spell--say a week."

He looked puzzled and then laughed.

"Oh, if you like I'll give you a chit to say you must go back to the country at once or I won't answer for the consequences."

"I'd like that, but not just yet. I'll ring you up when I want it. Meantime I can take it that there's nothing wrong with me?"

"Nothing that a game of squash and a little Eno won't cure."

"Well, when you send me that chit, say I've got to have a quiet week in bed at home--no visitors--regular rest cure."

"Right," he said. "It's a prescription that every son of Adam might follow with advantage four times a year."

When I got back to the Club I found Medina waiting for me. It was the first time he had visited me there, and I pretended to be delighted to see him--almost embarrassed with delight--and took him to the back smoking-room where I had talked with Sandy. I told him that I was out of sorts, and he was very sympathetic. Then, with a recollection of Sandy's last letter, I started out to blaspheme my gods. He commented on the snugness and seclusion of the little room, which for the moment we had to ourselves.

"It wasn't very peaceful when I was last in it," I said. "I had a row here with that lunatic Arbuthnot before he went abroad."

He looked up at the name.

"You mean you quarrelled. I thought you were old friends."

"Once we were. Now I never want to see the fellow again." I thought I might as well do the job thoroughly, though the words stuck in my throat.

I thought he seemed pleased.

"I told you," he said, "that he didn't attract me."

"Attract!" I cried. "The man has gone entirely to the devil. He has forgotten his manners, his breeding, and everything he once possessed. He has lived so long among cringing Orientals that his head is swollen like a pumpkin. He wanted to dictate to me, and I said I would see him further--and--oh well, we had the usual row. He's gone back to the East, which is the only place for him, and-- no! I never want to clap eyes on him again."

There was a purr of satisfaction in his voice, for he believed, as I meant him to, that his influence over me had been strong enough to shatter an ancient friendship. "I am sure you are wise. I have lived in the East and know something of its ways. There is the road of knowledge and the road of illusion, and Arbuthnot has chosen the second. . . . We are friends, Hannay, and I have much to tell you some day--perhaps very soon. I have made a position for myself in the world, but the figure which the world sees is only a little part of me. The only power is knowledge, and I have attained to a knowledge compared with which Arbuthnot's is the merest smattering."

I noticed that he had dropped the easy, well-bred, deprecating manner which I had first noted in him. He spoke to me now magisterially, arrogantly, almost pompously.

"There has never been a true marriage of East and West," he went on. "To-day we incline to put a false interpretation on the word Power. We think of it in material terms like money, or the control of great patches of inanimate nature. But it still means, as it has always meant, the control of human souls, and to him who acquires that everything else is added. How does such control arise? Partly by knowledge of the intricacies of men's hearts, which is a very different thing from the stock platitudes of the professional psychologists. Partly by that natural dominion of spirit which comes from the possession of certain human qualities in a higher degree than other men. The East has the secret knowledge, but, though it can lay down the practice, it cannot provide the practitioners. The West has the tools, but not the science of their use. There has never, as I have said, been a true marriage of East and West, but when there is, its seed will rule the world."

I was drinking this in with both ears, and murmuring my assent. Now at last I was to be given his confidence, and I prayed that he might be inspired to go on. But he seemed to hesitate, till a glance at my respectful face reassured him. "The day after to- morrow a man will be in London, a man from the East, who is a great master of this knowledge. I shall see him, and you will accompany me. You will understand little, for you are only at the beginning, but you will be in the presence of wisdom."

I murmured that I should feel honoured.

"You will hold yourself free for all that day. The time will probably be the evening."

After that he left with the most perfunctory good-bye. I congratulated myself on having attained to just the kind of position I wanted--that of a disciple whose subjection was so much taken for granted that he was treated like a piece of furniture. From his own point of view Medina was justified; he must have thought the subconscious control so strong, after all the tests I had been through, that my soul was like putty in his hands.

Next day I went down to Fosse and told Mary to expect me back very soon for a day or two. She had never plagued me with questions, but something in my face must have told her that I was hunting a trail, for she asked me for news and looked as if she meant to have it. I admitted that I had found out something, and said I would tell her everything when I next came back. That would only have been prudent, for Mary was a genius at keeping secrets and I wanted some repository of my knowledge in case I got knocked on the head.

When I returned to town I found another note from Sandy, also from France, signed "Alan Breck"--Sandy was terribly out with his Derby winners. It was simply two lines imploring me again to make Medina believe I had broken with him and that he had gone east of Suez for good.

There was also a line from Macgillivray, saying that Dr. Newhover had taken a passage on the Gudrun, leaving Hull at 6.30 p.m. on the 21st, and that a passage had been booked for C. Brand, Esqre, by the same boat. That decided me, so I wrote to my own doctor asking for the chit he had promised, to be dated the 19th. I was busy with a plan, for it seemed to me that it was my duty to follow up the one trail that presented itself, though it meant letting the rest of the business sleep. I longed more than I could say for a talk with Sandy, who was now playing the fool in France and sending me imbecile notes. I also rang up Archie Roylance, and found to my delight that he had not left town, for I ran him to ground at the Travellers', and fixed a meeting for next morning.

"Archie," I said, when we met, "I want to ask a great favour from you. Are you doing anything special in the next fortnight?"

He admitted that he had thought of getting back to Scotland to watch a pair of nesting greenshanks.

"Let the greenshanks alone, like a good fellow. I've probably got to go to Norway on the 21st, and I shall want to get home in the deuce of a hurry. The steamer's far too slow."

"Destroyer," he suggested.

"Hang it, this is not the War. Talk sense. I want an aeroplane, and I want you to fetch me."

Archie whistled long and loud.

"You're a surprisin' old bird, Dick. It's no joke bein' a pal of yours. . . . I dare say I could raise a bus all right. But you've got to chance the weather. And my recollection of Norway is that it's not very well provided with landin' places. What part do you favour?"

I told him the mouth of the Merdalfjord.

"Lord! I've been there," he said. "It's all as steep as the side of a house."

"Yes, but I've been studying the map, and there are some eligible little islands off the mouth, which look flattish from the contouring. I'm desperately serious, old man. I'm engaged on a job where failure means the loss of innocent lives. I'll tell you all about it soon, but meantime you must take my word for it."

I managed to get Archie suitably impressed, and even to interest him in the adventure, for he was never the man to lag behind in anything that included risk and wanted daring. He promised to see Hansen, who had been in his squadron and was believed to have flown many times across the North Sea. As I left him I could see that he was really enormously cheered by the prospect, for if he couldn't watch his blessed birds the next best thing was to have a chance of breaking his neck.

I had expected to be bidden by Medina to meet his necromancer in some den in the East End or some Bloomsbury lodging-house. Judge of my surprise, then, when I was summoned to Claridge's for nine- thirty that evening. When I got to the hotel it was difficult to believe that a place so bright and commonplace could hold any mystery. There was the usual dancing going on, and squads of people who had dined well were sitting around watching. Medina was standing by a fireplace talking to a man who wore a long row of miniature medals and a star, and whom I recognised as Tom Machin, who had commanded a cavalry brigade in France. Medina nodded casually to me, and Tom, whom I had not seen for years, made a great fuss.

"Regimental dinner," he explained. "Came out for a moment to give instructions about my car. Been telling Medina here of the dirty trick the Government have played on my old crowd. I say it's up to the few sahibs like him in that damned monkey-house at Westminster to make a row about it. You back me up, Hannay. What I say is . . ." and so on with all the eternal iteration of "abso-lutely" and "If you follow me" and "You see what I mean" of the incoherent British regular.

Medina gently disengaged himself. "Sorry, Tom, but I must be off now. You're dining with Burminster on Thursday aren't you? We'll talk about that business then. I agree it's an infernal shame."

He signed to me and we went together to the lift. On the first floor, where the main suites are, a turbaned Indian waited for us in the corridor. He led us into a little ante-room, and then disappeared through big folding-doors. I wondered what kind of swell this Oriental necromancer must be who could take rooms like these, for the last time I had been in them was when they were occupied by a Crown Prince who wanted to talk to me about a certain little problem in Anatolia.

"You are about to see Kharáma," Medina whispered, and there was an odd exaltation in his voice. "You do not know his name, but there are millions in the East who reverence it like that of a god. I last saw him in a hut on the wildest pass in the Karakoram, and now he is in this gilded hotel with the dance-music of the West jigging below. It is a parable of the unity of all Power."

The door was opened, and the servant beckoned us to enter. It was a large room furnished with the usual indifferent copies of French furniture--very hot and scented, just the kind of place where international financiers make their deals over liqueur brandy and big cigars, or itinerant stars of the cinema world receive their friends. Bright, hard and glossy, you would have said that no vulgarer environment could be found. . . . And yet after the first glance I did not feel its commonness, for it was filled with the personality of the man who sat on a couch at the far end. I realised that here was one who carried with him his own prepotent atmosphere, and who could transform his surroundings, whether it was a Pamir hut or a London restaurant.

To my surprise he was quite young. His hair was hidden by a great turban, but the face was smooth and hairless, and the figure, so far as I could judge, had not lost the grace of youth. I had imagined someone immensely venerable and old with a beard to his girdle, or, alternately, an obese babu with a soft face like a eunuch. I had forgotten that this man was of the hills. To my amazement he wore ordinary evening dress, well-cut too, I thought, and over it a fine silk dressing-gown. He had his feet tucked up on the couch, but he did not sit cross-legged. At our entrance he slightly inclined his head, while we both bowed. Medina addressed him in some Indian tongue, and he replied, and his voice was like the purr of a big cat.

He motioned us to sit down, looking not so much at us as through us, and while Medina spoke I kept my eyes on his face. It was the thin, high-boned, high-bred face of the hillman; not the Mongolian type, but that other which is like an Arab, the kind of thing you can see in Pathan troops. And yet, though it was as hard as flint and as fierce as Satan, there was a horrid feline softness in it, like that of a man who would never need to strike a blow in anger, since he could win his way otherwise. The brow was straight and heavy, such as I had always associated with mathematical talent, and broader than is common with Orientals. The eyes I could not see, for he kept them half shut, but there was something uncanny in the way they were chased in his head, with an odd slant the opposite from what you see in the Chinaman. His mouth had a lift at each corner as if he were perpetually sneering, and yet there was a hint of humour in the face, thought it was as grave as a stone statue.

I have rarely seen a human being at once so handsome and so repulsive, but both beauty and horror were merged in the impression of ruthless power. I had been sceptical enough about this Eastern image, as I had been sceptical about Medina's arts, because they had failed with me. But as I looked on that dark countenance I had a vision of a world of terrible knowledge, a hideousness like an evil smell, but a power like a blasting wind or a pestilence. . . . Somehow Sandy's talk at the Thursday Club dinner came back to me, about the real danger to the world lying in the constraint of spirit over spirit. This swarthy brute was the priest of that obscene domination, and I had an insane desire there and then to hammer him into pulp.

He was looking at me, and seemed to be asking a question to which Medina replied. I fancy he was told that I was a chela, or whatever was the right name, a well-broken and submissive disciple.

Then to my surprise he spoke in English--good English, with the chi-chi accent of the Indian.

"You have followed far in the path of knowledge, brother. I did not think a son of the West could have travelled so far and so soon. You have won two of the three keys to Mastery, if you can make a man forget his past, and begin life anew subject to your will. But what of the third key?"

I thought Medina's voice had a tinge of disappointment. "It is the third key which I look for, master. What good is it to wipe out the past and establish my control if it is only temporary? I want the third key, to lock the door, so that I have my prisoner safe for ever. Is there such a key?"

"The key is there, but to find it is not easy. All control tends to grow weak and may be broken by an accident, except in the case of young children, and some women, and those of feeble mind."

"That I know," said Medina almost pettishly. "But I do not want to make disciples only of babes, idiots, and women."

"Only some women, I said. Among our women perhaps all, but among Western women, who are hard as men, only the softer and feebler."

"That is my trouble. I wish to control for ever, and to control without constant watching on my part. I have a busy life and time is precious. Tell me, master, is there a way?"

I listened to this conversation with feelings of genuine horror. Now I saw Medina's plans, and I realised that he and he alone was at the bottom of the kidnapping. I realised, too, how he had dealt with the three hostages, and how he proposed to deal. Compared to him a murderer was innocent, for a murderer only took life, while he took the soul. I hated him and that dark scoundrel more intensely than I think I have ever hated man; indeed it was only by a great effort that I checked myself from clutching the two by the throat. The three stories, which had been half forgotten and overlaid by my recent experiences, returned sharp and clear to my memory. I saw again Victor's haggard face, I heard Sir Arthur Warcliff's voice break; and my wrath rose and choked me. This stealing of souls was the worst infamy ever devised by devils among mankind. I must have showed my emotion, but happily the two had no eyes for me.

"There is a way, a sure way," the Indian was saying, and a wicked half-smile flitted over his face. "But it is a way which, though possible in my own country, may be difficult in yours. I am given to understand that your police are troublesome, and you have a public repute, which it is necessary to cherish. There is another way which is slower, but which is also sure, if it is boldly entered upon."

The sage seemed to open his half-shut eyes, and I thought I saw the opaque brightness which comes from drug-taking.

"Him whom you would make your slave," he said, "you first strip of memory, and then attune to your own will. To keep him attuned you must be with him often and reinforce the control. But this is burdensome, and if the slave be kept apart and seen rarely the influence will ebb--except, as I have said, in the case of a young child. There is a way to rivet the bondage and it is this. Take him or her whom you govern into the same life as they have been accustomed to live before, and there, among familiar things, assert your control. Your influence will thus acquire the sanction of familiarity--for though the conscious memory has gone, the unconscious remains--and presently will be a second nature."

"I see," said Medina abstractedly. "I had already guessed as much. Tell me, master, can the dominion, once it is established, be shaken off?"

"It cannot save by the will of him who exercises it. Only the master can release."

After that they spoke again in the foreign tongue of I know not what devilry. It seemed to me that the sage was beginning to tire of the interview, for he rang a bell and when the servant appeared gave him some rapid instructions. Medina rose, and kissed the hand which was held out to him, and I, of course, followed suit.

"You stay here long, master?" he asked.

"Two days. Then I have business in Paris and elsewhere. But I return in May, when I will summon you again. Prosper, brother. The God of Wisdom befriend you."

We went downstairs to the dancing and the supper parties. The regimental dinner was breaking up and Tom Machin was holding forth in the hall to a knot of be-medalled friends. I had to say something to Medina to round off the evening, and the contrast of the two scenes seemed to give me a cue. As we were putting on our coats I observed that it was like coming from light to darkness. He approved. "Like falling from a real world into shadows," he said.

He evidently wished to follow his own thoughts, for he did not ask me to walk home with him. I, too, had a lot to think about. When I got back to the Club I found a note signed "Spion Kop," and with an English postmark.

"Meet me," it said, "on the 21st for breakfast at the inn called 'The Silent Woman' on the Fosse Way as you go over from Colne to Windrush. I have a lot to tell you."

I thanked Heaven that Sandy was home again, though he chose fantastic spots for his assignations. I, too, had something to say to him. For that evening had given me an insight into Medina's mind, and, what was more, the glimmerings of a plan of my own.

CHAPTER X

CONFIDENCES AT A WAYSIDE INN

My first impulse was to go to Macgillivray about this Kharáma fellow, who I was certain was up to mischief. I suspected him of some kind of political intrigue; otherwise what was he doing touring the capitals of Europe and putting up at expensive hotels? But on second thoughts I resolved to let the police alone. I could not explain about Kharáma without bringing in Medina, and I was determined to do nothing which would stir a breath of suspicion against him. But I got the chit from my doctor, recommending a week's rest, and I went round to see Medina on the morning of the 19th. I told him I had been feeling pretty cheap for some days and that my doctor ordered me to go home and go to bed. He didn't look pleased, so I showed him the doctor's letter, and made a poor mouth, as if I hated the business but was torn between my inclinations and my duty. I think he liked my producing that chit, like a second-lieutenant asking for leave, anyhow he made the best of it and was quite sympathetic. "I'm sorry you're going out of town," he said, "for I want you badly. But it's as well to get quite fit, and to lie up for a week ought to put you all right. When am I to expect you back?" I told him that without fail I would be in London on the 29th. "I'm going to disappear into a monastery," I said. "Write no letters, receive none, not at home to visitors, only sleep and eat. I can promise you that my wife will watch me like a dragon."

Then I hunted up Archie Roylance, whom I found on the very top of his form. He had seen Hansen, and discovered that on the island of Flacksholm, just off the mouth of the Merdalfjord, there was good landing. It was a big flattish island with a loch in the centre, and entirely uninhabited except for a farm at the south end. Archie had got a machine, a Sopwith, which he said he could trust, and I arranged with him to be at Flacksholm not later than the 27th, and to camp there as best he could. He was to keep watch by day for a motor-boat from the Merdalfjord, and at night if he saw a green light he was to make for it. I told him to take ample supplies, and he replied that he wasn't such a fool as to neglect the commissariat. He said he had been to Fortnum & Mason and was going to load up with liqueurs and delicatessen. "Take all the clothes you've got, Dick," he added. "It will be perishing cold in those parts at this time of year." He arranged, too, to cable through Hansen for a motor-launch to be ready at Stavanger for a Mr. Brand who was due by the Hull steamer on the morning of the 23rd. If I had to change my plans I was to wire him at once.

That evening I went down to Fosse a little easier in my mind. It was a blessed relief to get out of London and smell clean air, and to reflect that for a week at any rate I should be engaged in a more congenial job than loafing about town. I found Peter John in the best of health and the Manor garden a glory of spring flowers.

I told Mary that I was ordered by my doctor to go to bed for a week and take a rest cure.

"Dick," she asked anxiously, "you're not ill, are you?"

"Not a bit, only a trifle stale. But officially I'm to be in bed for a week and not a blessed soul is to be allowed to come near me. Tell the servants, please, and get the cook on to invalid dishes. I'll take Paddock into my confidence, and he'll keep up a show of waiting on me."

"A show?"

"Yes, for you see I'm going to put in a week in Norway--that is, unless Sandy has anything to say against it."

"But I thought Colonel Arbuthnot was still abroad?"

"So he is--officially. But I'm going to breakfast with him the day after to-morrow at The Silent Woman--you remember, the inn we used to have supper at last summer when I was fishing the Colne."

"Dick," she said solemnly, "isn't it time you told me a little more about what you're doing?"

"I think it is," I agreed, and that night after dinner I told her everything.

She asked a great many questions, searching questions, for Mary's brain was about twice as good as mine. Then she sat pondering for a long time with her chin on her hand.

"I wish I had met Mr. Medina," she said at last. "Aunt Claire and Aunt Doria know him. . . . I am afraid of him, terribly afraid, and I think I should be less afraid if I could just see him once. It is horrible, Dick, and you are fighting with such strange weapons. Your only advantage is that you're such a gnarled piece of oak. I wish I could help. It's dreadful to have to wait here and be tortured by anxiety for you, and to be thinking all the time of those poor people. I can't get the little boy out of my head. I often wake in a terror, and have to go up to the night-nursery to hug Peter John. Nanny must think I'm mad. . . . I suppose you're right to go to Norway?"

"I see no other way. We have a clue to the whereabouts of one of the hostages--I haven't a notion which. I must act on that, and besides, if I find one it may give me a line on the others."

"There will still be two lost," she said, "and the time grows fearfully short. You are only one man. Can you not get helpers? Mr. Macgillivray?"

"No. He has his own job, and to let him into mine would wreck both."

"Well, Colonel Arbuthnot? What is he doing?"

"Oh, Sandy's busy enough, and, thank God! he's back in England. I'll know more about his game when I see him, but you may be sure it's a deep one. While I'm away Sandy will be working all the time."

"Do you know, I have never met him. Couldn't I see him some time when you're away? It would be a great comfort to me. And, Dick, can't I help somehow? We've always shared everything, even before we were married, and you know I'm dependable."

"Indeed I do, my darling," I said. "But I can't see how you can help--yet. If I could, I would inspan you straight off, for I would rather have you with me than a regiment."

"It's the poor little boy. I could endure the rest, but the thought of him makes me crazy. Have you seen Sir Arthur?"

"No, I have avoided him. I can stand the sight of Victor and the Duke, but I swear I shall never look Sir Arthur in the face unless I can hand him over his son."

Then Mary got up and stood over me like a delivering angel.

"It is going to be done," she cried. "Dick, you must never give up. I believe in my heart we shall win. We must win or I shall never be able to kiss Peter John again with a quiet mind. Oh, I wish--I wish I could do something."

I don't think Mary slept that night, and next morning she was rather pale and her eyes had that funny long-sighted look that they had had when I said good-bye to her at Amiens in March '18, before going up to the line.

I spent a blissful day with her and Peter John wandering round our little estate. It was one of those April days which seem to have been borrowed from late May, when you have the warmth of summer joined with the austerity and fresh colouring of spring. The riot of daffodils under the trees was something to thank God for, the banks of the little lake were one cascade of grape hyacinths, blue and white, and every dell in the woods was bright with primroses. We occupied the morning deepening the pools in a tiny stream which was to be one of the spawning-grounds for the new trout in the lake, and Peter John showed conspicuous talent as a hydraulic engineer. His nurse, who was a middle-aged Scotswoman from the Cheviots, finally carried him off for his morning rest, and when he had gone, Mary desisted from her watery excavations and sat down on a bank of periwinkles.

"What do you really think of Nanny?" she asked.

"About as good as they make," I replied.

"That's what I think too. You know, Dick, I feel I'm far too fussy about Peter John. I give hours of my time to him, and it's quite unnecessary. Nanny can do everything better than I can. I scarcely dare let him out of my sight, and yet I'm certain that I could safely leave him for weeks with Nanny and Paddock--and Dr. Greenslade within call."

"Of course you could," I agreed, "but you'd miss him, as I do, for he's jolly good company."

"Yes, he's jolly good company, the dear fellow," she said.

In the afternoon we went for a canter on the downs, and I came back feeling as fit as a race-horse and keyed up for anything. But that evening, as we walked in the garden before dinner, I had another fit of longing to be free of the business and to return to my quiet life. I realised that I had buried my heart in my pleasant acres, and the thought of how much I loved them made me almost timid. I think Mary understood what I was feeling, for she insisted on talking about David Warcliff, and before I went to bed had worked me into that honest indignation which is the best stiffener of resolution. She went over my plans with me very carefully. On the 28th, if I could manage it, I was to come home, but if I was short of time I was to send her a wire and go straight to London. The pretence of my being in bed was to be religiously kept up. For safety's sake I was to sign every wire with the name of Cornelius.

Very early next morning, long before anyone was stirring, I started the big Vauxhall with Paddock's assistance, and, accompanied by a very modest kit, crept down the avenue. Paddock, who could drive a car, was to return to the house about ten o'clock, and explain to my chauffeur that by my orders he had taken the Vauxhall over to Oxford as a loan for a week to a friend of mine. I drove fast out of the silent hill roads and on to the great Roman way which lay like a strap across the highlands. It was not much after six o'clock when I reached The Silent Woman, which sat like an observation post on a ridge of down, at a junction of four roads. Smoke was going up from its chimneys, so I judged that Sandy had ordered early breakfast. Presently, as I was garaging the car in an outhouse, Sandy appeared in flannel bags and a tweed jacket, looking as fresh as paint and uncommonly sunburnt.

"I hope you're hungry," he said. "Capital fellow the landlord! He knows what a man's appetite is. I ordered eggs, kidneys, sausages and cold ham, and he seemed to expect it. Yes. These are my headquarters for the present, though Advanced G.H.Q. is elsewhere. By the by, Dick, just for an extra precaution, my name's Thomson--Alexander Thomson--and I'm a dramatic critic taking a belated Easter holiday."

The breakfast was as good as Sandy had promised, and what with the run in the fresh air and the sight of him opposite me I began to feel light-hearted.

"I got your letters," I said, "but, I say, your knowledge of Derby winners is pretty rocky. I thought that was the kind of information no gentleman was without."

"I'm the exception. Did you act on them?"

"I told Medina I had broken with you for good and never wanted to see your face again. But why did you make such a point of it?"

"Simply because I wanted to be rid of his attentions, and I reckoned that if he thought we had quarrelled and that I had gone off for good, he might let me alone. You see he has been trying hard to murder me."

"Good Lord!" I exclaimed. "When?"

"Four times," said Sandy calmly, counting on his fingers. "Once before I left London. Oh, I can tell you I had an exciting departure. Three times in Paris, the last time only four days ago. I fancy he's off my trail now, for he really thinks I sailed from Marseilles the day before yesterday."

"But why on earth?"

"Well, I made some ill-advised remarks at the Thursday Club dinner. He believes that I'm the only man alive who might uncover him, and he won't sleep peacefully till he knows that I am out of Europe and is convinced that I suspect nothing. I sent you those letters because I wanted to be let alone, seeing I had a lot to do, and nothing wastes time like dodging assassins. But my chief reason was to protect YOU. You mayn't know it, Dick, but you've been walking for three weeks on the edge of a precipice with one foot nearly over. You've been in the most hideous danger, and I was never more relieved in my life than when I saw your solemn old face this morning. You were only safe when he regarded our friendship as broken and me out of the way and you his blind and devoted slave."

"I'm that all right," I said. "There's been nothing like it since Uncle Tom's Cabin."

"Good. That's the great thing, for it gives us a post in the enemy's citadel. But we're only at the beginning of a tremendous fight and there's no saying how it will go. Have you sized up Medina?"

"Only a little bit. Have you?"

"I'm on the road. He's the most complex thing I've ever struck. But now we've got to pool our knowledge. Shall I start?"

"Yes. Begin at the Thursday dinner. What started you off then? I could see that something he said intrigued you."

"I must begin before that. You see, I'd heard a good deal about Medina up and down the world and couldn't for the life of me place him. Everybody swore by him, but I had always a queer feeling about the man. I told you about Lavater. Well, I had nothing to go upon there except the notion that his influence upon my friend had been bad. So I began making inquiries, and, as you know, I've more facilities than most people for finding things out. I was curious to know what he had been doing during the War. The ordinary story was that he had been for the first two years pretty well lost in Central Asia, where he had gone on a scientific expedition, and that after that he has been with the Russians, and had finished up by doing great work with Denikin. I went into that story and discovered that he had been in Central Asia all right, but had never been near any fighting front and had never been within a thousand miles of Denikin. That's what I meant when I told you that I believed the man was one vast lie."

"He made everybody believe it."

"That's the point. He made the whole world believe what he wanted. Therefore he must be something quite out of the common--a propagandist of genius. That was my first conclusion. But how did he work? He must have a wonderful organisation, but he must have something more--the kind of personality which can diffuse itself like an atmosphere and which, like an electric current, is not weakened by distance. He must also have unique hypnotic powers. I had made a study of that in the East and had discovered how little we know here about the compulsion of spirit by spirit. That, I have always believed, is to-day, and ever has been, the true magic. You remember I said something about that at the Thursday dinner?"

I nodded. "I suppose you did it to try him?"

"Yes. It wasn't very wise, for I might easily have frightened him. But I was luckier than I deserved, and I drew from him a tremendous confession."

"The Latin quotation?"

"The Latin quotation. Sit vini abstemius qui hermeneuma tentat aut hominum petit dominatum. I nearly had a fit when I heard it. Listen, Dick. I've always had a craze for recondite subjects, and when I was at Oxford I wasted my time on them when I should have been working for my schools. I only got a third in Greats, but I acquired a lot of unusual information. One of my subjects was Michael Scott. Yes--the wizard, only he wasn't a wizard, but a very patient and original thinker. He was a Borderer like me, and I started out to write a life of him. I kept up the study, and when I was at the Paris Embassy I spent my leisure tracking him through the libraries of Europe. Most of his works were published in the fifteenth and sixteenth centuries, and mighty dull they are, but there are some still in manuscript, and I had always the hope of discovering more, for I was positive that the real Michael Scott was something far bigger than the translator and commentator whom we know. I believed that he taught the mad Emperor Ferdinand some queer things, and that the centre of his teaching was just how one human soul could control another. Well, as it turned out, I was right. I found some leaves of manuscript in the Bibliothèque Nationale, which I was certain were to be attributed to Michael. One of his best-known works, you remember, is the Physionomia, but that is only a version of Aristotle. This, too, was part of a Physionomia, and a very different thing from the other, for it purported to give the essence of the Secreta Secretorum--it would take too long to explain about that--and the teaching of the Therapeutae, with Michael's own comments. It is a manual of the arts of spiritual control--oh, amazingly up-to-date, I assure you, and a long way ahead of our foolish psycho-analysts. Well, that quotation of Medina's comes from that fragment--the rare word 'hermeneuma' caught my attention as soon as he uttered it. That proved that Medina was a student of Michael Scott, and showed me what was the bent of his mind."

"Well, he gave himself away then, and you didn't."

"Oh yes, I did. You remember I asked him if he knew the guru who lived at the foot of the Shansi pass as you go over to Kaikand? That was a bad blunder, and it is on account of that question that he has been trying to remove me from the earth. For it was from that guru that he learned most of his art."

"Was the guru's name Kharáma?" I asked.

Sandy stared as if he had seen a ghost.

"Now how on earth do you know that?"

"Simply because I spent an hour with him and Medina a few nights ago."

"The devil you did! Kharáma in London! Lord, Dick, this is an awesome business. Quick, tell me every single thing that passed."

I told him as well as I remembered, and he seemed to forget his alarm and to be well satisfied. "This is tremendously important. You see the point of Medina's talk? He wants to rivet his control over those three unfortunate devils, and to do that he is advised to assert it in some environment similar to that of their past lives. That gives us a chance to get on their track. And the control can only be released by him who first imposed it! I happened to know that, but I was not sure that Medina knew it. It is highly important to have found this out."

"Finish your story," I begged him. "I want to know what you have been doing abroad?"

"I continued my studies in the Bibliothèque Nationale, and I found that, as I suspected, Medina, or somebody like him, had got on to the Michael Scott MS. and had had a transcript made of it. I pushed my researches further, for Michael wasn't the only pebble on the beach, though he was the biggest. Lord, Dick, it's a queer business in a problem like ours to have to dig for help in the debris of the Middle Ages. I found out something--not much, but something."

"And then?"

"Oh, all the time I was making inquiries about Medina's past--not very fruitful--I've told you most of the results. Then I went to see Ram Dass--you remember my speaking about him. I thought he was in Munich, but I found him in Westphalia, keeping an eye on the German industrials. Don't go to Germany for a holiday, Dick; it's a sad country and a comfortless. I had to see Ram Dass, for he happens to be the brother of Kharáma."

"What size of a fellow is Kharáma?" I asked.

Sandy's reply was: "For knowledge of the practice unequalled but only a second-class practitioner"--exactly what Medina had said.

"Ram Dass told me most of what I wanted to know. But he isn't aware that his brother is in Europe. I rather fancy he thinks he is dead. . . . That's all I need tell you now. Fire away, Dick, and give me an exact account of your own doings."

I explained as best I could the gradual change in Medina's manner from friendship to proprietorship. I told how he had begun to talk freely to me, as if I were a disciple, and I described that extraordinary evening in Hill Street when I had met his mother."

"His mother!" Sandy exclaimed, and made me go over every incident several times--the slap in the face, the spitting, my ultimate fainting. He seemed to enjoy it immensely. "Good business," he said. "You never did a better day's work, old man."

"I have found the Blind Spinner at any rate," I said.

"Yes. I had half guessed it. I didn't mention it, but when I got into the house in Gospel Oak as the electric light man, I found a spinning-wheel in the back room, and they had been burning peat on the hearth. Well, that's Number One."

"I think I am on my way to find Number Two," I said, and I told him of the talk I had overheard between the two about secundus and sending "the doctor" somewhere, and of how I had discovered that Dr. Newhover was starting this very day for the Skarso. "It's the first clear clue," I said, "and I think I ought to follow it up."

"Yes. What do you propose to do?"

"I am travelling this evening on the Gudrun and I'm going to trail the fellow till I find out his game. I'm bound to act upon what little information we've got."

"I agree. But this means a long absence from London, and secundus is only one of three."

"Just a week," I said. "I've got sick leave from Medina for a week, and I'm supposed to be having a rest cure at Fosse, with Mary warding off visitors. I've arranged with Archie Roylance to pick me up in an aeroplane about the 28th and bring me back. It doesn't allow me much time, but an active man can do the deuce of a lot in a week."

"Bravo!" he cried. "That's your old moss-trooping self!"

"Do you approve?"

"Entirely. And, whatever happens, you present yourself to Medina on the 29th? That leaves us about six weeks for the rest of the job."

"More like five," I said gloomily, and I told him how I had learnt that the gang proposed to liquidate by midsummer, and that Macgillivray had therefore moved the date when he would take action ten days forward. "You see how we are placed. He must collect all the gang at the same moment, and we must release all three hostages, if we can, at the same time. The releasing mustn't be done too soon or it will warn the gang. Therefore if Macgillivray strikes on the 10th of June, we must be ready to strike not earlier than the 9th and, of course, not later."

"I see," he said, and was silent for a little. "Have you anything more to tell me?"

I ransacked my memory and remembered about Odell. He wrote down the name of the dancing club where I had seen that unprepossessing butler. I mentioned that I had asked Macgillivray to get on to his dossier.

"You haven't told Macgillivray too much?" he inquired anxiously and seemed relieved when I replied that I had never mentioned the Medina business.

"Well, here's the position," he said at last. "You go off for a week hunting Number Two. We are pretty certain that we have got Number One. Number Three--that nonsense about the fields of Eden and the Jew with a dyed beard in a curiosity shop in Marylebone-- still eludes us. And of course we have as yet no word of any of the three hostages. There's a terrible lot still to do. How do you envisage the thing, Dick? Do you think of the three, the girl, the young man, and the boy, shut up somewhere and guarded by Medina's minions? Do you imagine that if we find their places of concealment we shall have done the job?"

"That was my idea."

He shook his head. "It is far subtler than that. Did no one ever tell you that the best way of hiding a person is to strip him of his memory? Why is it that when a man loses his memory he is so hard to find? You see it constantly in the newspapers. Even a well-known figure, if he loses his memory and wanders away, is only discovered by accident. The reason is that the human personality is identified far less by appearance than by its habits and mind. Loss of memory means the loss of all true marks of identification, and the physical look alters to correspond. Medina has stolen these three poor souls' memories and set them adrift like waifs. David Warcliff may at this moment be playing in a London gutter along with a dozen guttersnipes and his own father could scarcely pick him out from the rest. Mercot may be a dock labourer or a deck hand, whom you wouldn't recognise if you met him, though you had sat opposite him in a college hall every night for a year. And Miss Victor may be in a gaiety chorus or a milliner's assistant or a girl in a dancing saloon. . . . Wait a minute. You saw Odell at a dance-club? There may be something in that." I could see his eyes abstracted in thought.

"There's another thing I forgot to mention," I said. "Miss Victor's fiancé is over here, staying in Carlton

House Terrace. He is old Turpin, who used to be with the division--the Marquis de la Tour du Pin."

Sandy wrote the name down. "Her fiancé. He may come in useful. What sort of fellow?"

"Brave as a lion, but he'll want watching, for he's a bit of a Gascon."

We went out after breakfast and sat in an arbour looking down a shallow side-valley to the upper streams of the Windrush. The sounds of morning were beginning to rise from the little village far away in the bottom, the jolt of a wagon, the "clink-clenk" from the smithy, the babble of children at play. In a fortnight the may-fly would be here, and every laburnum and guelder rose in bloom. Sandy, who had been away from England for years, did not speak for a long time, but drank in the sweet-scented peace of it. "Poor devil," he said at last. "He has nothing like this to love. He can only hate."

I asked whom he was talking about, and he said "Medina."

"I'm trying to understand him. You can't fight a man unless you understand him, and in a way sympathise with him."

"Well, I can't say I sympathise with him, and I most certainly don't understand him."

"Do you remember once telling me that he had no vanity? You were badly out there. He has a vanity which amounts to delirium.

"This is how I read him," he went on. "To begin with, there's a far-away streak of the Latin in him, but he is mainly Irish, and that never makes a good cross. He's the déraciné Irish, such as you find in America. I take it that he imbibed from that terrible old woman--I've never met her, but I see her plainly and I know that she is terrible--he imbibed that venomous hatred of imaginary things--an imaginary England, an imaginary civilisation, which they call love of country. There is no love in it. They think there is, and sentimentalise about an old simplicity, and spinning wheels and turf fires and an uncouth language, but it's all hollow. There's plenty of decent plain folk in Ireland, but his kind of déraciné is a ghastly throw-back to something you find in the dawn of history, hollow and cruel like the fantastic gods of their own myths. Well, you start with this ingrained hate."

"I agree about the old lady. She looked like Lady Macbeth."

"But hate soon becomes conceit. If you hate, you despise, and when you despise you esteem inordinately the self which despises. This is how I look at it, but remember, I'm still in the dark and only feeling my way to an understanding. I see Medina growing up--I don't know in what environment--conscious of great talents and immense good looks, flattered by those around him till he thinks himself a god. His hatred does not die, but it is transformed into a colossal egotism and vanity, which, of course, is a form of hate. He discovers quite early that he has this remarkable hypnotic power--Oh, you may laugh at it, because you happen to be immune from it, but it is a big thing in the world for all that. He discovers another thing--that he has an extraordinary gift of attracting people and making them believe in him. Some of the worst scoundrels in history have had it. Now, remember his vanity. It makes him want to play the biggest game. He does not want to be a king among pariahs; he wants to be the ruler of what is most strange to him, what he hates and in an unwilling bitter way admires. So he aims at conquering the very heart, the very soundest part of our society. Above all he wants to be admired by men and admitted into the innermost circle."

"He has succeeded all right," I said.

"He has succeeded, and that is the greatest possible tribute to his huge cleverness. Everything about him is dead right--clothes, manner, modesty, accomplishments. He has made himself an excellent sportsman. Do you know why he shoots so well, Dick? By faith--or fatalism, if you like. His vanity doesn't allow him to believe that he could miss. . . . But he governs himself strictly. In his life he is practically an ascetic, and though he is adored by women he doesn't care a straw for them. There are no lusts of the flesh in that kind of character. He has one absorbing passion which subdues all others--what our friend Michael Scott called 'hominum dominatus.'"

"I see that. But how do you explain the other side?"

"It is all the ancestral hate. First of all, of course, he has got to have money, so he gets it in the way Macgillivray knows about. Second, he wants to build up a regiment of faithful slaves. That's where you come in, Dick. There is always that inhuman hate at the back of his egotism. He wants to conquer in order to destroy, for destruction is the finest meat for his vanity. You'll find the same thing in the lives of Eastern tyrants, for when a man aspires to be like God he becomes an incarnate devil."

"It is a tough proposition," I observed dismally.

"It would be an impossible proposition, but for one thing. He is always in danger of giving himself away out of sheer arrogance. Did you ever read the old Irish folk-lore? Very beautiful it is, but there is always something fantastic and silly which mars the finest stories. They lack the grave good-sense which you find in the Norse sagas and, of course, in the Greek. Well, he has this freakish element in his blood. That is why he sent out that rhyme about the three hostages, which by an amazing concatenation of chances put you on to his trail. Our hope is--and, mind you, I think it is a slender hope--that his vanity may urge him to further indiscretions."

"I don't know how you feel about it," I said, "but I've got a pretty healthy hatred for that lad. I'm longing for a quiet life, but I swear I won't settle down again till I've got even with him."

"You never will," said Sandy solemnly. "Don't let's flatter ourselves that you and I are going to down Medina. We are not. A very wise man once said to me that in this life you could often get success, if you didn't want victory. In this case we're out for success only. We want to release the hostages. Victory we can never hope for. Why, man, supposing we succeed fully, we'll never be able to connect Medina with the thing. His tools are faithful, because he has stolen their souls and they work blindly under him. Supposing Macgillivray rounds up all the big gang and puts the halter round their necks. There will be none of them to turn King's evidence and give Medina away. Why? Because none of them KNOW anything against him. They're his unconscious agents, and very likely most have never seen him. And you may be pretty sure that his banking accounts are too skilfully arranged to show anything."

"All the same," I said stubbornly, "I have a notion that I'll be able to put a spoke in his wheel."

"Oh, I dare say we can sow suspicion, but I believe he'll be too strong for us. He'll advance in his glorious career, and may become Prime Minister--or Viceroy of India--what a chance the second would be for him!--and publish exquisite little poetry books, as finished and melancholy as The Shropshire Lad. Pessimism, you know, is often a form of vanity."

At midday it was time for me to be off, if I was to be at Hull by six o'clock. I asked Sandy what he proposed to do next, and he said he was undecided. "My position," he said, "badly cramps my form. It would be ruination if Medina knew I was in England-- ruination for both you and me. Mr. Alexander Thomson must lie very low. I must somehow get in touch with Macgillivray to hear if he has anything about Odell. I rather fancy Odell. But there will probably be nothing doing till you come back, and I think I'll have a little fishing."

"Suppose I want to get hold of you?"

"Suppose nothing of the kind. You mustn't make any move in my direction. That's our only safety. If I want you I'll come to you."

As I was starting he said suddenly: "I've never met your wife, Dick. What about my going over to Fosse and introducing myself?"

"The very thing," I cried. "She is longing to meet you. But remember that I'm supposed to be lying sick upstairs."

As I looked back he was waving his hand, and his face wore its familiar elfish smile.

CHAPTER XI

HOW A GERMAN ENGINEER FOUND STRANGE FISHING

I got to Hull about six o'clock, having left my car at a garage in York, and finished the journey by train. I had my kit in a small suit-case and rucksack, and I waited on the quay till I saw Dr. Newhover arrive with a lot of luggage and a big rod-box. When I reckoned he would be in his cabin arranging his belongings, I went on board myself, and went straight to my own cabin, which was a comfortable two-berthed one well forward. There I had sandwiches brought me, and settled myself to doze and read for thirty-six hours.

All that night and all next day it blew fairly hard, and I remained quietly in my bunk, trying to read Boswell's Life of Johnson, and thanking my stars that I hadn't lived a thousand years earlier and been a Viking. I didn't see myself ploughing those short steep seas in an open galley. I woke on the morning of the 23rd to find the uneasy motion at an end, and, looking out of my port-hole, saw a space of green sunlit water, a rocky beach, and the white and red of a little town. The Gudrun waited about an hour at Stavanger, so I gave Dr. Newhover time to get on shore, before I had a hurried breakfast in the saloon and followed him. I saw him go off with two men, and get on board a motor-launch which was lying beside one of the jetties. The coast was now clear, so I went into the town, found the agents to whom Archie Roylance had cabled, and learned that my own motor-launch was ready and waiting in the inner harbour where the fishing-boats lie. A clerk took me down there, and introduced me to Johan, my skipper, a big, cheerful, bearded Norwegian, who had a smattering of English. I bought a quantity of provisions, and by ten o'clock we were on the move. I asked Johan about the route to Merdal, and he pointed out a moving speck a couple of miles ahead of us. "That is Kristian Egge's boat," he said. "He carries an English fisherman to Merdal and we follow." I got my glasses on the craft, and made out Newhover smoking in the stern.

It was a gorgeous day, with that funny Northern light which makes noon seem like early morning. I enjoyed every hour of it, partly because I had now a definite job before me, and partly because I was in the open air to which I properly belonged. I got no end of amusement watching the wild life--the cormorants and eider-duck on the little islands, and the seals, with heads as round as Medina's, that slipped off the skerries at our approach. The air was chilly and fresh, but when we turned the corner of the Merdalfjord out of the sea-wind and the sun climbed the sky it was as warm as June. A big flat island we passed, all short turf and rocky outcrops, was pointed out to me by Johan as Flacksholm. Soon we were shaping due east in an inlet which was surrounded by dark steep hills, with the snow lying in the gullies. I had Boswell with me in two volumes; the first I had read in the steamer, and the second I was now starting on, when it fell overboard, through my getting up in a hurry to look at a flock of duck. So I presented the odd volume to Johan, and surrendered myself to tobacco and meditation.

In the afternoon the inlet narrowed to a fjord, and the walls of hill grew steeper. They were noble mountains, cut sharp like the edge of the Drakensberg, and crowned with a line of snow, so that they looked like a sugar-coated cake that had been sliced. Streams came out of the upper snow-wreaths and hurled themselves down the steeps--above a shimmering veil of mist, and below a torrent of green water tumbling over pebbles to the sea. The landscape and the weather lulled me into a delectable peace which refused to be disturbed by any "looking before or after," as some poet says. Newhover was ahead of me--we never lost track of his launch--and it was my business to see what he was up to and to keep myself out of his sight. The ways and means of it I left to fortune to provide.

By and by the light grew dimmer, and the fjord grew narrower, so that dusk fell on us, though, looking back down the inlet, we could see a bright twilight. I assumed that Newhover would go on to Merdal and the fjord's head, where the Skarso entered the sea, and had decided to stop at Hauge, a village two miles short of it, on the south shore. We came to Hauge about half-past eight, in a wonderful purple dusk, for the place lay right under the shadow of a great cliff. I gave Johan full instructions: he was to wait for me and expect me when I turned up, and to provision himself from the village. On no account must he come up to Merdal, or go out of sight or hail of the boat. He seemed to relish the prospect of a few days' idleness, for he landed me at a wooden jetty in great good-humour, and wished me sport. What he thought I was after I cannot imagine, for I departed with a rucksack on my back and a stout stick in my hand, which scarcely suggested the chase.

I was in good spirits myself as I stretched my legs on the road which led from Hauge to Merdal. The upper fjord lay black on my left hand, the mountains rose black on my right, but though I walked in darkness I could see twilight ahead of me, where the hills fell back from the Skarso valley, that wonderful apple-green twilight which even in spring is all the northern night. I had never seen it before, and I suppose something in my blood answered to the place--for my father used to say that the Hannays came originally from Norse stock. There was a jolly crying of birds from the waters, ducks and geese and oyster-catchers and sandpipers, and now and then would come a great splash as if a salmon were jumping in the brackish tides on his way to the Skarso. I was thinking longingly of my rods left behind, when on turning a corner the lights of Merdal showed ahead, and it seemed to me that I had better be thinking of my next step.

I knew no Norwegian, but I counted on finding natives who could speak English, seeing so many of them have been in England or America. Newhover, I assumed, would go to the one hotel, and it was for me to find lodgings elsewhere. I began to think this spying business might be more difficult than I had thought, for if he saw me he would recognise me, and that must not happen. I was ready, of course, with a story of a walking tour, but he would be certain to suspect, and certain to let Medina know. . . . Well, a lodging for the night was my first business, and I must start inquiries. Presently I came to the little pier of Merdal, which was short of the village itself. There were several men sitting smoking on barrels and coils of rope, and one who stood at the end looking out to where Kristian Egge's boat, which had brought Newhover, lay moored. I turned down the road to it, for it seemed a place to gather information.

I said good evening to the men, and was just about to ask them for advice about quarters, when the man who had been looking out to sea turned round at the sound of my voice. He seemed an oldish fellow, with rather a stoop in his back, wearing an ancient shooting-jacket. The light was bad, but there was something in the cut of his jib that struck me as familiar, though I couldn't put a name to it.

I spoke to the Norwegians in English, but it was obvious that I had hit on a bunch of indifferent linguists. They shook their heads, and one pointed to the village, as if to tell me that I would be better understood there. Then the man in the shooting-jacket spoke.

"Perhaps I can help," he said. "There is a good inn in Merdal, which at this season is not full."

He spoke excellent English, but it was obvious that he wasn't an Englishman. There was an unmistakable emphasis of the gutturals.

"I doubt the inn may be too good for my purse," I said. "I am on a walking-tour and must lodge cheaply."

He laughed pleasantly. "There may be accommodation elsewhere. Peter Bojer may have a spare bed. I am going that way, sir, and can direct you."

He had turned towards me, and his figure caught the beam of the riding-light of the motor-launch. I saw a thin sunburnt face with a very pleasant expression, and an untidy grizzled beard. Then I knew him, and I could have shouted with amazement at the chance which had brought us two together again.

We walked side by side up the jetty road and on to the highway.

"I think," I said, "that we have met before, Herr Gaudian."

He stopped short. "That is my name . . . but I do not . . . I do not think . . ."

"Do you remember a certain Dutchman called Cornelius Brandt whom you entertained at your country house one night in December '15?"

He looked searchingly in my face.

"I remember," he said. "I also remember a Mr. Richard Hanau, one of Guggenheim's engineers, with whom I talked at Constantinople."

"The same," I said. For a moment I was not clear how he was going to take the revelation, but his next action reassured me, and I saw that I had not been wrong in my estimate of the one German I have ever wholeheartedly liked. He began to laugh, a friendly tolerant laugh.

"Kritzi Turken!" he cried. "It is indeed romantic. I have often wondered whether I should see or hear of you again, and behold! you step out of the darkness on a Norwegian fjord."

"You bear no malice?" I said. "I served my country as you served yours. I played fair, as you played fair."

"Malice!" he cried. "But we are gentlemen; also we are not children. I rejoice to see that you have survived the War. I have always wished you well, for you are a very bold and brave man."

"Not a bit of it," I said--"only lucky."

"By what name shall I call you now--Brandt or Hanau?"

"My name is Richard Hannay, but for the present I am calling myself Cornelius Brand--for a reason which I am going to tell you." I had suddenly made up my mind to take Gaudian into my full confidence. He seemed to have been sent by Providence for that purpose, and I was not going to let such a chance slip.

But at my words he stopped short.

"Mr. Hannay," he said, "I do not want your confidence. You are still engaged, I take it, in your country's service? I do not question your motive, but remember I am a German, and I cannot be party to the pursuit of one of my countrymen, however base I may think him."

I could only stare. "But I am not in my country's service," I stammered. "I left it at the Armistice, and I'm a farmer now."

"Do English farmers travel in Norway under false names?"

"That's a private business which I want to explain to you. I assure you there is no German in it. I want to keep an eye on the doings of a fashionable English doctor."

"I must believe you," he said after a pause. "But two hours ago a man arrived in the launch you see anchored out there. He is a fisherman and is now at the inn. That man is known to me--too well known. He is a German, who during the War served Germany in secret ways, in America and elsewhere. I did not love him and I think he did my country grievous ill, but that is a matter for us Germans to settle, and not for foreigners."

"I know your man as Dr. Newhover of Wimpole Street."

"So?" he said. "He has taken again his father's name, which was Neuhofer. We knew him as Kristoffer. What do you want with him?"

"Nothing that any honest German wouldn't approve," and there and then I gave him a sketch of the Medina business. He exclaimed in horror.

"Mr. Hannay," he said hesitatingly, "you are being honest with me?"

"I swear by all that's holy I am telling you the plain truth, and the full truth. Newhover may have done anything you jolly well like in the War. That's all washed out. I'm after him to get a line on a foul business which is English in origin. I want to put a spoke in the wheel of English criminals, and to save innocent lives. Besides, Newhover is only a subordinate. I don't propose to raise a hand against him, only to find out what he is doing."

He held out his hand. "I believe you," he said, "and if I can I will help you."

He conducted me through the long street of the village, past the inn, where I supposed Newhover was now going to bed, and out on to the road which ran up the Skarso valley. We came in sight of the river, a mighty current full of melted snow, sweeping in noble curves through the meadowland in that uncanny dusk. It appeared that he lodged with Peter Bojer, who had a spare bed, and when we reached the cottage, which stood a hundred yards from the highway on the very brink of the stream, Peter was willing to let me have it. His wife gave us supper--an omelette, smoked salmon, and some excellent Norwegian beer--and after it I got out my map and had a survey of the neighbourhood.

Gaudian gave me a grisly picture of the condition of his own country. It seemed that the downfall of the old régime had carried with it the decent wise men like himself, who had opposed its follies, but had lined up with it on patriotic grounds when the War began. He said that Germany was no place for a moderate man, and that the power lay with the bloated industrials, who were piling up fortunes abroad while they were wrecking their country at home. The only opposition, he said, came from the communists, who were half-witted, and the monarchists, who wanted the impossible. "Reason is not listened to, and I fear there is no salvation till my poor people have passed through the last extremity. You foreign Powers have hastened our destruction, when you had it in your hands to save us. I think you have meant well, but you have been blind, for you have not supported our moderate men and have by your harshness played the game of the wreckers among us."

It appeared that he was very poor now, like all the professional classes. I thought it odd that this man, who had a world-wide reputation as an engineer, couldn't earn a big income in any country he chose. Then I saw that it was because he had lost the wish to make money. He had seen too deep into the vanity of human wishes to have any ambition left. He was unmarried, with no near relations, and he found his pleasure in living simply in remote country places and watching flowers and beasts. He was a keen fisherman, but couldn't afford a good beat, so he leased a few hundred yards from a farmer, who had not enough water to get a proper rent for it, and he did a lot of trout fishing in the tarns high up in the hills and in the Skarso above the foss. As he sat facing me beyond the stove, with his kind sad brown eyes and his rugged face, I thought how like he was to a Scottish moorland shepherd. I had liked him when I first saw him in Stumm's company, but now I liked him so much that because of him I was prepared to think better of the whole German race.

I asked him if he had heard of any other Englishman in the valley-- anyone of the name of Jason, for instance. He said no; he had been there for three weeks, but the fishing did not begin for another fortnight, and foreign visitors had not yet arrived. Then I asked him about the saeter farms, and he said that few of these were open yet, since the high pastures were not ready. One or two on the lower altitudes might be already inhabited, but not many, though the winter had been a mild one and the spring had come early. "Look at the Skarso," he said. "Usually in April it is quite low, for the snowfields have not begun to melt. But to-day it is as brimming as if it were the middle of May."

He went over the map with me--an inch-to-a-mile one I had got in London--and showed me the lie of the land. The saeters were mostly farther up the river, reached by paths up the tributary glens. There was a good road running the length of the valley, but no side roads to connect with the parallel glens, the Uradal and the Bremendal. I found indeed one track marked on the map, which led to the Uradal by a place called Snaasen. "Yes," said Gaudian, "that is the only thing in the way of what you soldiers would call lateral communications. I've walked it, and I'm sorry for the man who tries the road in bad weather. You can see the beginning of the track from this house; it climbs up beside the torrent just across the valley. Snaasen is more or less inhabited all the year round, and I suppose you would call it a kind of saeter. It is a sort of shelter hut for travellers taking that road, and in summer it is a paradise for flowers. You would be surprised at the way the natives can cross the hills even in winter. Snaasen belongs to the big farm two miles upstream, which carries with it the best beat on the Skarso. Also there is said to be first-class ryper- shooting later in the year, and an occasional bear. By the way, I rather fancy someone told me that the whole thing was owned by, or had been leased to, an Englishman. . . .

You are rich, you see, and you do not leave much in Norway for poor people."

I slept like a log on a bed quite as hard as a log, and woke to a brilliant blue morning, with the birds in the pine-woods fairly riotous, and snipe drumming in the boggy meadows, and the Skarso coming down like a sea. I could see the water almost up to the pathway of a long wooden bridge that led to the big farm Gaudian had spoken of. I got my glass on the torrent opposite, and saw the track to Snaasen winding up beside it till it was lost in a fold of the ravine. Above it I scanned the crown of the ridge, which was there much lower than on the sides of the fjord. There was no snow to be seen, and I knew by a sort of instinct that if I got up there I should find a broad tableland of squelching pastures with old snowdrifts in the hollows and tracts of scrubby dwarf birch.

While I was waiting for breakfast I heard a noise from the high- road, and saw a couple of the little conveyances they call stolkjaeres passing. My glass showed me Dr. Newhover in the first and a quantity of luggage in the second. They took the road across the wooden bridge to the big farm, and I could see the splash of their wheels at the far end of it, where the river was over the road. So Dr. Newhover, or some friend of his, was the lessee of this famous fishing, which carried with it the shooting on the uplands behind it. I rather thought I should spend the day finding out more about Snaasen, and I counted myself lucky to have got quarters in such an excellent observation-post as Peter Bojer's cottage.

I wouldn't go near the track to Snaasen till I saw what Newhover did, so Gaudian and I sat patiently at Peter Bojer's window. About ten o'clock a couple of ponies laden with kit in charge of a tow- headed boy appeared at the foot of the track and slowly climbed up the ravine. An hour later came Dr. Newhover, in a suit that looked like khaki and wearing a long mackintosh cape. He strode out well and breasted the steep path like a mountaineer. I wanted to go off myself in pursuit of him, keeping well behind, but Gaudian very sensibly pointed out how sparse the cover was, and that if he saw a man on that lonely road he would certainly want to know all about him.

We sat out-of-doors after luncheon in a pleasant glare of sun, and by and by were rewarded by the sight of the pack-ponies returning, laden with a different size and shape of kit. They did not stop at the big farm, but crossed the wooden bridge and took the high-road for Merdal. I concluded that this was the baggage of the man whom Newhover had replaced, and that he was returning to Stavanger in Kristian Egge's boat. About tea-time the man himself appeared-- Jason, or whatever his name was. I saw two figures come down the ravine by the Snaasen road, and stop at the foot and exchange farewells. One of them turned to go back, and I saw that this was Newhover, climbing with great strides like a man accustomed to hills. The other crossed the bridge, and passed within hail of us-- a foppish young man, my glass told me, wearing smart riding- breeches and with an aquascutum slung over his shoulder.

I was very satisfied with what I had learned. I had seen Newhover relieve his predecessor, just as Medina had planned, and I knew where he was lodged. Whatever his secret was it was hidden in Snaasen, and to Snaasen I would presently go. Gaudian advised me to wait till after supper, when there would be light enough to find the way and not too much to betray us. So we both lay down and slept for four hours, and took the road about ten-thirty as fresh as yearlings.

It was a noble night, windless and mild, and, though darkness lurked in the thickets and folds of hill, the sky was filled with a translucent amethyst glow. I felt as if I were out on some sporting expedition and enjoyed every moment of the walk with that strung-up expectant enjoyment which one gets in any form of chase. The torrent made wild music on our left hand, grumbling in pits and shooting over ledges with a sound like a snowslip. There was every kind of bird about, but I had to guess at them by their sounds and size, for there was no colour in that shadowy world.

By and by we reached the top and had a light cold wind in our faces blowing from the snowy mountains to the north. The place seemed a huge broken tableland and every hollow glistened as if filled with snow or water. There were big dark shapes ahead of us which I took to be the hills beyond the Uradal. Here it was not so easy to follow the track, which twined about in order to avoid the boggy patches, and Gaudian and I frequently strayed from it and took tosses over snags of juniper. Once I was up against an iron pole, and to my surprise saw wires above. Gaudian nodded. "Snaasen is on the telephone," he said.

I had hoped to see some light in the house, so as to tell it from a distance. But we did not realise its presence till we were close upon it, standing a little back from the path, as dark as a tombstone. The inhabitants must have gone early to bed, for there was no sign of life within. It was a two-storeyed erection of wood, stoutly built, with broad eaves, to the roof. Adjacent there stood a big barn or hayshed, and behind it some other outbuildings which might have been byres or dairies. We walked stealthily round the place, and were amazed at its utter stillness. There was no sound of an animal moving in the steading, and when a brace of mallards flew overhead we started at the noise like burglars at the creaking of a board.

Short of burglary there was nothing further to be done, so we took the road home and scrambled at a great pace down the ravine, for it was chilly on the tableland. Before we went to bed, we had settled that next day Gaudian should go up to Snaasen like an ordinary tourist and make some excuse to get inside, while I would take a long tramp over the plateau, keeping well away from the house in case there might be something ado in that barren region.

Next morning saw the same cloudless weather, and we started off about ten o'clock. I had a glorious but perfectly futile day. I went up the Skarso to well above the foss, and then climbed the north wall of the valley by a gulley choked with brushwood, which gave out long before the top and left me to finish my ascent by way of some very loose screes and unpleasant boiler-plates. I reached the plateau much farther to the east, where it was at a greater altitude, so that I looked down upon the depression where ran the track to Uradal. I struck due north among boggy meadows and the remains of old snowdrifts, through whose fringes flowers were showing, till I was almost on the edge of Uradal, and looked away beyond it to a fine cluster of rock peaks streaked and patched with ice. The Uradal glen was so deep cut that I could not see into it, so I moved west and struck the Merdal track well to the north of Snaasen. After that I fetched a circuit behind Snaasen, and had a good view of the house from the distance of about half a mile. Two of its chimneys were smoking, and there were sounds of farm work from the yard. There was no sign of live stock, but it looked as if someone was repairing the sheds against the summer season. I waited for more than an hour, but I saw no human being, so I turned homeward, and made a careful descent by the ravine, reconnoitring every corner in case I should run into Newhover.

I found that Gaudian had returned before me. When I asked him what luck he had had he shook his head.

"I played the part of a weary traveller, and asked for milk. An ugly woman gave me beer. She said she had no milk, till the cattle came up from the valleys. She would not talk and she was deaf. She said an English Herr had the ryper shooting, but lived at Tryssil. That is the name of the big farm by the Skarso. She would tell me no more, and I saw no other person. But I observed that Snaasen is larger than I thought. There are rooms built out at the back, which we thought were barns. There is ample space there for a man to be concealed."

I asked him if he had any plan, and he said he thought of going boldly up next day and asking for Newhover, whom he could say he had seen passing Peter Bojer's cottage. He disliked the man, but had never openly quarrelled with him. I approved of that, but in the meantime I resolved to do something on my own account that night. I was getting anxious, for I felt that my time was growing desperately short; it was now the 25th of April and I was due back in London on the 29th, and, if I failed to turn up, Medina would make inquiries at Fosse Manor and suspect. I had made up my mind to go alone that night to Snaasen and do a little pacific burgling.

I set out about eleven, and I put my pistol in my pocket, as well as my flask and sandwiches and electric torch, for it occurred to me that anything might happen. I made good going across the bridge and up the first part of the track, for I wanted to have as much time as possible for my job. My haste was nearly my undoing, for instead of reconnoitring and keeping my ears open, I strode up the hill as if I had been walking to make a record. It was by the mercy of Heaven that I was at a point where an outjutting boulder made a sharp corner when I was suddenly aware that someone was coming down the road. I flattened myself into the shadow, and saw Newhover.

He did not see or hear me, for he, too, was preoccupied. He was descending at a good pace, and he must have started in a hurry, for he had no hat. His longish blond locks were all tousled, and his face seemed sharper than usual with anxiety.

I wondered what on earth had happened, and my first notion was to follow him downhill. And then it occurred to me that his absence gave me a sovereign chance at Snaasen. But if the household was astir there might be other travellers on the road and it behoved me to go warily. Now, near the top of the ravine, just under the edge of the tableland, there was a considerable patch of wood--birches, juniper, and wind-blown pines--for there the torrent flowed in a kind of cup, after tumbling off the plateau and before hurling itself down to the valley. Here it was possible to find an alternative road to the path, so I dived in among the matted whortleberries and moss-covered boulders.

I had not gone ten yards before I realised that there was somebody or something else in the thicket. There was a sound of plunging ahead of me, then the crack of a rotten log, then the noise of a falling stone. It might be a beast, but it struck me that no wild thing would move so awkwardly. Only human boots make that kind of clumsy slipping.

If this was somebody from Snaasen, what was he doing off the track? Could he be watching me? Well, I proposed to do a little stalking on my own account. I got down on all-fours and crawled in cover in the direction of the sound. It was very dark there, but I could see a faint light where the scrub thinned round the stream.

Soon I was at the edge of the yeasty water. The sounds had stopped, but suddenly they began again a little farther up, and there was a scuffle as if part of the bank had given way. The man, whoever he was, seemed to be trying to cross. That would be a dangerous thing to do, for the torrent was wide and very strong. I crawled a yard or two up-stream, and then in an open patch saw what was happening.

A fallen pine made a crazy bridge to a great rock, from which the rest of the current might conceivably be leaped. A man was kneeling on the trunk and beginning to move along it. . . . But as I looked the rotten thing gave way and the next I saw he was struggling in the foam. It was all the matter of a fraction of a second, and before I knew I was leaning over the brink and clutching at an arm. I gripped it, braced one leg against a rock, and hauled the owner close into the edge out of the main current. He seemed to have taken no hurt, for he found a foothold, and scarcely needed my help to scramble up beside me.

Then to my surprise he went for me tooth and nail. It was like the assault of a wild beast, and its suddenness rolled me on my back. I felt hands on my throat, and grew angry, caught the wrists and wrenched them away. I flung a leg over his back and got uppermost, and after that he was at my mercy. He seemed to realise it, too, for he lay quite quiet and did not struggle.

"What the devil do you mean?" I said angrily. "You'd have been drowned but for me, and then you try to throttle me."

I got out my torch and had a look at him. It was the figure of a slight young man, dressed in rough homespun such as Norwegian farm lads wear. His face was sallow and pinched, and decorated with the most preposterous wispish beard, and his hair was cut roughly as if with garden shears. The eyes that looked up at me were as scared and wild as a deer's.

"What the devil do you mean?" I repeated, and then to my surprise he replied in English.

"Let me up," he said, "I'm too tired to fight. I'll go back with you."

Light broke in on me.

"Don't you worry, old chap," I said soothingly. "You're going back with me, but not to that infernal saeter. We've met before, you know. You're Lord Mercot, and I saw you ride 'Red Prince' last year at the 'House' Grind."

He was sitting up, staring at me like a ghost.

"Who are you? Oh, for God's sake, who are you?"

"Hannay's my name. I live at Fosse Manor in the Cotswolds. You once came to dine with us before the Heythrop Ball."

"Hannay!" He repeated stumblingly--"I remember--I think--remember-- remember Lady Hannay. Yes--and Fosse. It's on the road between--"

He scrambled to his feet.

"Oh, sir, get me away. He's after me--the new devil with the long face, the man who first brought me here. I don't know what has happened to me, but I've been mad a long time, and I've only got sane in the last days. Then I remembered--and I ran away. But they're after me. Oh, quick, quick! Let's hide."

"See here, my lad," I said, and I took out my pistol. "The first man that lays a hand on you I shoot, and I don't miss. You're as safe now as if you were at home. But this is no place to talk, and I've the devil of a lot to tell you. I'm going to take you down with me to my lodging in the valley. But they're hunting you, so we've got to go cannily. Are you fit to walk? Well, do exactly as I tell you, and in an hour you'll be having a long drink and looking up time-tables."

I consider that journey back a creditable piece of piloting. The poor boy was underfed and shaking with excitement, but he stepped out gallantly, and obeyed me like a lamb. We kept off the track so as to muffle our steps in grass, and took every corner like scouts in a reconnaissance. We met Newhover coming back, but we heard him a long way off and were in good cover when he passed. He was hurrying as furiously as ever and I could hear his laboured breathing. After that we had a safe road over the meadow, but we crossed the bridge most circumspectly, making sure that there was no one in the landscape. About half-past one I pushed open Gaudian's bedroom window, woke him, and begged him to forage for food and drink.

"Did you get into Snaasen?" he asked sleepily.

"No, but I've found what we've been looking for. One of the three hostages is at this moment sitting on your cabin-box."

CHAPTER XII

I RETURN TO SERVITUDE

We fed Mercot with tinned meats and biscuits and bottled beer, and he ate like a famished schoolboy. The odd thing was that his terror had suddenly left him. I suppose the sight of me, which had linked him up definitely with his past, had made him feel a waif no more, and, once he was quite certain who he was, his natural courage returned. He got great comfort from looking at Gaudian, and indeed I could not imagine a better sedative than a sight of that kind, wise old face. I lent him pyjamas, rubbed him down to prevent a chill from his ducking, put him in my bed, and had the satisfaction of seeing him slip off at once into deep slumber.

Next morning Gaudian and I interviewed Peter Bojer and explained that a young English friend of ours had had an accident, while on a walking tour, and might be with us for a day or two. It was not likely that Newhover would advertise his loss, and in any case Peter was no gossip, and Gaudian, who had known him for years, let him see that we wanted the fact of a guest being with us kept as quiet as possible. The boy slept till nearly midday, while I kept a watch on the road. Newhover appeared early, and went down to Merdal village, where he spent the better part of the forenoon. He was probably making inquiries, but they were bound in his own interest to be discreet ones. Then he returned to Tryssil, and later I saw a dejected figure tramping up the Snaasen track. He may have thought that the body of the fugitive was in some pool of the torrent or being swirled down by the Skarso to the sea, and I imagined that that scarcely fitted in with his instructions.

When Mercot awoke at last and had his breakfast he looked a different lad. His eyes had lost their fright, and though he stuttered badly and seemed to have some trouble in collecting his wits, he had obviously taken hold of himself. His great desire was to get clean, and that took some doing, for he could not have had a bath for weeks. Then he wanted to borrow my razor and shave his beard, but I managed to prevent him in time, for I had been thinking the thing out, and I saw that that would never do. So far as I could see, he had recovered his memory, but there were still gaps in it; that is to say, he remembered all his past perfectly well till he left Oxford on February 17th, and he remembered the events of the last few days, but between the two points he was still hazy.

On returning to his rooms that February evening he had found a note about a horse he was trying to buy, an urgent note asking him to come round at once to certain stables. He had just time for this, before dressing for dinner, so he dashed out of the house--meeting nobody, as it chanced, on the stairs, and, as the night was foggy, being seen by no one in the streets. After that his memory was a blank. He had wakened in a room in

London, which he thought was a nursing home, and had seen a doctor--I could picture that doctor-- and had gone to sleep again. After that his recollection was like a black night studded with little points of light which were physical sensations. He remembered being very cold and sometimes very tired, he recollected the smell of paraffin, and of mouldy hay, and of a treacly drink which made him sick. He remembered faces, too, a cross old woman who cursed him, a man who seemed to be always laughing, and whose laugh he feared more than curses. . . .

I suppose that Medina's spell must have been wearing thin during these last days, and that the keeper, Jason, or whoever he was, could not revive it. For Mercot had begun to see Jason no longer as a terror but as an offence--an underbred young bounder whom he detested. And with this clearing of the foreground came a lightening of the background. He saw pictures of his life at Alcester, at first as purely objective things, but soon as in some way connected with himself. Then longing started, passionate longing for something which he knew was his own. . . . It was a short step from that to the realisation that he was Lord Mercot, though he happened to be clad like a tramp and was as dirty as a stoker. And then he proceeded to certain halting deductions. Something bad had happened to him: he was in a foreign land--which land he didn't know: he was being ill-treated and kept prisoner; he must escape and get back to his old happy world. He thought of escape quite blindly, without any plan; if only he could get away from that accursed saeter, he would remember better, things would happen to him, things would come back to him.

Then Jason went and Newhover came, and Newhover drove him half crazy with fear, for the doctor's face was in some extraordinary way mixed up with his confused memory of the gaps between the old world and the new. He was mad to escape now, but rather to escape from Newhover than to reach anywhere. He watched for his chance, and found it about eight o'clock the evening before, when the others in the house were at supper. Some instinct had led him towards Merdal. He had heard footsteps behind him and had taken to the thicket. . . . I appeared, an enemy as he thought, and he had despairingly flung himself on me. Then I had spoken his name, and that fixed the wavering panorama of his memory. He "came to himself" literally, and was now once more the undergraduate of Christ Church, rather shell-shocked and jumpy, but quite sane.

The question which worried me was whether the cure was complete, whether Newhover could act as Medina's deputy and resurrect the spell. I did not believe that he could, but I wasn't certain. Anyhow it had to be risked.

Mercot repeated his request for the loan of my razor. He was smoking a Turkish cigarette as if every whiff took him nearer Elysium. Badly shorn, ill-clad, and bearded as he was, he had still the ghost of the air of the well-to-do, sporting young men. He wanted to know when the steamer sailed, but there seemed no panic now in his impatience.

"Look here," I said. "I don't think you can start just yet. There's a lot I want to tell you now you're able to hear it."

I gave him a rough summary of Macgillivray's story, and the tale of the three hostages. I think he found it comforting to know that there were others in the same hole as himself. "By Jove!" he said, "what a damnable business! And I'm the only one you've got on the track of. No word of the girl and the little boy?"

"No word!"

"Poor devils," he said, but I do not think he really took in the situation.

"So you see how we are placed. Macgillivray's round-up is fixed for the 10th of June. We daren't release the hostages till the 9th, for otherwise the gang would suspect. They have everything ready, as I've told you, for their own liquidation. Also we can't release one without the others, unless by the 9th of June we have given up hope of the others. Do you see what I mean?"

He didn't. "All I want is to get home in double-quick time," he said.

"I don't wonder. But you must see that that is impossible, unless we chuck in our hand."

He stared at me, and I saw fright beginning to return to his eyes.

"Do you mean that you want me to go back to that bloody place?"

"That's what I mean. If you think it out, you'll see it's the only way. We must do nothing to spoil the chances of the other two. You're a gentleman, and are bound to play the game."

"But I can't," he cried. "Oh, my God, you can't ask me to." There were tears in his voice, and his eyes were wild.

"It's a good deal to ask, but I know you will do it. There's not a scrap of danger now, for you have got back your memory, and you know where you are. It's up to you to play a game with your gaoler. He is the dupe now. You fill the part of the half-witted farm-boy and laugh at him all the time in your sleeve. Herr Gaudian will be waiting down here to keep an eye on you, and when the time is ripe--and it won't be more than five weeks--I give you full permission to do anything you like with Dr. Newhover."

"I can't, I can't," he wailed, and his jaw dropped like a scared child's.

Then Gaudian spoke. "I think we had better leave the subject for the present. Lord Mercot will do precisely what he thinks right. You have sprung the thing on him too suddenly. I think it might be a good plan if you went for a walk, Hannay. Try the south side of the foss--there's some very pretty scrambling to be had there."

He spoke to me at the door. "The poor boy is all in pieces. You cannot ask him for a difficult decision when his nerves are still raw. Will you leave him with me? I have had some experience in dealing with such cases."

When I got back for supper, after a climb which exercised every muscle in my body, I found Gaudian teaching Mercot a new patience game. We spent a very pleasant evening, and I noticed that Gaudian led the talk to matters in which the boy could share, and made him speak of himself. We heard about his racing ambitions, his desire to ride in the Grand National, his hopes for his polo game. It appeared that he was destined for the Guards, but he was to be allowed a year's travel when he left the 'Varsity, and we planned out an itinerary for him. Gaudian, who had been almost everywhere in the world, told him of places in Asia where no tourist had ever been and where incredible sport was to be had in virgin forest, and I pitched him some yarns about those few districts of Africa which are still unspoiled. He got very keen, for he had a bit of the explorer in him, and asked modestly if we thought he could pull off certain plans we had suggested. We told him there was no doubt about it. "It's not as tough a proposition as riding in the National," I said.

When we had put him to bed, Gaudian smiled as if well pleased. "He has begun to get back his confidence," he said.

He slept for twelve hours, and when he woke I had gone out, for I thought it better to leave him in Gaudian's hands. I had to settle the business that day, for it was now the 27th. I walked down the fjord to Hauge, and told Johan to be ready to start next morning. I asked him about the weather, which was still cloudless, and he stared at the sky and sniffed, and thought it would hold for a day or two. "But rain is coming," he added, "and wind. The noise of the foss is too loud."

When I returned Gaudian met me at the door. "The boy has recovered," he said. "He will speak to you himself. He is a brave boy and will do a hard task well."

It was a rather shy and self-conscious Mercot that greeted me.

"I'm afraid I behaved rather badly yesterday, sir. I was feeling a bit rattled, and I'm ashamed of myself, for I've always rather fancied my nerve."

"My dear chap," I said, "you've been through enough to crack the nerve of a buffalo."

"I want to say that of course I'll do what you want. I must play the game by the others. That poor little boy! And I remember Miss Victor quite well--I once stayed in the same house with her. I'll go back to the saeter when you give the word. Indeed, I'm rather looking forward to it. I promise to play the half-wit so that Dr. Newhover will think me safe in the bag. All I ask is that you let me have my innings with him when the time comes. I've a biggish score to settle."

"Indeed I promise that. Look here, Mercot, if you don't mind my saying it, I think you're behaving uncommonly well. You're a gallant fellow."

"Oh, that's all right," he said, blushing. "When do you want me to start? If it's possible, I'd like another night in a decent bed."

"You shall have it. Early to-morrow morning we'll accompany you to the prison door. You've got to gibber when you see Newhover, and pretend not to be able to give any account of your doings. I leave you to put up a camouflage. The next five weeks will be infernally dull for you, but you must just shut your teeth and stick it out. Remember, Gaudian will be down here all the time and in touch with your friends, and when the day comes you will take your instructions from him. And, by the way, I'm going to leave you my pistol. I suppose you can keep it concealed, for Newhover is not likely to search your pockets. Don't use it, of course, but it may be a comfort to you to know that you have it."

He took it gladly. "Don't be afraid I'll use it. What I'm keeping for Newhover is the best hiding man ever had. He's a bit above my weight, but I don't mind that."

Very early next morning we woke Mercot, and, while the sky was turning from sapphire to turquoise, took our way through the hazy meadows and up the Snaasen track. We left it at the summit, and fetched a circuit round by the back of the saeter, but first we made Mercot roll in the thicket till he had a very grubby face and plenty of twigs and dust in his untidy hair. Then the two of us shook hands with him, found a lair in a patch of juniper, and watched him go forward.

A forlorn figure he looked in that cold half-light as he approached the saeter door. But he was acting his part splendidly, for he stumbled with fatigue, dropped heavily against the door, and beat on it feebly. It seemed a long time till it opened, and then he appeared to shrink back in terror. The old woman cried out shrilly to summon someone from within, and presently Newhover came out in a dressing-gown. He caught Mercot by the shoulder and shook him, and that valiant soul behaved exactly like a lunatic, shielding his head and squealing like a rabbit. Finally we saw him dragged indoors. . . . It was horrible to leave him like that, but I comforted myself with the thought of what Newhover would be like in five weeks' time.

We raced back to Peter Bojer's and after a hasty breakfast started off for Hauge. I settled with Gaudian that he was to report any developments to me by cable, and I was to do the same to him. When the day of release was fixed, he was to go boldly up to Snaasen and deal with the doctor as he liked, making sure that he could not communicate with Medina for a day or two. A motor-launch would be waiting at Merdal to take the two to Stavanger, for I wanted him to see Mercot on board the English steamer. I arranged, too, that he should be supplied with adequate funds, for Mercot had not a penny.

We pushed off at once, for I had to be at Flacksholm in good time, and as the morning advanced I did not feel so sure of the weather. What wind we had had these last days had been mild breezes from the west, but now it seemed to be shifting more to the north, and increasing in vehemence. Down in that deep-cut fjord it was calm enough, but up on the crest of the tableland on the northern shore I could see that it was blowing hard, for my glass showed me little tourmentes of snow. Also it had suddenly got much colder. I made Johan force the pace, and early in the afternoon we were out of the shelter of the rock walls in the inlet into which the fjord broadened. Here it was blowing fairly hard, and there was a stiff sea running. Flying squalls of rain beat down on us from the north, and for five minutes or so would shut out the view. It was a regular gusty April day, such as you find in spring salmon- fishing in Scotland, and had my job been merely to catch the boat at Stavanger I should not have minded it at all. But there was no time for the boat, for in little more than twenty-four hours I had to meet Medina. I wondered if Archie Roylance had turned up. I wondered still more how an aeroplane was to make the return journey over these stormy leagues of sea.

Presently the low green lines of Flacksholm showed through the spray, and when Johan began to shape his course to the south-west for Stavanger, I bade him go straight forward and land me on the island. I told him I had a friend who was camping there, and that we were to be picked up in a day or two by an English yacht. Johan obviously thought me mad, but he did as he was told. "There will be no one on the island yet," he said. "The farmer from Rosmaer does not come till June, when the haymaking begins. The winter pasture is poor and sour." That was all to the good, for I did not want any spectator of our madness.

As we drew nearer I could see no sign of life on the low shore, except an infinity of eider-ducks, and a fine osprey which sat on a pointed rock like a heraldic griffin. I was watching the bird, for I had only seen an osprey twice before, when Johan steered me into a creek, where there was deep water alongside a flat reef. This, he told me, was the ordinary landing-place from the mainland. I flung my suit-case and rucksack on shore, said good-bye to Johan and tipped him well, and watched the little boat ploughing south till it was hidden by a squall. Then, feeling every kind of a fool, I seized my baggage and proceeded, like Robinson Crusoe, into the interior.

It was raining steadily, a fine thin rain, and every now and then a squall would burst on me and ruffle the sea. Jolly weather for flying, I reflected, especially for flying over some hundreds of miles of ocean! . . . I found the farm, a few rough wooden buildings and a thing like a stone cattle-pen, but there was no sign of human life there. Then I got out my map, and concluded that I had better make for the centre of the island, where there seemed to be some flat ground at one end of the loch. I was feeling utterly depressed, walking like a bagman with my kit in my hand in an uninhabited Norwegian isle, and due in London the next evening. London seemed about as inaccessible in the time as the moon.

When I got to the rim of the central hollow there was a brief clearing of the weather, and I looked down on a little grey tarn set in very green meadows. In the meadows at the north end I saw to my joy what looked like an aeroplane picketed down, and a thing like a small tent near it. Also I could see smoke curling up from a group of boulders adjoining. The gallant Archie had arrived, and my spirits lightened. I made good going down the hill, and, as I shouted, a figure like an Arctic explorer crawled out of the tent.

"Hullo, Dick," it cried. "Any luck?"

"Plenty," I said. "And you?"

"Famous. Got here last night after a clinkin' journey with the bus behavin' like a lamb. Had an interestin' evenin' with the birds-- Lord! such a happy huntin'-ground for 'em. I've been doin' sentry- go on the tops all mornin' lookin' for you, but the weather got dirty, so I returned to the wigwam. Lunch is nearly ready."

"What about the weather?" I asked anxiously.

"Pas si bête," he said, sniffing. "The wind is pretty sure to go down at sunset. D'you mind a night journey?"

Archie's imperturbable good humour cheered me enormously. I must say he was a born campaigner, for he had made himself very snug, and gave me as good a meal as I have ever eaten--a hot stew of tinned stuff and curry, a plum-pudding, and an assortment of what he called "delicatessen." To keep out the cold we drank benedictine in horn mugs. He could talk about nothing but his blessed birds, and announced that he meant to come back to Flacksholm and camp for a week. He had seen a special variety-- some kind of phalarope--that fairly ravished his heart. When I asked questions about the journey ahead of us, he scarcely deigned to answer, so busy he was with speculation on the feathered fauna of Norway.

"Archie," I said, "are you sure you can get me across the North Sea?"

"I won't say 'sure.' There's always a lottery in this game, but with any luck we ought to manage it. The wind will die down, and besides it's a ground wind, and may be quiet enough a few hundred feet up. We'll have to shape a compass course anyhow, so that darkness won't worry us."

"What about the machine?" I asked. I don't know why, but I felt horribly nervous.

"A beauty. But of course you never know. If we were driven much out of a straight course, our petrol might run short."

"What would that mean?"

"Forced landin'."

"But supposing we hadn't reached land?"

"Oh, then we'd be for it," said Archie cheerfully. He added, as if to console me: "We might be picked up by a passin' steamer or a fishin' smack. I've known fellows that had that luck."

"What are the chances of our getting over safely?"

"Evens. Never better or worse than evens in this flyin' business. But it will be all right. Dash it all, a woodcock makes the trip constantly in one flight."

After that I asked no more questions, for I knew I could not get him past the woodcock. I was not feeling happy, but Archie's calm put me to shame. We had a very good tea, and then, sure enough, the wind began to die down, and the clouds opened to show clear sky. It grew perishing cold, and I was glad of every stitch of clothing, and envied Archie his heavy skin coat. We were all ready about nine, and in a dead calm cast loose, taxied over a stretch of turf, rose above the loch so as to clear the hill, and turned our faces to the west, which was like a shell of gold closing down upon the molten gold of the sea.

Luck was with us that night, and all my qualms were belied. Apart from the cold, which was savage, I enjoyed every moment of the trip, till in the early dawn we saw a crawling black line beneath us which was the coast of Aberdeen. We filled up with petrol at a place in Kincardine, and had an enormous breakfast at the local hotel. Everything went smoothly and it was still early in the day when I found we were crossing the Cheviots. We landed at York about noon, and, while Archie caught the London train, I got my car from the garage and started for Oxford. But first I wired to Mary asking her to wire to Medina in my name that I would reach London by the seven-fifteen. I had a pleasant run south, left the car at Oxford, and duly emerged on the platform at Paddington to find Medina waiting for me.

His manner was almost tender.

"My dear fellow, I do hope you are better?"

"Perfectly fit again, thank you. Ready for anything."

"You look more sunburnt than when you left town."

"It's the wonderful weather we've had. I've been lying basking on the verandah."

CHAPTER XIII

I VISIT THE FIELDS OF EDEN

There was a change in Medina. I noticed it the following day when I lunched with him, and very particularly at the next dinner of the Thursday Club to which I went as his guest. It was a small change, which nobody else would have remarked, but to me, who was watching him like a lynx, it was clear enough. His ease of manner towards the world was a little less perfect, and when we were alone he was more silent than before. I did not think that he had begun to suspect any danger to his plans, but the day for their consummation was approaching, and even his cold assurance may have been flawed by little quivers of nervousness. As I saw it, once the big liquidation took place and he realised the assets which were to be the foundation of his main career, it mattered little what became of the hostages. He might let them go; they would wander back to their old world unable to give any account of their absence, and, if the story got out, there would be articles in the medical journals about these unprecedented cases of lost memory. So far I was certain that they had taken no lasting harm. But if the liquidation failed, God knew what their fate would be. They would never be seen again, for if his possession of them failed to avert disaster to his plans, he would play for safety, and, above all, for revenge. Revenge to a mind like his would be a consuming passion.

The fact that I had solved one conundrum and laid my hand on one of the hostages put me in a perfect fever of restlessness. Our time was very short, and there were still two poor souls hidden in his black underworld. It was the little boy I thought most of, and perhaps my preoccupation with him made me stupid about other things. My thoughts were always on the Blind Spinner, and there I could not advance one single inch. Macgillivray's watchers had nothing to report. It was no use my paying another visit to Madame Breda, and going through the same rigmarole. I could only stick to Medina and pray for luck. I had resolved that if he asked me again to take up my quarters with him in Hill Street I would accept, though it might be hideously awkward in a score of ways.

I longed for Sandy, but no word came from him, and I had his strict injunctions not to try to reach him. The only friend I saw in those early days of May was Archie Roylance who seemed to have forgotten his Scotch greenshanks and settled down in London for the season. He started playing polo, which was not a safe game for a man with a crocked leg, and he opened his house in Grosvenor Street and roosted in a corner of it. He knew I was busy in a big game, and he was mad to be given a share in it, but I had to be very careful with Archie. He was the best fellow alive, but discretion had never been his strong point. So I refused to tell him anything at present, and I warned Turpin, who was an ancient friend of his, to do the same. The three of us dined together one night, and poor old Turpin was rallied by Archie on his glumness.

"You're a doleful bird, you know," he told him. "I heard somewhere you were goin' to be married and I expect that's the cause. What do you call it--ranger yourself? Cheer up, my son. It can't be as bad as it sounds. Look at Dick there."

I switched him on to other subjects, and we got his opinion on the modern stage. Archie had been doing a course of plays, and had very strong views on the drama. Something had got to happen, he said, or he fell asleep in the first act, and something very rarely happened, so he was left to slumber peacefully till he was awakened and turned out by the attendants. He liked plays with shooting in them, and knockabout farce--anything indeed with a noise in it. But he had struck a vein of serious drama which he had found soporific. One piece in especial, which showed the difficulties of a lady of fifty who fell in love with her stepson, he seriously reprobated.

"Rotten," he complained. "What did it matter to anyone what the old cat did? But I assure you, everybody round me was gloatin' over it. A fellow said to me it was a masterpiece of tragic irony. What's irony, Dick? I thought it was the tone your commandin' officer adopted, when you had made an ass of yourself, and he showed it by complimentin' you on your intelligence. . . . Oh, by the way, you remember the girl in green we saw at that dancin' place? Well, I saw her at the show--at least I'm pretty sure it was her--in a box with the black-bearded fellow. She didn't seem to be takin' much of it in. Wonder who she is and what she was doin' there? Russian, d'you think? I believe the silly play was translated from the Russian. I want to see that girl dance again."

The next week was absolutely blank, except for my own perpetual worrying. Medina kept me close to him, and I had to relinquish any idea of going down to Fosse for an occasional night. I longed badly for the place and for a sight of Peter John, and Mary's letters didn't comfort me, for they were getting scrappier and scrappier. My hope was that Medina would act on Kharáma's advice, and in order to establish his power over his victims bring them into the open and exercise it in the environment to which they had been accustomed. That wouldn't help me with the little boy, but it might give me a line on Miss Victor. I rather hoped that at some ball I would see him insisting on some strange woman dancing with him, or telling her to go home, or something, and then I would have cause to suspect. But no such luck. He never spoke to a woman in my presence who wasn't somebody perfectly well known. I began to think that he had rejected the Indian's advice as too dangerous.

Kharáma, more by token, was back in town, and Medina took me to see him again. The fellow had left Claridge's and was living in a little house in Eaton Place, and away from the glitter of a big hotel he looked even more sinister and damnable. We went there one evening after dinner, and found him squatting on the usual couch in a room lit by one lamp and fairly stinking with odd scents. He seemed to have shed his occidental dress, for he wore flowing robes, and I could see his beastly bare feet under the skirts of them, when he moved to rearrange a curtain.

They took no more notice of me than if I had been a grandfather's clock, and to my disgust they conducted the whole conversation in some Eastern tongue. I gathered nothing from it, except a deduction as to Medina's state of mind. There was an unmistakable hint of nervousness in his voice. He seemed to be asking urgent questions, and the Indian was replying calmly and soothingly. By and by Medina's voice became quieter, and suddenly I realised that the two were speaking of me. Kharáma's heavy eyes were raised for a second in my direction, and Medina turned ever so little towards me. The Indian asked some question about me, and Medina replied carelessly with a shrug of his shoulders and a slight laugh. The laugh rasped my temper. He was evidently saying that I was packed up and sealed and safe on the shelf.

That visit didn't make me feel happier, and next day, when I had a holiday from Medina's company, I had nothing better to do than to wander about London and think dismal thoughts. Yet, as luck would have it, that aimless walk had its consequences. It was a Sunday, and on the edge of Battersea Park I encountered a forlorn little company of Salvationists conducting a service in the rain. I stopped to listen--I always do--for I am the eternal average man who is bound to halt at every street show, whether it be a motor accident or a Punch and Judy. I listened to the tail-end of an address from a fat man who looked like a reformed publican, and a few words from an earnest lady in spectacles. Then they sang a hymn to a trombone accompaniment, and lo and behold, it was my old friend, which I had last whistled in Tom Greenslade's bedroom at Fosse. "There is rest for the weary," they sang:

"On the other side of Jordan, In the green fields of Eden, Where the Tree of Life is blooming, There is rest for you."

I joined heartily in the singing, and contributed two half-crowns to the collecting box, for somehow the thing seemed to be a good omen.

I had been rather neglecting that item in the puzzle, and that evening and during the night I kept turning it over till my brain was nearly addled.

"Where the sower casts his seed in Furrows of the fields of Eden."

That was the version in the rhyme, and in Tom Greenslade's recollection the equivalent was a curiosity shop in North London kept by a Jew with a dyed beard.

Surely the two must correspond, though I couldn't just see how. The other two items had panned out so well that it was reasonable to suppose that the third might do the same. I could see no light, and I finally dropped off to sleep with that blessed "fields of Eden" twittering about my head.

I awoke with the same obsession, but other phrases had added themselves to it. One was the "playing-fields of Eton," about which some fellow had said something, and for a moment I wondered if I hadn't got hold of the right trail. Eton was a school for which Peter John's name was down, and therefore it had to do with boys, and might have to do with David Warcliff. But after breakfast I gave up that line, for it led nowhere. The word was "Eden," to rhyme with "seed in." There were other fields haunting me--names like Tothill Fields and Bunhill Fields. These were places in London, and that was what I wanted. The Directory showed no name like that of "Fields of Eden," but was it not possible that there had once in old days been a place called by that odd title?

I spent the morning in the Club library, which was a very good one, reading up Old London. I read all about Vauxhall Gardens and Ranelagh and Cremorne, and a dozen other ancient haunts of pleasure, but I found nothing to my purpose. Then I remembered that Bullivant--Lord Artinswell--had had for one of his hobbies the study of bygone London, so I telephoned to him and invited myself to lunch.

He was very pleased to see me, and it somehow comforted me to find myself again in the house in Queen Anne's Gate where I had spent some of the most critical moments of my life.

"You've taken on the work I wrote to you about," he said. "I knew you would. How are you getting on?"

"So-so. It's a big job and there's very little time. I want to ask you a question. You're an authority on Old London. Tell me, did you ever come across in your researches the name of the 'Fields of Eden'?"

He shook his head. "Not that I remember. What part of London?"

"I fancy it would be somewhere north of Oxford Street."

He considered. "No. What is your idea? A name of some private gardens or place of amusement?"

"Yes. Just like Cremorne or Vauxhall."

"I don't think so, but we'll look it up. I've a good collection of old maps and plans, and some antique directories."

So after luncheon we repaired to his library and set to work. The maps showed nothing, nor did the books at first. We were searching too far back, in the seventeenth and early eighteenth centuries, when you went fox-hunting in what is now Regent's Park and Tyburn gallows stood near the Marble Arch. Then, by sheer luck, I tried a cast nearer our own time, and found a ribald work belonging to about the date of the American War, which purported to be a countryman's guide to the amusements of town. There was all sorts of information about "Cider Cellars" and "Groves of Harmony," which must have been pretty low pubs, and places in the suburbs for cock- fighting and dog-fighting. I turned up the index, and there to my joy I saw the word "Eden."

I read the passage aloud, and I believe my hands were shaking. The place was, as I hoped, north of Oxford Street in what we now call Marylebone. "The Fields of Eden," said the book, "were opened by Mr. Askew as a summer resort for the gentlemen and sportsmen of the capital. There of a fine afternoon may be seen Lord A-- and the Duke of B-- roving among the shady, if miniature, groves, not unaccompanied by the fair nymphs of the garden, while from adjacent arbours comes the cheerful tinkle of glasses and the merry clatter of dice, and the harmonious strains of Signora F--'s Italian choir." There was a good deal more of it, but I stopped reading. There was a plan of London in the book, and from it I was able to plot out the boundaries of that doubtful paradise.

Then I got a modern map, and fixed the location on it. The place had been quite small, only a few acres, and to-day it was covered by the block defined by Wellesley

Street, Apwith Lane, Little Fardell Street, and the mews behind Royston Square. I wrote this down in my note-book and took my leave.

"You look pleased, Dick. Have you found what you want? Curious that I never heard the name, but it seems to have belonged to the dullest part of London at the dullest period of its history." Lord Artinswell, I could see, was a little nettled, for your antiquary hates to be caught out in his own subject.

I spent the rest of the afternoon making a very thorough examination of a not very interesting neighbourhood. What I wanted was a curiosity shop, and at first I thought I was going to fail. Apwith Lane was a kind of slum, with no shops but a disreputable foreign chemist's and a small dirty confectioner's, round the door of which dirty little children played. The inhabitants seemed to be chiefly foreigners. The mews at the back of Royston Square were of course useless; it was long since any dweller in that square had kept a carriage, and they seemed to be occupied chiefly with the motor vans of a steam laundry and the lorries of a coal merchant. Wellesley Street, at least the part of it in my area, was entirely occupied with the show-rooms of various American automobile companies. Little Fardell Street was a curious place. It had one odd building which may have been there when the Fields of Eden flourished, and which now seemed to be a furniture repository of a sort, with most of the windows shuttered. The other houses were perhaps forty years old, most of them the offices of small wholesale businesses, such as you find in back streets in the City. There was one big French baker's shop at the corner, a picture- framer's, a watch-maker's and a small and obviously decaying optician's. I walked down the place twice, and my heart sank, for I could see nothing in the least resembling an antique-shop.

I patrolled the street once more, and then I observed that the old dwelling, which looked like a furniture depository, was also some kind of shop. Through a dirty lower window I caught a glimpse of what seemed to be Persian rugs and the bland face of a soap-stone idol. The door had the air of never having been used, but I tried it and it opened, tinkling a bell far in the back premises. I found myself in a small dusty place, littered up like a lumber room with boxes and carpets and rugs and bric-a-brac. Most of the things were clearly antiques, though to my inexpert eye they didn't look worth much. The Turcoman rugs, especially, were the kind of thing you can buy anywhere in the Levant by the dozen.

A dishevelled Jewess confronted me, wearing sham diamond earrings.

"I'm interested in antiques," I said pleasantly, taking off my hat to her. "May I look round?"

"We do not sell to private customers," she said. "Only to the trade."

"I'm sorry to hear that. But may I look round? If I fancied something, I dare say I could get some dealer I know to offer for it."

She made no answer, but fingered her earrings with her plump grubby hands.

I turned over some of the rugs and carpets, and my first impression was confirmed. They were mostly trash, and a lacquer cabinet I uncovered was a shameless fake.

"I like that," I said, pointing to a piece of Persian embroidery. "Can't you put a price on it for me?"

"We only sell to the trade," she repeated, as if it were a litany. Her beady eyes, which never left my face, were entirely without expression.

"I expect you have a lot of things upstairs," I said. "Do you think I might have a look at them? I'm only in London for the day, and I might see something I badly wanted. I quite understand that you are wholesale people, but I can arrange any purchase through a dealer. You see, I'm furnishing a country house."

For the first time her face showed a certain life. She shook her head vigorously. "We have no more stock at present. We do not keep a large stock. Things come in and go out every day. We only sell to the trade."

"Well, I'm sorry to have taken up your time. Good afternoon." As I left the shop, I felt that I had made an important discovery. The business was bogus. There was very little that any dealer would touch, and the profits from all the trade done would not keep the proprietor in Virginian cigarettes.

I paid another visit to the neighbourhood after dinner. The only sign of life was in the slums of Apwith Lane, where frowsy women were chattering on the kerb. Wellesley Street was shuttered and silent from end to end. So was Little Fardell Street. Not a soul was about in it, not a ray of light was seen at any window, in the midst of the din of London it made a little enclave like a graveyard. I stopped at the curiosity shop, and saw that the windows were heavily shuttered and that the flimsy old door was secured by a strong outer frame of iron which fitted into a groove at the edge of the pavement and carried a stout lock. The shutters on the ground-floor windows were substantial things, preposterously substantial for so worthless a show. As I looked at them I had a strong feeling that the house behind that palisade was not as dead as it looked, that somewhere inside it there was life, and that in the night things happened there which it concerned me tremendously to know. Next morning I went to see Macgillivray. "Can you lend me a first-class burglar?" I asked. "Only for one night. Some fellow who won't ask any questions and will hold his tongue."

"I've given up being surprised when you're about," he said. "No. We don't keep tame burglars here, but I can find you a man who knows rather more about the art than any professional. Why?"

"Simply because I want to get inside a certain house to-night, and I see no chance of doing it except by breaking my way in. I suppose you could so arrange it that the neighbouring policemen would not interfere. In fact I want them to help to keep the coast clear."

I went into details with him, and showed him the lie of the land. He suggested trying the back of the house, but I had reconnoitred that side and seen that it was impossible, for the building seemed to join on with the houses in the street behind. In fact there was no back door. The whole architecture was extremely odd, and I had a notion that the entrance in Little Fardell Street might itself be a back door. I told Macgillivray that I wanted an expert who could let me in by one of the ground-floor windows, and replace everything so that there should be no trace next morning. He rang a bell and asked for Mr. Abel to be sent for. Mr. Abel was summoned, and presently appeared, a small wizened man, like a country tradesman. Macgillivray explained what was required of him, and Mr. Abel nodded. It was a job which offered no difficulties, he said, to an experienced man. He would suggest that he investigated the place immediately after closing time, and began work about ten o'clock. If I arrived at ten-thirty, he promised to have a means of entrance prepared. He inquired as to who were the constables at the nearest points, and asked that certain special ones should be put on duty, with whom he could arrange matters. I never saw anyone approach what seemed to me to be a delicate job with such businesslike assurance.

"Do you want anyone to accompany you inside?" Macgillivray asked.

I said no. I thought I had better explore the place alone, but I wanted somebody within call in case there was trouble, and of course if I didn't come back, say within two hours, he had better come and look for me."

"We may have to arrest you as a housebreaker," he said. "How are you going to explain your presence if there's nothing wrong indoors and you disturb the sleep of a respectable caretaker?"

"I must take my chance," I said. I didn't feel nervous about that point. The place would either be empty, or occupied by those who would not invite the aid of the police.

After dinner I changed into an old tweed suit and rubber-soled shoes, and as I sat in the taxi I began to think that I had entered too lightly on the evening's business. How was that little man Abel to prepare an entrance without alarming the neighbourhood, even with the connivance of the police; and if I found anybody inside, what on earth was I to say? There was no possible story to account for a clandestine entry into somebody else's house, and I had suddenly a vision of the earringed Jewess screeching in the night and my departure for the cells in the midst of a crowd of hooligans from Apwith Lane. Even if I found something very shady indoors it would only be shady in my own mind in connection with my own problem, and would be all right in the eyes of the law. I was not likely to hit on anything patently criminal, and, even if I did, how was I to explain my presence there? I suffered from a bad attack of cold feet, and would have chucked the business there and then but for that queer feeling at the back of my head that it was my duty to risk it--that if I turned back I should be missing something of tremendous importance. But I can tell you I was feeling far from happy when I dismissed the taxi at the corner of Royston Square, and turned into Little Fardell Street.

It was a dark cloudy evening, threatening rain, and the place was none too brilliantly lit. But to my disgust I saw opposite the door of the curiosity shop a brazier of hot coals and the absurd little shelter which means that part of the street is up. There was the usual roped-in enclosure, decorated with red lamps, a heap of debris, and a hole where some of the setts had been lifted. Here was bad luck with a vengeance, that the Borough Council should have chosen this place and moment of all others for investigating the drains. And yet I had a kind of shamefaced feeling of relief, for this put the lid on my enterprise. I wondered why Macgillivray had not contrived the thing better.

I found I had done him an injustice. It was the decorous face of Mr. Abel which regarded me out of the dingy pent-house.

"This seemed to me the best plan, sir," he said respectfully. "It enables me to wait for you here without exciting curiosity. I've seen the men on point duty, and it is all right in that quarter. This street is quiet enough, and taxis don't use it as a short cut. You'll find the door open. The windows might have been difficult, but I had a look at the door first, and that big iron frame is a piece of bluff. The bolt of the lock runs into the side-bar of the frame, but the frame itself is secured to the wall by another much smaller lock which you can only detect by looking closely. I have opened that for you--quite easily done."

"But the other door--the shop door--that rings a bell inside."

"I found it unlocked," he said, with the ghost of a grin. "Whoever uses this place after closing hours doesn't want to make much noise. The bell is disconnected. You have only to push it open and walk in."

Events were forcing me against all my inclinations to go forward.

"If anyone enters when I am inside? . . ." I began.

"You will hear the sound and must take measures accordingly. On the whole, sir, I am inclined to think that there's something wrong with the place. You are armed? No. That is as well. Your position is unauthorised, as one would say, and arms might be compromising."

"If you hear me cry?"

"I will come to your help. If you do not return within--shall we say?--two hours, I will make an entrance along with the nearest constable. The unlocked door will give us a pretext."

"And if I come out in a hurry?"

"I have thought of that. If you have a fair start there is room for you to hide here," and he jerked his thumb towards the pent- house. "If you are hard-pressed I will manage to impede the pursuit."

The little man's calm matter-of-factness put me on my mettle. I made sure that the street was empty, opened the iron frame, and pushed through the shop-door, closing it softly behind me.

The shop was as dark as the inside of a nut, not a crack of light coming through the closely-shuttered windows. I felt very eerie, as I tiptoed cautiously among the rugs and tables. I listened, but there was no sound of any kind either from within or without, so I switched on my electric torch and waited breathlessly. Still no sound or movement. The conviction grew upon me that the house was uninhabited, and with a little more confidence I started out to explore.

The place did not extend far to the back, as I had believed. Very soon I came upon a dead wall against which every kind of litter was stacked, and that way progress was stopped. The door by which the Jewess had entered lay to the right, and that led me into a little place like a kitchen, with a sink, a cupboard or two, a gas-fire, and in the corner a bed--the kind of lair which a caretaker occupies in a house to let. I made out a window rather high up in the wall, but I could discover no other entrance save that by which I had come. So I returned to the shop and tried the passage to the left.

Here at first I found nothing but locked doors, obviously cupboards. But there was one open, and my torch showed me that it contained a very steep flight of stairs--the kind of thing that in old houses leads to the attics. I tried the boards, for I feared that they would creak, and I discovered that all the treads had been renewed. I can't say I liked diving into that box, but there was nothing else for it unless I were to give up.

At the top I found a door, and I was just about to try to open it when I heard steps on the other side.

I stood rigid in that narrow place, wondering what was to happen next. The man--it was a man's foot--came up to the door and to my consternation turned the handle. Had he opened it I would have been discovered, for he had a light, and Lord knows what mix-up would have followed. But he didn't; he tried the handle and then turned a key in the lock. After that I heard him move away.

This was fairly discouraging, for it appeared that I was now shut off from the rest of the house. When I had waited for a minute or two for the coast to clear, I too tried the handle, expecting to find it fast. To my surprise the door opened; the man had not locked, but unlocked it. This could mean only one of two things. Either he intended himself to go out by this way later, or he expected someone and wanted to let him in.

From that moment I recovered my composure. My interest was excited, there was a game to play and something to be done. I looked round the passage in which I found myself and saw the explanation of the architecture which had puzzled me. The old building in Little Fardell Street was the merest slip, only a room thick, and it was plastered against a much more substantial and much newer structure in which I now found myself. The passage was high and broad, and heavily carpeted, and I saw electric fittings at each end. This alarmed me, for if anyone came along and switched on the light, there was not cover to hide a cockroach. I considered that the boldest plan would be the safest, so I tiptoed to the end, and saw another passage equally bare going off at right angles. This was no good, so I brazenly assaulted the door of the nearest room. Thank Heaven! it was empty, so I could have a reconnoitring base.

It was a bedroom, well furnished in the Waring & Gillow style, and to my horror I observed that it was a woman's bedroom. It was a woman's dressing-table I saw, with big hair-brushes and oddments of scents and powders. There was a wardrobe with the door ajar full of hanging dresses. The occupant had been there quite lately, for wraps had been flung on the bed and a pair of slippers lay by the dressing-table, as if they had been kicked off hurriedly.

The place put me into the most abject fright. I seemed to have burgled a respectable flat and landed in a lady's bedroom, and I looked forward to some appalling scandal which would never be hushed up. Little Abel roosting in his pent-house seemed a haven of refuge separated from me by leagues of obstacles. I reckoned I had better get back to him as soon as possible, and I was just starting, when that happened which made me stop short. I had left the room door ajar when I entered, and of course I had switched off my torch after my first look round. I had been in utter darkness, but now I saw a light in the passage.

It might be the confounded woman who owned the bedroom, and my heart went into my boots. Then I saw that the passage lights had not been turned on, and that whoever was there had a torch like me. The footsteps were coming by the road I had come myself. Could it be the man for whom the staircase door had been unlocked?

It was a man all right, and, whatever his errand, it was not with my room. I watched him through the crack left by the door, and saw his figure pass. It was someone in a hurry who walked swiftly and quietly, and, beyond the fact that he wore a dark coat with the collar turned up and a black soft hat, I could make out nothing. The figure went down the corridor, and at the end seemed to hesitate. Then it turned into a room on the left and disappeared.

There was nothing to do but wait, and happily I had not to wait long, for I was becoming pretty nervous. The figure reappeared, carrying something in its hand, and as it came towards me I had a glimpse of its face. I recognised it at once as that of the grey melancholy man whom I had seen the first night in Medina's house, when I was coming out of my stupor. For some reason or another that face had become stamped on my memory, and I had been waiting to see it again. It was sad, forlorn, and yet in a curious way pleasant; anyhow there was nothing repellent in it. But he came from Medina, and at that thought every scrap of hesitation and funk fled from me. I had been right in my instinct; this place was Medina's, it was the Fields of Eden of the rhyme. A second ago I had felt a futile blunderer; now I was triumphant.

He passed my door and turned down the passage which ran at right angles. I stepped after him and saw the light halt at the staircase door, and then disappear. My first impulse was to follow, tackle him in the shop, and get the truth out of him, but I at once discarded that notion, which would have given the whole show away. My business was to make further discoveries. I must visit the room which had been the object of his visit.

I was thankful to be out of that bedroom. In the passage I listened, but could hear no sound anywhere. There was indeed a sound in the air, but it appeared to come from the outer world, a sound like an organ or an orchestra a long way off. I concluded that there must be a church somewhere near where the choir-boys were practising.

The room I entered was a very queer place. It looked partly like a museum, partly like an office, and partly like a library. The curiosity shop had been full of rubbish, but I could see at a glance that there was no rubbish here. There were some fine Italian plaques--I knew something about these, for Mary collected them--and a set of green Chinese jars which looked the real thing. Also, there was a picture which seemed good enough to be a Hobbema. For the rest there were several safes of a most substantial make; but there were no papers lying about, and every drawer of a big writing-table was locked. I had not the wherewithal to burgle the safes and the table, even if I had wanted to. I was certain that most valuable information lurked somewhere in that place, but I did not see how I could get at it.

I was just about to leave, when I realised that the sound of music which I had heard in the passage was much louder here. It was no choir-boys' practising, but strictly secular music, apparently fiddles and drums, and the rhythm suggested a dance. Could this odd building abut on a dance-hall? I looked at my watch and saw that it was scarcely eleven and that I had only been some twenty minutes indoors. I was now in a mood of almost foolhardy confidence, so I determined to do a little more research.

The music seemed to come from somewhere to the left. The windows of the room, so far as I could judge, must look into Wellesley Street, which showed me how I had misjudged that thoroughfare. There might be a dancing-hall tucked in among the automobile shops. Anyhow I wanted to see what lay beyond this room, for there must be an entrance to it other than by the curiosity shop. Sure enough I found a door between two bookcases covered with a heavy portière, and emerged into still another passage.

Here the music sounded louder, and I seemed to be in a place like those warrens behind the stage in a theatre, where rooms are of all kinds of shapes and sizes. The door at the end was locked, and another door which I opened gave on a flight of wooden steps. I did not want to descend just yet, so I tried another door, and then shut it softly. For the room it opened upon was lighted, and I had the impression of human beings not very far off. Also the music, as I opened the door, came out in a great swelling volume of sound.

I stood for a moment hesitating, and then I opened that door again. For I had a notion that the light within did not come from anything in the room. I found myself in a little empty chamber, dusty and cheerless, like one of those cubby-holes you see in the Strand, where the big plate-glass front window reaches higher than the shop, and there is a space between the ceiling and the next floor. All one side was of glass, in which a casement was half open, and through the glass came the glare of a hundred lights from somewhere beyond. Very gingerly I moved forward, till I could look down on what was happening below.

For the last few seconds I think I had known what I was going to see. It was the dancing-club which I had visited some weeks before with Archie Roylance. There were the sham Chinese decorations, the blaze of lights, the nigger band, the whole garish spectacle. Only the place was far more crowded than on my previous visit. The babble of laughter and talk which rose from it added a further discord to the ugly music, but there was a fierce raucous gaiety about it all, an overpowering sense of something which might be vulgar but was also alive and ardent. Round the skirts of the hall was the usual rastaquouère crowd of men and women drinking liqueurs and champagne, and mixed with fat Jews and blue-black dagos the flushed faces of boys from barracks or college who imagined they were seeing life. I thought for a moment that I saw Archie, but it was only one of Archie's kind, whose lean red visage made a queer contrast with the dead white of the woman he sat by.

The dancing was madder and livelier than on the last occasion. There was more vigour in the marionettes, and I was bound to confess that they knew their trade, little as I valued it. All the couples were expert, and when now and then a bungler barged in he did not stay long. I saw no sign of the girl in green whom Archie had admired, but there were plenty like her. It was the men I most disliked, pallid skeletons or puffy Latins, whose clothes fitted them too well, and who were sometimes as heavily made-up as the women.

One especially I singled out for violent disapproval. He was a tall young man, with a waist like a wasp, a white face, and hollow drugged eyes. His lips were red like a chorus-girl's, and I would have sworn that his cheeks were rouged. Anyhow he was a loathsome sight. But ye gods! he could dance. There was no sign of animation in him, so that he might have been a corpse, galvanised by some infernal power and compelled to move through an everlasting dance of death. I noticed that his heavy eyelids were never raised.

Suddenly I got a bad shock. For I realised that this mannequin was no other than my ancient friend, the Marquis de la Tour du Pin.

I hadn't recovered from that when I got a worse. He was dancing with a woman whose hair seemed too bright to be natural. At first I could not see her face clearly, for it was flattened against his chest, but she seemed to be hideously and sparsely dressed. She too knew how to dance, and the slim grace of her body was conspicuous even in her vulgar clothes. Then she turned her face to me, and I could see the vivid lips and the weary old pink and white enamel of her class. Pretty, too . . .

And then I had a shock which nearly sent me through the window. For in this painted dancer I recognised the wife of my bosom and the mother of Peter John.

CHAPTER XIV

SIR ARCHIBALD ROYLANCE PUTS HIS FOOT IN IT

Three minutes later I was back in the curiosity shop. I switched off my light, and very gently opened the street door. There was a sound of footsteps on the pavement, so I drew back till they had passed. Then I emerged into the quiet street, with Abel's little brazier glowing in front of me, and Abel's little sharp face poked out of his pent-house.

"All right, sir?" he asked cheerfully.

"All right," I said. "I have found what I wanted."

"There was a party turned up not long after you had gone in. Lucky I had locked the door after you. He wasn't inside more than five minutes. A party with a black topcoat turned up at the collar-- respectable party he looked--oldish--might have been a curate. Funny thing, sir, but I guessed correctly when you were coming back, and had the door unlocked ready for you. . . . If you've done with me I'll clear off."

"Can you manage alone?" I asked. "There's a good deal to tidy up."

He winked solemnly. "In an hour there won't be a sign of anything. I have my little ways of doing things. Good night, sir, and thank you." He was like a boots seeing a guest off from an hotel.

I found that the time was just after half-past eleven, so I walked to Tottenham Court Road and picked up a taxi, telling the man to drive to Great Charles Street in Westminster. Mary was in London, and I must see her at once. She had chosen to take a hand in the game, probably at Sandy's instigation, and I must find out what exactly she was doing. The business was difficult enough already with Sandy following his own trail and me forbidden to get into touch with him, but if Mary was also on the job it would be naked chaos unless I knew her plans. I own I felt miserably nervous. There was nobody in the world whose wisdom I put higher than hers, and I would have trusted her to the other side of Tophet, but I hated to think of a woman mixed up in something so ugly and perilous. She was far too young and lovely to be safe on the back- stairs. And yet I remembered that she had been in uglier affairs before this and I recalled old Blenkiron's words: "She can't scare and she can't soil." And then I began to get a sort of comfort from the feeling that she was along with me in the game; it made me feel less lonely. But it was pretty rough luck on Peter John. Anyhow I must see her, and I argued that she would probably be staying with her Wymondham aunts, and that in any case I could get news of her there.

The Misses Wymondham were silly ladies, but their butler would have made Montmartre respectable. He and I had always got on well, and I think the only thing that consoled him when Fosse was sold was that Mary and I were to have it. The house in Great Charles Street was one of those tremendously artistic new dwellings with which the intellectual plutocracy have adorned the Westminster slums.

"Is her ladyship home yet?" I asked.

"No, Sir Richard, but she said she wouldn't be late. I expect her any moment."

"Then I think I'll come in and wait. How are you, Barnard? Found your city legs yet?"

"I am improving, Sir Richard, I thank you. Very pleased to have Miss Mary here, if I may take the liberty of so speaking of her. Miss Claire is in Paris still, and Miss Wymondham is dancing to- night, and won't be back till very late. How are things at Fosse, sir, if I may make so bold? And how is the young gentleman? Miss Mary has shown me his photograph. A very handsome young gentleman, sir, and favours yourself."

"Nonsense, Barnard. He's the living image of his mother. Get me a drink, like a good fellow. A tankard of beer, if you have it, for I've a throat like a grindstone."

I drank the beer and waited in a little room which would have been charming but for the garish colour scheme which Mary's aunts had on the brain. I was feeling quite cheerful again, for Peter John's photograph was on the mantelpiece and I reckoned that any minute Mary might be at the doorway.

She came in just before midnight. I heard her speak to Barnard in the hall, and then her quick step outside the door. She was preposterously dressed, but she must have done something to her face in the taxi, for the paint was mostly rubbed from it, leaving it very pale.

"Oh, Dick, my darling," she cried, tearing off her cloak and running to my arms. "I never expected you. There's nothing wrong at home?"

"Not that I know of, except that it's deserted. Mary, what on earth brought you here?"

"You're not angry, Dick?"

"Not a bit--only curious."

"How did you know I was here?"

"Guessed. I thought it the likeliest cover to draw. You see I've been watching you dancing to-night. Look here, my dear, if you put so much paint and powder on your face and jam it so close to old Turpin's chest, it won't be easy for the poor fellow to keep his shirt-front clean."

"You--watched--me--dancing! Were you in that place?"

"Well, I wouldn't say IN it. But I had a prospect of the show from the gallery. And it struck me that the sooner we met and had a talk the better."

"The gallery! Were you in the house? I don't understand."

"No more do I. I burgled a certain house in a back street for very particular reasons of my own. In the process I may mention that I got one of the worst frights of my life. After various adventures I came to a place where I heard the dickens of a row which I made out to be dance music. Eventually I found a dirty little room with a window and to my surprise looked down on a dancing-hall. I know it, for I had once been there with Archie Roylance. That was queer enough, but imagine my surprise when I saw my wedded wife, raddled like a geisha, dancing with an old friend who seemed to have got himself up to imitate a wax-work."

She seemed scarcely to be listening. "But in the house! Did you see no one?"

"I saw one man and I heard another. The fellow I saw was a man I once met in the small hours with Medina."

"But the other? You didn't see him? You didn't hear him go out?"

"No." I was puzzled at her excitement. "Why are you so keen about the other?"

"Because I think--I'm sure--it was Sandy--Colonel Arbuthnot."

This was altogether beyond me. "Impossible!" I cried. "The place is a lair of Medina's. The man I saw was Medina's servant or satellite. Do you mean to say that Sandy has been exploring that house?"

She nodded. "You see it is the Fields of Eden."

"Oh, I know. I found that out for myself. Do you tell me that Sandy discovered it too?"

"Yes. That is why I was there. That is why I have been living a perfectly loathsome life and am now dressed like a chorus girl."

"Mary," I said solemnly, "my fine brain won't support any more violent shocks. Will you please to sit down beside me, and give me the plain tale of all you have been doing since I said good-bye to you at Fosse?"

"First," she said, "I had a visit from a dramatic critic on holiday, Mr. Alexander Thomson. He said he knew you and that you had suggested that he should call. He came three times to Fosse, but only once to the house. Twice I met him in the woods. He told me a good many things, and one was that he couldn't succeed and you couldn't succeed, unless I helped. He thought that if a woman was lost only a woman could find her. In the end he persuaded me. You said yourself, Dick, that Nanny was quite competent to take charge of Peter John, with Dr. Greenslade so close at hand. And I hear from her every day, and he is very well and happy."

"You came to London. But when?"

"The day you came back from Norway."

"But I've been having letters regularly from you since then."

"That is my little arrangement with Paddock. I took him into my confidence. I send him the letters in batches and he posts one daily."

"Then you've been here more than a fortnight. Have you seen Sandy?"

"Twice. He has arranged my life for me, and has introduced me to my dancing partner, the Marquis de la Tour du Pin, whom you call Turpin. I think I have had the most horrible, the most wearing time that any woman ever had. I have moved in raffish circles and have had to be the most raffish of the lot. Do you know, Dick, I believe I'm really a good actress? I have acquired a metallic voice, and a high silly laugh, and hard eyes, and when I lie in bed at night I blush all over for my shamelessness. I know you hate it, but you can't hate it more than I do. But it had to be done. I couldn't be a 'piker,' as Mr. Blenkiron used to say."

"Any luck?"

"Oh, yes," she said wearily. "I have found Miss Victor. It wasn't very difficult, really. When I had made friends with the funny people that frequent these places it wasn't hard to see who was different from the others. They're all mannequins, but the one I was looking for was bound to be the most mannequinish of the lot. I wanted someone without mind or soul, and I found her. Besides, I had a clue to start with. Odell, you know."

"It was the green girl."

She nodded. "I couldn't be certain, of course, till I had her lover to help me. He is a good man, your French Marquis. He has played his part splendidly. You see, it would never do to try to AWAKE Adela Victor now. We couldn't count on her being able to keep up appearances without arousing suspicion, till the day of release arrived. But something had to be done, and that is my business especially. I have made friends with her, and I talk to her and I have attached her to me just a little, like a dog.

That will give me the chance to do the rest quickly when the moment comes. You cannot bring back a vanished soul all at once unless you have laid some foundation. We have to be very, very careful, for she is keenly watched, but I think--yes, I am sure--it is going well."

"Oh, bravo!" I cried. "That makes Number Two. I may tell you that I have got Number One." I gave her a short account of my doings in Norway. "Two of the poor devils will get out of the cage anyhow. I wonder if it wouldn't be possible to pass the word to Victor and the Duke. It would relieve their anxiety."

"I thought of that," she replied, "but Colonel Arbuthnot says No, on no account. He says it might ruin everything. He takes a very solemn view of the affair, you know. And so do I. I have seen Mr. Medina."

"Where?" I asked in astonishment.

"I got Aunt Doria to take me to a party where he was to be present. Don't be worried. I wasn't introduced to him, and he never heard my name. But I watched him, and knowing what I did I was more afraid than I have ever been in my life. He is extraordinarily attractive--no, not attractive--seductive, and he is as cold and hard as chilled steel. You know these impressions I get of people which I can't explain--you say they are always right. Well, I felt him almost superhuman. He exhales ease and power like a god, but it is a god from a lost world. I can see that, like a god too, it is souls that he covets. Ordinary human badness seems decent in comparison with that Lucifer's pride of his. I think if I ever could commit murder it would be his life I would take. I should feel like Charlotte Corday. Oh, I'm dismally afraid of him."

"I'm not," I said stoutly, "and I see him at closer quarters than most people." The measure of success we had attained was beginning to make me confident.

"Colonel Arbuthnot is afraid for you," she said. "The two times I have seen him in London he kept harping on the need of your keeping very near to him. I think he meant me to warn you. He says that when you are fighting a man with a long-range weapon the only chance is to hug him. Dick, didn't you tell me that Mr. Medina suggested that you should stay in his house? I have been thinking a lot about that, and I believe it would be the safest plan. Once he saw you secure in his pocket he might forget about you."

"It would be most infernally awkward, for I should have no freedom of movement. But all the same I believe you are right. Things may grow very hectic as we get near the day."

"Besides, you might find out something about Number Three. Oh, it is the little boy that breaks my heart. The others might escape on their own account--some day, but unless we find HIM he is lost for ever. And Colonel Arbuthnot says that, even if we found him, it might be hard to restore the child's mind. Unless--unless--"

Mary's face had become grim, if one could use the word of a thing so soft and gentle. Her hands were tightly clasped, and her eyes had a strained far-away look.

"I am going to find him," she cried. "Listen, Dick. That man despises women and rules them out of his life, except in so far as he can make tools of them. But there is one woman who is going to stop at nothing to beat him. . . . When I think of that little David I grow mad and desperate. I am afraid of myself. Have you no hope to give me?"

"I haven't the shadow of a clue," I said dolefully. "Has Sandy none?"

She shook her head. "He is so small, the little fellow, and so easy to hide."

"If I were in Central Africa, I would get Medina by the throat, and peg him down and torture him till he disgorged."

Again she shook her head. "Those methods are useless here. He would laugh at you, for he isn't a coward--at least I think not. Besides, he is certain to be magnificently guarded. And for the rest he has the entrenchments of his reputation and popularity, and a quicker brain than any of us. He can put a spell of blindness on the world--on all men and nearly all women."

The arrival of Miss Wymondham made me get up to leave. She was still the same odd-looking creature, with a mass of tow-coloured hair piled above her long white face. She had been dancing somewhere, and looked at once dog-tired and excited. "Mary has been having such a good time," she told me. "Even I can scarcely keep pace with her ardent youth. Can't you persuade her to do her hair differently? The present arrangement is so démodé and puts her whole figure out of drawing. Nancy Travers was speaking about it only to-night. Properly turned out, she said, Mary would be the most ravishing thing in London. By the way, I saw your friend Sir Archie Roylance at the Parminters'. He is lunching here on Thursday. Will you come, Richard?"

I told her that my plans were vague and that I thought I might be out of town. But I arranged with Mary before I left to keep me informed at the Club of any news that came from Sandy. As I walked back I was infected by her distress over little David Warcliff. That was the most grievous business of all, and I saw no light in it, for though everything else happened according to plan, we should never be able to bring Medina to book. The more I thought of it the more hopeless our case against him seemed to be. We might free the hostages, but we could never prove that he had had anything to do with them. I could give damning evidence, to be sure, but who would take my word against his? And I had no one to confirm me. Supposing I indicted him for kidnapping and told the story of what I knew about the Blind Spinner and Newhover and Odell? He and the world would simply laugh at me, and I should probably have to pay heavy damages for libel. None of his satellites, I was certain, would ever give him away; they couldn't, even if they wanted to, for they didn't know anything. No, Sandy was right. We might have a measure of success, but there would be no victory. And yet only victory would give us full success, for only to get him on his knees, gibbering with terror, would restore the poor little boy. I strode through the empty streets with a sort of hopeless fury in my heart.

One thing puzzled me. What was Sandy doing in that house behind the curiosity shop, if indeed it was Sandy? Whoever had been there had been in league with the sad grey man whom I watched from behind the bedroom door. Now the man was part of Medina's entourage: I had no doubt about the accuracy of my recollection. Had Sandy dealings with someone inside the enemy's citadel? I didn't see how that was possible, for he had told me he was in deadly danger from Medina, and that his only chance was to make him believe that he was out of Europe. . . . As I went to bed, one thing was very clear in my mind. If Medina asked me to stay with him, I would accept. It would probably be safer, though I wasn't so much concerned about that, and it would possibly be more fruitful. I might find out something about the grey man.

Next day I went to see Medina, for I wanted him to believe that I couldn't keep away from him. He was in tremendous spirits about something or other, and announced that he was going off to the country for a couple of days. He made me stay to luncheon, when I had another look at Odell, who seemed to be getting fat. "Your wind, my lad," I said to myself, "can't be as good as it should be. You wouldn't have my money in a scrap." I hoped that Medina was going to have a holiday, for he had been doing a good deal lately in the way of speaking, but he said "No such luck." He was going down to the country on business--an estate of which he was a trustee wanted looking into. I asked in what part of England, and he said Shropshire. He liked that neighbourhood and had an idea of buying a place there when he had more leisure.

Somehow that led me to speak of his poetry. He was surprised to learn that I had been studying the little books, and I could see took it as a proof of my devotion. I made a few fulsome observations on their merits, and said that even an ignorant fellow like me could see how dashed good they were. I also remarked that they seemed to me a trifle melancholy.

"Melancholy!" he said. "It's a foolish world, Hannay, and a wise man must have his moods of contempt. Victory loses some of its salt when it is won over fools."

And then he said what I had been waiting for. "I told you weeks ago that I wanted you to take up your quarters with me. Well, I repeat the offer and will take no refusal."

"It is most awfully kind of you," I stammered. "But wouldn't I be in the way?"

"Not in the least. You see the house--it's as large as a barracks. I'll be back from Shropshire by Friday, and I expect you to move in here on Friday evening. We might dine together."

I was content, for it gave me a day or two to look about me. Medina went off that afternoon, and I spent a restless evening. I wanted to be with Mary, but it seemed to me that the less I saw her the better. She was going her own way, and if I showed myself in her neighbourhood it might ruin all. Next day was no better; I actually longed for Medina to return so that I might feel I was doing something, for there was nothing I could turn my hand to, and when I was idle the thought of David Warcliff was always present to torment me. I went out to Hampton Court and had a long row on the river; then I dined at the Club and sat in the little back smoking-room, avoiding anyone I knew, and trying to read a book of travels in Arabia. I fell asleep in my chair, and, waking about half-past eleven, was staggering off to bed, when a servant came to tell me that I was wanted on the telephone.

It was Mary; she was speaking from Great Charles Street and her voice was sharp with alarm.

"There's been an awful mishap, Dick," she said breathlessly. "Are you alone? You're sure there's no one there? . . . Archie Roylance has made a dreadful mess of things. . . . He came to that dancing-place to-night, and Adela Victor was there, and Odell with her. Archie had seen her before, you know, and apparently was much attracted. No! He didn't recognise me, for when I saw him I kept out of range. But of course he recognised the Marquis. He danced with Adela, and I suppose he talked nonsense to her--anyhow he made himself conspicuous. The result was that Odell proposed to take her away--I suppose he was suspicious of anybody of Archie's world--and, well, there was a row. The place was very empty--only about a dozen, and mostly a rather bad lot. Archie asked what right he had to carry off the girl, and lost his temper, and the manager was called in--the man with the black beard. He backed up Odell, and then Archie did a very silly thing. He said he was Sir Archibald Roylance and wasn't going to be dictated to by any Jew, and, worse, he said his friend was the Marquis de la Tour du Pin, and that between them they would burst up this show, and that he wouldn't have a poor girl ordered about by a third-rate American bully. . . . I don't know what happened afterwards. The women were hustled out, and I had to go with the rest. . . . But, Dick, it's bad trouble. I'm not afraid so much for Archie, though he has probably had a bad mauling, but the Marquis. They're sure to know who he is and all about him and remember his connection with Adela. They're almost certain to make certain in some horrible way that he can't endanger them again.

"Lord," I groaned, "what a catastrophe! And what on earth can I do? I daren't take any part!"

"No," came a hesitating voice. "I suppose not. But you can warn the Marquis--if nothing has happened to him already."

"Precious poor chance. These fellows don't waste time. But go to bed and sleep, my dear. I'll do my best."

My best at that time of night was pretty feeble. I rang up Victor's house and found, as I expected, that Turpin had not returned. Then I rang up Archie's house in Grosvenor Street and got the same answer about him. It was no good my going off to the back streets of Marylebone, so I went to bed and spent a wretched night.

Very early next morning I was in Grosvenor Street, and there I had news. Archie's man had just had a telephone message from a hospital to say that his master had had an accident, and would he come round and bring clothes. He packed a bag and he and I drove there at once, and found the miserable Archie in bed, the victim officially of a motor accident. He did not seem to be very bad, but it was a rueful face, much battered about the eyes and bandaged as to the jaw, which was turned on me when the nurse left us.

"You remember what I said about the pug with the diamond studs," he whistled through damaged teeth.

"Well, I took him on last night and got tidily laid out. I'm not up to professional standards, and my game leg made me slow."

"You've put your foot into it most nobly," I said. "What do you mean by brawling in a dance-club? You've embarrassed me horribly in the job I'm on."

"But how?" he asked, and but for the bandage his jaw would have dropped.

"Never mind how at present. I want to know exactly what happened. It's more important than you think."

He told me the same story that I had heard from Mary, but much garlanded with objurgations. He denied that he had dined too well-- "nothing but a small whisky-and-soda and one glass of port." He had been looking for the girl in green for some time, and having found her, was not going to miss the chance of making her acquaintance. "A melancholy little being with nothin' to say for herself. She's had hard usage from some swine--you could see it by her eyes--and I expect the pug's the villain. Anyway, I wasn't goin' to stand his orderin' her about like a slave. So I told him so, and a fellow with a black beard chipped in and they began to hustle me. Then I did a dam' silly thing. I tried to solemnise 'em by sayin' who I was, and old Turpin was there, so I dragged his name in. Dashed caddish thing to do, but I thought a Marquis would put the wind up that crowd."

"Did he join in?"

"I don't know--I rather fancy he got scragged at the start. Anyhow I found myself facin' the pug, seein' bright red, and inclined to fight a dozen. I didn't last for more than one round--my game leg cramped me, I suppose. I got in one or two on his ugly face, and then I suppose I took a knock-out. After that I don't remember anything till I woke up in this bed feelin' as if I had been through a mangle. The people here say I was brought in by two bobbies and a fellow with a motor-car, who said I had walked slap into his bonnet at a street corner and hurt my face. He was very concerned about me, but omitted to leave his name and address. Very thoughtful of the sweeps to make sure there would be no scandal. . . . I say, Dick, you don't suppose this will get into the newspapers? I don't want to be placarded as havin' been in such a vulgar shindy just as I'm thinkin' of goin' in for Parliament."

"I don't think there's the remotest chance of your hearing another word about it, unless you talk too much yourself. Look here, Archie, you've got to promise me never to go near that place again, and never on any account whatever to go hunting for that girl in green. I'll tell you my reasons some day, but you can take it that they're good ones. Another thing. You've got to keep out of Turpin's way. I only hope you haven't done him irreparable damage because of your idiocy last night."

Archie was desperately penitent. "I know I behaved like a cad. I'll go and grovel to old Turpin as soon as they let me up. But he's all right--sure to be. He wasn't lookin' for a fight like me. I expect he only got shoved into the street and couldn't get back again."

I did not share Archie's optimism, and very soon my fear was a certainty. I went straight from the hospital to Carlton House Terrace, and found Mr. Victor at breakfast. I learned that the Marquis de la Tour du Pin had been dining out on the previous evening and had not returned.

CHAPTER XV

HOW A FRENCH NOBLEMAN DISCOVERED FEAR

I have twice heard from Turpin the story I am going to set down-- once before he understood much of it, a second time when he had got some enlightenment--but I doubt whether to his dying day he will ever be perfectly clear about what happened to him.

I have not had time to introduce Turpin properly, and in any case I am not sure that the job is not beyond me. My liking for the French is profound, but I believe there is no race on earth which the average Briton is less qualified to comprehend. For myself, I could far more easily get inside the skin of a Boche. I knew he was as full of courage as a Berserker, pretty mad, but with that queer core of prudence which your Latin possesses and which in the long run makes his madness less dangerous than an Englishman's. He was high-strung, excitable, imaginative, and I should have said in a general way very sensitive to influences such as Medina wielded. But he was forewarned. Mary had told him the main lines of the business, and he was playing the part she had set him as dutifully as a good child. I had not done justice to his power of self- control. He saw his sweetheart leading that blind unearthly life, and it must have been torture to him to do nothing except look on. But he never attempted to wake her memory, but waited obediently till Mary gave orders, and played the part to perfection of the ordinary half-witted dancing mountebank.

When the row with Archie started, and the scurry began, he had the sense to see that he must keep out of it. Then he heard Archie speak his real name, and saw the mischief involved in that, for nobody knew him except Mary, and he had passed as a Monsieur Claud Simond from Buenos Aires. When he saw his friend stand up to the bruiser, he started off instinctively to his help, but stopped in time and turned to the door. The man with the black beard was looking at him, but said nothing.

There seemed to be a good deal of racket at the foot of the stairs. One of the girls caught his arm. "No good that way," she whispered. "It's a raid all right. There's another road out. You don't want your name in to-morrow's papers."

He followed her into a little side passage, which was almost empty and very dark, and there he lost her. He was just starting to prospect, when he saw a little dago whom he recognised as one of the bar-tenders. "Up the stairs, monsieur," the man said. "Then first to the left and down again. You come out in the yard of the Apollo Garage. Quick, monsieur, or les flics will be here."

Turpin sped up the steep wooden stairs, and found himself in another passage fairly well lit, with a door at each end. He took the one to the left, and dashed through, wondering how he was to recover his hat and coat, and also what had become of Mary. The door opened easily enough, and in his haste he took two steps forward. It swung behind him, so that he was in complete darkness, and he turned back to open it again to give him light. But it would not open. With the shutting of that door he walked clean out of the world.

At first he was angry, and presently, when he realised his situation, a little alarmed. The place seemed to be small, it was utterly dark, and as stuffy as the inside of a safe. His chief thought at the moment was that it would never do for him to be caught in a raid on a dance-club, for his true name might come out and the harm which Archie's foolish tongue had wrought might be thereby aggravated. But soon he saw that he had stepped out of one kind of danger into what was probably a worse. He was locked in an infernal cupboard in a house which he knew to have the most unholy connections.

He started to grope around, and found that the place was larger than he thought. The walls were bare, the floor seemed to be of naked boards, and there was not a stick of furniture anywhere, nor, so far as he could see, any window. He could not discover the door he had entered by, which on the inside must have been finished dead level with the walls. Presently he found that his breathing was difficult, and that almost put him in a panic, for the dread of suffocation had always been for him the private funk from which the bravest man is not free. To breathe was like having his face tightly jammed against a pillow. He made an effort and controlled himself, for he realised that if he let himself become hysterical he would only suffocate the faster. . . .

Then he declares that he felt a hand pressing on his mouth. . . . It must have been imagination, for he admits that the place was empty, but all the same the hand came again and again--a large soft hand smelling of roses. His nerves began to scream, and his legs to give under him. The roses came down on him in a cloud, and that horrible flabby hand, as big as a hill, seemed to smother him. He tried to move, to get away from it, and before he knew he found himself on his knees. He struggled to get up, but the hand was on him, flattening him out, and that intolerable sweet sickly odour swathed him in its nauseous folds. . . . And then he lost consciousness. . . .

How long he was senseless he doesn't know, but he thinks it must have been a good many hours. When he came to he was no longer in the cupboard. He was lying on what seemed to be a couch in a room which felt spacious, for he could breathe freely, but it was still as black as the nether pit. He had a blinding headache, and felt rather sick and as silly as an owl. He couldn't remember how he had come there, but as his hand fell on his shirt-front, and he realised he was in dress clothes, he recollected Archie's cry. That was the last clear thing in his head, but it steadied him, for it reminded him how grave was his danger. He has told me that at first he was half stifled with panic, for he was feeling abominably weak; but he had just enough reason left in him to let him take a pull on his nerves. "You must be a man," he repeated to himself. "Even if you have stumbled into hell, you must be a man."

Then a voice spoke out of the darkness, and at the sound of it most of his fright disappeared. It was no voice that he knew, but a pleasant voice, and it spoke to him in French. Not ordinary French, you understand, but the French of his native valley in the South, with the soft slurring patois of his home. It seemed to drive away his headache and nausea, and to soothe every jangled nerve, but it made him weaker. Of that he has no doubt. This friendly voice was making him a child again.

His memory of what it said is hopelessly vague. He thinks that it reminded him of the life of his boyhood--the old chateau high in a fold of the limestone hills, the feathery chestnuts in the valley bottom, the clear pools where the big trout lived, the snowy winters when the wolves came out of the forests to the farmyard doors, the hot summers when the roads were blinding white and the turf on the downs grew as yellow as corn. The memory of it was all jumbled, and whatever the voice said its effect was more like music than spoken words. It smoothed out the creases in his soul, but it stole also the manhood from him. He was becoming limp and docile and passive like a weak child.

The voice stopped and he felt a powerful inclination to sleep. Then suddenly, between sleeping and waking, he became aware of a light, a star which glowed ahead of him in the darkness. It waxed and then waned, and held his eyes like a vice. At the back of his head he knew that there was some devilry in the business, that it was something which he ought to resist, but for the life of him he could not remember why.

The light broadened till it was like the circle which a magic- lantern makes on a screen. Into the air there crept a strange scent--not the sickly smell of roses, but a hard pungent smell which tantalised him with its familiarity. Where had he met it before? . . . Slowly out of it there seemed to shape a whole world of memories.

Now Turpin before the War had put in some years' service in Africa with the Armée Coloniale as a lieutenant of Spahis, and had gone with various engineering and military expeditions south of the Algerian frontier into the desert. He used to rave to me about the glories of those lost days, that first youth of a man which does not return. . . . This smell was the desert, that unforgettable, untameable thing which stretches from the Mediterranean to the Central African forests, the place where, in the days when it was sea, Ulysses wandered, and where the magic of Circe and Calypso for all the world knows may still linger.

In the moon of light a face appeared, a face so strongly lit up that every grim and subtle line of it was magnified. It was an Eastern face, a lean high-boned Arab face, with the eyes set in a strange slant. He had never seen it before, but he had met something like it when he had dabbled in the crude magic of the sands, the bubbling pot, and the green herb fire. At first it was only a face, half averted, and then it seemed to move so that the eyes appeared, like lights suddenly turned on at night as one looks from without at a dark house.

He felt in every bone a thing he had almost forgotten, the spell and the terror of the desert. It was a cruel and inhuman face, hiding God knows what of ancient horror and sin, but wise as the Sphinx and eternal as the rocks. As he stared at it the eyes seemed to master and envelop him, and, as he put it, suck the soul out of him.

You see he had never been told about Kharáma. That was the one mistake Mary made, and a very natural one, for it was not likely that he and the Indian would foregather. So he had nothing in his poor muddled head to help him to combat this mastering presence. He didn't try. He said he felt himself sinking into a delicious lethargy, like the coma which overtakes a man who is being frozen to death.

I could get very little out of Turpin about what happened next. The face spoke to him, but whether in French or some African tongue he didn't know--French, he thought--certainly not English. I gather that, while the eyes and the features were to the last degree awe-inspiring, the voice was, if anything, friendly. It told him that he was in instant danger, and that the only hope lay in utter impassivity. If he attempted to exercise his own will, he was doomed, and there was sufficient indication of what that doom meant to shake his lethargy into spasms of childish fear. "Your body is too feeble to move," said the voice, "for Allah has laid His hand on it." Sure enough Turpin realised that he hadn't the strength of a kitten. "You have surrendered your will to Allah till He restores it to you." That also was true, for Turpin knew he could not summon the energy to brush his hair, unless he was ordered to. "You will be safe," said the voice, "so long as you sleep. You will sleep till I bid you awake."

Sleep he probably did, for once again came a big gap in his consciousness. . . . The next he knew he was being jolted in something that ran on wheels, and he suddenly rolled over on his side, as the vehicle took a sharp turn. This time it didn't take him quite so long to wake up. He found he was in a big motor-car, with his overcoat on, and his hat on the seat beside him. He was stretched out almost at full length, and comfortably propped up with cushions. All this he realised fairly soon, but it was some time before he could gather up the past, and then it was all blurred and sketchy. . . . What he remembered most clearly was the warning that he was in grave peril and was only safe while he did nothing. That was burned in on his mind, and the lesson was pointed by the complete powerlessness of his limbs. He could hardly turn over from his side to his back, and he knew that if he attempted to stand he would fall down in a heap. He shut his eyes and tried to think.

Bit by bit the past pieced itself together. He remembered Archie's cry--and things before that--Mary--the girl in green. Very soon the truth smote him in the face. He had been kidnapped like the rest, and had had the same tricks played on him. . . . But they had only affected his body. As he realised this tremendous fact Turpin swelled with pride. Some devilry had stolen his physical strength, but his soul was his own still, his memory and his will. A sort of miasma of past fear still clung about him, like the after-taste of influenza, but this only served to make him angry. He was most certainly not going to be beaten. The swine had miscalculated this time; they might have a cripple in their hands, but it would be a very watchful, wary, and determined cripple, quick to seize the first chance to be even with them. His anger made his spirits rise. All his life he had been a man of tropical loves and tempestuous hates. He had loathed the Boche, and free- masons, and communists and the deputies of his own land, and ever since Adela's disappearance he had nursed a fury against a person or persons unknown: and now every detestation of which he was capable had been focussed against those who were responsible for this night's work. The fools! They thought they had got a trussed sheep, when all the time it was a lame tiger.

The blinds of the car were down, but by small painful movements he managed to make out that there was a man in the front seat beside the chauffeur. By and by he got a corner of the right-hand blind raised, and saw that it was night time and that they were moving through broad streets that looked like a suburb. From the beat of the engine he gathered that the car was a Rolls-Royce, but not, he thought, one of the latest models. Presently the motion became less regular, and he realised that the suburban streets were giving place to country roads. His many expeditions in his Delage had taught him a good deal about the ways out of London, but, try as he might, he could not pick up any familiar landmark. The young moon had set, so he assumed that it was near midnight; it was a fine, clear night, not very dark, and he picked up an occasional inn and church, but they never seemed to pass through any village. Probably the driver was taking the less frequented roads--a view he was confirmed in by the frequent right-angled turns and the many patches of indifferent surface.

Very soon he found his efforts at reconnaissance so painful that he gave them up, and contented himself with planning his policy. Of course he must play the part of the witless sheep. That duty, he thought, presented no difficulties, for he rather fancied himself as an actor. The trouble was his bodily condition. He did not believe that a constitution as good as his could have taken any permanent damage from the night's work. . . . The night's! He must have been away for more than one night, for the row with Archie had taken place very near twelve o'clock. This must be the midnight following. He wondered what Mr. Victor was thinking about it--and Mary--and Hannay. The miserable Hannay had now four lost ones to look for instead of three! . . . Anyhow the devils had got an ugly prisoner in him. His body must soon be all right, unless of course they took steps to keep it all wrong. At that thought Turpin's jaw set. The rôle of the docile sheep might be difficult to keep up very long.

The next he knew the car had turned in at a gate and was following a dark tree-lined avenue. In another minute it had stopped before the door of a house, and he was being lifted out by the chauffeur and the man from the front seat, and carried into a hall. But first a dark bandanna was tied over his eyes, and, as he could do nothing with his arms or legs, he had to submit. He felt himself carried up a short staircase, and then along a corridor into a bedroom, where a lamp was lit. Hands undressed him--his eyes still bandaged--and equipped him with pyjamas which were not his own, and were at once too roomy and too short. Then food was brought, and an English voice observed that he had better have some supper before going to sleep. The bandage was taken off and he saw two male backs disappearing through the door.

Up till now he had felt no hunger or thirst, but the sight of food made him realise that he was as empty as a drum. By twisting his head he could see it all laid out on the table beside his bed--a good meal it looked--cold ham and galantine, an omelette, a salad, cheese and a small decanter of red wine. His soul longed for it, but what about his feeble limbs? Was this some new torture of Tantalus?

Desire grew, and like an automaton he moved to it. He felt all numbed, with needles and pins everywhere, but surely he was less feeble than he had been in the car. First he managed to get his right arm extended, and by flexing the elbow and wrist a certain life seemed to creep back. Then he did the same thing with his right leg, and presently found that he could wriggle by inches to the edge of the bed. He was soon out of breath, but there could be no doubt about it--he was getting stronger. A sudden access of thirst enabled him to grasp the decanter, and, after some trouble with the stopper, to draw it to his lips. Spilling a good deal, he succeeded in getting a mouthful. "Larose," he murmured, "and a good vintage. It would have been better if it had been cognac."

But the wine put new life into him. He found he could use both arms, and he began wolfishly on the omelette, making a rather messy job of it. By this time he was feeling a remarkably vigorous convalescent, and he continued with the cold meat, till the cramp in his left shoulder forced him to lie back on the pillow. It soon passed, and he was able in fair comfort to finish the meal down to the last lettuce leaf of the salad, and the last drop of the claret. The Turpin who reclined again on the bed was to all intents the same vigorous young man who the night before had stumbled through that fateful door into the darkness. But it was a Turpin with a profoundly mystified mind.

He would have liked to smoke, but his cigarettes were in the pocket of his dress clothes which had been removed. So he started to do for his legs what he had already achieved for his arms, and with the same happy results. It occurred to him that, while he was alone, he had better discover whether or not he could stand. He made the effort, rolled out of bed on to the floor, hit the little table with his head and set the dishes rattling.

But after a few scrambles he got to his feet and managed to shuffle round the room. The mischief was leaving his body--so much was plain, and but for a natural stiffness in the joints he felt as well as ever. But what it all meant he hadn't a notion. He was inclined to the belief that somehow he had scored off his enemies, and was a tougher proposition than they had bargained for. They had assuredly done no harm to his mind with their witchcraft, and it looked as if they had also failed with his body. The thought emboldened him. The house seemed quiet; why should he not do a little exploration?

He cautiously opened the door, finding it, somewhat to his surprise, unlocked. The passage was lit by a hanging oil-lamp, carpeted with an old-fashioned drugget, and its walls decorated with a set of flower pictures. Turpin came to the conclusion that rarely in his life had he been in a dwelling which seemed more innocent and homelike. He considered himself sensitive to the nuances of the sinister in an atmosphere, and there was nothing of that sort in this. He took a step or two down the passage, and then halted, for he thought he heard a sound. Yes, there could be no doubt of it. It was water gushing from a tap. Someone in the establishment was about to have a bath.

Then he slipped back to his room just in time. The someone was approaching with light feet and a rustle of draperies. He had his door shut when the steps passed, and then opened it and stuck his head out. He saw a pink dressing-gown, and above it a slender neck and masses of dark hair. It was the figure which he of all men was likely to know best.

It seemed that the place for him was bed, so he got between the sheets again and tried to think. Adela Victor was here; therefore he was in the hands of her captors, and made a fourth in their bag. But what insanity had prompted these wary criminals to bring the two of them to the same prison? Were they so utterly secure, so confident of their power, that they took this crazy risk? The insolence of it made him furious. In the name of every saint he swore that he would make them regret it. He would free the lady and himself, though he had to burn down the house and wring the neck of every inmate. And then he remembered the delicacy of the business, and the need of exact timing if the other two hostages were not to be lost, and at the thought he groaned.

There was a tap at the door, and a man entered to clear away the supper table. He seemed an ordinary English valet, with his stiff collar and decent black coat and smug expressionless face.

"Beg pardon, my lord," he said, "at what hour would you like your shavin' water? Seein' it's been a late night I make so bold as to suggest ten o'clock."

Turpin assented, and the servant had hardly gone when another visitor appeared. It was a slim pale man, whom he was not conscious of having seen before, a man with grey hair and a melancholy droop of the head. He stood at the foot of the bed, gazing upon the prostrate Turpin, and his look was friendly. Then he addressed him in French of the most Saxon type.

"Êtes-vous comfortable, monsieur? C'est bien. Soyez tranquille. Nous sommes vos amis. Bon soir."

CHAPTER XVI

OUR TIME IS NARROWED

I lunched that day with Mary--alone, for her aunts were both in Paris--and it would have been hard to find in the confines of the British islands a more dejected pair. Mary, who had always a singular placid gentleness, showed her discomposure only by her pallor. As for me I was as restless as a bantam.

"I wish I had never touched the thing," I cried. "I have done more harm than good."

"You have found Lord Mercot," she protested.

"Yes, and lost Turpin. The brutes are still three up on us. We thought we had found two, and now we have lost Miss Victor again. And Turpin! They'll find him an ugly customer, and probably take strong measures with him. They'll stick to him and the girl and the little boy now like wax; for last night's performance is bound to make them suspicious."

"I wonder," said Mary, always an optimist. "You see, Sir Archie only dragged him in because of his rank. It looked odd his being in Adela's company, but then all the times he has seen her he never spoke a word to her. They must have noticed that. I'm anxious about Sir Archie. He ought to leave London."

"Confound him! He's going to, as soon as he gets out of hospital, which will probably be this afternoon. I insisted on it, but he meant to in any case. He's heard an authentic report of a green sandpiper nesting somewhere. It would be a good thing if Archie would stick to birds. He has no head for anything else. . . . And now we've got to start again at the beginning."

"Not quite the beginning," she interposed.

"Dashed near it. They won't bring Miss Victor into that kind of world again, and all your work goes for nothing, my dear. It's uncommon bad luck that you didn't begin to wake her up, for then she might have done something on her own account. But she's still a dummy, and tucked away, you may be sure, in some place where we can never reach her. And we have little more than three weeks left."

"It is bad luck," Mary agreed. "But, Dick, I've a feeling that I haven't lost Adela Victor. I believe that somehow or other we'll soon get in touch with her again. You remember how children when they lose a ball sometimes send another one after it in the hope that one will find the other. Well, we've sent the Marquis after Adela, and I've a notion we may find them both together. We always did that as children." . . . She paused at the word 'children' and I saw pain in her eyes. "Oh, Dick, the little boy! We're no nearer him, and he's far the most tragic of all."

The whole business looked so black that I had no word of comfort to give her.

"And to put the lid on it," I groaned, "I've got to settle down in Medina's house this evening. I hate the idea like poison."

"It's the safest way," she said.

"Yes, but it puts me out of action. He'll watch me like a lynx, and I won't be able to take a single step on my own--simply sit there and eat and drink and play up to his vanity. Great Scott, I swear I'll have a row with him and break his head."

"Dick, you're not going to--how do you say it?--chuck in your hand? Everything depends on you. You're our scout in the enemy's headquarters. Your life depends on your playing the game. Colonel Arbuthnot said so. And you may find out something tremendous. It will be horrible for you, but it isn't for long, and it's the only way."

That was Mary all over. She was trembling with anxiety for me, but she was such a thorough sportsman that she wouldn't take any soft option.

"You may hear something about David Warcliff," she added.

"I hope to God I do. Don't worry, darling. I'll stick it out. But, look here, we must make a plan. I shall be more or less shut off from the world, and I must have a line of communication open. You can't telephone to me at that house, and I daren't ring you up from there. The only chance is the Club. If you have any message, ring up the head porter and make him write it down. I'll arrange that he keeps it quiet, and I'll pick up the messages when I get the chance. And I'll ring you up occasionally to give you the news. But I must be jolly careful, for, likely as not, Medina will keep an eye on me even there. You're in touch with Macgillivray?"

She nodded.

"And with Sandy?"

"Yes, but it takes some time--a day at least. We can't correspond direct."

"Well, there's the lay-out. I'm a prisoner--with qualifications. You and I can keep up some sort of communication. As you say, there's only about another three weeks."

"It would be nothing if only we had some hope."

"That's life, my dear. We've got to go on to the finish anyhow, trusting that luck will turn in the last ten minutes."

I arrived in Hill Street after tea and found Medina in the back smoking-room, writing letters.

"Good man, Hannay," he said; "make yourself comfortable. There are cigars on that table."

"Had a satisfactory time in Shropshire?" I asked.

"Rotten. I motored back this morning, starting very early. Some tiresome business here wanted my attention. I'm sorry, but I'll be out to dinner to-night. The same thing always happens when I want to see my friends--a hideous rush of work."

He was very hospitable, but his manner had not the ease it used to have. He seemed on the edge about something, and rather preoccupied. I guessed it was the affair of Archie Roylance and Turpin.

I dined alone and sat after dinner in the smoking-room, for Odell never suggested the library, though I would have given a lot to fossick about that place. I fell asleep over the Field and was wakened about eleven by Medina. He looked almost tired, a rare thing for him; also his voice was curiously hard. He made some trivial remark about the weather, and a row in the Cabinet which was going on. Then he said suddenly:

"Have you seen Arbuthnot lately?"

"No," I replied, with real surprise in my tone. "How could I? He has gone back to the East."

"So I thought. But I have been told that he has been seen again in England."

For a second I had a horrid fear that he had got on the track of my meeting with Sandy at the Cotswold inn and his visit to Fosse. His next words reassured me.

"Yes. In London. Within the last few days."

It was easy enough for me to show astonishment. "What a crazy fellow he is! He can't stay put for a week together. All I can say is that I hope he won't come my way. I've no particular wish to see him again."

Medina said no more. He accompanied me to my bedroom, asked if I had everything I wanted, bade me good night, and left me.

Now began one of the strangest weeks in my life. Looking back, it has still the inconsequence of a nightmare, but one or two episodes stand out like reefs in a tide-race. When I woke the first morning under Medina's roof I believed that somehow or other he had come to suspect me. I soon saw that that was nonsense, that he regarded me as a pure chattel; but I saw, too, that a most active suspicion of something had been awakened in his mind. Probably Archie's fiasco, together with the news of Sandy, had done it, and perhaps there was in it something of the natural anxiety of a man nearing the end of a difficult course. Anyhow I concluded that this tension of mind on his part was bound to make things more difficult for me. Without suspecting me, he kept me perpetually under his eye. He gave me orders as if I were a child, or rather he made suggestions, which in my character of worshipping disciple I had to treat as orders.

He was furiously busy night and day, and yet he left me no time to myself. He wanted to know everything I did, and I had to give an honest account of my doings, for I had a feeling that he had ways of finding out the truth. One lie discovered would, I knew, wreck my business utterly, for if I were under his power, as he believed I was, it would be impossible for me to lie to him. Consequently I dared not pay many visits to the Club, for he would want to know what I did there. I was on such desperately thin ice that I thought it best to stay most of my time in Hill Street, unless he asked me to accompany him. I consulted Mary about this, and she agreed that it was the wise course.

Apart from a flock of maids, there was no other servant in the house but Odell. Twice I met the grey, sad-faced man on the stairs, the man I had seen on my first visit, and had watched a week before in thc housc behind the curiosity shop. I asked who he was, and was told a private secretary, who helped Medina in his political work. I gathered that he did not live regularly in the house, but only came there when his services were required.

Now Mary had said that the other man that evening in Little Fardell Street had been Sandy. If she was right, this fellow might be a friend, and I wondered if I could get in touch with him. The first time I encountered him he never raised his eyes. The second time I forced him by some question to look at me, and he turned on me a perfectly dead expressionless face like a codfish. I concluded that Mary had been in error, for this was the genuine satellite, every feature of whose character had been steam-rollered out of existence by Medina's will.

I was seeing Medina now at very close quarters, and in complete undress, and the impression he had made on me at our first meeting-- which had been all overlaid by subsequent happenings--grew as vivid again as daylight. The "good fellow," of course, had gone; I saw behind all his perfection of manner to the naked ribs of his soul. He would talk to me late at night in that awful library, till I felt that he and the room were one presence, and that all the diabolic lore of the ages had been absorbed by this one mortal. You must understand that there was nothing wrong in the ordinary sense with anything he said. If there had been a phonograph recording his talk it could have been turned on with perfect safety in a girls' school. . . . He never spoke foully, or brutally. I don't believe he had a shadow of those faults of the flesh which we mean when we use the word "vice." But I swear that the most wretched libertine before the bar of the Almighty would have shown a clean sheet compared to his.

I know no word to describe how he impressed me except "wickedness." He seemed to annihilate the world of ordinary moral standards, all the little rags of honest impulse and stumbling kindness with which we try to shelter ourselves from the winds of space. His consuming egotism made life a bare cosmos in which his spirit scorched like a flame. I have met bad men in my day, fellows who ought to have been quietly and summarily put out of existence, but if I had had the trying of them I would have found bits of submerged decency and stunted remnants of good feeling. At any rate they were human, and their beastliness was a degeneration of humanity, not its flat opposite. Medina made an atmosphere which was like a cold bright air in which nothing can live. He was utterly and consumedly wicked, with no standard which could be remotely related to ordinary life. That is why, I suppose, mankind has had to invent the notion of devils. He seemed to be always lifting the corner of a curtain and giving me peeps into a hoary mystery of iniquity older than the stars. . . . I suppose that someone who had never felt his hypnotic power would have noticed very little in his talk except its audacious cleverness, and that someone wholly under his dominion would have been less impressed than me because he would have forgotten his own standards, and been unable to make the comparison. I was just in the right position to understand and tremble. . . . Oh, I can tell you, I used to go to bed solemnised, frightened half out of my wits, and yet in a violent revulsion, and hating him like hell. It was pretty clear that he was mad, for madness means just this dislocation of the modes of thought which mortals have agreed upon as necessary to keep the world together. His head used to seem as round as a bullet, like nothing you find even in the skulls of cave-men, and his eyes to have a blue light in them like the sunrise of death in an arctic waste.

One day I had a very narrow escape. I went to the Club, to see if there was anything from Mary, and received instead a long cable from Gaudian in Norway. I had just opened it, when I found Medina at my elbow. He had seen me enter, and followed me, in order that we should walk home together.

Now I had arranged a simple code with Gaudian for his cables, and by the mercy of Heaven that honest fellow had taken special precautions, and got some friend to send this message from Christiania. Had it borne the Merdal stamp it would have been all up with me.

The only course was the bold one, though I pursued it with a quaking heart.

"Hullo," I cried, "here's a cable from a pal of mine in Norway. Did I tell you I had been trying to get a beat on the Leardal for July? I had almost forgotten about the thing. I started inquiring in March, and here's my first news."

I handed him the two sheets and he glanced at the place of dispatch.

"Code," he said. "Do you want to work it out now?"

"If you don't mind waiting a few seconds. It's a simple code of my own invention, and I ought to be able to decipher it pretty fast."

We sat down at one of the tables in the hall, and I took up a pen and a sheet of notepaper. As I think I have mentioned before, I am rather a swell at codes, and this one in particular I could read without much difficulty. I jotted down some letters and numbers, and then wrote out a version which I handed to Medina. This was what he read:

"Upper beat Leardal available from first of month. Rent two hundred and fifty with option of August at one hundred more. No limit to rods. Boat on each pool. Tidal waters can also be got for sea trout by arrangement. If you accept please cable word 'Yes.' You should arrive not later than June 29th. Bring plenty of bottled prawns. Motor boat can be had from Bergen. Andersen, Grand Hotel, Christiania."

But all the time I was scribbling this nonsense, I was reading the code correctly and getting the message by heart. Here is what Gaudian really sent:

"Our friend has quarrelled with keeper and beaten him soundly. I have taken charge at farm and frightened latter into docility. He will remain prisoner in charge of ally of mine till I give the word to release. Meantime, think it safer to bring friend to England and start on Monday. Will wire address in Scotland and wait your instructions. No danger of keeper sending message. Do not be anxious, all is well."

Having got that clear in my head, I tore the cable into small pieces and flung them into the waste-paper basket.

"Well, are you going?" Medina asked.

"Not I. I'm off salmon-fishing for the present." I took a cable form from the table and wrote: "Sorry, must cancel Leardal plan," signed it "Hannay," addressed it to "Andersen, Grand Hotel, Christiania," and gave it to the porter to send off. I wonder what happened to that telegram. It is probably still stuck up on the hotel-board, awaiting the arrival of the mythical Andersen.

On our way back to Hill Street Medina put his arm in mine, and was very friendly. "I hope to get a holiday," he said, "perhaps just after the beginning of June. Only a day or two off now. I may go abroad for a little. I would like you to come with me."

That puzzled me a lot. Medina could not possibly leave town before the great liquidation, and there could be no motive in his trying to mislead me on such a point, seeing that I was living in his house. I wondered if something had happened to make him change the date. It was of the first importance that I should find this out, and I did my best to draw him about his plans. But I could get nothing out of him except that he hoped for an early holiday, and "early" might apply to the middle of June as well as to the beginning, for it was now the 27th of May.

Next afternoon at tea-time to my surprise Odell appeared in the smoking-room, followed by the long lean figure of Tom Greenslade. I never saw anybody with greater pleasure, but I didn't dare to talk to him alone. "Is your master upstairs?" I asked the butler. "Will you tell him that Dr. Greenslade is here? He is an old friend of his."

We had rather less than two minutes before Medina appeared. "I come from your wife," Greenslade whispered. "She has told me all about the business, and she thought this was the safest plan. I was to tell you that she has news of Miss Victor and the Marquis. They are safe enough. Any word of the little boy?"

He raised his voice as Medina entered. "My dear fellow, this is a great pleasure. I had to be in London for a consultation, and I thought I would look up Hannay. I hardly hoped to have the luck to catch a busy man like you."

Medina was very gracious--no, that is not the word, for there was nothing patronising in his manner. He asked in the most friendly way about Greenslade's practice, and how he liked English country life after his many wanderings. He spoke with an air of regret of the great valleys of loess and the windy Central Asian tablelands where they had first foregathered. Odell brought in tea, and we made as pleasant a trio of friends as you could find in London. I asked a few casual questions about Fosse, and then I mentioned Peter John. Here Greenslade had an inspiration; he told me afterwards that he thought it might be a good thing to open a channel for further communications.

"I think he's all right," he said slowly. "He's been having occasional stomach-aches, but I expect that is only the result of hot weather and the first asparagus. Lady Hannay is a little anxious--you know what she is, and all mothers to-day keep thinking about appendicitis. So I'm keeping my eye on the little man. You needn't worry, Dick."

I take credit to myself for having divined the doctor's intention. I behaved as if I scarcely heard him, and as if Fosse Manor and my family were things infinitely remote. Indeed I switched off the conversation to where Medina had last left it, and I behaved towards Tom Greenslade as if his presence rather bored me, and I had very little to say to him. When he got up to go, it was Medina who accompanied him to the front door. All this was a heavy strain upon my self-command, for I would have given anything for a long talk with him--though I had the sense not to believe his news about Peter John.

"Not a bad fellow, that doctor of yours," Medina observed on his return.

"No," I said carelessly. "Rather a dull dog all the same, with his country gossip. But I wish him well, for it is to him that I owe your friendship."

I must count that episode one of my lucky moments, for it seemed to give Medina some special satisfaction. "Why do you make this your only sitting-room?" he asked. "The library is at your disposal, and it is pleasanter in summer than any other part of the house."

"I thought I might be disturbing your work," I said humbly.

"Not a bit of it. Besides, I've nearly finished my work. After to-night I can slack off, and presently I'll be an idle man."

"And then the holiday?"

"Then the holiday." He smiled in a pleasant boyish way, which was one of his prettiest tricks.

"How soon will that be?"

"If all goes well, very soon. Probably after the second of June. By the way, the Thursday Club dines on the first. I want you to be my guest again."

Here was more food for thought. The conviction grew upon me that he and his friends had put forward the date of liquidation; they must have suspected something--probably from Sandy's presence in England--and were taking no risks. I smoked that evening till my tongue was sore and went to bed in a fever of excitement. The urgency of the matter fairly screamed in my ears, for Macgillivray must know the truth at once, and so must Mary. Mercot was safe, and there was a chance apparently of Turpin and Miss Victor, which must be acted upon instantly if the main date were changed. Of the little boy I had given up all hope. . . . But how to find the truth! I felt like a man in a bad dream who is standing on the line with an express train approaching, and does not know how to climb back on to the platform.

Next morning Medina never left me. He took me in his car to the City, and I waited while he did his business, and then to call in Carlton House Terrace a few doors from the Victors' house. I believe it was the residence of the man who led his party in the Lords. After luncheon he solemnly installed me in the library. "You're not much of a reader, and in any case you would probably find my books dull. But there are excellent arm-chairs to doze in."

Then he went out and I heard the wheels of his car move away. I felt a kind of awe creeping over me when I found myself left alone in the uncanny place, which I knew to be the devil's kitchen for all his schemes. There was a telephone on his writing-table, the only one I had seen in the house, though there was no doubt one in the butler's pantry. I turned up the telephone book and found a number given, but it was not the one on the receiver. This must be a private telephone, by means of which he could ring up anybody he wanted, but of which only his special friends knew the number. There was nothing else in the room to interest me, except the lines and lines of books, for his table was as bare as a bank-manager's.

I tried the books, but most of them were a long sight too learned for me. Most were old, and many were in Latin, and some were evidently treasures, for I would take one down and find it a leather box with inside it a slim battered volume wrapped in wash- leather. But I found in one corner a great array of works of travel, so I selected one of Aurel Stein's books and settled down in an arm-chair with it. I tried to fix my attention, but found it impossible. The sentences would not make sense to my restless mind, and I could not follow the maps. So I got up again, replaced the work on its shelf, and began to wander about. It was a dull close day, and out in the street a water-cart was sprinkling the dust and children were going park-wards with their nurses. . . . I simply could not account for my disquiet, but I was like a fine lady with the vapours. I felt that somewhere in that room there was something that it concerned me deeply to know.

I drifted towards the bare writing-table. There was nothing on it but a massive silver inkstand in the shape of an owl, a silver tray of pens and oddments, a leather case of notepaper and a big blotting-book. I would never have made a good thief, for I felt both nervous and ashamed as, after listening for steps, I tried the drawers.

They were all locked--all, that is, except a shallow one at the top which looked as if it were meant to contain one of those big engagement tablets which busy men affect. There was no tablet there, but there were two sheets of paper.

Both had been torn from a loose-leaf diary, and both covered the same dates--the fortnight between Monday the 29th of May, and Sunday the 11th of June. In the first the space for the days was filled with entries in Medina's neat writing, entries in some sort of shorthand. These entries were close and thick up to and including Friday the 2nd of June; after that there was nothing. The second sheet of paper was just the opposite. The spaces were virgin up to and including the 2nd of June; after that, on till the 11th, they were filled with notes.

As I stared at these two sheets, some happy instinct made me divine their meaning. The first sheet contained the steps that Medina would take up to the day of liquidation, which was clearly the 2nd of June. After that, if all went well, came peace and leisure. But if it didn't go well, the second sheet contained his plans--plans I have no doubt for using the hostages, for wringing safety out of certain great men's fears. . . . My interpretation was confirmed by a small jotting in long-hand on the first sheet in the space for 2nd June. It was the two words "Dies irae," which my Latin was just good enough to construe.

I had lost all my tremors now, but I was a thousandfold more restless. I must get word to Macgillivray at once--no, that was too dangerous--to Mary. I glanced at the telephone and resolved to trust my luck.

I got through to the Wymondhams' house without difficulty. Barnard the butler answered, and informed me that Mary was at home. Then after a few seconds I heard her voice.

"Mary," I said, "the day is changed to the 2nd of June. You understand, warn everybody . . . I can't think why you are worrying about that child."

For I was conscious that Medina was entering the room. I managed with my knee to close the shallow drawer with the two sheets in it, and I nodded and smiled to him, putting my hand over the receiver.

"Forgive me using your telephone. Fact is, my wife's in London and she sent me round a note here asking me to ring her up. She's got the boy on her mind."

I put the tube to my ear again. Mary's voice sounded sharp and high-pitched.

"Are you there? I'm in Mr. Medina's library and I can't disturb him talking through this machine. There's no cause to worry about Peter John. Greenslade is usually fussy enough, and if he's calm there's no reason why you shouldn't be. But if you want another opinion, why not get it? We may as well get the thing straightened out now, for I may be going abroad early in June. . . . Yes, some time after the 2nd."

Thank God Mary was quick-witted.

"The 2nd is very near. Why do you make such sudden plans, Dick? I can't go home without seeing you. I think I'll come straight to Hill Street."

"All right," I said, "do as you please." I rang off and looked at Medina with a wry smile. "What fussers women are! Do you mind if my wife comes round here? She won't be content till she has seen me. She has come up with a crazy notion of taking down a surgeon to give an opinion on the child's appendix. Tommy rot! But that's a woman's way."

He clearly suspected nothing. "Certainly let Lady Hannay come here. We'll give her tea. I'm sorry that the drawing-room is out of commission just now. She might have liked to see my miniatures."

Mary appeared in ten minutes, and most nobly she acted her part. It was the very model of a distraught silly mother who bustled into the room. Her eyes looked as if she had been crying and she had managed to disarrange her hat and untidy her hair.

"Oh, I've been so worried," she wailed, after she had murmured apologies to Medina. "He really has had a bad tummy pain, and nurse thought last night that he was feverish. I've seen Mr. Dobson-Wray, and he can come down by the four-forty-five. . . . He's such a precious little boy, Mr. Medina, that I feel we must take every precaution with him. If Mr. Dobson-Wray says it is all right, I promise not to fuss any more. I think a second opinion would please Dr. Greenslade, for he too looked rather anxious. . . . Oh, no, thank you so much, but I can't stay for tea. I have a taxi waiting, and I might miss my train. I'm going to pick up Mr. Dobson-Wray in Wimpole Street."

She departed in the same tornado in which she had come, just stopping to set her hat straight at one of the mirrors in the hall.

"Of course I'll wire when the surgeon has seen him. And, Dick, you'll come down at once if there's anything wrong, and bring nurses. Poor, poor little darling! . . . Did you say after the 2nd of June, Dick? I do hope you'll be able to get off. You need a holiday away from your tiresome family. . . . Good-bye, Mr. Medina. It was so kind of you to be patient with a silly mother. Look after Dick and don't let him worry."

I had preserved admirably the aloof air of the bored and slightly ashamed husband. But now I realised that Mary was not babbling at large, but was saying something which I was meant to take in.

"Poor, poor little darling!" she crooned as she got into the taxi. "I do pray he'll be all right--I THINK he may, Dick. . . . I hope, oh I hope . . . to put your mind at ease . . . before the 2nd of June."

As I turned back to Medina I had a notion that the poor little darling was no longer Peter John.

CHAPTER XVII

THE DISTRICT-VISITOR IN PALMYRA SQUARE

During the last fortnight a new figure had begun to appear in Palmyra Square. I do not know if Macgillivray's watchers reported its presence, for I saw none of their reports, but they must have been cognisant of it, unless they spent all their time in the nearest public-house. It was a district-visitor of the familiar type--a woman approaching middle age, presumably a spinster, who wore a plain black dress and, though the weather was warm, a cheap fur round her neck, and carried a rather old black silk satchel. Her figure was good, and had still a suggestion of youth, but her hair, which was dressed very flat and tight and coiled behind in an unfashionable bun, seemed--the little that was seen of it--to be sprinkled with grey. She was dowdy, and yet not altogether dowdy, for there was a certain faded elegance in her air, and an observer might have noted that she walked well. Besides the black satchel she carried usually a sheaf of papers, and invariably and in all weathers a cheap badly-rolled umbrella.

She visited at the doctor's house with the brass plate, and the music-teacher's, and at the various lodging-houses. She was attached, it appeared, to the big church of St. Jude's a quarter of a mile off, which had just got a new and energetic vicar. She was full of enthusiasm for her vicar, praised his earnestness and his eloquence, and dwelt especially, after the way of elderly maiden ladies, on the charm of his youth. She was also very ready to speak of herself, and eager to explain that her work was voluntary-- she was a gentlewoman of modest but independent means, and had rooms in Hampstead, and her father had been a clergyman at Eastbourne. Very full of her family she was to those who would hear her. There was a gentle simplicity about her manners, and an absence of all patronage, which attracted people and made them willing to listen to her when they would have shut the door on another, for the inhabitants of Palmyra Square are not a courteous or patient or religious folk.

Her aim was to enlist the overworked general servants of the Square in some of the organisations of St. Jude's. There were all kinds of activities in that enlightened church--choral societies, and mothers' meetings, and country holiday clubs, and classes for adult education. She would hand out sheaves of literature about the Girls' Friendly Society, and the Mothers' Union, and such-like, and try to secure a promise of attendance at some of the St. Jude's functions. I do not think she had much success at the doctor's and the music-teacher's, though she regularly distributed her literature there. The wretched little maids were too downtrodden and harassed to do more than listen dully on the doorstep and say "Yes'm." Nor was she allowed to see the mistresses, except one of the lodging-house keepers, who was a Primitive Methodist and considered St. Jude's a device of Satan. But she had better fortune with the maid at No. 4.

The girl belonged to a village in Kent, and the district-visitor, it seemed, had been asked to look her up by the rector of her old parish. She was a large flat-faced young woman, slow of speech, heavy of movement, and suspicious of nature. At first she greeted the district-visitor coldly, but thawed at the mention of familiar names and accepted a copy of the St. Jude's Magazine. Two days later, when on her afternoon out, she met the district-visitor and consented to walk a little way with her. Now the girl's hobby was dress, and her taste was better than most of her class and aspired to higher things. She had a new hat which her companion admired, but she confessed that she was not quite satisfied with it. The district-visitor revealed a knowledge of fashions which one would have scarcely augured from her own sombre clothes. She pointed out where the trimming was wrong, and might easily be improved, and the girl--her name was Elsie Outhwaite--agreed. "I could put it right for you in ten minutes," she was told. "Perhaps you would let me come and see you when you have a spare half-hour, and we could do it together. I'm rather clever at hats, and used to help my sisters."

The ice was broken and the aloof Miss Outhwaite became confidential. She liked her place, had no cause to complain, received good wages, and above all was not fussed. "I minds my own business, and Madame minds 'ers," she said. Madame was a foreigner, and had her queer ways, but had also her good points. She did not interfere unnecessarily, and was not mean. There were handsome presents at Christmas, and every now and then the house would be shut up and Miss Outhwaite returned to Kent on generous board wages. It was not a hard billet, though of course there were a lot of visitors, Madame's clients. "She's a massoose, you know, but very respectable." When asked if there were no other inmates of the house she became reticent. "Not what you would call reg'lar part of the family," she admitted. "There's an old lady, Madame's aunt, that stops with us a but, but I don't see much of 'er. Madame attends to 'er 'erself, and she 'as her private room. And of course there's . . ." Miss Outhwaite seemed suddenly to recollect something, and changed the subject.

The district-visitor professed a desire to make Madame's acquaintance, but was not encouraged. "She's not the sort for the likes of you. She don't 'old with churches and God and such-like-- I've 'eard 'er say so. You won't be getting 'er near St. Jude's, miss."

"But if she is so clever and nice I would like to meet her. She could advise me about some of the difficult questions in this big parish. Perhaps she would help with our Country Holidays."

Miss Outhwaite primmed her lips and didn't think so. "You've got to be ill and nervy for Madame to have an interest in you. I'll take in your name if you like, but I expect Madame won't be at 'ome to you."

It was eventually arranged that the district-visitor should call at No. 4 the following afternoon and bring the materials for the reconstructed hat. She duly presented herself, but was warned away by a flustered Miss Outhwaite. "We're that busy to-day I 'aven't a minute to myself." Sunday was suggested, but it appeared that that was the day when the district-visitor was fully occupied, so a provisional appointment was made for the next Tuesday evening.

This time all went well. Madame was out, and the district-visitor spent a profitable hour in Miss Outhwaite's room. Her nimble fingers soon turned the hat, purchased in Queen's Crescent for ten and sixpence, into a distant imitation of a costlier mode. She displayed an innocent interest in the household, and asked many questions which Miss Outhwaite, now in the best of tempers, answered readily. She was told of Madame's habits, her very occasional shortness of temper, her love of every tongue but English. "The worst of them furriners," said Miss Outhwaite, "is that you can't never be sure what they thinks of you. Half the time I'm with Madame and her aunt they're talking some 'eathen language."

As she departed the district-visitor was given a sketch of the topography of the house about which she showed an unexpected curiosity. Before she left there was a slight contretemps. Madame's latch-key was heard in the door and Miss Outhwaite had a moment of panic. "Here, miss, I'll let you out through the kitchen," she whispered. But her visitor showed no embarrassment. "I'd like to meet Madame Breda," she declared. "This is a good chance."

Madame's plump dark face showed surprise, and possibly annoyance, as she observed the two. Miss Outhwaite hastened to explain the situation with a speed which revealed nervousness. "This is a lady from St. Jude's, Madame," she said. "She comes 'ere districk-visiting and she knows the folk in Radhurst, where I comes from, so I made bold to ask her in."

"I am very glad to meet you, Madame Breda," said the district- visitor. "I hope you don't mind my calling on Elsie Outhwaite. I want her to help in our Girls' Friendly Society work."

"You have been here before, I think," was the reply in a sufficiently civil tone. "I have seen you in the Square sometimes. There is no objection on my part to Outhwaite's attending your meetings, but I warn you that she has very little free time." The woman was a foreigner, no doubt, but on this occasion her English showed little trace of accent.

"That is very good of you. I should have asked your permission first, but you were unfortunately not at home when I called, and Elsie and I made friends by accident. I hope you will let me come again."

As the visitor descended the steps and passed through the bright green gate into the gathering dusk of the Square, Madame Breda watched her contemplatively from one of the windows.

The lady came again four days later--it must, I think, have been the 29th of May. Miss Outhwaite, when she opened the door, looked flustered. "I can't talk to you to-night, miss. Madame's orders is that when you next came you was to be shown in to her room."

"How very kind of her!" said the lady. "I should greatly enjoy a talk with her. And, Elsie--I've got such a nice present for you--a hat which a friend gave me and which is too young--really too young--for me to wear. I'm going to give it you, if you'll accept it. I'll bring it in a day or two."

The district-visitor was shown into the large room on the right- hand side of the hall where Madame received her patients. There was no one there except a queer-looking little girl in a linen smock, who beckoned her to follow to the folding-doors which divided the apartment from the other at the back. The lady did a strange thing, for she picked up the little girl, held her a second in her arms, and kissed her--after the emotional habit of the childless dévote. Then she passed through the folding-doors.

It was an odd apartment in which she found herself--much larger than could have been guessed from the look of the house, and, though the night was warm, there was a fire lit, a smouldering fire which gave off a fine blue smoke. Madame Breda was there, dressed in a low-cut gown as if she had been dining out, and looking handsome and dark and very foreign in the light of the shaded lamps. In an armchair by the hearth sat a wonderful old lady, with a thing like a mantilla over her snow-white hair. It was a room so unlike anything in her narrow experience that the newcomer stood hesitating as the folding-doors shut behind her.

"Oh, Madame Breda, it is so very kind of you to see me," she faltered.

"I do not know your name," Madame said, and then she did a curious thing, for she lifted a lamp and held it in the visitor's face, scrutinising every line of her shabby figure.

"Clarke--Agnes Clarke. I am the eldest of three sisters--the other two are married--you may have heard of my father--he wrote some beautiful hymns, and edited--"

"How old are you?" Madame broke in, still holding up the lamp.

The district-visitor gave a small nervous laugh. "Oh, I am not so very old--just over forty--well, to be quite truthful, nearly forty-seven. I feel so young sometimes that I cannot believe it, and then--at other times--when I am tired--I feel a hundred. Alas! I have many useless years behind me. But then we all have, don't you think? The great thing is to be resolved to make the most of every hour that remains to us. Mr. Empson at St. Jude's preached such a beautiful sermon last Sunday about that. He said we must give every unforgiving minute its sixty seconds' worth of distance run--I think he was quoting poetry. It is terrible to think of unforgiving minutes."

Madame did not appear to be listening. She said something to the older lady in a foreign tongue.

"May I sit down, please?" the visitor asked. "I have been walking a good deal to-day."

Madame waved her away from the chair she seemed about to take. "You will sit there, if you please," she said, pointing to a low couch beside the old woman.

The visitor was obviously embarrassed. She sat down on the edge of the couch, a faded nervous figure compared to the two masterful personages, and her fingers played uneasily with the handle of her satchel.

"Why do you come to this house?" Madame asked, and her tone was almost menacing. "We have nothing to do with your church."

"Oh, but you live in the parish, and it's such a large and difficult parish, and we want help from everyone. You cannot imagine how horrible some of the slums are-

-what bitter poverty in these bad times--and the worn-out mothers and the poor little neglected children. We are trying to make it a brighter place."

"Do you want money?"

"We always want money." The district-visitor's face wore an ingratiating smile. "But we want chiefly personal service. Mr. Empson always says that one little bit of personal service is better than a large subscription--better for the souls of the giver and the receiver."

"What do you expect to get from Outhwaite?"

"She is a young girl from a country village and alone in London. She is a good girl, I think, and I want to give her friends and innocent amusement. And I want her help too in our work."

The visitor started, for she found the hand of the old woman on her arm. The long fingers were running down it and pressing it. Hitherto the owner of the hand had not spoken, but now she said:

"This is the arm of a young woman. She has lied about her age. No woman of forty-seven ever had such an arm."

The soft passage of the fingers had suddenly become a grip of steel, and the visitor cried out.

"Oh, please, please, you are hurting me. . . . I do not tell lies. I am proud of my figure--just a little. It is like my mother's, and she was so pretty. But oh! I am not young. I wish I was. I'm afraid I'm quite old when you see me by daylight."

The grip had relaxed, and the visitor moved along the couch to be out of its reach. She had begun to cry in a helpless silly way, as if she were frightened. The two other women spoke to each other in a strange tongue, and then Madame said:

"I will not have you come here. I will not have you meddle with my servants. I do not care a fig for your church. If you come here again you will repent it."

Her tone was harsh, and the visitor looked as if her tears would begin again. Her discomposure had deprived her of the faded grace which had been in her air before, and she was now a pathetic and flimsy creature, like some elderly governess pleading against dismissal.

"You are cruel," she sighed. "I am so sorry if I have done anything wrong, but I meant it for the best. I thought that you might help me, for Elsie said you were clever and kind. Won't you think of poor Elsie? She is so young and far from her people. Mayn't she come to St. Jude's sometimes?"

"Outhwaite has her duties at home, and so I dare say have you, if truth was spoken. Bah! I have no patience with restless English old maids. They say an Englishman's house is his castle, and yet there is a plague of barren virgins always buzzing round it in the name of religion and philanthropy. Listen to me. I will not have you in this house. I will not have you talking to Outhwaite. I will not have an idle woman spying on my private affairs."

The visitor dabbed her eyes with a wisp of handkerchief. The old woman had stretched out her hand again and would have laid it on her breast, but she had started up violently. She seemed to be in a mood between distress and fear. She swallowed hard before her voice came, and then it quavered.

"I think I had better go. You have wounded me very deeply. I know I'm not clever, but I try so hard . . . and . . . and--it pains me to be misunderstood. I am afraid I have been tactless, so please forgive me . . . I won't come again . . . I'll pray that your hearts may some day be softened."

She seemed to make an effort to regain composure, and with a final dab at her eyes smiled shakily at the unrelenting Madame, who had touched an electric bell. She closed the folding-doors gently behind her, like a repentant child who has been sent to bed. The front room was in darkness, but there was a light in the hall where Miss Outhwaite waited to show her out.

At the front door the district-visitor had recovered herself.

"Elsie," she whispered, "Madame Breda does not want me to come again. But I must give you the hat I promised you. I'll have it ready by Thursday night. I'm afraid I may be rather late--after eleven perhaps--but don't go to bed till I come. I'll go round to the back door. It's such a smart pretty hat. I know you'll love it."

Once in the Square she looked sharply about her, cast a glance back at No. 4, and then walked away briskly. There was a man lounging at the corner to whom she spoke; he nodded and touched his hat, and a big motor car, which had been waiting in the shadows on the other side, drew up at the kerb. It seemed a strange conveyance for the district-visitor, but she entered it as if she were used to it, and when it moved off it was not in the direction of her rooms in Hampstead.

CHAPTER XVIII

THE NIGHT OF THE FIRST OF JUNE

The last two days of May were spent by me in the most miserable restlessness and despondency. I was cut off from all communications with my friends and I did not see how I could reopen them. For Medina, after his late furious busyness, seemed to have leisure again, and he simply never let me out of his sight. I dare say I might have managed a visit to the Club and a telephone message to Mary, but I durst not venture it, for I realised as I had never done before how delicate was the ground I walked on and how one false step on my part might blow everything sky-high. It would have mattered less if I had been hopeful of success, but a mood of black pessimism had seized me. I could count on Mary passing on my news to Macgillivray and on Macgillivray's taking the necessary steps to hasten the rounding-up; by the second of June Mercot would be restored to his friends, and Miss Victor too, if Mary had got on her track again. But who was arranging all that? Was Mary alone in the business, and where was Sandy? Mercot and Gaudian would be arriving in Scotland, and telegraphing to me any moment, and I could not answer them. I had the maddening feeling that everything was on a knife edge, that the chances of a blunder were infinite, and that I could do nothing. To crown all, I was tortured by the thought of David Warcliff. I had come to the conclusion that Mary's farewell words at Hill Street had meant nothing: indeed, I couldn't see how she could have found out anything about the little boy, for as yet we had never hit on the faintest clue, and the thought of him made success with the other two seem no better than failure. Likewise I was paying the penalty for the assurance about Medina which I had rashly expressed to Mary. I felt the terror of the man in a new way; he seemed to me impregnable beyond the hope of assault; and while I detested him I also shuddered at him--a novel experience, for hitherto I had always found that hatred drove out fear.

He was abominable during those two days--abominable but also wonderful. He seemed to love the sight of me, as if I were a visible and intimate proof of his power, and he treated me as an Oriental tyrant might treat a favourite slave. He unbent to me as a relief to his long spiritual tension, and let me see the innermost dreams of his heart. I realised with a shudder that he thought me a part of that hideous world he had created, and--I think for the first time in the business--I knew fear on my own account. If he dreamed I could fail him he would become a ravening beast. . . . I remember that he talked a good deal of politics, but, ye gods! what a change from the respectable conservative views which he had once treated me to--a Tory revival owing to the women and that sort of thing! He declared that behind all the world's creeds, Christianity, Buddhism, Islam and the rest, lay an ancient devil-worship and that it was raising its head again. Bolshevism, he said, was a form of it, and he attributed the success of Bolshevism in Asia to a revival of what he called Shamanism--I think that was the word. By his way of it the War had cracked the veneer everywhere and the real stuff was showing through. He rejoiced in the prospect, because the old faiths were not ethical codes but mysteries of the spirit, and they gave a chance for men who had found the ancient magic. I think he wanted to win everything that civilisation would give him, and then wreck it, for his hatred of Britain was only a part of his hatred of all that most men hold in love and repute. The common anarchist was a fool to him, for the cities and temples of the whole earth were not sufficient sacrifice to appease his vanity. I knew now what a Goth and a Hun meant, and what had been the temper of scourges like Attila and Timour. . . . Mad, you will say. Yes, mad beyond doubt, but it was the most convincing kind of madness. I had to fight hard by keeping my mind firm on my job, to prevent my nerve giving.

I went to bed on the last night of May in something very near despair, comforting myself, I remember, by what I had said to Mary, that one must go on to the finish and trust to luck changing in the last ten minutes. I woke to a gorgeous morning, and when I came down to breakfast I was in a shade better spirits. Medina proposed a run out into the country and a walk on some high ground. "It will give us an appetite for the Thursday dinner," he said. Then he went upstairs to telephone, and I was in the smoking-room filling my pipe when suddenly Greenslade was shown in.

I didn't listen to what he had to say, but seized a sheet of paper and scribbled a note: "Take this to the head porter at the Club and he will give you any telegram there is for me. If there is one from Gaudian, as there must be, wire him to start at once and go straight to Julius Victor. Then wire the Duke to meet him there. Do you understand? Now, what have you to tell me?"

"Only that your wife says things are going pretty well. You must turn up to-night at ten-thirty at the Fields of Eden. Also somehow you must get a latch-key for this house, and see that the door is not chained."

"Nothing more?"

"Nothing more."

"And Peter John?"

Greenslade was enlarging on Peter John's case when Medina entered. "I came round to tell Sir Richard that it was all a false alarm. Only the spring fret. The surgeon was rather cross at being taken so far on a fool's errand. Lady Hannay thought he had better hear it from me personally, for then he could start on his holiday with an easy mind."

I was so short with him that Medina must have seen how far my thoughts were from my family. As we motored along the road to Tring I talked of the approaching holiday, like a toadying schoolboy who has been asked to stay for a cricket week with some senior. Medina said he had not fixed the place, but it must be somewhere south in the sun--Algiers, perhaps, and the fringes of the desert, or better still some remote Mediterranean spot where we could have both sunlight and blue sea. He talked of the sun like a fire-worshipper. He wanted to steep his limbs in it, and wash his soul in light, and swim in wide warm waters. He rhapsodised like a poet, but what struck me about his rhapsodies was how little sensuous they were. The man's body was the most obedient satellite of his mind, and I don't believe he had any weakness of the flesh. What he wanted was a bath of radiance for his spirit.

We walked all day on the hills around Ivinghoe, and had a late lunch in the village inn. He spoke very little, but strode over the thymy downs with his eyes abstracted. Once, as we sat on the summit, he seemed to sigh and his face for a moment was very grave.

"What is the highest pleasure?" he asked suddenly. "Attainment? . . . No. Renunciation."

"So I've heard the parsons say," I observed.

He did not heed me. "To win everything that mankind has ever striven for, and then to cast it aside. To be Emperor of the Earth and then to slip out of the ken of mankind and take up the sandals and begging-bowl. The man who can do that has conquered the world-- he is not a king but a god. Only he must be a king first to achieve it."

I cannot hope to reproduce the atmosphere of that scene, the bare top of the hill in the blue summer weather, and that man, nearing, as he thought, the summit of success, and suddenly questioning all mortal codes of value. In all my dealings with Medina I was obsessed by the sense of my inferiority to him, that I was like a cab horse compared to an Arab stallion, and now I felt it like a blow in the face. That was the kind of thing Napoleon might have said--and done--had his schemes not gone astray. I knew I was contending with a devil, but I know also that it was a great devil.

We returned to town just in time to dress for dinner, and all my nervousness revived a hundredfold. This was the night of crisis, and I loathed having to screw myself up to emergencies late in the day. Such things should take place in the early morning. It was like going over the top in France; I didn't mind it so much when it happened during a drizzling dawn, when one was anyhow depressed and only half-awake, but I abominated an attack in the cold-blooded daylight, or in the dusk when one wanted to relax.

That evening I shaved, I remember, very carefully, as if I were decking myself out for a sacrifice. I wondered what would be my feelings when I next shaved. I wondered what Mary and Sandy were doing. . . .

What Mary and Sandy were doing at that precise moment I do not know, but I can now unfold certain contemporary happenings which were then hid from me. . . . Mercot and Gaudian were having a late tea in the Midland express, having nearly broken their necks in a furious motor race to catch the train at Hawick. The former was clean and shaven, his hair nicely cut, and his clothes a fairly well-fitting ready-made suit of flannels. He was deeply sunburnt, immensely excited, and constantly breaking in on Gaudian's study of the works of Sir Walter Scott.

"Newhover is to be let loose to-day. What do you suppose he'll do?" he asked.

"Nothing--yet awhile," was the answer. "I said certain things to him. He cannot openly go back to Germany, and I do not think he dare come to England. He fears the vengeance of his employer. He will disappear for a little, and then emerge in some new crime with a new name and a changed face. He is the eternal scoundrel."

The young man's face lighted up pleasantly. "If I live to be a hundred," he said, "I can't enjoy anything half as much as that clip I gave him on the jaw."

* * * * *

In a room in a country house on the Middlesex and Bucks borders Turpin was talking to a girl. He was in evening dress, a very point-device young man, and she was wearing a wonderful gown, grass-green in colour and fantastically cut. Her face was heavily made up, and her scarlet lips and stained eyebrows stood out weirdly against the dead white of her skin. But it was a different face from that which I first saw in the dancing-hall. Life had come back to it, the eyes were no longer dull like pebbles, but were again the windows of a soul. There was still fear in those eyes and bewilderment, but they were human again, and shone at this moment with a wild affection.

"I am terrified," she said. "I have to go to that awful place with that awful man. Please, Antoine, please, do not leave me. You have brought me out of a grave, and you cannot let me slip back again."

He held her close to him and stroked her hair.

"I think it is--how do you say it?--the last lap. My very dear one, we cannot fail our friends. I follow you soon. The grey man-- I do not know his name--he told me so, and he is a friend. A car is ordered for me half an hour after you drive off with that Odell."

"But what does it all mean?" she asked.

"I do not know, but I think--I am sure--it is the work of our friends. Consider, my little one. I am brought to the house where you are, but those who have charge of you do not know I am here. When Odell comes I am warned and locked in my room. I am not allowed out of it. I have had no exercise except sparring with that solemn English valet. He indeed has been most amiable, and has allowed me to keep myself in form. He boxes well, too, but I have studied under our own Jules and he is no match for me. But when the coast is clear I am permitted to see you, and I have waked you from sleep, my princess. Therefore so far it is good. As to what will happen to-night I do not know, but I fancy it is the end of our troubles. The grey man has told me as much. If you go back to that dance place, I think I follow you, and then we shall see something. Have no fear, little one. You go back as a prisoner no more, but as an actress to play a part, and I know you will play the part well. You will not permit the man Odell to suspect. Presently I come, and I think there will be an éclaircissement-- also, please God, a reckoning."

The wooden-faced valet entered and signed to the young man, who kissed the girl and followed him. A few minutes later Turpin was in his own room, with the door locked behind him. Then came a sound of the wheels of a car outside, and he listened with a smile on his face. As he stood before the glass putting the finishing touches to his smooth hair he was still smiling--an ominous smile.

* * * * *

Other things, which I did not know about, were happening that evening. From a certain modest office near Tower Hill a gentleman emerged to seek his rooms in Mayfair. His car was waiting for him at the street corner, but to his surprise as he got into it someone entered also from the other side, and the address to which the car ultimately drove was not Clarges Street. The office, too, which he had left locked and bolted was presently open, and men were busy there till far into the night--men who did not belong to his staff. An eminent publicist, who was the special patron of the distressed populations of Central Europe, was starting out to dine at his club, when he was unaccountably delayed, and had to postpone his dinner. The Spanish copper company in London Wall had been doing little business of late, except to give luncheons to numerous gentlemen, but that night its rooms were lit, and people who did not look like city clerks were investigating its documents. In Paris a certain French count of royalist proclivities, who had a box that night for the opera and was giving a little dinner beforehand, did not keep his appointment, to the discomfiture of his guests, and a telephone message to his rooms near the Champs Elysées elicited no reply. There was a gruff fellow at the other end who discouraged conversation. A worthy Glasgow accountant, an elder of the kirk and a prospective candidate for Parliament, did not return that evening to his family, and the police, when appealed to, gave curious answers. The office, just off Fleet Street, of the Christian Advocate of Milwaukee, a paper which cannot have had much of a circulation in England, was filled about six o'clock with silent preoccupied people, and the manager, surprised and rather wild of eye, was taken off in a taxi by two large gentlemen who had not had previously the honour of his acquaintance. Odd things seemed to be happening up and down the whole world. More than one ship did not sail at the appointed hour because of the interest of certain people in the passenger lists; a meeting of decorous bankers in Genoa was unexpectedly interrupted by the police; offices of the utmost respectability were occupied and examined by the blundering minions of the law; several fashionable actresses did not appear to gladden their admirers, and more than one pretty dancer was absent from the scene of her usual triumphs; a Senator in Western America, a high official in Rome, and four deputies in France found their movements restricted, and a Prince of the Church, after receiving a telephone message, fell to his prayers. A mining magnate in Westphalia, visiting Antwerp on business, found that he was not permitted to catch the train he had settled on. Five men, all highly placed, and one woman, for no cause apparent to their relatives, chose to rid themselves of life between the hours of six and seven. There was an unpleasant occurrence in a town on the Loire, where an Englishman, motoring to the south of France--a typical English squire, well known in hunting circles in Shropshire--was visited at his hotel by two ordinary Frenchmen, whose conversation seemed unpalatable to him. He was passing something from his waistcoat pocket to his mouth, when they had the audacity to lay violent hands on him, and to slip something over his wrists.

* * * * *

It was a heavenly clear evening when Medina and I set out to walk the half-mile to Mervyn Street. I had been so cloistered and harassed during the past weeks that I had missed the coming of summer. Suddenly the world seemed to have lighted up, and the streets were filled with that intricate odour of flowers, scent, hot wood pavements and asphalt which is the summer smell of London. Cars were waiting at house-doors, and women in pretty clothes getting into them; men were walking dinner-wards, with some of whom we exchanged greetings; the whole earth seemed full of laughter and happy movement. And it was shut off from me. I seemed to be living on the other side of a veil from this cheerful world, and I could see nothing but a lonely old man with a tragic face waiting for a lost boy. There was one moment at the corner of Berkeley Square when I accidentally jostled Medina, and had to clench my hands and bite my lips to keep myself from throttling him there and then.

The dining-room in Mervyn Street looked west, and the evening light strove with the candles on the table, and made a fairy-like scene of the flowers and silver. It was a full meeting--fifteen, I think--and the divine weather seemed to have put everybody in the best of spirits. I had almost forgotten Medina's repute with the ordinary man, and was staggered anew at the signs of his popularity. He was in the chair that evening, and a better chairman of such a dinner I have never seen. He had the right word for everybody, and we sat down to table like a party of undergraduates celebrating a successful cricket-match.

I was on the chairman's right hand, next to Burminster, with Palliser-Yeates opposite me. At first the talk was chiefly about the Derby and Ascot entries, about which Medina proved uncommonly well posted. He had a lot of inside knowledge from the Chilton stables, and showed himself a keen critic of form; also he was a perfect pundit about the pedigree of race-horses, and made Burminster, who fancied himself in the same line, gape with admiration. I suppose a brain like his could get up any subject at lightning speed, and he thought this kind of knowledge useful to him, for I don't believe he cared more for a horse than for a cat.

Once, during the Somme battle, I went to dine at a French château behind the lines, as the guest of the only son of the house. It was an ancient place, with fishponds and terraces, and there were only two people in it, an old Comtesse and a girl of fifteen called Simone. At dinner, I remember, a decrepit butler filled for me five glasses of different clarets, till I found the one I preferred. Afterwards I walked in the garden with Simone in a wonderful yellow twilight, watching the fat carp in the ponds, and hearing the grumbling of the distant guns. I felt in that hour the poignant contrast of youth and innocence and peace with that hideous world of battle a dozen miles off. To-night I had the same feeling--the jolly party of clean, hard, decent fellows, and the abominable hinterland of mystery and crime of which the man at the head of the table was the master. I must have been poor company, but happily everybody was talkative, and I did my best to grin at Burminster's fooling.

Presently the talk drifted away from sport. Palliser-Yeates was speaking, and his fresh boyish colour contrasted oddly with his wise eyes and grave voice.

"I can't make out what is happening," he said in reply to a remark of Leithen's. "The City has suddenly become jumpy, and there's no reason in the facts that I can see for it. There's been a good deal of realisation of stocks, chiefly by foreign holders, but there are a dozen explanations of that. No, there's a kind of malaise about, and it's unpleasantly like what I remember in June 1914. I was in Whittingtons' then, and we suddenly found the foundations beginning to crumble--oh yes, before the Serajevo murders. You remember Charlie Esmond's smash--well, that was largely due to the spasm of insecurity that shook the world. People now and then get a feeling in their bones that something bad is going to happen. And probably they are right, and it has begun to happen."

"Good Lord!" said Leithen. "I don't like this. Is it another war?"

Palliser-Yeates did not answer at once. "It looks like it. I admit it's almost unthinkable, but then all wars are really unthinkable, till you're in the middle of them."

"Nonsense!" Medina cried. "There's no nation on the globe fit to go to war, except half-civilised races with whom it is the normal condition. You forget how much we know since 1914. You couldn't get even France to fight without provoking a revolution--a middle- class revolution, the kind that succeeds."

Burminster looked relieved. "The next war," he said, "will be a dashed unpleasant affair. So far as I can see there will be very few soldiers killed, but an enormous number of civilians. The safest place will be the front. There will be such a rush to get into the army that we'll have to have conscription to make people remain in civil life. The embusqués will be the regulars."

As he spoke someone entered the room, and to my amazement I saw that it was Sandy.

He was looking extraordinarily fit and as brown as a berry. He murmured an apology to the chairman for being late, patted the bald patch on Burminster's head, and took a seat at the other end of the table. "I'll cut in where you've got to," he told the waiters. "No--don't bother about fish. I want some English roast beef and a tankard of beer."

There was a chorus of questions.

"Just arrived an hour ago. I've been in the East--Egypt and Palestine. Flew most of the way back."

He nodded to me, and smiled at Medina and raised his tankard to him.

I was not in a good position for watching Medina's face, but so far as I could see it was unchanged. He hated Sandy, but he didn't fear him now, when his plans had practically come to fruition. Indeed he was very gracious to him, and asked in his most genial tones what he had been after.

"Civil aviation," said Sandy. "I'm going to collar the pilgrim traffic to the Holy Places. You've been in Mecca?" he asked Pugh, who nodded. "You remember the hamelidari crowd who used to organise the transport from Mespot. Well, I'm a hamelidari on a big scale. I am prepared to bring the rank of hadji within reach of the poorest and feeblest. I'm going to be the great benefactor of the democracy of Islam, by means of a fleet of patched-up 'planes and a few kindred spirits that know the East. I'll let you fellows in on the ground-floor when I float my company. John"--he addressed Palliser-Yeates--"I look to you to manage the flotation."

Sandy was obviously ragging, and no one took him seriously. He sat there with his merry brown face, looking absurdly young and girlish, so that the most suspicious could have seen nothing more in him than the ordinary mad Englishman who lived for adventure and novelty. Me he never addressed, and I was glad of it, for I was utterly at sea. What did he mean by turning up now? What part was he to play in the events of the night? I could not have controlled the anxiety in my voice if I had been forced to speak to him.

A servant brought Medina a note, which he opened at leisure and read. "No answer," he said, and stuffed it into his pocket. I had a momentary dread that he might have got news of Macgillivray's round-up, but his manner reassured me.

There were people there who wanted to turn Sandy to other subjects, especially Fulleylove and the young Cambridge don, Nightingale. They wanted to know about South Arabia, of which at the time the world was talking. Some fellow, I forget his name, was trying to raise an expedition to explore it.

"It's the last geographical secret left unriddled," he said, and now he spoke seriously. "Well, perhaps not quite the last. I'm told there's still something to be done with the southern tributaries of the Amazon. Mornington, you know, believes there's a chance of finding some of the Inca people still dwelling in the unexplored upper glens. But all the rest have gone. Since the beginning of the century we've made a clean sweep of the jolly old mysteries that made the world worth living in. We have been to both the Poles, and to Lhasa, and to the Mountains of the Moon. We haven't got to the top of Everest yet, but we know what it is like. Mecca and Medina are as stale as Bournemouth. We know that there's nothing very stupendous in the Brahmaputra gorges. There's little left for a man's imagination to play with, and our children will grow up in a dull, shrunken world. Except, of course, the Great Southern Desert of Arabia."

"Do you think it can be crossed?" Nightingale asked.

"It's hard to say, and the man who tried it would take almighty risks. I don't fancy myself pinning my life to milk camels. They're chancy brutes."

"I don't believe there's anything there," said Fulleylove, "except eight hundred miles of soft sand."

"I'm not so sure. I've heard strange stories. There was a man I met once in Oman, who went west from the Manah oasis . . ."

He stopped to taste the club madeira, then set down the glass and looked at his watch.

"Great Scott!" he said. "I must be off. I'm sorry, Mr. President, but I felt I must see you all again. You don't mind my butting in?"

He was half-way to the door, when Burminster asked where he was going.

"To seek the straw in some sequestered grange. . . . Meaning the ten-thirty from King's Cross. I'm off to Scotland to see my father. Remember, I'm the last prop of an ancient house. Good- bye, all of you. I'll tell you about my schemes at the next dinner."

As the door closed on him I had a sense of the blackest depression and loneliness. He was my one great ally, and he came and disappeared like a ship in the night, without a word to me. I felt like a blind bat, and I must have showed my feeling in my face, for Medina saw it and put it down, I dare say, to my dislike of Sandy. He asked Palliser-Yeates to take his place. "It's not the Scotch express, like Arbuthnot, but I'm off for a holiday very soon, and I have an appointment I must keep." That was all to the good, for I had been wondering how I was to make an excuse for my visit to the Fields of Eden. He asked me when I would be back and I said listlessly within the next hour. He nodded. "I'll be home by then, and can let you in if Odell has gone to bed." Then with a little chaff of Burminster he left, so much at ease that I was positive he had had no bad news. I waited for five minutes and followed suit. The time was a quarter past ten.

* * * * *

At the entrance to the Club in Wellesley Street I expected to have some difficulty, but the man in the box at the head of the stairs, after a sharp glance at me, let me pass. He was not the fellow who had been there on my visit with Archie Roylance and yet I had a queer sense of having seen his face before. I stepped into the dancing-room with its heavy flavour of scent and its infernal din of mountebank music, sat down at a side table and ordered a liqueur.

There was a difference in the place, but at first I could not put my finger on it. Everything seemed the same; the only face I knew was Miss Victor's, and that had the same mask-like pallor; she was dancing with a boy, who seemed to be trying to talk to her and getting few replies. Odell I did not see, nor the Jew with the beard. I observed with interest the little casement above from which I had looked when I burgled the curiosity shop. There were fewer people to-night, but apparently the same class.

No, not quite the same class. The women were the same, but the men were different. They were older and more--how shall I put it?-- responsible-looking, and had not the air of the professional dancing partner or the young man on the spree. They were heavier footed, too, though good enough performers. Somehow I got the notion that most of them were not habitués of this kind of place and were here with a purpose.

As soon as this idea dawned on me I began to notice other things. There were fewer foreign waiters, and their number was steadily decreasing. Drinks would be ordered and would be long in coming; a servant, once he left the hall, seemed to be unaccountably detained. And then I observed another thing. There was a face looking down from the casement above; I could see it like a shadow behind the dirty glass.

Presently Odell appeared, a resplendent figure in evening dress, with a diamond solitaire in his shirt and a red silk handkerchief in his left sleeve. He looked massive and formidable, but puffier than ever, and his small pig's eyes were very bright. I fancied he had been having a glass or two, just enough to excite him. He swaggered about among the small tables, turning now and then to stare at the girl in green, and then went out again. I looked at my watch, and saw that it was a quarter to eleven.

When I lifted my head Mary had arrived. No more paint and powder and bizarre clothes. She was wearing the pale blue gown she had worn at our Hunt Ball in March, and her hair was dressed in the simple way I loved, which showed all the lights and shadows in the gold. She came in like a young queen, cast a swift glance round the room, and then, shading her eyes with her hand, looking up towards the casement. It must have been a signal, for I saw a hand wave.

As she stood there, very still and poised like a runner, the music stopped suddenly. The few men who were still dancing spoke to their partners and moved towards the door. I observed the bearded Jew hurry in and look round. A man touched him on the arm and drew him away, and that was the last I saw of him.

Suddenly Odell reappeared. He must have had some warning which required instant action. I shall never know what it was, but it may have announced the round-up, and the course to be followed towards the hostages. He signed peremptorily to Miss Victor and went forward as if to take her arm. "You gotta come along," I heard, when my eyes were occupied with a new figure.

Turpin was there, a pale taut young man with his brows knit, as I remembered them in tight corners in France. The green girl had darted to Mary's side, and Turpin strode up to her.

"Adela, my dear," he said, "I think it is time for you to be going home."

The next I saw was Miss Victor's hand clutching his arm and Odell advancing with a flush on his sallow face.

"You letta go that goil," he was saying. "You got no business with her. She's my goil."

Turpin was smiling. "I think not, my friend." He disengaged Adela's arm and put her behind him, and with a swift step struck Odell a resounding smack on the cheek with the flat of his hand.

The man seemed to swell with fury. "Hell!" he cried, with a torrent of Bowery oaths. "My smart guy, I've got something in my mitt for you. You for the sleep pill."

I would have given a fortune to be in Turpin's place, for I felt that a scrap was what I needed to knit up my ragged nerves. But I couldn't chip in, for this was clearly his special quarrel, and very soon I saw that he was not likely to need my help.

Smiling wickedly, he moved round the pug, who had his fists up. "Fiche-moi la paix," he crooned. "My friend, I am going to massacre you."

I stepped towards Mary, for I wanted to get the women outside, but she was busy attending to Miss Victor, whom the strain of the evening had left on the verge of swooning. So I only saw bits of the fight. Turpin kept Odell at long range, for in-fighting would have been fatal, and he tired him with his lightning movements, till the professional's bad training told and his wind went. When the Frenchman saw his opponent puffing and his cheeks mottling he started to sail in. That part I witnessed, and I hope that Mary and Miss Victor did not understand old Turpin's language, for he spoke gently to himself the whole time, and it was the quintessence of all the esoteric abuse that the French poilu accumulated during the four years of war. His tremendous reach gave him an advantage, he was as light on his legs as a fencer, and his arms seemed to shoot out with the force of a steam-hammer. I realised what I had never known before, that his slimness was deceptive, and that stripped he would be a fine figure of sinew and bone. Also I understood that a big fellow, however formidable, if he is untrained and a little drunk, will go down before speed and quick wits and the deftness of youth.

They fought for just over six minutes. Turpin's deadliest blows were on Odell's body, but the knockout came with one on the point of the chin. The big man crumpled up in a heap, and the back of his head banged on the floor. Turpin wrapped a wisp of a handkerchief round his knuckles, which had suffered from Odell's solitaire, and looked about him.

"What is to become of this offal?" he asked.

One of the dancers replied. "We will look after him, sir. The whole house is in our hands. This man is wanted on a good many grounds."

I walked up to the prostrate Odell, and took the latch-key from his waistcoat pocket. Turpin and Adela had gone, and Mary stood watching me. I observed that she was very pale.

"I am going to Hill Street," I said.

"I will come later," was her answer. "I hope in less than an hour. The key will let you in. There will be people there to keep the door open for me."

Her facc had the alert and absorbed look that old Peter Pienaar's used to have when he was after big game. There was no other word spoken between us. She entered a big saloon-car which was waiting in the street below, and I walked to Royston Square to find a taxi. It was not yet eleven o'clock.

CHAPTER XIX

THE NIGHT OF THE FIRST OF JUNE--LATER

A little after eleven that night a late walker in Palmyra Square would have seen a phenomenon rare in the dingy neighbourhood. A large motor-car drew up at the gate of No. 7, where dwelt the teacher of music who had long retired to rest. A woman descended, wearing a dark cloak and carrying a parcel, and stood for a second looking across the road to where the lean elms in the centre of the square made a patch of shade. She seemed to find there what she expected, for she hastened to the gate of No. 4. She did not approach the front door, but ran down the path to the back where the tradesmen called, and as soon as she was out of sight several figures emerged from the shadow and moved towards the gate.

Miss Outhwaite opened to her tap. "My, but you're late, miss," she whispered, as the woman brushed past her into the dim kitchen. Then she gasped, for some transformation had taken place in the district-visitor. It was no longer a faded spinster that she saw, but a dazzling lady, gorgeously dressed as it seemed to her, and of a remarkable beauty.

"I've brought your hat, Elsie," she said. "It's rather a nice one, and I think you'll like it. Now go at once and open the front door."

"But Madame . . ." the girl gasped.

"Never mind Madame. You are done with Madame. To-morrow you will come and see me at this address," and she gave her a slip of paper. "I will see that you do not suffer. Now hurry, my dear."

The girl seemed to be mesmerised, and turned to obey. The district-visitor followed her, but did not wait in the hall. Instead, she ran lightly up the stairs, guiding herself by a small electric torch, and when the front door was open and four silent figures had entered she was nowhere to be seen.

For the next quarter of an hour an inquisitive passer-by would have noted lights spring out and then die away in more than one room of No. 4. He might have also heard the sound of low excited speech. At the end of that space of time he would have seen the district- visitor descend the steps and enter the big car which had moved up to the gate. She was carrying something in her arms.

Within, in a back room, a furious woman was struggling with a telephone, from which she got no answer, since the line had been cut. And an old woman sat in a chair by the hearth, raving and muttering, with a face like death.

When I got to Hill Street, I waited till the taxi had driven off before I entered. There was a man standing in the porch of the house opposite, and as I waited another passed me, who nodded. "Good evening, Sir Richard," he said, and though I did not recognise him I knew where he came from. My spirits were at their lowest ebb, and not even the sight of these arrangements could revive them. For I knew that, though we had succeeded with Miss Victor and Mercot, we had failed with the case which mattered most. I was going to try to scare Medina or to buy him, and I felt that both purposes were futile, for the awe of him was still like a black fog on my soul.

I let myself in with Odell's latch-key and left the heavy door ajar. Then I switched on the staircase lights and mounted to the library. I left the lights burning behind me, for they would be needed by those who followed.

Medina was standing by the fireplace, in which logs had been laid ready for a match. As usual, he had only the one lamp lit, that on his writing-table. He had a slip of paper in his hand, one of the two which had lain in the top drawer, as I saw by the dates and the ruled lines. I fancy he had been attempting in vain to ring up Palmyra Square. Some acute suspicion had been aroused in him, and he had been trying to take action. His air of leisure was the kind which is hastily assumed; a minute before I was convinced he had been furiously busy.

There was surprise in his face when he saw me.

"Hullo!" he said, "how did you get in? I didn't hear you ring. I told Odell to go to bed."

I was feeling so weak and listless that I wanted to sit down, so I dropped into a chair out of the circle of the lamp.

"Yes," I said. "Odell's in bed all right. I let myself in with his key. I've just seen that Bowery tough put to sleep with a crack on the chin from Turpin. You know--the Marquis de la Tour du Pin."

I had a good strategic position, for I could see his face clearly and he could only see the outline of mine.

"What on earth are you talking about?" he said.

"Odell has been knocked out. You see, Turpin has taken Miss Victor back to her father." I looked at my watch. "And by this time Lord Mercot should be in London--unless the Scotch express is late."

A great tide of disillusion must have swept over his mind, but his face gave no sign of it. It had grown stern, but as composed as a judge's.

"You're behaving as if you were mad. What has come over you? I know nothing of Lord Mercot--you mean the Alcester boy? Or Miss Victor."

"Oh yes, you do," I said wearily. I did not know where to begin, for I wanted to get him at once to the real business. "It's a long story. Do you want me to tell it when you know it all already?" I believe I yawned and I felt so tired I could hardly put the sentences together.

"I insist that you explain this nonsense," was his reply. One thing he must have realised by now, that he had no power over me, for his jaw was set and his eyes stern, as if he were regarding not a satellite, but an enemy and an equal.

"Well, you and your friends for your own purposes took three hostages, and I have made it my business to free them. I let you believe that your tomfoolery had mastered me--your performance in this room and Newhover and Madame Breda and the old blind lady and all the rest of it. When you thought I was drugged and demented I was specially wide awake. I had to abuse your hospitality--rather a dirty game, you may say, but then I was dealing with a scoundrel. I went to Norway when you thought I was in bed at Fosse, and I found Mercot, and I expect at this moment Newhover is feeling rather cheap. . . . Miss Victor, too. She wasn't very difficult, once we hit on the Fields of Eden. You're a very clever man, Mr. Medina, but you oughtn't to circulate doggerel verses. Take my advice and stick to good poetry."

By this time the situation must have been clear to him, but there was not a quiver in that set hard face. I take off my hat to the best actor I have ever met--the best but one, the German count who lies buried at the farm of Gavrelle. "You've gone off your head," he said, and his quiet considerate voice belied his eyes.

"Oh no! I rather wish I had. I hate to think that there can be so base a thing in the world as you. A man with the brains of a god and living only to glut his rotten vanity! You should be scotched like a snake."

For a moment I had a blessed thought that he was about to go for me, for I would have welcomed a scrap like nothing else on earth. There may have been a flicker of passion, but it was quickly suppressed. His eyes had become grave and reproachful.

"I have been kind to you," he said, "and have treated you as a friend. This is my reward. The most charitable explanation is that your wits are unhinged. But you had better leave this house."

"Not before you hear me out. I have something to propose, Mr. Medina. You have still a third hostage in your hands. We are perfectly aware of the syndicate you have been working with--the Barcelona nut business, and the Jacobite count, and your friend the Shropshire master-of-hounds. Scotland Yard has had its hand over the lot for months, and to-night the hand will be closed. That shop is shut for good. Now listen to me, for I have a proposal to make. You have the ambition of the devil, and have already made for yourself a great name. I will do nothing to smirch that name. I will swear a solemn oath to hold my tongue. I will go away from England, if you like. I will bury the memory of the past months, and my knowledge will never be used to put a spoke in your wheel. Also, since your syndicate is burst up, you will want money. Well, I will give you one hundred thousand pounds. And in return for my silence and my cash I ask you to restore to me David Warcliff, safe and sane. Sane, I say, for whatever you have made of the poor little chap you have got to unmake it."

I had made up my mind about this offer as I came along in the taxi. It was a big sum, but I had more money than I needed, and Blenkiron, who had millions, would lend a hand.

His face showed no response, no interest, only the same stern melancholy regard.

"Poor devil!" he said. "You're madder than I thought."

My lassitude was disappearing, and I began to get angry.

"If you do not agree," I said, "I will blacken your reputation throughout the civilised world. What use will England have for a kidnapper and a blackmailer and--a--a bogus magician?"

But as I spoke I knew that my threats were foolish. He smiled, a wise, pitying smile, which made me shiver with wrath.

"No, it is you who will appear as the blackmailer," he said softly. "Consider. You are making the most outrageous charges. I don't quite follow your meaning, but clearly they are outrageous--and what evidence have you to support them? Your own dreams. Who will believe you? I have had the good fortune to make many friends, and they are loyal friends." There was a gentle regret in his voice. "Your story will be laughed to scorn. Of course people will be sorry for you, for you are popular in a way. They will say that a meritorious soldier, more notable perhaps for courage than for brains, has gone crazy, and they will comment on the long-drawn-out effects of the War. I must of course protect myself. If you blackguard me I will prosecute you for slander and get your mental condition examined."

It was only too true. I had no evidence except my own word. I knew that it would be impossible to link up Medina with the doings of the syndicate--he was too clever for that. His blind mother would die on the rack before she spoke, and his tools could not give him away, because they were tools and knew nothing. The world would laugh at me if I opened my mouth. At that moment I think I had my first full realisation of Medina's quality. Here was a man who had just learned that his pet schemes were shattered, who had had his vanity wounded to the quick by the revelation of how I had fooled him, and yet he could play what was left of the game with coolness and precision. I had struck the largest size of opponent.

"What about the hundred thousand pounds, then?" I asked. "That is my offer for David Warcliff."

"You are very good," he said mockingly. "I might feel insulted, if I did not know you were a lunatic."

I sat there staring at the figure in the glow of the one lamp, which seemed to wax more formidable as I looked, and a thousandfold more sinister. I saw the hideous roundness of his head, the mercilessness of his eyes, so that I wondered how I had ever thought him handsome. But now that most of his game was spoiled he only seemed the greater, the more assured. Were there no gaps in his defences? He had kinks in him--witness the silly rhyme which had given me the first clue. . . . Was there no weakness in that panoply which I could use? Physical fear--physical pain--could anything be done with that?

I got to my feet with a blind notion of closing with him. He divined my intention, for he showed something in his hand which gleamed dully. "Take care," he said. "I can defend myself against any maniac."

"Put it away," I said hopelessly. "You're safe enough from me. My God, I hope that somewhere there is a hell." I felt as feeble as a babe, and all the while the thought of the little boy was driving me mad.

* * * * *

Suddenly I saw Medina's eyes look over my shoulder. Someone had come into the room, and I turned and found Kharáma.

He was in evening dress, wearing a turban, and in the dusk his dark malign face seemed an embodied sneer at my helplessness. I did not see how Medina took his arrival, for all at once something seemed to give in my head. For the Indian I felt now none of the awe which I had for the other, only a flaming, overpowering hate. That this foul thing out of the East should pursue his devilries unchecked seemed to me beyond bearing. I forgot Medina's pistol and everything else, and went for him like a wild beast.

He dodged me, and, before I knew, had pulled off his turban, and tossed it in my face.

"Don't be an old ass, Dick," he said.

Panting with fury, I stopped short and stared. The voice was Sandy's, and so was the figure. . . . And the face, too, when I came to look into it. He had done something with the corners of his eyebrows and tinted the lids with kohl, but the eyes, which I had never before seen properly opened, were those of my friend.

"What an artist the world has lost in me!" he laughed, and tried to tidy his disordered hair.

Then he nodded to Medina. "We meet again sooner than we expected. I missed my train, and came to look for Dick. . . . Lay down that pistol, please. I happen to be armed too, you see. It's no case for shooting anyhow. Do you mind if I smoke?"

He flung himself into an arm-chair and lit a cigarette. Once more I was conscious of my surroundings, for hitherto for all I knew I might have been arguing in a desert. My eyes had cleared and my brain was beginning to work again. I saw the great room with its tiers of books, some glimmering, some dusky; Sandy taking his ease in his chair and gazing placidly up into Medina's face; Medina with his jaw set but his eyes troubled--yes, for the first time I saw flickers of perplexity in those eyes.

"Dick, I suppose, has been reasoning with you," Sandy said mildly. "And you have told him that he was a madman? Quite right. He is. You have pointed out to him that his story rests on his unsupported evidence, which no one will believe, for I admit it is an incredible tale. You have warned him that if he opens his mouth you will have him shut up as a lunatic. Is that correct, Dick?

"Well," he continued, looking blandly at Medina, "that was a natural view for you to take. Only, of course, you made one small error. His evidence will not be unsupported."

Medina laughed, but there was no ease in his laugh. "Who are the other lunatics?"

"Myself for one. You have interested me for quite a long time, Mr. Medina. I will confess that one of my reasons for coming home in March was to have the privilege of your acquaintance. I have taken a good deal of pains about it. I have followed your own line of studies--indeed, if the present situation weren't so hectic, I should like to exchange notes with you as a fellow-inquirer. I have traced your career in Central Asia and elsewhere with some precision. I think I know more about you than anybody else in the world."

Medina made no answer. The tables were turning, and his eyes were chained to the slight figure in the arm-chair.

"All that is very interesting," Sandy went on, "but it is not quite germane to the subject before us. Kharáma, whom we both remember in his pride, unfortunately died last year. It was kept very secret for obvious reasons--the goodwill of his business was very valuable and depended upon his being alive--and I only heard of it by a lucky accident. So I took the liberty of borrowing his name, Mr. Medina. As Kharáma I was honoured with your confidence. Rather a cad's trick, you will say, and I agree, but in an affair like this one has no choice of weapons. . . . You did more than confide in me. You trusted me with Miss Victor and the Marquis de la Tour du Pin, when it was important that they should be in safe keeping. . . . I have a good deal of evidence to support Dick."

"Moonshine!" said Medina. "Two lunacies do not make sense. I deny every detail of your rubbish."

"Out of the mouth of two or three witnesses," said Sandy pleasantly. "There is still a third . . . Lavater," he cried, "come in, we're ready for you."

There entered the grey melancholy man, whom I had seen on my first visit here, and in the house behind Little Fardell Street. I noticed that he walked straight to Sandy's chair, and did not look at Medina.

"Lavater you know already, I think. He used to be a friend of mine, and lately we have resumed the friendship. He was your disciple for some time, but has now relinquished that honour. Lavater will be able to tell the world a good deal about you."

Medina's face had become like a mask, and the colour had gone out of it. He may have been a volcano within, but outside he was cold ice. His voice, acid and sneering, came out like drops of chilly water.

"Three lunatics," he said. "I deny every word you say. No one will believe you. It is a conspiracy of madmen."

"Let's talk business anyhow," said Sandy. "The case against you is proven to the hilt, but let us see how the world will regard it. The strong point on your side is that people don't like to confess they have been fools. You have been a very popular man, Mr. Medina, and your many friends will be loath to believe that you are a scoundrel. You've the hedge of your reputation to protect you. Again, our story is so monstrous that the ordinary Englishman may call it unbelievable, for we are not an imaginative nation. Again we can get no help from the principal sufferers. Miss Victor and Lord Mercot can tell an ugly story of kidnapping, which may get a life-sentence for Odell, and for Newhover if he is caught, but which does not implicate you. That will be a stumbling-block to most juries, who are not as familiar with occult science as you and I. . . . These are your strong points. But consider what we can bring on the other side. You are a propagandist of genius, as I once told Dick, and I can explain just how you have fooled the world--your exploits with Denikin and such-like. Then the three of us can tell a damning story, and tell it from close quarters. It may sound wild, but Dick has some reputation for good sense, and a good many people think that I am not altogether a fool. Finally we have on our side Scotland Yard, which is now gathering in your associates, and we have behind us Julius Victor, who is not without influence. . . . I do not say we can send you to prison, though I think it likely, but we can throw such suspicion on you that for the rest of your days you will be a marked man. You will recognise that for you that means utter failure, for to succeed you must swim in the glory of popular confidence."

I could see that Medina was shaken at last. "You may damage me with your lies," he said slowly, "but I will be even with you. You will find me hard to beat."

"I don't doubt it," was Sandy's answer. "I and my friends do not want victory, we want success. We want David Warcliff."

There was no answer, and Sandy went on.

"We make you a proposal. The three of us will keep what we know to ourselves. We will pledge ourselves never to breathe a word of it-- if you like we will sign a document to say that we acknowledge our mistake. So far as we are concerned you may go on and become Prime Minister of Britain or Archbishop of Canterbury, or anything you jolly well like. We don't exactly love you, but we will not interfere with the adoration of others. I'll take myself off again to the East with Lavater, and Dick will bury himself in Oxfordshire mud. And in return we ask that you hand over to us David Warcliff in his right mind."

There was no answer.

Then Sandy made a mistake in tactics. "I believe you are attached to your mother," he said. "If you accept our offer she will be safe from annoyance. Otherwise--well, she is an important witness."

The man's pride was stung to the quick. His mother must have been for him an inner sanctuary, a thing apart from and holier than his fiercest ambitions, the very core and shrine of his monstrous vanity. That she should be used as a bargaining counter stirred something deep and primeval in him, something--let me say it-- higher and better than I had imagined. A new and a human fury burned the mask off him like tissue paper.

"You fools!" he cried, and his voice was harsh with rage. "You perfect fools! You will sweat blood for that insult."

"It's a fair offer," said Sandy, never moving a muscle. "Do I understand that you refuse?"

Medina stood on the hearthrug like an animal at bay, and upon my soul I couldn't but admire him. The flame in his face would have scorched most people into abject fear.

"Go to hell, the pack of you! Out of this house! You will never hear a word from me till you are bleating for mercy. Get out . . ."

* * * * *

His eyes must have been dimmed by his rage, for he did not see Mary enter. She had advanced right up to Sandy's chair before even I noticed her. She was carrying something in her arms, something which she held close as a mother holds a child.

It was the queer little girl from the house in Palmyra Square. Her hair had grown longer and fell in wisps over her brow and her pale tear-stained cheeks. A most piteous little object she was, with dull blind eyes which seemed to struggle with perpetual terror. She still wore the absurd linen smock, her skinny little legs and arms were bare, and her thin fingers clutched at Mary's gown.

Then Medina saw her, and Sandy ceased to exist for him. He stared for a second uncomprehendingly, till the passion in his face turned to alarm. "What have you done with her?" he barked, and flung himself forward.

I thought he was going to attack Mary, so I tripped him up. He sprawled on the floor, and since he seemed to have lost all command of himself I reckoned that I had better keep him there. I looked towards Mary, who nodded. "Please tie him up," she said, and passed me the turban cloth of the late Kharáma.

He fought like a tiger, but Lavater and I with a little help from Sandy managed to truss him fairly tight, supplementing the turban with one of the curtain cords. We laid him in an arm-chair.

"What have you done with her?" he kept on, screwing his head round to look at Mary.

I could not understand his maniacal concern for the little girl, till Mary answered, and I saw what he meant by "her."

"No one has touched your mother. She is in the house in Palmyra Square."

Then Mary laid the child down very gently in the chair where Sandy had been sitting and stood erect before Medina.

"I want you to bring back this little boy's mind," she said.

I suppose I should have been astonished, but I wasn't--at least not at her words, though I had not had an inkling beforehand of the truth. All the astonishment I was capable of was reserved for Mary. She stood there looking down on the bound man, her face very pale, her eyes quite gentle, her lips parted as if in expectation. And yet there was something about her so formidable, so implacable, that the other three of us fell into the background. Her presence dominated everything, and the very grace of her body and the mild sadness of her eyes seemed to make her the more terrifying. I know now how Joan of Arc must have looked when she led her troops into battle.

"Do you hear me?" she repeated. "You took away his soul and you can give it back again. That is all I ask of you."

He choked before he replied. "What boy? I tell you I know nothing. You are all mad."

"I mean David Warcliff. The others are free now, and he must be free to-night. Free, and in his right mind, as when you carried him off. Surely you understand."

There was no answer.

"That is all I ask. It is such a little thing. Then we will go away."

I broke in. "Our offer holds. Do as she asks, and we will never open our mouths about to-night's work."

He was not listening to me, nor was she. It was a duel between the two of them, and as she looked at him, his face seemed to grow more dogged and stone-like. If ever he had felt hatred it was for this woman, for it was a conflict between two opposite poles of life, two worlds eternally at war.

"I tell you I know nothing of the brat . . ."

She stopped him with lifted hand. "Oh, do not let us waste time, please. It is far too late for arguing. If you do what I ask we will go away, and you will never be troubled with us again. I promise--we all promise. If you do not, of course we must ruin you."

I think it was the confidence in her tone which stung him.

"I refuse," he almost screamed. "I do not know what you mean . . . I defy you. . . . You can proclaim your lies to the world. . . . You will not crush me. I am too strong for you."

There was no mistaking the finality of that defiance. I thought it put the lid on everything. We could blast the fellow's reputation no doubt, and win victory; but we had failed, for we were left with that poor little mindless waif. Mary's face did not change.

"If you refuse, I must try another way"; her voice was as gentle as a mother's. "I must give David Warcliff back to his father. . . . Dick," she turned to me, "will you light the fire."

I obeyed, not knowing what she meant, and in a minute the dry faggots were roaring up the chimney, lighting up our five faces and the mazed child in the chair.

"You have destroyed a soul," she said, "and you refuse to repair the wrong. I am going to destroy your body, and nothing will ever repair it."

Then I saw her meaning, and both Sandy and I cried out. Neither of us had led the kind of life which makes a man squeamish, but this was too much for us. But our protests died half-born, after one glance at Mary's face. She was my own wedded wife, but in that moment I could no more have opposed her than could the poor bemused child. Her spirit seemed to transcend us all and radiate an inexorable command. She stood easily and gracefully, a figure of motherhood and pity rather than of awe. But all the same I did not recognise her; it was a stranger that stood there, a stern goddess that wielded the lightnings. Beyond doubt she meant every word she said, and her quiet voice seemed to deliver judgment as aloof and impersonal as Fate. I could see creeping over Medina's sullenness the shadow of terror.

"You are a desperate man," she was saying. "But I am far more desperate. There is nothing on earth that can stand between me and the saving of this child. You know that, don't you? A body for a soul--a soul for a body--which shall it be?"

The light was reflected from the steel fire-irons, and Medina saw it and shivered.

"You may live a long time, but you will have to live in seclusion. No woman will ever cast eyes on you except to shudder. People will point at you and say 'There goes the man who was maimed by a woman-- because of the soul of a child.' You will carry your story written on your face for the world to read and laugh and revile."

She had got at the central nerve of his vanity, for I think that he was ambitious less of achievement than of the personal glory that attends it. I dared not look at her, but I could look at him, and I saw all the passions of hell chase each other over his face. He tried to speak, but only choked. He seemed to bend his whole soul to look at her, and to shiver at what he saw.

She turned her head to glance at the clock on the mantelpiece.

"You must decide before the quarter strikes," she said. "After that there will be no place for repentance. A body for a soul--a soul for a body."

Then from her black silk reticule she took a little oddly-shaped green bottle. She held it in her hand as if it had been a jewel, and I gulped in horror.

"This is the elixir of death--of death in life, Mr. Medina. It makes comeliness a mockery. It will burn flesh and bone into shapes of hideousness, but it does not kill. Oh no--it does not kill. A body for a soul--a soul for a body."

It was that, I think, which finished him. The threefold chime which announced the quarter had begun when out of his dry throat came a sound like a clucking hen's. "I agree," a voice croaked, seeming to come from without, so queer and far away it was.

"Thank you," she said, as if someone had opened a door for her. "Dick, will you please make Mr. Medina more comfortable. . . ."

The fire was not replenished, so the quick-burning faggots soon died down. Again the room was shadowy, except for the single lamp that glowed behind Medina's head.

I cannot describe that last scene, for I do not think my sight was clear, and I know that my head was spinning. The child sat on Mary's lap, with its eyes held by the glow of light. "You are Gerda . . . you are sleepy . . . now you sleep"--I did not heed the patter, for I was trying to think of homely things which would keep my wits anchored. I thought chiefly of Peter John.

Sandy was crouched on a stool by the hearth. I noticed that he had his hands on his knees, and that from one of them protruded something round and dark, like the point of a pistol barrel. He was taking no chances, but the thing was folly, for we were in the presence of far more potent weapons. Never since the world began was there a scene of such utter humiliation. I shivered at the indecency of it. Medina performed his sinister ritual, but on us spectators it had no more effect than a charade. Mary especially sat watching it with the detachment with which one watches a kindergarten play. The man had suddenly become a mountebank under those fearless eyes.

The voices droned on, the man asking questions, the child answering in a weak unnatural voice. "You are David Warcliff . . . you lost your way coming from school . . . you have been ill and have forgotten. . . . You are better now . . . you remember Haverham and the redshanks down by the river. . . . You are sleepy . . . I think you would like to sleep again."

Medina spoke. "You can wake him now. Do it carefully."

I got up and switched on the rest of the lights. The child was peacefully asleep in Mary's arms, and she bent and kissed him. "Speak to him, Dick," she said.

"Davie," I said loudly. "Davie, it's about time for us to get home."

He opened his eyes and sat up. When he found himself on Mary's knee, he began to clamber down. He was not accustomed to a woman's lap, and felt a little ashamed.

"Davie," I repeated. "Your father will be getting tired waiting for us. Don't you think we should go home?"

"Yes, sir," he said, and put his hand in mine.

* * * * *

To my dying day I shall not forget my last sight of that library-- the blazing lights which made the books, which I had never seen before except in shadow, gleam like a silk tapestry, the wood-fire dying on the hearth, and the man sunk in the chair. It may sound odd after all that had happened, but my chief feeling was pity. Yes, pity! He seemed the loneliest thing on God's earth. You see he had never had any friends except himself, and his ambitions had made a barrier between him and all humanity. Now that they were gone he was stripped naked, and left cold and shivering in the arctic wilderness of his broken dreams.

Mary leaned back in the car.

"I hope I'm not going to faint," she said. "Give me the green bottle, please."

"For Heaven's sake!" I cried.

"Silly!" she said. "It's only eau-de-cologne."

She laughed, and the laugh seemed to restore her a little though she still looked deadly pale. She fumbled in her reticule, and drew out a robust pair of scissors.

"I'm going to cut Davie's hair. I can't change his clothes, but at any rate I can make his head like a boy's again, so that his father won't be shocked."

"Does he know we are coming?"

"Yes. I telephoned to him after dinner, but of course I said nothing about Davie."

She clipped assiduously, and by the time we came to the Pimlico square where Sir Arthur Warcliff lived she had got rid of the long locks, and the head was now that of a pallid and thin but wonderfully composed little boy. "Am I going back to Dad?" he had asked, and seemed content.

I refused to go in--I was not fit for any more shocks--so I sat in the car while Mary and David entered the little house. In about three minutes Mary returned. She was crying, and yet smiling too.

"I made Davie wait in the hall, and went into Sir Arthur's study alone. He looked ill--and oh, so old and worn. I said: 'I have brought Davie. Never mind his clothes. He's all right!' Then I fetched him in. Oh, Dick, it was a miracle. That old darling seemed to come back to life. . . . The two didn't run into each other's arms . . . they shook hands . . . and the little boy bowed his head and Sir Arthur kissed the top of it, and said 'Dear Mouse- head, you've come back to me.' . . . And then I slipped away."

* * * * *

There was another scene that night in which I played a part, for we finished at Carlton House Terrace. Of what happened there I have only a confused recollection. I remember Julius Victor kissing Mary's hand, and the Duke shaking mine as if he would never stop. I remember Mercot, who looked uncommonly fit and handsome, toasting me in champagne, and Adela Victor sitting at a piano and singing to us divinely. But my chief memory is of a French nobleman whirling a distinguished German engineer into an extemporised dance of joy.

CHAPTER XX

MACHRAY

A week later, after much consultation with Sandy, I wrote Medina a letter. The papers said he had gone abroad for a short rest, and I could imagine the kind of mental purgatory he was enduring in some Mediterranean bay. We had made up our mind to be content with success. Victory meant a long campaign in the courts and the Press, in which no doubt we should have won, but for which I at any rate had no stomach. The whole business was a nightmare which I longed to shut the door on; we had drawn his fangs, and for all I cared he might go on with his politics and dazzle the world with his gifts, provided he kept his hands out of crime. I wrote and told him that; told him that the three people who knew everything would hold their tongues, but that they reserved the right to speak if he ever showed any sign of running crooked. I had no reply and did not expect one. I had lost all my hate for the man, and, so strangely are we made, what I mostly felt was compassion. We are all, even the best of us, egotists and self-deceivers, and without a little comfortable make-believe to clothe us we should freeze in the outer winds. I shuddered when I thought of the poor devil with his palace of cards about his ears and his naked soul. I felt that further triumph would be an offence against humanity.

He must have got my message, for in July he was back at his work, and made a speech at a big political demonstration which was highly commended in the papers. Whether he went about in society I do not know, for Sandy was in Scotland and I was at Fosse, and not inclined to leave it. . . . Meantime Macgillivray's business was going on, and the Press was full of strange cases, which no one seemed to think of connecting. I gathered from Macgillivray that though the syndicate was smashed to little bits he had failed to make the complete bag of malefactors that he had hoped. In England there were three big financial exposures followed by long sentences; in Paris there was a first-rate political scandal and a crop of convictions; a labour agitator and a copper magnate in the Middle West went to gaol for life, and there was the famous rounding-up of the murder gang in Turin. But Macgillivray and his colleagues, like me, had success rather than victory; indeed in this world I don't think you can get both at once--you must make your choice.

We saw Mercot at the "House" Ball at Oxford, none the worse for his adventures, but rather the better, for he was a man now and not a light-witted boy. Early in July Mary and I went to Paris for Adela Victor's wedding, the most gorgeous show I have ever witnessed, when I had the privilege of kissing the bride and being kissed by the bridegroom. Sir Arthur Warcliff brought David to pay us a visit at Fosse, where the boy fished from dawn to dusk, and began to get some flesh on his bones. Archie Roylance arrived and the pair took such a fancy to each other that the three of them went off to Norway to have a look at the birds on Flacksholm.

I was busy during those weeks making up arrears of time at Fosse, for my long absence had put out the whole summer programme. One day, as I was down in the Home Meadow, planning a new outlet for one of the ponds, Sandy turned up, announcing that he must have a talk with me and could only spare twenty minutes.

"When does your tenancy of Machray begin?" he asked.

"I have got it now--ever since April. The sea-trout come early there."

"And you can go up whenever you like?"

"Yes. We propose starting about the 5th of August."

"Take my advice and start at once," he said.

I asked why, though I guessed his reason.

"Because I'm not very happy about you here. You've insulted to the marrow the vainest and one of the cleverest men in the world. Don't imagine he'll take it lying down. You may be sure he is spending sleepless nights planning how he is to get even with you. It's you he is chiefly thinking about. Me he regards as a rival in the same line of business--he'd love to break me, but he'll trust to luck for the chance turning up. Lavater has been his slave and has escaped--but at any rate he once acknowledged his power. YOU have fooled him from start to finish and left his vanity one raw throbbing sore. He won't be at ease till he has had his revenge on you--on you and your wife."

"Peter John!" I exclaimed.

He shook his head. "No, I don't think so. He won't try that line again--at any rate not yet awhile. But he would be much happier, Dick, if you were dead."

The thought had been in my own mind for weeks, and had made me pretty uncomfortable. It is not pleasant to walk in peril of your life, and move about in constant expectation of your decease. I had considered the thing very carefully, and had come to the conclusion that I could do nothing but try to forget the risk. If I ever allowed myself to think about it, my whole existence would be poisoned. It was a most unpleasant affair, but after all the world is full of hazards. I told Sandy that.

"I'm quite aware of the danger," I said. "I always reckoned that as part of the price I had to pay for succeeding. But I'm hanged if I'm going to allow the fellow to score off me to the extent of disarranging my life."

"You've plenty of fortitude, old fellow," said Sandy, "but you owe a duty to your family and your friends. Of course you might get police protection from Macgillivray, but that would be an infernal nuisance for you, and, besides, what kind of police protection would avail against an enemy as subtle as Medina? . . . No, I want you to go away. I want you to go to Machray now, and stay there till the end of October."

"What good would that do? He can follow me there, if he wants to, and anyhow the whole thing would begin again when I came back."

"I'm not so sure," he said. "In three months' time his wounded vanity may have healed. It's no part of his general game to have a vendetta with you, and only a passion of injured pride would drive him to it. Presently that must die down, and he will see his real interest. Then as for Machray--why a Scotch deer-forest is the best sanctuary on earth. Nobody can come up that long glen without your hearing about it, and nobody can move on the hills without half a dozen argus-eyed stalkers and gillies following him. They're the right sort of police protection. I want you for all our sakes to go to Machray at once."

"It looks like funking," I objected.

"Don't be an old ass. Is there any man alive, who is not a raving maniac, likely to doubt your courage? You know perfectly well that it is sometimes a brave man's duty to run away."

I thought for a bit. "I don't think he'll hire ruffians to murder me," I said.

"Why."

"Because he challenged me to a duel. Proposed a place in the Pyrenees and offered to let me choose both seconds."

"What did you reply?"

"I wired, 'Try not to be a fool.' It looks as if he wanted to keep the job of doing me in for himself."

"Very likely, and that doesn't mend matters. I'd rather face half a dozen cut-throats than Medina. What you tell me strengthens my argument."

I was bound to admit that Sandy talked sense, and after he had gone I thought the matter out and decided to take his advice. Somehow the fact that he should have put my suspicions into words made them more formidable, and I knew again the odious feeling of the hunted. It was hardly fear, for I think that, if necessary, I could have stayed on at Fosse and gone about my business with a stiff lip. But all the peace of the place had been spoiled. If a bullet might at any moment come from a covert--that was the crude way I envisaged the risk--then good-bye to the charm of my summer meadows.

The upshot was that I warned Tom Greenslade to be ready to take his holiday, and by the 20th of July he and I and Mary and Peter John were settled in a little white-washed lodge tucked into the fold of a birch-clad hill, and looking alternately at a shrunken river and a cloudless sky, while we prayed for rain.

Machray in calm weather is the most solitary place on earth, lonelier and quieter even than a Boer farm lost in some hollow of the veld. The mountains rise so sheer and high, that it seems that only a bird could escape, and the road from the sea-loch ten miles away is only a strip of heather-grown sand which looks as if it would end a mile off at the feet of each steep hill-shoulder. But when the gales come, and the rain is lashing the roof, and the river swirls at the garden-edge, and the birches and rowans are tossing, then a thousand voices talk, and one lives in a world so loud that one's ears are deafened and one's voice acquires a sharp pitch of protest from shouting against the storm.

We had few gales, and the last week of July was a very fair imitation of the Tropics. The hills were cloaked in a heat haze, the Aicill river was a chain of translucent pools with a few reddening salmon below the ledges, the burns were thin trickles, the sun drew hot scents out of the heather and bog-myrtle, and movement was a weariness to man and beast. That was for the day- time; but every evening about five o'clock there would come a light wind from the west, which scattered the haze, and left a land swimming in cool amber light. Then Mary and Tom Greenslade and I would take to the hills, and return well on for midnight to a vast and shameless supper. Sometimes in the hot noontides I went alone, with old Angus the head stalker, and long before the season began I had got a pretty close knowledge of the forest.

The reader must bear with me while I explain the lie of the land. The twenty thousand acres of Machray extend on both sides of the Aicill glen, but principally to the south. West lies the Machray sea-loch, where the hills are low and green and mostly sheep- ground. East, up to the river-head, is Glenaicill Forest, the lodge of which is beyond the watershed on the shore of another sea- loch, and on our side of the divide there is only a stalker's cottage. Glenaicill is an enormous place, far too big to be a single forest. It had been leased for years by Lord Glenfinnan, an uncle of Archie Roylance, but he was a frail old gentleman of over seventy who could only get a stag when they came down to the low ground in October. The result was that the place was ridiculously undershot, and all the western end, which adjoined Machray, was virtually a sanctuary. It was a confounded nuisance, for it made it impossible to stalk our northern beat except in a south-west wind, unless you wanted to shift the deer on to Glenaicill, and that beat had all our best grazing and seemed to attract all our best heads.

Haripol Forest to the south was not so large, but I should think it was the roughest ground in Scotland. Machray had good beats south of the Aicill right up to the watershed, and two noble corries, the Corrie-na-Sidhe and the Corrie Easain. Beyond the watershed was the glen of the Reascuill, both sides of which were Haripol ground. The Machray heights were all over the 3,000 feet, but rounded and fairly easy going, but the Haripol peaks beyond the stream were desperate rock mountains--Stob Bán, Stob Coire Easain, Sgurr Mor--comprising some of the most difficult climbing in the British Isles. The biggest and hardest top of all was at the head of the Reascuill--Sgurr Dearg, with its two pinnacle ridges, its three prongs, and the awesome precipice of its eastern face. Machray marched with Haripol on its summit, but it wasn't often that any of our stalkers went that way. All that upper part of the Reascuill was a series of cliffs and chasms, and the red deer--who is no rock-climber--rarely ventured there. For the rest these four southern beats of ours were as delightful hunting-ground as I have ever seen, and the ladies could follow a good deal of the stalking by means of a big telescope in the library window of the Lodge. Machray was a young man's forest, for the hills rose steep almost from the sea-level, and you might have to go up and down 3,000 feet several times in a day. But Haripol--at least the north and east parts of it--was fit only for athletes, and it seemed to be its fate to fall to tenants who were utterly incapable of doing it justice. In recent years it had been leased successively to an elderly distiller, a young racing ne'er-do-well who drank, and a plump American railway king. It was now in the hands of a certain middle-aged Midland manufacturer, Lord Claybody, who had won an easy fortune and an easier peerage during the War. "Ach, he will be killed," Angus said. "He will never get up a hundred feet of Haripol without being killed." So I found myself, to my disgust, afflicted with another unauthorised sanctuary.

Angus was very solemn about it. He was a lean anxious man, just over fifty, with a face not unlike a stag's, amazingly fast on the hills, a finished cragsman, and with all the Highlander's subtle courtesy. Kennedy, the second stalker, was of Lowland stock; his father had come to the North from Galloway in the days of the boom in sheep, and had remained as a keeper when sheep prices fell. He was a sturdy young fellow, apt to suffer on steep slopes on a warm day, but strong as an ox and with a better head than Angus for thinking out problems of weather and wind. Though he had the Gaelic, he was a true Lowlander, plain-spoken and imperturbable. It was a contrast of new and old, for Kennedy had served in the War, and learned many things beyond the other's ken. He knew, for example, how to direct your eye to the point he wanted, and would give intelligent directions like a battery observer, whereas with Angus it was always "D'ye see yon stone? Ay, but d'ye see another stone?"--and so forth. Kennedy, when we sat down to rest, would smoke a cigarette in a holder, while Angus lit the dottle in a foul old pipe.

In the first fortnight of August we had alternate days of rain, real drenching torrents, and the Aicill rose and let the fish up from the sea. There were few sea-trout that year, but there was a glorious run of salmon.

Greenslade killed his first, and by the end of a week had a bag of twelve, while Mary, with the luck which seems to attend casual lady anglers, had four in one day to her own rod. Those were pleasant days, though there were mild damp afternoons when the midges were worse than tropical mosquitoes. I liked it best when a breeze rose and the sun was hot and we had all our meals by the waterside. Once at luncheon we took with us an iron pot, made a fire, and boiled a fresh-killed salmon "in his broo"--a device I recommend to anyone who wants the full flavour of that noble fish.

Archie Roylance arrived on August 16th, full of the lust of hunting. He reported that they had seen nothing remarkable in the way of birds at Flacksholm, but that David Warcliff had had great sport with the sea-trout. "There's a good boy for you," he declared. "First-class little sportsman, and to see him and his father together made me want to get wedded straight off. I thought him a bit hipped at Fosse, but the North Sea put him right, and I left him as jolly as a grig. By the way, what was the matter with him in the summer? I gathered that he had been seedy or something, and the old man can't let him out of his sight. . . . Let's get in Angus, and talk deer."

Angus was ready to talk deer till all hours. I had fixed the 21st for the start of the season, though the beasts were in such forward condition that we might have begun four days earlier. Angus reported that he had already seen several stags clear of velvet. But he was inclined to be doleful about our neighbours.

"My uncle Alexander is past prayin' for," said Archie. "He lives for that forest of his, and he won't have me there early in the season, for he says I have no judgment about beasts and won't listen to the stalkers. In October, you see, he has me under his own eye. He refuses to let a stag be killed unless it's a hummel or a diseased ancient. Result is, the place is crawlin' with fine stags that have begun to go back and won't perish till they're fairly moulderin'. Poor notion of a stud has my uncle Alexander. . . . What about Haripol? Who has it this year?"

When he heard he exclaimed delightedly. "I know old Claybody. Rather a good old fellow in his way, and uncommon free-handed. Rum old bird, too! He once introduced his son to me as 'The Honourable Johnson Claybody.' Fairly wallows in his peerage. You know he wanted to take the title of Lord Oxford, because he had a boy goin' up to Magdalen, but even the Heralds' College jibbed at that. But he'll never get up those Haripol hills. He's a little fat puffin' old man. I'm not very spry on my legs now, but compared to Claybody I'm a gazelle."

"He'll maybe have veesitors," said Angus.

"You bet he will. He'll have the Lodge stuffed with young men, for there are various Honourable Claybody daughters. Don't fancy they'll be much good on the hill, though."

"They will not be good, Sir Archibald," said the melancholy Angus. "There will have been some of them on the hill already. They will be no better than towrists."

"Towrists" I should explain were the poison in Angus's cup. By that name he meant people who trespassed on a deer forest during, or shortly before, the stalking season, and had not the good manners to give him notice and ask his consent. He distinguished them sharply from what he called "muntaneers," a class which he respected, for they were modest and civil folk who came usually with ropes and ice axes early in the spring, and were accustomed to feast off Angus's ham and eggs and thaw their frozen limbs by Angus's fire. If they came at other seasons it was after discussing their routes with Angus. They went where no deer could travel, and spent their time, as he said, "shamming themselves into shimneys." But the "towrist" was blatant and foolish and abundantly discourteous. He tramped, generally in a noisy party, over deer-ground, and, if remonstrated with, became truculent. A single member of the species could wreck the stalking on a beat for several days. "The next I see on Machray," said Angus, "I will be rolling down a big stone on him." Some of the Haripol guests, it appeared, were of this malign breed, and had been wandering thoughtlessly over the forest, thereby wrecking their own sport-- and mine.

"They will have Alan Macnicol's heart broke," he concluded. "And Alan was saying to me that they was afful bad shots. They was shooting at a big stone and missing it. And they will have little ponies to ride on up to the tops, for the creatures is no use at walking. I hope they will fall down and break their necks."

"They can't all be bad shots," said Archie. "By the way, Dick, I forgot to tell you. You know Medina, Dominick Medina? You once told me you knew him. Well, I met him on the steamer, and he said he was going to put in a week with old Claybody."

That piece of news took the light out of the day for me. If Medina was at Haripol it was most certainly with a purpose. I had thought little about the matter since I arrived at Machray, for the place had an atmosphere of impregnable seclusion, and I seemed to have shut a door on my recent life. I had fallen into a mood of content and whole-hearted absorption in the ritual of wild sport. But now my comfort vanished. I looked up at the grim wall of hills towards Haripol and wondered what mischief was hatching behind it.

I warned Angus and Kennedy and the gillies to keep a good look-out for trespassers. Whenever one was seen, they were to get their glasses on him and follow him and report his appearance and doings to me. Then I went out alone to shoot a brace of grouse for the pot, and considered the whole matter very carefully. I had an instinct that Medina had come to these parts to have a reckoning with me, and I was determined not to shirk it. I could not go on living under such a menace; I must face it and reach a settlement. To Mary, of course, I could say nothing, and I saw no use in telling either Archie or Greenslade. It was, metaphorically, and perhaps literally, my own funeral. But next morning I did not go fishing. Instead, I stayed at home and wrote out a full account of the whole affair up to Medina's appearance at Haripol, and I set down baldly what I believed to be his purpose. This was in case I went out one day and did not return. When I finished it, I put the document in my dispatch-box, and felt easier, as a man feels when he has made his will. I only hoped the time of waiting would not be prolonged.

The 21st was a glorious blue day, with a morning haze which promised heat. What wind there was came from the south-east, so I sent Archie out on the Corrie Easain beat, and went myself, with one gillie, to Clach Glas, which is the western peak on the north bank of the Aicill. I made a practice of doing my own stalking, and by this time I knew the ground well enough to do it safely. I saw two shootable stags, and managed to get within range of one of them, but spared him for the good of the forest, as he was a young beast whose head would improve. I had a happy and peaceful day, and found to my relief that I wasn't worrying about the future. The clear air and the great spaces seemed to have given me the placid fatalism of an Arab.

When I returned I was greeted by Mary with the news that Archie had got a stag, and that she had followed most of his stalk through the big telescope. Archie himself arrived just before dinner, very cheerful and loquacious. He found that his game leg made him slow, but he declared that he was not in the least tired. At dinner we had to listen to every detail of his day, and we had a sweep on the beast's weight, which Mary won. Afterwards in the smoking-room he told me more.

"Those infernal tailors from Haripol were out to-day. Pretty wild shots they must be. When we were lunchin' a spent bullet whistled over our heads--a long way off, to be sure, but I call it uncommon bad form. You should have heard Angus curse in Gaelic. Look here, Dick, I've a good mind to drop a line to old Claybody and ask him to caution his people. The odds are a million to one, of course, against their doin' any harm, but there's always that millionth chance. I had a feelin' to-day as if the War had started over again."

I replied that if anything of the sort happened a second time I would certainly protest, but I pretended to make light of it, as a thing only possible with that particular brand of wind. But I realised now what Medina's plans were. He had been tramping about Haripol, getting a notion of the lie of the land, and I knew that he had a big-game hunter's quick eye for country. He had fostered the legend of wild shooting among the Haripol guests, and probably he made himself the wildest of the lot. The bullet which sang over Archie's head was a proof, but he waited on the chance of a bullet which would not miss. If a tragedy happened, everyone would believe it was a pure accident, there would be heart-broken apologies, and, though Sandy and one or two others would guess the truth, nothing could be proved, and in any case it wouldn't help ME. . . . Of course I could stalk only on the north beats of Machray, but the idea no sooner occurred to me than I dismissed it. I must end this hideous suspense. I must accept Medina's challenge and somehow or other reach a settlement.

When Angus came in for orders, I told him that I was going stalking on the Corrie-na-Sidhe beat the day after to-morrow, and I asked him to send word privately to Alan Macnicol at Haripol.

"It will be no use, sir," he groaned. "The veesitors will no heed Alan."

But I told him to send word nevertheless. I wanted to give Medina the chance he sought. It was my business to draw his fire.

Next day we slacked and fished. In the afternoon I went a little way up the hill called Clach Glas, from which I could get a view of the ground on the south side of the Aicill. It was a clear quiet day, with the wind steady in the south-east, and promising to continue there. The great green hollow of Corrie-na-Sidhe was clear in every detail; much of it looked like a tennis-court, but I knew that what seemed smooth sward was really matted blaeberries and hidden boulders, and that the darker patches were breast-high bracken and heather. Corrie Easain I could not see, for it was hidden by the long spur of Bheinn Fhada, over which peeped the cloven summit of Sgurr Dearg. I searched all the ground with my glasses, and picked up several lots of hinds, and a few young stags, but there was no sign of human activity. There seemed to be a rifle out, however, on Glenaicill Forest, for I heard two far- away shots towards the north-east. I lay a long time amid the fern, with bees humming around me and pipits calling, and an occasional buzzard or peregrine hovering in the blue, thinking precisely the same thoughts that I used to have in France the day before a big action. It was not exactly nervousness that I felt, but a sense that the foundations of everything had got loose, and that the world had become so insecure that I had better draw down the blinds on hoping and planning and everything, and become a log. I was very clear in my mind that next day was going to bring the crisis.

Of course I didn't want Mary to suspect, but I forgot to caution Archie, and that night at dinner, as ill luck would have it, he mentioned that Medina was at Haripol. I could see her eyes grow troubled, for I expect she had been having the same anxiety as myself those past weeks, and had been too proud to declare it. As we were going to bed she asked me point-blank what it meant. "Nothing in the world," I said. "He is a great stalker and a friend of the Claybodys. I don't suppose he has the remotest idea that I am here. Anyhow that affair is all over. He is not going to cross our path if he can help it. The one wish in his heart is to avoid us."

She appeared to be satisfied, but I don't know how much she slept that night. I never woke till six o'clock, but when I opened my eyes I felt too big a load on my heart to let me stay in bed, so I went down to the Garden Pool and had a swim. That invigorated me, and indeed it was not easy to be depressed in that gorgeous morning, with the streamers of mist still clinging to the high tops, and the whole glen a harmony of singing birds and tumbling waters. I noticed that the wind, what there was of it, seemed to have shifted more to the east--a very good quarter for the Corrie- na-Sidhe beat.

Angus and Kennedy were waiting outside the smoking-room, and even the pessimism of the head stalker was mellowed by the weather. "I think," he said slowly, "we will be getting a sta-ag. There was a big beast on Bheinn Fhada yesterday--Kennedy seen him--a great beast he was--maybe nineteen stone, but Kennedy never right seen his head. . . . We'd better be moving on, sir."

Mary whispered in my ear. "There's no danger, Dick? You're sure?" I have never heard her voice more troubled.

"Not a scrap," I laughed. "It's an easy day and I ought to be back for tea. You'll be able to follow me all the time through the big telescope."

We started at nine. As I left, I had a picture of Greenslade sitting on a garden-seat busy with fly-casts, and Archie smoking his pipe and reading a three-days-old Times, and Peter John going off with his nurse, and Mary looking after me with a curious tense gaze. Behind, the smoke of the chimneys was rising straight into the still air, and the finches were twittering among the Prince Charlie roses. The sight gave me a pang. I might never enter my little kingdom again. Neither wife nor friends could help me: it was my own problem, which I must face alone.

We crossed the bridge, and began to plod upwards through a wood of hazels. In such fashion I entered upon the strangest day of my life.

CHAPTER XXI

HOW I STALKED WILDER GAME THAN DEER

I

9 A.M. TO 2.15 P.M.

Obviously I could make no plan, and I had no clear idea in my head as to what kind of settlement I wanted with Medina. I was certain that I should find him somewhere on the hill, and that, if he got a chance, he would try to kill me. The odds were, of course, against his succeeding straight off, but escape was not what I sought--I must get rid of this menace for ever. I don't think that I wanted to kill him, but indeed I never tried to analyse my feelings. I was obeying a blind instinct, and letting myself drift on the tides of fate.

Corrie-na-Sidhe is an upper corrie, separated from the Aicill valley by a curtain of rock and scree which I dare say was once the moraine of a glacier and down which the Alt-na-Sidhe tumbled in a fine chain of cascades. So steep is its fall that no fish can ascend it, so that, while at the foot it is full of sizable trout, in the Corrie itself it holds nothing, as Greenslade reported, but little dark fingerlings. It was very warm as we mounted the chaos of slabs and boulders, where a very sketchy and winding track had been cut for bringing down the deer. Only the toughest kind of pony could make that ascent.

Though the day was young the heat was already great, and the glen behind us swam in a glassy sheen. Kennedy, as usual, mopped his brow and grunted, but the lean Angus strode ahead as if he were on the flat.

At the edge of the corrie we halted for a spy. Deep hollows have a trick of drawing the wind, and such faint currents of air as I could detect seemed to be coming on our left rear from the north- east. Angus was positive, however, that though the south had gone out of the wind, it was pretty well due east, with no north in it, and maintained that when we were farther up the corrie we would have it fair on our left cheek. We were not long in finding beasts. There was a big drove of hinds on the right bank of the burn, and another lot, with a few small stags, on the left bank, well up on the face of Bheinn Fhada. But there was nothing shootable there.

"The big stags will be all on the high tops," said Angus. "We must be getting up to the burnhead."

It was easier said than done, for there were the hinds to be circumvented, so we had to make a long circuit far up the hill called Clonlet, which is the westernmost of the Machray tops south of the Aicill. It was rough going, for we mounted to about the 3,000 feet level, and traversed the hill-side just under the upper scarp of rock. Presently we were looking down upon the cup which was the head of the corrie, and over the col could see the peak of Stob Coire Easain and the ridge of Stob Bán, both on Haripol and beyond the Reascuill. We had another spy, and made out two small lots of stags on the other side of the Alt-na-Sidhe. They were too far off to get a proper view of them, but one or two looked good beasts, and I decided to get nearer.

We had to make a cautious descent of the hill-side in case of deer lying in pockets, for the place was seamed with gullies. Before we were half-way down I got my telescope on one of the lots, and picked out a big stag with a poor head, which clearly wanted shooting. Angus agreed, and we started down a sheltering ravine to get to the burnside. The sight of a quarry made me forget everything else, and for the next hour and a half I hadn't a thought in the world except how to get within range of that beast. One stalk is very much like another, and I am not going to describe this. The only trouble came from a small stag in our rear, which had come over Clonlet and got the scent of our track on the hill- face. This unsettled him and he went off at a great pace towards the top of the burn. I thought at first that the brute would go up Bheinn Fhada and carry off our lot with him, but he came to a halt, changed his mind, and made for the Haripol march and the col.

After that it was plain sailing. We crawled up the right of the Alt-na-Sidhe, which was first-class cover, and then turned up a tributary gully which came down from Bheinn Fhada. Indeed the whole business was too simple to be of much interest to anyone, except the man with the rifle. When I judged I was about the latitude of my stag, I crept out of the burn and reached a hillock from which I had a good view of him. The head, as I suspected, was poor--only nine points, though the horns were of the rough, thick, old Highland type, but the body was heavy, and he was clearly a back-going beast. After a wait of some twenty minutes he got up and gave me a chance at about two hundred yards, and I dropped him dead with a shot in the neck, which was the only part of him clear.

It was for me the first stag of the season, and it is always a pleasant moment when the tension relaxes and you light your pipe and look around you. As soon as the gralloch was over I proposed lunch, and we found for the purpose a little nook by a spring. We were within a few hundred yards of the Haripol march, which there does not run along the watershed but crosses the corrie about half a mile below the col. In the old days of sheep there had been a fence, the decaying posts of which could be observed a little way off on a knoll. Between the fence and the col lay some very rough ground, where the Alt-na-Sidhe had its source, ground so broken that it was impossible, without going a good way up the hill, to see from it the watershed ridge.

I finished Mary's stuffed scones and ginger biscuits, and had a drink of whisky and spring water, while Angus and Kennedy ate their lunch a few yards off in the heather. I was just lighting my pipe, when a sound made me pause with the match in my hand. A rifle bullet sang over my head. It was not very near--fifty feet or so above me, and a little to the left.

"The tamned towrists!" I heard Angus exclaim.

I knew it was Medina as certainly as if I had seen him. He was somewhere in the rough ground between the Haripol march and the col--probably close to the col, for the sound of the report seemed to come from a good way off. He could not have been aiming at me, for I was perfectly covered, but he must have seen me when I stalked the stag. He had decided that his chance was not yet come, and the shot was camouflage--to keep up the reputation of Haripol for wild shooting.

"It would be the staggie that went over the march," grunted Angus. "The towrists--to be shooting at such a wee beast!"

I had suddenly made up my mind. I would give Medina the opportunity he sought. I would go and look for him.

I got up and stretched my legs. "I'm going to try a stalk on my own," I told Angus. "I'll go over to Corrie Easain. You had better pull this beast down to the burnside, and then fetch the pony. You might send Hughie and the other pony up Glenaicill to the Mad Burn. If I get a stag I'll gralloch him and get him down somehow to the burn, so tell Hughie to look out for my signal. I'll wave a white handkerchief. The wind is backing round to the north, Angus. It should be all right for Corrie Easain, if I take it from the south."

"It would be better for Sgurr Dearg," said Angus, "but that's ower far. Have you the cartridges, sir?"

"Plenty," I said, patting a side pocket. "Give me that spare rope, Kennedy. I'll want it for hauling down my stag, if I get one."

I put my little .240 into its cover, nodded to the men, and turned down the gully to the main burn. I wasn't going to appear on the bare hill-side so long as it was possible for Medina to have a shot at me. But soon a ridge shut off the view from the Haripol ground, and I then took a slant up the face of Bheinn Fhada.

Mary had spent most of the morning at the big telescope in the library window. She saw us reach the rim of the corrie and lost us when we moved up the side of Clonlet. We came into view again far up the corrie, and she saw the stalk and the death of the stag. Then she went to luncheon, but hastened back in the middle of it in time to see me scrambling alone among the screes of Bheinn Fhada. At first she was reassured because she thought I was coming home. But when she realised that I was mounting higher and was making for Corrie Easain her heart sank, and, when I had gone out of view, she could do nothing but range miserably about the garden.

II

2.15 P.M. TO ABOUT 5 P.M.

It was very hot on Bheinn Fhada, for I was out of the wind, but when I reached the ridge and looked down on Corrie Easain I found a fair breeze, which had certainly more north than east in it. There was not a cloud in the sky, and every top for miles round stood out clear, except the Haripol peaks which were shut off by the highest part of the ridge I stood on. Corrie Easain lay far below--not a broad cup like Corrie-na-Sidhe, but a deep gash in the hills, inclined at such an angle that the stream in it was nothing but white water. We called it the Mad Burn--its Gaelic name, I think, was the Alt-a-mhuillin--and half-way up and just opposite me a tributary, the Red Burn, came down from the cliffs of Sgurr Dearg. I could see the northern peak of that mountain, a beautiful cone of rock, rising like the Matterhorn from its glacis of scree.

I argued that Medina would have seen me going up Bheinn Fhada and would assume that I was bound for Corrie Easain. He would re-cross the col and make for the Haripol side of the beallach which led from that corrie to the Reascuill. Now I wanted to keep the higher ground, where I could follow his movements, so it was my aim to get to the watershed ridge looking down on Haripol before he did. The wind was a nuisance, for it was blowing from me and would move any deer towards him, thereby giving him a clue to my whereabouts. So I thought that if I could once locate him, I must try to get the lee side of him. At that time I think I had a vague notion of driving him towards Machray.

I moved at my best pace along the east face of Bheinn Fhada towards the beallach--which was a deep rift in the grey rock-curtain through which deer could pass. My only feeling was excitement, such as I had never known before in any stalk. I slipped and sprawled among the slabs, slithered over the screes, had one or two awkward traverses round the butt-end of cliffs, but in about twenty minutes I was at the point where the massif of Bheinn Fhada joined the watershed ridge. The easy way was now to get on to the ridge, but I dared not appear on the sky-line, so I made a troublesome journey along the near side of the ridge-wall, sometimes out on the face of sheer precipices, but more often involved in a chaos of loose boulders which were the debris of the upper rocks. I was forced pretty far down, and eventually struck the beallach path about five hundred feet below the summit.

At the crest I found I had no view of the Reascuill valley--only a narrow corrie blocked by a shoulder of hill and the bald top of Stob Coire Easain beyond. A prospect I must have, so I turned east along the watershed ridge in the direction of Sgurr Dearg. I was by this time very warm, for I had come at a brisk pace; I had a rifle to carry, and had Angus's rope round my shoulders like a Swiss guide; I was wearing an old grey suit, which, with bluish stockings, made me pretty well invisible on that hill-side. Presently as I mounted the ridge, keeping of course under the sky- line, I came to a place where a lift of rock enabled me to clear the spurs and command a mile or so of the Reascuill.

The place was on the sky-line, bare and exposed, and I crawled to the edge where I could get a view. Below me, after a few hundred yards of rocks and scree, I saw a long tract of bracken and deep heather sweeping down to the stream. Medina, I made sure, was somewhere thereabouts, watching the ridge. I calculated that, with his re-crossing of the col at the head of Corrie-na-Sidhe and his working round the south end of Bheinn Fhada, he could not have had time to get to the beallach, or near the beallach, before me, and must still be on the lower ground. Indeed I hoped to catch sight of him, for, while I was assured he was pursuing me, he could not know that I was after him, and might be off his guard.

But there was no sign of life in that sunny stretch of green and purple, broken by the grey of boulders. I searched it with my glass and could see no movement except pipits, and a curlew by a patch of bog. Then it occurred to me to show myself. He must be made to know that I had accepted his challenge.

I stood up straight on the edge of the steep, and decided to remain standing till I had counted fifty. It was an insane thing to do, I dare say, but I was determined to force the pace. . . . I had got to forty-one without anything happening. Then a sudden instinct made me crouch and step aside. That movement was my salvation. There was a sound like a twanged fiddle-string, and a bullet passed over my left shoulder. I felt the wind of it on my cheek.

The next second I was on my back wriggling below the sky-line. Once there I got to my feet and ran--up the ridge on my left to get a view from higher ground. The shot, so far as I could judge, had come from well below and a little to the east of where I had been standing. I found another knuckle of rock, and crept to the edge of it, so that I looked from between two boulders into the glen.

The place was still utterly quiet. My enemy was hidden there, probably not half a mile off, but there was nothing to reveal his presence. The light wind stirred the bog cotton, a merlin sailed across to Stob Coire Easain, a raven croaked in the crags, but these were the only sounds. There was not even a sign of deer.

My glass showed that half-way down an old ewe was feeding--one of those melancholy beasts which stray into a forest from adjacent sheep-ground, and lead a precarious life among the rocks, lean and matted and wild, till some gillie cuts their throats. They are far sharper-eyed and quicker of hearing than a stag, and an unmitigated curse to the stalker. The brute was feeding on a patch of turf near a big stretch of bracken, and suddenly I saw her raise her head and stare. It was the first time I had ever felt well disposed towards a sheep.

She was curious about something in a shallow gully which flanked the brackens, and so was I. I kept my glass glued on her, and saw her toss her disreputable head, stamp her foot, and then heard her whistle through her nose. This was a snag Medina could not have reckoned with. He was clearly in that gully, working his way upward in its cover, unwitting that the ewe was giving him away. I argued that he must want to reach the high ground as soon as possible. He had seen me on the ridge, and must naturally conclude that I had beaten a retreat. My first business, therefore, was to reassure him.

I got my rifle out of its cover, which I stuffed into my pocket. There was a little patch of gravel just on the lip of the gully, and I calculated that he would emerge beside it, under the shade of a blaeberry-covered stone. I guessed right . . . I saw first an arm, and then a shoulder part the rushes, and presently a face which peered uphill. My glass showed me that the face was Medina's, very red, and dirty from contact with the peaty soil. He slowly reached for his glass, and began to scan the heights.

I don't know what my purpose was at this time, if indeed I had any purpose. I didn't exactly mean to kill him, I think, though I felt it might come to that. Vaguely I wanted to put him out of action, to put the fear of God into him, and make him come to terms. Of further consequences I never thought. But now I had one clear intention--to make him understand that I accepted his challenge.

I put a bullet neatly into the centre of the patch of gravel, and then got my glass on it. He knew the game all right. In a second like a weasel he was back in the gully.

I reckoned that now I had my chance. Along the ridge I went, mounting fast, and keeping always below the skyline. I wanted to get to the lee side of him and so be able to stalk him up-wind, and I thought that I had an opportunity now to turn the head of the Reascuill by one of the steep corries which descend from Sgurr Dearg. Looking back, it all seems very confused and amateurish, for what could I hope to do, even if I had the lee side, beyond killing or wounding him? and I had a chance of that as long as I had the upper ground. But in the excitement of the chase the mind does not take long views, and I was enthralled by the crazy sport of the thing. I did not feel any fear, because I was not worrying about consequences.

Soon I came to the higher part of the ridge and saw frowning above me the great rock face of Sgurr Dearg. I saw, too, a thing I had forgotten. There was no way up that mountain direct from the ridge, for the tower rose as perpendicular as a house-wall. To surmount it a man must traverse on one side or the other--on the Machray side by a scree slope, or on the Haripol side by a deep gully which formed the top of the corrie into which I was now looking. Across that corrie was the first of the great buttresses which Sgurr Dearg sends down to the Reascuill. It was the famous Pinnacle Ridge (as mountaineers called it); I had climbed it three weeks before and found it pretty stiff; but then I had kept the ridge all the way from the valley bottom, and I did not see any practicable road up the corrie face of it, which seemed nothing but slabs and rotten rocks, while the few chimneys had ugly overhangs.

I lay flat and reconnoitred. What was Medina likely to do? After my shot he could not follow up the ridge--the cover was too poor on the upper slopes. I reasoned that he would keep on in the broken ground up the glen till he reached this corrie, and try to find a road to the high ground either by the corrie itself or by one of the spurs. In that case it was my business to wait for him. But first I thought I had better put a fresh clip in my magazine, for the shot I had fired had been the last cartridge in the old clip.

It was now that I made an appalling discovery. I had felt my pockets and told Angus that I had plenty of cartridges. So I had, but they didn't fit. . . . I remembered that two days before I had lent Archie my .240 and had been shooting with a Mannlicher. What I had in my pocket were Mannlicher clips left over from that day. . . . I might chuck my rifle away, for it was no more use than a poker.

At first I was stunned by the fatality. Here was I, engaged in a duel on a wild mountain with one of the best shots in the world, and I had lost my gun! The sensible course would have been to go home. There was plenty of time for that, and long before Medina reached the ridge I could be in cover in the gorge of the Mad Burn. But that way out of it never occurred to me. I had chosen to set the course, and the game must be played out here and now. But I confess I was pretty well in despair and could see no plan. I think I had a faint hope of protracting the thing till dark and then trusting to my hill-craft to get even with him, but I had an unpleasant feeling that he was not likely to oblige me with so long a delay.

I forced myself to think, and decided that Medina would either come up the corrie or take the steep spur which formed the right-hand side of it and ran down to the Reascuill. The second route would give him cover, but also render him liable to a surprise at close quarters if I divined his intention, for I might suddenly confront him four yards off at the top of one of the pitches. He would therefore prefer the corrie, which was magnificently broken up with rocks, and seamed with ravines, and at the same time gave a clear view of all the higher ground.

With my face in a clump of louse-wort I raked the place with my glass; and to my delight saw deer feeding about half-way down in the right-hand corner. Medina could not ascend the corrie without disturbing these deer--a batch of some thirty hinds, with five small and two fairish stags among them. Therefore I was protected from that side, and had only the ridge to watch.

But as I lay there I thought of another plan. Medina, I was pretty certain, would try the corrie first, and would not see the deer till he was well inside it, for they were on a kind of platform which hid them from below. Opposite me across the narrow corrie rose the great black wall of the Pinnacle Ridge, with the wind blowing from me towards it. I remembered a trick which Angus had taught me--how a stalker might have his wind carried against the face of an opposite mountain and then, so to speak, reflected from it and brought back to his own side, so that deer below him would get it and move away from it up TOWARDS HIM. If I let my scent be carried to the Pinnacle Ridge and diverted back, it would move the deer on the platform up the corrie towards me. It would be a faint wind, so they would move slowly away from it--no doubt towards a gap under the tower of Sgurr Dearg which led to the little corrie at the head of the Red Burn. We never stalked that corrie, because it was impossible to get a stag out of it without cutting him up, so the place was a kind of sanctuary to which disturbed deer would naturally resort.

I stood on the sky-line, being confident that Medina could not yet be within sight, and let the wind, which was now stronger and nearly due north, ruffle my hair. I did this for about five minutes, and then lay down to watch the result, with my glass on the deer. Presently I saw them become restless, first the hinds and then the small stags lifting their heads and looking towards the Pinnacle Ridge. Soon a little fellow trotted a few yards up- hill; then a couple of hinds moved after him; and then by a sudden and simultaneous impulse the whole party began to drift up the corrie. It was a quiet steady advance; they were not scared, only a little doubtful. I saw with satisfaction that their objective seemed to be the gap which led over to the Red Burn.

Medina must see this and would assume that wherever I was I was not ahead of the deer. He might look for me on the other side, but more likely would follow the beasts so as to get the high ground. Once there he could see my movements, whether I was on the slopes of the Pinnacle Ridge, or down on the Machray side. He would consider no doubt that his marksmanship was so infinitely better than mine that he had only to pick me out from the landscape to make an end of the business.

What I exactly intended I do not know. I had a fleeting notion of lying hidden and surprising him, but the chances against that were about a million to one, and even if I got him at close quarters he was armed and I was not. I moved a little to the right so as to keep my wind from the deer, and waited with a chill beginning to creep over my spirit. . . . My watch told me it was five o'clock. Mary and Peter John would be having tea among the Prince Charlie roses, and Greenslade and Archie coming up from the river. It would be heavenly at Machray now among greenery and the cool airs of evening. Up here there was loveliness enough, from the stars of butterwort and grass of Parnassus by the wellheads to the solemn tops of Sgurr Dearg, the colour of stormy waves against a faint turquoise sky. But I knew now that the beauty of earth depends on the eye of the beholder, for suddenly the clean airy world around me had grown leaden and stifling.

III

5 P.M. TO ABOUT 7.30 P.M.

It was a good hour before he came. I had guessed rightly, and he had made the deduction I hoped for. He was following the deer towards the gap, assuming that I was on the Machray side. I was in a rushy hollow at a junction of the main ridge and the spur I have mentioned, and I could see him clearly as, with immense circumspection and the use of every scrap of cover, he made his way up the corrie. Once he was over the watershed, I would command him from the higher ground and have the wind to my vantage. I had some hope now, for I ought to be able to keep him on the hill till the light failed, when my superior local knowledge would come to my aid. He must be growing tired, I reflected, for he had had far more ground to cover. For myself I felt that I could go on for ever.

That might have been the course of events but for a second sheep. Sgurr Dearg had always been noted for possessing a few sheep even on its high rocks--infernal tattered outlaws, strays originally from some decent flock, but now to all intents a new species, unclassified by science. How they lived and bred I knew not, but there was a legend of many a good stalk ruined by their diabolical cunning. I heard something between a snort and a whistle behind me, and, screwing my head round, saw one of these confounded animals poised on a rock and looking in my direction. It could see me perfectly, too, for on that side I had no cover.

I lay like a mouse watching Medina. He was about half a mile off, almost on the top of the corrie, and he had halted for a rest and a spy. I prayed fervently that he would not see the sheep.

He heard it. The brute started its whistling and coughing, and a novice could have seen that it suspected something and knew where that something was. I observed him get his glass on my lair, though from the place where he was he could see nothing but rushes. Then he seemed to make up his mind and suddenly disappeared from view.

I knew what he was after. He had dropped into a scaur, which would take him to the sky-line and enable him to come down on me from above, while he himself would be safe from my observation.

There was nothing to do but to clear out. The spur dropping to the Reascuill seemed to give me the best chance, so I started off, crouching and crawling, to get round the nose of it and on to the steep glen-ward face.

It was a miserable job till I had turned the corner, for I expected every moment a bullet in my back. Nothing happened, however, and soon I was slithering down awesome slabs on to insecure ledges of heather. I am a fairly experienced mountaineer, and a lover of rock, but I dislike vegetation mixed up with a climb, and I had too much of it now. There was perhaps a thousand feet of that spur, and I think I must hold the speed record for its descent. Scratched, bruised, and breathless, I came to anchor on a bed of screes, with the infant Reascuill tumbling below me, and beyond it, a quarter of a mile off, the black cliffs of the Pinnacle Ridge.

But what was my next step to be? The position was reversed. Medina was above me with a rifle, and my own weapon was useless. He must find out the road I had taken and would be after me like a flame. . . . It was no good going down the glen; in the open ground he would get the chance of twenty shots. It was no good sticking to the spur or the adjacent ridge, for the cover was bad. I could not hide for long in the corrie. . . . Then I looked towards the Pinnacle Ridge and considered that, once I got into those dark couloirs, I might be safe. The Psalmist had turned to the hills for his help--I had better look to the rocks.

I had a quarter of a mile of open to cross, and a good deal more if I was to reach the ridge at a point easy of ascent. There were chimneys in front of me, deep black gashes, but my recollection of them was that they had looked horribly difficult, and had been plentifully supplied with overhangs. Supposing I got into one of them and stuck. Medina would have me safe enough. . . . But I couldn't wait to think. With an ugly cold feeling in my inside I got into the ravine of the burn, and had a long drink from a pool. Then I started down-stream, keeping close to the right-hand bank, which mercifully was high and dotted with rowan saplings. And as I went I was always turning my head to see behind and above me what I feared.

I think Medina, who of course did not know about my rifle, may have suspected a trap, for he came on slowly, and when I caught sight of him it was not on the spur I had descended but farther up the corrie. Two things I now realised. One was that I could not make the easy end of the Pinnacle Ridge without exposing myself on some particularly bare ground. The other was that to my left in the Ridge was a deep gully which looked climbable. Moreover, the foot of that gully was not a hundred yards from the burn, and the mouth was so deep that a man would find shelter as soon as he entered it.

For the moment I could not see Medina, and I don't thing he had yet caught sight of me. There was a trickle of water coming down from the gully to the burn, and that gave me an apology for cover. I ground my nose into the flowe-moss and let the water trickle down my neck, as I squirmed my way up, praying hard that my enemy's eyes might be sealed.

I think I had got about half-way, when a turn gave me a view of the corrie, and there was Medina halted and looking towards me. By the mercy of Providence my boots were out of sight, and my head a little lower than my shoulders, so that I suppose among the sand and gravel and rushes I must have been hard to detect. Had he used his telescope I think he must have spotted me, though I am not certain. I saw him staring. I saw him half-raise his rifle to his shoulder, while I heard my heart thump. Then he lowered his weapon, and moved out of sight.

Two minutes later I was inside the gully.

The place ran in like a cave with a sandy floor, and then came a steep pitch of rock, while the sides narrowed into a chimney. This was not very difficult. I swung myself up into the second storey, and found that the cleft was so deep that the back wall was about three yards from the opening, so that I climbed in almost complete darkness and in perfect safety from view. This went on for about fifty feet, and then, after a rather awkward chockstone, I came to a fork. The branch on the left looked hopeless, while that on the right seemed to offer some chances. But I stopped to consider, for I remembered something.

I remembered that this was the chimney which I had prospected three weeks before when I climbed the Pinnacle Ridge. I had prospected it from above, and had come to the conclusion that, while the left fork MIGHT be climbed, the right was impossible or nearly so, for, modestly as it began, it ran out into a fearsome crack on the face of the cliff, and did not become a chimney again till after a hundred feet of unclimbable rotten granite.

So I tried the left fork, which looked horribly unpromising. The first trouble was a chockstone, which I managed to climb round, and then the confounded thing widened and became perpendicular. I remembered that I had believed a way could be found by taking to the right-hand face, and in the excitement of the climb I forgot all precautions. It simply did not occur to me that this face route might bring me in sight of eyes which at all costs I must avoid.

It was not an easy business, for there was an extreme poverty of decent holds. But I have done worse pitches in my time, and had I not had a rifle to carry (I had no sling), might have thought less of it. Very soon I was past the worst, and saw my way to returning to the chimney, which had once more become reasonable. I stopped for a second to prospect the route, with my foot on a sound ledge, my right elbow crooked round a jag of rock, and my left hand, which held the rifle, stretched out so that my fingers could test the soundness of a certain handhold.

Suddenly I felt the power go out of those fingers. The stone seemed to crumble and splinters flew into my eye. There was a crashing of echoes, which drowned the noise of my rifle as it clattered down the precipice. I remember looking at my hand spread-eagled against the rock, and wondering why it looked so strange.

The light was just beginning to fail, so it must have been about half-past seven.

IV

7.30 P.M. AND ONWARDS

Had anything of the sort happened to me during an ordinary climb I should beyond doubt have lost my footing with the shock and fallen. But, being pursued, I suppose my nerves were keyed to a perpetual expectancy, and I did not slip. The fear of a second bullet saved my life. In a trice I was back in the chimney, and the second bullet spent itself harmlessly on the granite.

Mercifully it was now easier going--honest knee-and-back work, which I could manage in spite of my shattered fingers. I climbed feverishly with a cold sweat on my brow, but every muscle was in order, and I knew I would make no mistake. The chimney was deep, and a ledge of rock hid me from my enemy below. . . . Presently I squeezed through a gap, swung myself up with my right hand and my knees to a shelf, and saw that the difficulties were over. A shallow gully, filled with screes, led up to the crest of the ridge. It was the place I had looked down on three weeks before.

I examined my left hand, which was in a horrid mess. The top of my thumb was blown off, and the two top joints of my middle and third fingers were smashed to pulp. I felt no pain in them, though they were dripping blood, but I had a queer numbness in my left shoulder. I managed to bind the hand up in a handkerchief, where it made a gory bundle. Then I tried to collect my wits.

Medina was coming up the chimney after me. He knew I had no rifle. He was, as I had heard, an expert cragsman, and he was the younger man by at least ten years. My first thought was to make for the upper part of the Pinnacle Ridge, and try to hide or to elude him somehow till the darkness. But he could follow me in the transparent Northern night, and I must soon weaken from loss of blood. I could not hope to put sufficient distance between us for safety, and he had his deadly rifle. Somewhere in the night or in the dawning he would get me. No, I must stay and fight it out.

Could I hold the chimney? I had no weapon but stones, but I might be able to prevent a man ascending by those intricate rocks. In the chimney at any rate there was cover, and he could not use his rifle. . . . But would he try the chimney? Why should he not go round by the lower slopes of the Pinnacle Ridge and come on me from above?

It was the dread of his bullets that decided me. My one passionate longing was for cover. I might get him in a place where his rifle was useless and I had a chance to use my greater muscular strength. I did not care what happened to me provided I got my hands on him. Behind all my fear and confusion and pain there was now a cold fury of rage.

So I slipped back into the chimney and descended it to where it turned slightly to the left past a nose of rock. Here I had cover, and could peer down into the darkening deeps of the great couloir.

A purple haze filled the corrie, and the Machray tops were like dull amethysts. The sky was a cloudy blue sprinkled with stars, and mingled with the last flush of sunset was the first tide of the afterglow. . . . At first all was quiet in the gully. I heard the faint trickle of stones which are always falling in such a place, and once the croak of a hungry raven. . . . Was my enemy there? Did he know of the easier route up the Pinnacle Ridge? Would he not assume that if I could climb the cleft he could follow, and would he feel any dread of a man with no gun and a shattered hand?

Then from far below came a sound I recognised--iron hobnails on rock. I began to collect loose stones and made a little pile of such ammunition beside me. . . . I realised that Medina had begun the ascent of the lower pitches. Every breach in the stillness was perfectly clear--the steady scraping in the chimney, the fall of a fragment of rock as he surmounted the lower chockstone, the scraping again as he was forced out on to the containing wall. The light must have been poor, but the road was plain. Of course I saw nothing of him, for a bulge prevented me, but my ears told me the story. Then there was silence. I realised that he had come to the place where the chimney forked.

I had my stones ready, for I hoped to get him when he was driven out on the face at the overhang, the spot where I had been when he fired.

The sounds began again, and I waited in a desperate choking calm. In a minute or two would come the crisis. I remember that the afterglow was on the Machray tops and made a pale light in the corrie below. In the cleft there was still a kind of dim twilight. Any moment I expected to see a dark thing in movement fifty feet below, which would be Medina's head.

But it did not come. The noise of scraped rock still continued, but it seemed to draw no nearer. Then I realised that I had misjudged the situation. Medina had taken the right-hand fork. He was bound to, unless he had made, like me, an earlier reconnaissance. My route in the half-light must have looked starkly impossible.

The odds were now on my side. No man in the fast-gathering darkness could hope to climb the cliff face and rejoin that chimney after its interruption. He would go on till he stuck--and then it would not be too easy to get back. I reascended my own cleft, for I had a notion that I might traverse across the space between the two forks, and find a vantage point for a view.

Very slowly and painfully, for my left arm was beginning to burn like fire and my left shoulder and neck to feel strangely paralysed, I wriggled across the steep face till I found a sort of gendarme of rock, beyond which the cliff fell smoothly to the lip of the other fork. The great gully below was now a pit of darkness, but the afterglow still lingered on this upper section and I saw clearly where Medina's chimney lay, where it narrowed and where it ran out. I fixed myself so as to prevent myself falling, for I feared I was becoming light-headed. Then I remembered Angus's rope, got it unrolled, took a coil round my waist, and made a hitch over the gendarme.

There was a smothered cry from below, and suddenly came the ring of metal on stone, and then a clatter of something falling. I knew what it meant. Medina's rifle had gone the way of mine and lay now among the boulders at the chimney foot. At last we stood on equal terms, and, befogged as my mind was, I saw that nothing now could stand between us and a settlement.

It seemed to me that I saw something moving in the half-light. If it was Medina, he had left the chimney and was trying the face. That way I knew there was no hope. He would be forced back, and surely would soon realise the folly of it and descend. Now that his rifle had gone my hatred had ebbed. I seemed only to be watching a fellow-mountaineer in a quandary.

He could not have been forty feet from me, for I heard his quick breathing. He was striving hard for holds, and the rock must have been rotten, for there was a continuous dropping of fragments, and once a considerable boulder hurtled down the couloir.

"Go back, man," I cried instinctively. "Back to the chimney. You can't get further that way."

I suppose he heard me, for he made a more violent effort, and I thought I could see him sprawl at a foothold which he missed, and then swing out on his hands. He was evidently weakening, for I heard a sob of weariness. If he could not regain the chimney, there was three hundred feet of a fall to the boulders at the foot.

"Medina," I yelled, "I've a rope. I'm going to send it down to you. Get your arm in the loop."

I made a noose at the end with my teeth and my right hand, working with a maniac's fury.

"I'll fling it straight out," I cried. "Catch it when it falls to you."

My cast was good enough, but he let it pass, and the rope dangled down into the abyss.

"Oh, damn it, man," I roared, "you can trust me. We'll have it out when I get you safe. You'll break your neck if you hang there."

Again I threw, and suddenly the rope tightened. He believed my word, and I think that was the greatest compliment ever paid me in all my days.

"Now you're held," I cried. "I've got a belay here. Try and climb back into the chimney."

He understood and began to move. But his arms and legs must have been numb with fatigue, for suddenly that happened which I feared. There was a wild slipping and plunging, and then he swung out limply, missing the chimney, right on to the smooth wall of the cliff.

There was nothing for it but to haul him back. I knew Angus's ropes too well to have any confidence in them, and I had only the one good hand. The rope ran through a groove of stone which I had covered with my coat, and I hoped to work it even with a single arm by moving slowly upwards.

"I'll pull you up," I yelled, "but for God's sake give me some help. Don't hang on the rope more than you need."

My loop was a large one and I think he had got both arms through it. He was a monstrous weight, limp and dead as a sack, for though I could feel him scraping and kicking at the cliff face, the rock was too smooth for fissures. I held the rope with my feet planted against boulders, and wrought till my muscles cracked. Inch by inch I was drawing him in, till I realised the danger.

The rope was grating on the sharp brink beyond the chimney and might at any moment be cut by a knife-edge.

"Medina"--my voice must have been like a wild animal's scream-- "this is too dangerous. I'm going to let you down a bit so that you can traverse. There's a sort of ledge down there. For Heaven's sake go canny with this rope."

I slipped the belay from the gendarme, and hideously difficult it was. Then I moved farther down to a little platform nearer the chimney. This gave me about six extra yards.

"Now," I cried, when I had let him slip down, "a little to your left. Do you feel the ledge?"

He had found some sort of foothold, and for a moment there was a relaxation of the strain. The rope swayed to my right towards the chimney. I began to see a glimmer of hope.

"Cheer up," I cried. "Once in the chimney you're safe. Sing out when you reach it."

The answer out of the darkness was a sob. I think giddiness must have overtaken him, or that atrophy of muscle which is the peril of rock-climbing. Suddenly the rope scorched my fingers and a shock came on my middle which dragged me to the very edge of the abyss.

I still believe that I could have saved him if I had had the use of both my hands, for I could have guided the rope away from that fatal knife-edge. I knew it was hopeless, but I put every ounce of strength and will into the effort to swing it with its burden into the chimney. He gave me no help, for I think--I hope--that he was unconscious. Next second the strands had parted, and I fell back with a sound in my ears which I pray God I may never hear again-- the sound of a body rebounding dully from crag to crag, and then a long soft rumbling of screes like a snowslip.

* * * * *

I managed to crawl the few yards to the anchorage of the gendarme before my senses departed. There in the morning Mary and Angus found me.

THE END

The Island of Sheep

By

John Buchan

TO

J.N.S.B.

WHO KNOWS THE NORLANDS AND THE
WAYS OF THE WILD GEESE

PART I. Fosse

CHAPTER I

Lost Gods

I have never believed, as some people do, in omens and forewarnings, for the dramatic things in my life have generally come upon me as suddenly as a tropical thunderstorm. But I have observed that in a queer way I have been sometimes prepared for them by my mind drifting into an unexpected mood. I would remember something I had not thought of for years, or start without reason an unusual line of thought. That was what happened to me on an October evening when I got into the train at Victoria.

That afternoon I had done what for me was a rare thing, and attended a debate in the House of Commons. Lamancha was to make a full-dress speech, and Lamancha on such an occasion is worth hearing. But it was not my friend's eloquence that filled my mind or his deadly handling of interruptions, but a reply which the Colonial Secretary gave to a question before the debate began. A name can sometimes be like a scent or a tune, a key to long-buried memories. When old Melbury spoke the word 'Lombard,' my thoughts were set racing down dim alleys of the past. He quoted a memorandum written years ago and incorporated in the report of a certain Commission; 'A very able memorandum,' he called it, 'by a certain Mr. Lombard,' which contained the point he wished to make. Able! I should think it was. And the writer! To be described as 'a certain Mr. Lombard' showed how completely the man I once knew had dropped out of the world's ken.

I did not do justice to Lamancha's speech, for I thought of Lombard all through it. I thought of him in my taxi going to the station, and, when I had found my compartment, his face came between me and the pages of my evening paper. I had not thought much about him for years, but now Melbury's chance quotation had started a set of pictures which flitted like a film series before my eyes. I saw Lombard as I had last seen him, dressed a little differently from to-day, a little fuller in the face than we lean kine who have survived the War, with eyes not blurred from motoring, and voice not high-pitched like ours to override the din of our environment. I saw his smile, the odd quick lift of his chin--and I realized that I was growing old and had left some wonderful things behind me.

The compartment filled up with City men going home to their comfortable southern suburbs. They all had evening papers, and some had morning papers to finish. Most of them appeared to make this journey regularly, for they knew each other, and exchanged market gossip or commented on public affairs. A friendly confidential party; and I sat in my corner looking out of the window at another landscape than what some poet has called 'smoky dwarf houses,' and seeing a young man's face which was very different from theirs.

Lombard had come out to East Africa as secretary to a Government Commission, a Commission which he very soon manipulated as he pleased. I met him there when I was sent up on a prospecting job. He was very young then, not more than twenty-five, and he was in his first years at the Bar. He had been at one of the lesser public schools and at Cambridge, had been a good scholar, and was as full as he could hold of books. I remembered our first meeting in a cold camp on the Uasin Gishu plateau, when he quoted and translated a Greek line about the bitter little wind before dawn. But he never paraded his learning, for his desire was to be in complete harmony with his surroundings, and to look very much the pioneer. Those were the old days in East Africa, before the 'Happy Valley' and the remittance man and settlers who wanted self- government, and people's hopes were high. He was full of the heroes of the past, like Roddy Owen and Vandeleur and the Portals, and, except that he was a poor horseman, he had something in common with them. With his light figure and bleached fair hair and brown skin he looked the very model of the adventurous Englishman. I thought that there might be a touch of the Jew in his ancestry--something high-coloured and foreign at any rate, for he was more expansive and quickly fired than the rest of us. But on the whole he was as English as a Hampshire water-meadow. . . .

The compartment was blue with pipe-smoke. My companions were talking about rock-gardens. The man in the corner opposite me was apparently an authority on the subject, and he had much to say about different firms of nursery gardeners. He was blond, plump, and baldish, and had a pleasant voice whose tones woke a recollection which I could not fix. I thought that I had probably seen him at some company meeting. . . .

My mind went back to Lombard. I remembered how we had sat on a rock one evening looking over the trough of Equatoria, and, as the sun crimsoned the distant olive-green forests, he had told me his ambitions. In those days the after-glow of Cecil Rhodes's spell still lay on Africa, and men could dream dreams. Lombard's were majestic. 'I have got my inspiration,' he told me. His old hankerings after legal or literary or political success at home had gone. He had found a new and masterful purpose.

It was a very young man's talk. I was about his own age, but I had knocked about a bit and saw its crudity. Yet it most deeply impressed me. There were fire and poetry in it, and there was also a pleasant shrewdness. He had had his 'call' and was hastening to answer it. Henceforth his life was to be dedicated to one end, the building up of a British Equatoria, with the highlands of the East and South as the white man's base. It was to be both white man's and black man's country, a new kingdom of Prester John. It was to link up South Africa with Egypt and the Sudan, and thereby complete

Rhodes's plan. It was to be a magnet to attract our youth and a settlement ground for our surplus population. It was to carry with it a spiritual renaissance for England. 'When I think,' he cried, 'of the stuffy life at home! We must bring air into it, and instead of a blind alley give 'em open country. . . .'

The talk in the compartment was now of golf. Matches were being fixed up for the following Sunday. My vis-à-vis had evidently some repute as a golfer, and was describing how he had managed to lower his handicap. Golf 'shop' is to me the most dismal thing on earth, and I shut my ears to it. 'So I took my mashie, you know, my LITTLE mashie'--the words seemed to have all the stuffiness of which Lombard had complained. Here in perfection was the smug suburban life from which he had revolted. My thoughts went back to that hilltop three thousand miles and thirty years away. . . .

All of us at that time had talked a little grandiloquently, but with Lombard it was less a rhapsody than a passionate confession of faith. He was not quite certain about the next step in his own career. He had been offered a post on the staff of the Governor of X--, which might be a good jumping-off ground. There was the business side, too. He had the chance of going into the firm of Y--, which was about to spend large sums on African development. Money was important, he said, and cited Rhodes and Beit. He had not made up his mind, but ways and means did not greatly trouble him. His goal was so clear that he would find a road to it.

I do not think that I have ever had a stronger impression of a consuming purpose. Here was one who would never be content to settle among the fatted calves of the world. He might fail, but he would fail superbly.

'Some day,' I said, 'there will be a new British Dominion, and it will be called Lombardy. You have the right sort of name for Empire-making.'

I spoke quite seriously, and he took it seriously.

'Yes, I have thought of that,' he said, 'but it would have to be Lombardia.'

That was not the last time I saw him, for a year later he came down to Rhodesia, again on Government business, and we went through a rather odd experience together. But it was that hour in the African twilight that stuck in my memory. Here was a man dedicated to a crusade, ready to bend every power of mind and body to a high ambition, and to sacrifice all the softer things of life. I had felt myself in the presence of a young knight-errant, gravely entering upon his vows of service. . . .

I looked round the compartment at the flabby eupeptic faces which offered so stark a contrast to the one I remembered. The talk was still of golf, and the plump man was enlarging on a new steel- shafted driver. Well, it required all kinds to make a world. . . .

I had not seen Lombard for more than a quarter of a century. I had not even heard his name till that afternoon when Melbury mentioned him in the House. But at first I had often thought of him and waited for his avatar. I felt about him as Browning felt about Waring in the poem, for I believed that sooner or later--and rather soon than late--he would in some way or other make for himself a resounding name. I pictured him striding towards his goal, scorning half-achievements and easy repute, waiting patiently on the big chance and the great moment. Death alone, I was convinced, would stop him. And then the War came. . . .

The compartment had nearly emptied. Only my vis-à-vis remained. He had put up his feet on the seat and was skimming a motoring journal. . . .

Yes, I decided, the War had done it. Lombard would of course have fought--he was the kind of man who must--and in some obscure action in some part of the world-wide battlefield death had closed his dreams. Another case of unfulfilled renown. The thought made me melancholy. The fatted calves had always the best of it. Brains and high ambitions had perished, and the world was for the comfortable folk like the man opposite me.

We passed a station, and the next was obviously my companion's destination, for he got up, stretched his legs, and took down a parcel from the rack. He was carrying back the fish for dinner. He folded up his papers and lit a cigarette. Then for the first time he had a proper look at me, and in his face I saw slowly the dawning of recognition. He hesitated, and then he spoke my name.

'Hannay?' he said. 'Isn't it Dick Hannay?'

The voice did the trick with me, for I remembered those precise tones which he had never managed to slur and broaden after our outland fashion. My eyes cleared, and a response clicked in my brain. I saw, behind the well-covered cheeks and the full chin and the high varnish of good living, a leaner and younger face.

'Lombard!' I cried. 'I haven't seen or heard of you for twenty years. Do you know that the Colonial Secretary referred to you in the House this afternoon? I have been thinking of you ever since.'

He grinned and he held out his hand.

'What did he say? Nothing uncomplimentary, I hope. We've been having a bit of a controversy with his department over Irak. I've often heard of YOU, and read about you in the papers, and I've been hoping to run across you some day. You made some splash in the War. You're a K.C.B., aren't you? They offered me a knighthood too, but my firm thought I'd better stand out. Bad luck we didn't spot each other sooner, for I should have liked a yarn with you.'

'So should I,' was my answer. 'We have plenty to talk about.'

He replied to the question in my eye.

'Those were funny old times we had together. Lord, they seem a long way off now. What have I been doing since? Well, I went in for oil. I wish I had taken it up sooner, for I wasted several years chasing my tail. My firm made a pot of money in the War, and we haven't done so badly since.'

He was friendly and obviously glad to see me, but after so long a gap in our acquaintance he found it difficult to come to close quarters. So did I. I could only stare at his bland comfortable face and try in vain to recapture in it something that had gone for ever.

He felt the constraint. As we slackened speed, he dusted his hat, adjusted an aquascutum on his arm, and looked out of the window. I seemed to detect some effort in his geniality.

'I live down here,' he said. 'We mustn't lose sight of each other now we have foregathered. What about lunching together one day--my club's the Junior

Carlton? Or better still, come down to us for a week-end. I can give you quite a decent game of golf.'

The train drew up at a trim little platform covered with smooth yellow gravel, and a red station house, like a Wesleyan chapel, which in June would be smothered with Dorothy Perkins roses. There was a long line of fading geraniums, and several plots of chrysanthemums. Beyond the fence I could see a glistening tarmac road and the trees and lawns of biggish villas. I noticed a shining Daimler drawn up at the station entrance, and on the platform was a woman like a full-blown peony, to whom Lombard waved his hand.

'My wife,' he said, as he got out. 'I'd like you to meet her. . . . It's been great seeing you again. I've got a nice little place down here. . . . Promise you'll come to us for some week-end. Beryl will write to you.'

I continued my journey--I was going down to the Solent to see about laying up my boat, for I had lately taken to a mild sort of yachting--in an odd frame of mind. I experienced what was rare with me--a considerable dissatisfaction with life. Lombard had been absorbed into the great, solid, complacent middle class which he had once despised, and was apparently happy in it. The man whom I had thought of as a young eagle was content to be a barndoor fowl. Well, if he was satisfied, it was no business of mine, but I had a dreary sense of the fragility of hopes and dreams.

It was about myself that I felt most dismally. Lombard's youth had gone, but so had my own. Lombard was settled like Moab on his lees, but so was I. We all make pictures of ourselves that we try to live up to, and mine had always been of somebody hard and taut who could preserve to the last day of life a decent vigour of spirit. Well, I kept my body in fair training by exercise, but I realized that my soul was in danger of fatty degeneration. I was too comfortable. I had all the blessings a man can have, but I wasn't earning them. I tried to tell myself that I deserved a little peace and quiet, but I got no good from that reflection, for it meant that I had accepted old age. What were my hobbies and my easy days but the consolations of senility? I looked at my face in the mirror in the carriage back, and it disgusted me, for it reminded me of my recent companions who had pattered about golf. Then I became angry with myself. 'You are a fool,' I said. 'You are becoming soft and elderly, which is the law of life, and you haven't the grit to grow old cheerfully.' That put a stopper on my complaints, but it left me dejected and only half convinced.

CHAPTER II

Hanham Flats

All that autumn and early winter I had an uneasy feeling at the back of my mind. I had my pleasant country-gentleman's existence, but some of the zest had gone out of it. Instead of feeling, as I usually did, that it was the only life for a white man, I had an ugly suspicion that satisfaction with it meant that I had grown decrepit. And at the same time I had a queer expectation that an event was about to happen which would jog me out of my rut into something much less comfortable, and that I had better bask while the sun shone, for it wouldn't shine long. Oddly enough, that comforted me. I wasn't looking for any more difficult jobs in this world, but the mere possibility of one coming along allowed me to enjoy my slippered days with a quieter conscience.

In the week before Christmas came the second of the chain of happenings which were the prelude to this story. My son came into it, and here I must beg leave to introduce Peter John, now in his fourteenth year.

The kind of son I had hoped for when he was born was the typical English boy, good at games, fairly intelligent, reasonably honest and clean, the kind of public-school product you read about in books. I say had 'hoped for,' for it was the conventional notion most fathers entertain, though I doubt if I should have had much patience with the reality. Anyhow, Peter John was nothing like that. He didn't care a rush for the public-school spirit. He was rather a delicate child, but after he had passed his seventh birthday his health improved, and at his preparatory school he was a sturdy young ruffian who had no ailments except the conventional mumps and measles. He was tall for his age and rather handsome in his own way. Mary's glorious hair in him took the form of a sandy thatch inclining to red, but he had her blue eyes and her long, slim hands and feet. He had my mouth and my shape of head, but he had a slightly sullen air which he could have got from neither of us. I have seen him when he was perfectly happy looking the picture of gloom. He was very quiet in his manner; had a pleasant, low voice; talked little, and then with prodigiously long words. That came of his favourite reading, which was the Prophet Isaiah, Izaak Walton, and an eighteenth-century book on falconry translated from the French. One of his school reports said he spoke to his masters as Dr. Johnson might have addressed a street-arab.

He was never meant for any kind of schoolboy, for talk about 'playing the game' and the 'team spirit' and 'the honour of the old House' simply made him sick. He was pretty bad at his books, though he learned to slog along at them, but he was a hopeless duffer at games, which indeed he absolutely refused to learn. He detested his preparatory school, and twice ran away from it. He took the lowest form at his public school, where, however, he was happier, since he was left more to himself. He was the kind of boy who is the despair of masters, for he kept them at arm's length, and, though very gentle and well-mannered, could not help showing that he didn't think much of them. He didn't think much of the other boys either, but most were wise enough not to resent this, for he was for his weight one of the handiest people with his fists I have ever seen.

Peter John's lack of scholastic success used to worry Mary sometimes, but I felt that he was going his own way and picking up a pretty good education. He was truthful and plucky and kindly, and that was what I chiefly cared about. Also his mind never stopped working on his own subjects. He scarcely knew a bat from a ball, but he could cast a perfect dry-fly. He was as likely to be seen with a doll as with a tennis-racquet, but before he was twelve he was a good enough shot with his 16-bore to hold his own at any covert shoot. He had a funny aversion to horses, and wouldn't get into a saddle, but he was a genius with other animals. He could last out a long day in a deer forest when he had just entered his teens. Also he had made himself a fine field naturalist, and even Archie Roylance respected his knowledge of birds. He took up boxing very early and entirely of his own accord, because he didn't like the notion of being hit in the face, and thought that he had better conquer that funk. It proved to be a game in which he was a natural master, for he had a long reach and was wonderfully light on his feet. I would add that in his solemn way he was the friendliest of souls. The whole countryside within twenty miles of Fosse had a good word for him. One habit of his was to call everybody 'Mr.' and it was a queer thing to hear him 'mistering' some ragamuffin that I had helped on the Bench to send to jail a few months before. Peter John was getting his education from wild nature and every brand of country folk, and I considered that it was about as good a kind as any.

But it made him rather a misfit as a schoolboy, since he had none of the ordinary ambitions. He wouldn't have thanked you for putting him into the Eleven or the Boat, and the innocent snobbery of boys left him untouched. He simply wasn't running for the same stakes. I think he was respected by other boys, and on the whole rather liked by the masters, for he was always being forgiven for his breaches of discipline. Certainly he had an amazing knack of getting away with things. He twice stayed out all night, and wasn't expelled for it, since no one thought of disbelieving his explanation that in one case he had been timing a badger, and in the other waiting for an expected flight of grey-lags. He must have poached and never been caught, for he once sent his mother a brace of woodcock with his compliments, after she had complained in a letter that the birds were scarce with us. Also he kept hawks from his second week as a lower boy and nobody seemed to mind. At the date of which I write he was in his fourth half at school, and had at various times possessed goshawks, sparrow-hawks, merlins, and innumerable kestrels. The whole aviary in bandboxes used to accompany him backwards and forwards in the car. He had generally a hawk of sorts tucked away in his change coat, and once a party of American tourists got the surprise of their lives when they stopped a gentle-looking child to ask some question about the chapel, and suddenly saw a bird come out of the heavens and dive under his jacket.

Mary announced at breakfast that Peter John was cutting down costs and reducing his establishment. Archie Roylance, who was staying with us, looked up sympathetically from his porridge bowl.

'What? Sending his horses to Tattersall's and shutting up the old home? Poor old chap!'

'He has lost his she-goshawk, Jezebel,' Mary said, 'and can't afford another. Also white horse-leather for jesses costs too much. He has nothing left now except a couple of kestrels. If you want to live with death, Archie, keep hawks. They perish at the slightest provocation. Hang themselves, or have apoplexy, or a clot or something, or they get lost and catch their jesses in a tree and die of starvation. I'm always being heartbroken by Peter John coming in with a sad face in the morning to tell me that another bird is dead. Last summer he had four kestrels, called Violet, Slingsby, Guy, and Lionel. The most beloved little birds. They sat all day on their perches on the lawn, and scolded like fishwives if one of Dick's cockers came near them, for they couldn't abide black dogs. Not one is left. Jezebel killed one, two died of heart-disease, and one broke its neck in the stable-yard. Peter John got two eyasses to take their place from the Winstanleys' keeper, but they'll go the same road. And now Jezebel is a corpse. I never liked her, for she was as big as an eagle and had a most malevolent eye, but she was the joy of his soul, and it was wonderful to see her come back to the lure out of the clouds. Now he says he can't afford to buy any more and is putting down his establishment. He spent most of his allowance on hawks, and was always corresponding with distressed Austrian noblemen about them.'

Just then Peter John came in. He was apt to be late for breakfast, for, though he rose early, he had usually a lot to do in the morning. He was wearing old beagling breeches, and a leather- patched jacket which a tramp would have declined.

'I say, I'm sorry about your bad luck,' Archie told him. 'But you mustn't chuck falconry. Did you ever have a peregrine?'

'You mustn't talk like that,' Mary said. 'Say tassel-gentle or falcon-gentle, according to the sex. Peter John likes the old names, which he gets out of Gervase Markhan.'

'Because,' Archie continued, 'if you'd like it I can get you one.'

Peter John's eye brightened.

'Eyass or passage-hawk?' he asked.

'Eyass,' said Archie, who understood the language. 'Wattie Laidlaw got it out of a nest last spring. It's a female--a falcon, I suppose you'd call it--and an uncommon fine bird. She has been well manned too, and Wattie has killed several brace of grouse with her. But she can't go on with him, for he has too much to do, and he wrote last week that he wanted to find a home for her. I thought of young David Warcliff, but he has gone to France to cram for the Diplomatic. So what about it, my lad? She's yours for the taking.'

The upshot was that Peter John had some happy days making new hoods and leashes and jesses, and that a week later the peregrine arrived in a box from Crask. She was in a vile temper, and had damaged two of her tail feathers, so that he had to spend a day with the imping needle. If you keep hawks you have to be a pretty efficient nursemaid, and feed them and wash them and mend for them. She hadn't a name, so Peter John christened her Morag, as a tribute to her Highland ancestry. He spent most of his time in solitary communion with her till she got to know him, and in the first days of the New Year he had her in good train.

Always in January, if the weather is right, I go down to the Norfolk coast for a few days' goose-shooting. This year I had meant to take Peter John with me, for I thought that it would be a sport after his own heart. But it was plain that he couldn't leave Morag, and, as I wanted company, I agreed to her coming. So on the night of January 7 Peter John, his bird, and myself found ourselves in the Rose and Crown at Hanham, looking out over darkening mudflats which were being scourged by a south-west gale.

Peter John found quarters for Morag in an outhouse, and after supper went to bed, for he had to be up at four next morning. I looked into the bar for a word with the old fowlers, particularly my own man, Samson Grose, whom I had appointed to meet me there. There were only two in the place besides Samson, Joe Whipple and the elder Green, both famous names on the Hanham Flats, for the rest were at the evening flight and would look in later on their way home for the fowler's jorum of hot rum-and-milk. All three were elderly--two had fought in the Boer War--and they had the sallow skins and yellowish eyeballs of those who spend their lives between the Barrier Sands and the sea. I never met a tougher, and I never saw a less healthy-looking, breed than the Hanham men. They are a class by themselves, neither quite of the land nor quite of the water.

Samson had good news. The Baltic must be freezing, for wild fowl were coming in plentifully, though too thin to be worth shooting. Chiefly widgeon and teal, but he had seen a little bunch of pintail. I asked about geese. Plenty of brent, he said, which were no good, for they couldn't be eaten, and a few barnacle and bean. The white-fronts and the pink-foot were there, though they had been mortal hard to get near, but this gale was the right thing to keep them low. The evening flight was the better just now, Samson thought, for there was no moon, and geese, whose eyesight is no keener than yours or mine, left the shore fields early to get back to the sea, and one hadn't to wait so long. He fixed 4.15 as the time he was to meet us at the inn-door next morning; for dawn would not be till close on eight, and that gave us plenty of time to get well out into the mud and dig our 'graves.'

The three fowlers left for home, and I went into the bar-parlour to have a talk with the hostess, Mrs. Pottinger. When I first visited Hanham she and Job her husband were a handsome middle-aged pair, but Job had had his back broken in Hanham Great Wood when he was drawing timber, and his widow had suddenly become an old woman. It was a lonely business at the Rose and Crown, on the edge of the salt marshes and a couple of miles from any village, but that she minded not at all. Grieving for Job, and a kind of recurring fever which is common in those parts in the autumn, a sort of mild malaria, had taken the vigour out of her, and put a pathos like a dog's into her fine dark eyes. She ran the little inn for the fowlers, who had been Joe's friends, and did a small transport business with a couple of barges in the creek and an ancient carrier's cart along the shore. She took me in as a guest because Job had liked me, but, though the house had three or four snug little bedrooms, she did not hold it out as a place for visitors, and would have shut the door in the face of an inquisitive stranger.

I found her having a late cup of tea and looking better than I remembered her last time. A fire burned pleasantly, and window and roof-beams shook in the gale. She was full of inquiries about Peter John, who in his old-fashioned way had at once paid his respects to her and begged her tolerance for Morag. She shook her head when she heard that he was going out next morning. 'Pore little lad,' she said. 'Young bones want long lays abed.' Then she broke to me what I should never have suspected, that there was another guest in the Rose and Crown.

'Nice, quiet, young gentleman,' she said, 'and not so young neither, for he'll never see thirty-five again. Name of Smith--Mr. James Smith. He has been ill and wanted a place where folks wouldn't worrit him, and he heard of this house through my cousin Nance, her that's married on a groom at Lord Hanham's racin' stables. He wrote to me that pleadingly that I hadn't the heart to refuse, and now he's been a fortnight in the red room and become, as you might say, a part of the 'ousehold. Keeps hisself to hisself, but very pleasant when spoke to.'

I asked if Mr. Smith was a sportsman.

'No. He ain't no gunner. He lies late and goes early to bed, and in between walks up and down about the shore from Trim Head to Whaffle Creek. But this night he has gone out with the gunners-- for the first time. He persuaded Jeb Smart to take him, for, like your little gentleman son, he has a fancy for them wild birds.'

Mrs. Pottinger roused herself with difficulty out of her chair, for in spite of her grief she had put on weight since her husband's death.

'I think I hear them,' she said. 'Job always said I had the ears of a wild goose. I must see if Sue has kept up the fire in the bar, and got the milk 'ot. The pore things will be perished, for it's a wind to blow the tail off a cow, as folks say.'

Sure enough it was the returning fowlers. Two men, whose short frieze jackets made them seem as broad as they were long, were stamping their feet on the brick floor. A third was peeling off an airman's leather coat with a fleece lining, and revealing long legs in trench-boots and a long body in home-spun. I thought him one of the biggest fellows I had ever seen.

I knew the two Smarts, Jeb and Zeb--their shortened Christian names were a perpetual confusion--and they introduced me to the third, for Mrs. Pottinger, after satisfying herself that all was well, had retreated to her parlour. The fowlers drank their rum-and-milk and between gulps gave me their news. They had not done much--only a 'Charlie,' which is a goose that has been pricked by a shot and has dropped out of the flight. But they thought well of the chances in the morning, for the gale would last for twenty-four hours, there were plenty of white-fronts and pink-foot now out on the sea, and in that hurricane they would fly in low. Jeb and Zeb had never much conversation, and in three minutes they grunted good-night and took the road.

I was left with the third of the party. As I have said, he was a very big man, clean-shaven except for a small fair moustache, and with a shock of sandy hair which had certainly not been cut by a good barber. He was wearing an old suit of home-spun tweeds, and he had a pull-over of a coarse black-and-white pattern, the kind of thing you see in a Grimsby trawler. I would have set him down as a farmer of sorts, but for the fact that his skin was oddly pallid, and that his hands were not those of a man who had ever done manual toil. He had bowed to me in a way which was not quite English. I said something about the weather, and he replied in good English with just a suspicion of a foreign accent.

Clearly he had not expected to find another guest in the Rose and Crown, for his first glance at me had been one of extreme surprise. More than surprise. I could have sworn that it was alarm, almost panic, till something about me reassured him. But his eyes kept searching my face, as if they were looking for something which he dreaded to find there. Then, when I spoke, he appeared to be more at his ease. I told him that I had come to Hanham for some years, and that I had brought my boy with me, and hoped to show him a little sport.

'Your boy?' he asked. 'He is young?'

When I told him nearly fourteen, he seemed to be relieved.

'The boy--he is fond of shooting?'

I said that Peter John had never been after geese before, but that he was mad about birds.

'I too,' he said. 'I do not shoot, but I love to watch the birds. There are many here which I have not seen before, and some which I have seen rarely are here in multitudes.'

As I went to bed I speculated about Mr. Smith. That he was a foreigner I judged both from his slight accent and from his rather elaborate English. I thought that he might be a German or a Dutchman or a Swede, perhaps a field-naturalist who was visiting Hanham just as Archie Roylance used to visit Texel. I liked his face, which was kindly and shy, and I decided that, since he seemed to be a lonely fellow, Peter John and I would offer to take him out with us. But there were two things about him that puzzled me. One was that I had a dim consciousness of having seen him before, or at least some one very like him. The set of his jaw and the way his nose sprang sharply from below his forehead were familiar. The other was that spasm of fright in his eyes when he had first seen me. He could not be a criminal in hiding--he looked far too honest and wholesome for that--but he was in fear, in fear of some one or something coming suddenly upon him even in this outlandish corner of

England. I fell asleep wondering what might lurk in the past of this simple, substantial being.

At four o'clock we were called, and after a cup of tea joined Samson on the jetty, and by the light of an exiguous electric torch started to find our way over the dry sand, and out into the salt marshes. The gale had dropped a little, but the wind blew cruelly on our right cheek, and the whole dark world was an ice-box. Peter John and I wore rubber knee-boots, beastly things to walk in, and, not having Samson's experience, we plunged several times up to the waist in the little creeks. Both of us had 8-bore guns firing cartridges three and a half inches long, while Samson had a 12-bore with a barrel as long as a Boer roer. By and by we were free of the crab grass and out on the oozy mud-flats. There Samson halted us, and with the coal-shovels from our goose-bags we started to dig our 'graves,' piling up a rampart of mud on the sea side from which the birds were coming. After that there fell a silence like death, while each of us crouched in our holes about a hundred yards apart, peering up with chattering teeth into the thick darkness, and waiting for that slow lightening which would mean the dawn.

A little after six there came a sound above us like the roar of a second gale, the first having subsided to a fairly steady south- west wind. I knew from experience what it was, and I had warned Peter John about it. It was thousands and thousands of waders, stints and knots and redshanks and the like, flying in batches, each batch making the noise of a great wave on a beach. Then for a little there was stillness again, and the darkness thinned ever so little, so that I believed that I must be seeing at least fifty yards. But I wasn't, for when the duck began I could only hear the beat of their wings, though I knew that they were flying low.

There was another spell of eerie quiet, and then it seemed that the world was changing. The clouds were drifting apart, and I suddenly saw a brilliant star-sown patch of sky. Then the whole horizon turned from velvet-black to grey, grey rimmed in the east with a strip of intense yellow light. I looked behind me and could see the outlines of the low coast, with blurs which I knew were woods, and with one church-steeple pricking fantastically into the pale brume.

It was the time for the geese, and in an instant they were on us. They came in wedge after wedge, shadowy as ghosts against the faintly flushing clouds, but cut sharp against the violet lagoon of clear sky. They were not babbling, as they do in an evening flight from the fields to the sea, but chuckling and talking low to themselves. From the sound I knew they were pink-foot, for the white-fronts make a throatier noise. It was a sight that always takes my breath away, this multitude of wild living things surging out of the darkness and the deep, as steady in their discipline as a Guards battalion. I never wanted to shoot and I never shot first; it was only the thunder of Samson's 12-bore that woke me to my job.

An old gander, which was the leading bird in one wedge, suddenly trumpeted. Him Samson got; he fell with a thud five yards from my head, and the echo of the shot woke the marshes for miles. It was all our bag. The birds flew pretty high, and Peter John had the best chance, but no sign of life came from his trench. As soon as the geese had passed, and a double wedge of whistling widgeon had followed very high up, I walked over to investigate. I found my son sitting on his mud rampart with a rapt face. 'I couldn't shoot,' he stammered; 'they were too beautiful. To-morrow I'll bring Morag. I don't mind hawking a goose, for that's a fair fight, but I won't kill them with a gun.' I respected his feelings, but I thought him optimistic, for, till he had learned to judge their pace, I was pretty sure that he would never get near them.

We had a gargantuan breakfast, and then tumbled into bed for four hours. After luncheon we went out on the sand dunes with the falcon, where Peter John to his joy saw a ruff. He wouldn't fly Morag, because he said it was a shame to match a well-fed bird of prey against the thin and weary waders which had flown from the Baltic. On our road back we met Smith, who had been for a long walk, and I introduced Peter John. The two took to each other at once, in the way a shy man often makes friends with a boy. Smith obviously knew a good deal about birds, but I wondered what had been his observation ground, for he was keenly interested in ducks like teal and widgeon, which are common objects of the seashore, while he spoke of rarities like the purple sandpiper as if they were old acquaintances. Otherwise he was not communicative, and he had the same sad, watchful look that I had noticed the night before. But he brightened up when I suggested that he should come with us next morning.

That evening's flight was a wash-out. The wind capriciously died away, and out of the marshes a fog crept which the gunners call a 'thick.' We tried another part of the mud-flats, hoping that the weather would clear. Clear it did for about half an hour, when there was a wonderful scarlet and opal sunset. But the mist crept down again with the darkening, and all we could see was the occasional white glimmer of a duck's wing. The geese came from the shore about half-past five, not chuckling as in the morning, but making a prodigious clamour, and not in wedges, but in one continuous flight. We heard them right enough, but we could see nothing above us except a thing like a grey woollen comforter. At six o'clock we gave it up, and went back to supper, after which I read King Solomon's Mines aloud to Peter John before a blazing fire, and added comments on it from my own experience.

I thought that the weather was inclining to frost and had not much hope for next morning. But the gale had not finished, and I was awakened to the rattle of windows and the blatter of sleet on the roof. We found Smith waiting for us with Samson, looking as if he had been up for hours or had not slept, for his eyes were not gummy like Peter John's and mine. We had a peculiarly unpleasant walk over the crab grass, bent double to avoid the blizzard, and when we got to the mud our hands were so icy that they could hardly grip the coal-shovels. Smith, who had no gun, helped Peter John to dig his 'grave,' the latter being encumbered by Morag, who needed some attention. Never was an angrier bird, to judge by her vindictive squeaks and the glimpses I had in the fitful torchlight of her bright, furious eyes.

We had a miserable vigil, during which the sleet died away and the wind slightly abated. My hole was close to a creek, and I remember that, just as dawn was breaking, the shiny, water-proof head of a seal popped up beside me. After that came the usual ritual--the thunderous flocks of waders, the skeins of duck, and then in the first light the wedges of geese, this time mainly white-fronts. They were a little later than usual, for it must have been half- past seven before they came, and well after eight before they had passed.

The guns did nothing. Samson never fired, and though I had two shots at the tail birds of a wedge, I was well behind them. The birds were far out, and there was something mightily wrong with the visibility. . . . I was just getting up to shake the mud out of my boots when I squatted down again, for I was the spectator of a sudden marvellous sight. Smith, who shared the hole with me, also dropped on his knees.

Peter John had flown Morag, and the falcon had picked a gander out of a wedge and driven him beyond the echelon. The sky had lightened, and I saw the whole drama very clearly. Morag soared above her quarry, to prepare for her deadly stoop, but the goose had been at the game before and knew what to do. It dropped like a stone till it was only a couple of yards above the mud, and at that elevation made at its best pace for the shore. Fifty feet or so above it the falcon kept a parallel flight. She had easily the pace of the goose, but she did not dare to strike, for, if she had, she would have killed her prey, but, with the impetus of her stoop, would have also broken her own neck.

I have watched sensational horse-races and prize-fights in my time, but I have never seen anything more exciting than the finish of that contest. The birds shot past only about ten yards to my right, and I could easily have got the white-front, but I would as soon have shot my mother. This was a show in which I had no part, the kind of struggle of two wonderful winged things that had gone on since the creation of the world. I fairly howled in my enthusiasm for the old goose. Smith, too, was on his feet on the top of the rampart yelling like a dervish, and Peter John was squelching through the mud after the combatants. . . .

The whole business can scarcely have lasted a full minute, for the speed was terrific; but I seemed to be living through crowded hours. The white-front turned slightly to the left, rose a little to clear a hillock in the crab grass, and then the two became mere specks in the distance. But the light was good enough to show us the finish. The lower speck reached a pinewood and disappeared, and the upper speck was lost against the gloom of the trees. The goose had won sanctuary. I found myself babbling, 'Well done--oh, well done!' and I knew that Peter John, now frantically waving the lure, would be of the same mind.

Suddenly my attention was switched on to the man Smith. He was sitting in the mud, and he was weeping--yes, weeping. At first I thought it was only excitement, and wasn't much surprised, and then I saw that it was something more. I gave him a hand to help him up, and he clutched my arm.

'It is safe,' he stammered. 'Tell me, it is safe?'

'Safe as the Bank,' I said. 'No falcon can do anything against a bird in a wood.'

He gripped me harder.

'It is safe because it was humble,' he cried. 'It flew near the ground. It was humble and lowly, as I am. It is a message from Heaven.'

Then he seemed to be ashamed of himself, for he apologized for being a fool. But he scarcely spoke a word on the way back, and when I got out of bed in time for luncheon, Mrs. Pottinger brought me the news that he had left the Rose and Crown. . . . That moment on the mudflats had given me a line on Smith. He was a hunted man, in desperate terror of some pursuer and lying very low. The success of the old white-front had given him hope, for its tactics were his own. I wondered if I should ever meet him again.

CHAPTER III

The Tablet of Jade

The next chapter in this tale came at the end of March when the Clanroydens stayed with us at Fosse for a long week-end. Sandy, after his return from South America and his marriage, had settled down at Laverlaw as a Scots laird, and for the better part of a year you couldn't dig Barbara and him out of that heavenly fastness. Then came a crisis in the Near East on which he felt called upon to hold forth in the House of Lords, and gradually he was drawn more and more into public affairs. Also Barbara took a long time to recover from the birth of her daughter, and had to be much in London within reach of doctors. The consequence was that Mary and I saw a good deal of the Clanroydens. Mary was one of the daughter's godmothers, and Lady Clanroyden stayed at Fosse with us most of the time that Sandy was in China as chairman of an international Commission. He had only returned from the Far East at the end of February.

It was the most perfect kind of early spring weather. In February we had a fortnight's snow, so the ground was well moistened and the spring full, and in the first week of March we had drying blasts from the north-east. Then came mild south-west winds, and a sudden outburst of life. The blackthorn was in flower, the rooks were busy in the beeches, the elms were reddening, and the lawns at Fosse were framed in gold drifts of daffodils. On the Friday after tea Sandy and I went for a walk up on to the Sharway Downs, where you look east into the shallow Oxfordshire vales and north over ridge upon ridge of green, round-shouldered hills. As the twilight drew in there was a soft bloom like peach-blossom on the landscape, a thrush was pouring out his heart in a bush, and the wild cry of lapwings, mingled with the babble of young lambs, linked the untamable with our comfortable human uses.

Sandy, as he sniffed the scents coming up from the woods and the ploughlands, seemed to feel the magic of the place.

'Pretty good,' he said. 'England is the only really comfortable spot on earth--the only place where man can be utterly at home.'

'Too comfortable,' I said. 'I feel I'm getting old and soft and slack. I don't deserve this place, and I'm not earning it.'

He laughed. 'You feel like that? So do I, often. There are times at Laverlaw when it seems that that blessed glen is too perfect for fallen humanity, and that I'm not worthy of it. It was lucky that Adam was kicked out of Paradise, for he couldn't have enjoyed it if he had remained there. I've known summer mornings so beautiful that they depressed me to my boots. I suppose it is proper to feel like that, for it keeps you humble, and makes you count your mercies.'

'I don't know,' I said. 'It's not much good counting your mercies if you feel you have no right to them.'

'Oh, we've a right to them. Both of us have been through the hards. But there's no such thing as a final right. We have to go on earning them.'

'But we're not. I, at any rate. I'm sunk in cushions--lapped about in ease, like a man in a warm bath.'

'That's right enough, provided you're ready to accept the cold plunge when it comes. At least that's the way I look at it. Enjoy your comforts, but sit loose to them. You'll enjoy them all the more if you hold them on that kind of tenure, for you'll never take them for granted.'

We didn't talk much on the way home, for I was meditating on what Sandy had said and wondering if it would give me that philosophy for advancing age which I was seeking. The trouble was, that I couldn't be sure that I would ever be willing to give up my pleasant ways. Sandy would, for he would always have open ears, but I was getting pretty dull of hearing.

That night at dinner he was in his best form. Till last year he had never been farther east than India, though he knew the Near and Middle East like a book, and he was full of his new experiences. Sandy rarely talked politics, so he said nothing about the work of his Commission, but he revelled in all the whimsies and freaks of travel. Adventures are to the adventurous, and his acquaintance was so colossal that wherever he went he was certain to revive old contacts. He had something to tell me about common friends whom I had long lost sight of, and who had been washed up like driftwood on queer shores.

'Do you remember a man called Haraldsen?' he asked.

'Yes,' I said. 'I once knew a Haraldsen, a Dane. Marius Eliaser Haraldsen.'

He nodded. 'That's the chap.'

It was odd to hear that name spoken, for though I had not thought of it for years, just lately it had come back to my memory, since it was in a way connected with Lombard.

'I haven't seen him for a quarter of a century, and he was an old man then. What's he doing? Did you run across him?'

'No. He is dead. But I knew him at the end of the War--and after. I've got something to tell you about Haraldsen, and something to show you.'

After dinner we sat round the fire in the library, and Sandy went up to his bedroom and brought down a small flat object wrapped in chamois leather. 'First of all, Dick,' he said, 'what do you remember about Haraldsen?'

I remembered a good many things, especially a story into which Lombard came. But since I wanted to hear what Sandy had to tell, I only said that I had known him in Rhodesia as a rather lucky speculator in gold-mining propositions. He had been a long time in South Africa, and was believed to have made a pot of money in the earlier days of the Rand. But he was always looking for new fields, and might have dropped some of it in his Rhodesian ventures. When I had last seen him he had been exploring north of the Zambezi, and had a dozen prospectors working for him in the bend of the Kafue.

'Yes,' said Sandy. 'That was Haraldsen. Let me tell you something more about him. He was the professional gold-seeker in excelsis, with a wonderful nose for the stuff and the patience of Buddha. But he wasn't the ordinary treasure-hunter, for he had a purpose which he never lost sight of. He was a Dane, as you say, a native of Jutland, and he was bred a mining engineer. He was a pretty good mineralogist, too. But he was also, and principally, a poet. His youth was before the days of all this Nordic humbug, but he had got into his head the notion that the Northern culture was as great a contribution to civilization as the Greek and Roman, and that the Scandinavian peoples were destined to be the true leaders of Europe. He had their history at his fingers' ends, and he knew the Sagas better than any man I've ever met--I'm some judge of that, for I know them pretty well myself. He had a vision of a great Northern revival, when the spirit of Harald Fairhair would revive in Norway, and Gustavus Adolphus and Charles XII. would be reborn in Sweden, and Valdemar the Victorious in Denmark. Not that he wanted any conquests or federations--he wasn't interested in politics: his ideal was a revival of the Northern mind, a sort of Northern Renaissance of which he was to be the leader. You remember what a tough bird he was in any practical question, but how he could relax sometimes and become the simplest of souls when you pressed the right button.'

I certainly remembered one instance when Haraldsen had talked to me about a house he was building in a little island somewhere in the north, and had rhapsodized over it like a boy. Otherwise he was regarded as rather a hard citizen.

'Well, for his purpose he wanted money, and that would be difficult to come by if he stayed at home. So he started out like the gooseherd in Hans Andersen in search of fortune--a proper big fortune, for he had a lot to do with it. Somehow he drifted to Egypt, and he was one of the prospectors that Ismail sent out to look for an El Dorado in the Sudan. At that time he must have been in his early twenties. Then by way of Abyssinia and Madagascar he moved south, until he fetched up in

Mozambique, where he started out to look for the Queen of Sheba's gold-mines.

'He wasted a lot of time in that barren game, and more than once nearly had his throat cut, and then he was lucky enough to turn up on the Rand when that show was beginning. He did well--exceedingly well in a way, but not enough to satisfy him. He had still to find his own private special Golconda. So he went north into Rhodesia, where you met him, and farther north into the Eastern Congo. And then he decided that he had had enough of Africa, and would try Asia.'

'So that's where he went,' I said. 'The old hero! When I knew him he was nearer sixty than fifty.'

'I know. He was as tough as one of his own Saga-men. Well, he had a good many adventures in Asia--principally in Siberia and in the country east and south of the Caspian. When I came across him in Persia early in 1918 he was rather the worse for wear. You remember what a big fellow he was, with his enormous long arms and his great shoulders? When I met him he wasn't much more than a framework, and his clothes hung on him like the rags on the props of a scarecrow. But he wasn't ill, only indecently lean, and he was quite undefeated. He was still hunting for his Ophir.'

'That must have been during the War,' I put in. 'How on earth was he allowed to wander about in those parts?'

'He wasn't. He simply went--there were more of those uncharted libertines in the war zones than people imagined. You see, he was an impressive old gentleman, and he had money, and he knew the ropes--all the many ropes. He travelled in some style, too, with servants and a good cook and an armed escort who were more afraid of him than of any possible enemies. He wasn't a business man for nothing. I had about a week of his company, and in the cool of the morning, when we ate white mulberries together in the garden, he told me all about himself. He spoke to me freely, for we were two civilized men alone in the wilds, and he took a fancy to me, for I knew all about his blessed Sagas. How did he impress you, Dick, when you knew him?'

'I liked him--we all did, but we were a little puzzled about what he was after. We thought that a Rand magnate of well over fifty would be better employed enjoying himself in Europe than in fossicking about in the bush. He was very capable and ran his outfit beautifully. You would have had to rise uncommonly early to get the better of old Haraldsen.'

'He must have changed before I met him,' said Sandy. 'In Africa you have to fight hard to prevent matter dominating mind, but in Asia the trouble is to keep mind in reasonable touch with matter. Haraldsen, when I knew him, was about as much mystic as gold-hunter. He told me about his past life, as if it were a thing very far away. I mentioned your name, I remember, and he recollected you, but didn't seem greatly interested in anything that happened in Africa. He had a son somewhere in Europe, but he said very little about him--also a house, but I never discovered where. What filled his thoughts was this treasure which he was going to find some day, and which had been waiting for him since the foundation of the world. I gathered that he was a rich man, and that he was not looking for mere wealth. He told me about his dreams for the future of the Northern races, but rather as if he were repeating a lesson. The fact was that to find his Ophir had become for him an end in itself, quite apart from the use he meant to make of it. You sometimes find that in old men who have led a strenuous life. They become monomaniacs.'

'Did he find it?' I asked.

'Not in Persia. The Middle East at that time wasn't propitious for treasure-hunting. You must understand that Haraldsen wasn't looking for gold in the void. He was proceeding on a plan, and he had his data as carefully marshalled as any Intelligence Department. He was following the reports of a whole host of predecessors, whose evidence he had collected and analysed--chiefly the trail of old caravan-routes along which he knew that gold had been carried. Well, he failed in Persia, and the next I heard of him was in Sinkiang--what they used to call Chinese Turkestan. I was in India then, keeping a watchful eye on Central Asia, and my old friend managed to give me a good deal of trouble. He got into Kashgar, and we had the deuce of a job getting him out.

Sinkiang at that time was a kind of battleground between Moslem home-rulers and Soviet emissaries, with nobody to keep the peace except some weak Chinese officials and a ragtime Chinese army. However, in the end it was arranged that he should come to India, and I was looking forward to welcoming him at Simla, when news came that the Tungans had won, and that the garrison and the foreigners had been booted out and were fleeing eastward to China. I decided that it was all up with Haraldsen. He would never make the two thousand miles of desert that separated Sinkiang from China. I wrote something pious in my diary about the foolishness of treasure-hunting.'

'Poor old chap!' I murmured. 'It was the kind of end he was bound to have.'

'It wasn't the end,' said Sandy. 'That was twelve years ago. Haraldsen is dead, but after he left Sinkiang he lived for ten years. He must have been eighty when he died, so he had a goodish run for his money. Moreover, he found his Ophir.'

'How do you know?' I asked excitedly.

'It's a queer story,' said Sandy, and he took the object in his hands out of its chamois-leather wrappings. It was a tablet, about eight inches by six, of the most beautiful emerald jade I have ever seen. Sandy handed it to Mary, who handed it to me. I saw that it was covered on both sides with spidery marks, but if it was any known language it was one I couldn't read. Mary, who loved all jewels, exclaimed at its beauty.

'I got that in Peking,' he said. 'There were times when we weren't very busy, and I liked to go foraging about the city in the sharp, bright autumn afternoons. There was one junk-shop up near the An Ting gate where I made friends with the owner. He was an old Mohammedan from Kansu whose language I could make a shot at talking, and his place was an education in every corner and century of Asia. In the front, which was open to the street, there was a glorious muddle of saddlery and rugs and palanquins and bows and arrows and furs, and even a little livestock like red desert-hawks in bamboo cages. As you went farther in the stock got smaller in size, but more valuable, things like marvellously carved walking- sticks, and damascened swords, and mandarin hats, and temple furniture, and every sort of lacquer. Some outlandish things, too, like an ordinary English grandfather's clock marked 'London, 1782.' At the very back was the inner shrine which the old man only took you into when he knew all about you. It smelt of scented woods and spices and the dust of ages, and it was hard to find your way about in it with no light but the owner's little green lamp. Here were the small precious things, some on shelves, some in locked cabinets, and some in cheap glazed cases of deal. There was everything, from raw Bhotan turquoises to mandarin's buttons of flawed rubies, from tiny celadon cups to Ming bowls, from ivory Manchu combs to agate snuff-boxes. I was looking for something for Barbara when I found this.

'I always liked good jade, and even in that dusk I saw that this was a fine piece. The old fellow let me take it into the light in the front shop, and I had no doubts about it. It was an exquisite bit of the true imperial stone, with the famous kingfisher's-back colour. As you see, one side is covered with hieroglyphics which I can't read. The other side has also an inscription, which at first I took to be in the same jargon. I asked the shop-keeper what the writing meant, and he shook his head. It was some hieratic language, he thought, which the monks used on the Tibetan border.

'I took a tremendous fancy to the piece, and we chaffered over it for the better part of an afternoon. In the end I got it at quite a reasonable price--reasonable, that is, for jade, which would keep its value in China if the bottom dropped out of everything else. I think that the only reason why it was unsold was its size, which made it too clumsy for personal adornment, and because of the inscriptions on it which made it hard to fashion it into an ordinary jewel. The old fellow was doubtful about its provenance. From the quality of the stone he thought that it should have come from Siberia, from the Lake Baikal neighbourhood, but at the same time he was positive that the inscriptions belonged to the south- west corner of China. He couldn't read them, but he said he recognized the characters.

'That night in my hotel, when I examined the tablet by the light of a good lamp, I got the surprise of my life. The close lettering on one side, all whorls and twists, I could make nothing of. But on the other side the few lines inscribed were perfectly comprehensible. They consisted of a Latin sentence, a place-name, and a date. The Latin was "Marius Haraldsen moriturus haec scripsit thesauro feliciter invento"--"Marius Haraldsen, being on the point of death and having happily found his treasure, has written these words." The place-name was Gutok. The date was the fifteenth of October the year before last. What do you think of that for a yarn?'

I looked at the translucent green tablet in which the firelight woke wonderful glints of gold and ruby. I saw the maze of spidery writing on one side, and on the other the Latin words, not very neatly incised--probably with a penknife. It seemed a wonderful thing to get this news of my old friend out of the darkness four thousand miles from where I had known him. I handled it reverently, and passed it back to Sandy. 'What do you make of it?' I asked.

'I think it's simple,' he said. 'I raced back next morning to the old man to find out how he had got hold of it. But he could tell me nothing. It had come to him with other junk--he was always getting consignments--some caravan had picked it up--bought it from a pedlar or a thief. Then I went to the Embassy, and one of the secretaries helped me to hunt for Gutok. We ran it to earth at last--in a Russian gazetteer published just before the War. It was a little place down in the province of Shu-san, where a trade-route sent a fork south to Burma.

An active man with proper backing could have reached it in the old days from Shanghai in a month.'

'Are you going there?' I asked.

'Not I. I have never cared about treasure. But I think we can be certain what happened. Haraldsen found his Ophir--God knows what it was--an old mine or an outcrop or something--anyhow, it must have been the real thing, for he knew too much to make mistakes. But he discovered also that he was dying. Now Gutok is not exactly a convenient centre of transport. He probably wrote letters, but he couldn't be certain that they would ever get to their destination. Two years ago all that corner of Asia was a rabble of banditry and guerrillas. So he adopted the sound scheme of writing poorish Latin on a fine bit of jade, in the hope that sooner or later it would come into the hands of some one who could construe it and give his friends news of his fate. He probably entrusted it to a servant, who was robbed and murdered, but he knew that the jade was too precious to disappear, and he was pretty certain that it would drift east and fetch up in some junk-shop in Peking or Shanghai. That was rather his way of doing things, for he was a fatalist, and left a good deal to Providence.'

'Yes, that was the old chap,' I said. 'Well, he has won out. You and I were his friends, and we know when and where he died and that he had found what he was looking for. He'd have liked us to know the last part, for he wasn't fond of being beaten. But his treasure wasn't much use to him and his Northern races. It's buried again for good.'

'I don't know,' said Sandy. 'I'm fairly certain that that spidery stuff on the other side is an account of how to reach it. It was done at the same time as the Latin, either by Haraldsen himself or more likely by one of his Chinese assistants. I can't read it, but I expect I could find somebody who can, and I'm prepared to bet that if we had it translated we should know just what Haraldsen discovered. You're an idle man, Dick. Why not go out and have a shot at digging it up?'

'I'm too old,' I said, 'and too slack.'

I took the tablet in my hands again and examined it. It gave me a queer feeling to look at this last testament of my old friend, and to picture the conditions under which it had been inscribed in some godless mountain valley at the back of beyond, and to consider the vicissitudes it must have gone through before it reached the Peking curio-shop. Heaven knew what blood and tears it had drawn on its road. I felt too--I don't know why--that there was something in this for me, something which concerned me far more closely than Sandy. As I looked at my pleasant library, with the fire reflected from the book-lined walls, it seemed to dislimn and expand into the wild spaces where I had first known Haraldsen, and I was faced again by the man with his grizzled, tawny beard and his slow, emphatic speech. I suddenly saw him as I remembered him, standing in the African moonlight, swearing me to a pact which I hadn't remembered for twenty years.

'If you are not sleepy, I'll tell you a story about Haraldsen,' I said.

'Go on,' said Sandy, as he lit his pipe. He and Mary are the best listeners I know, and till well after midnight they gave their attention to the tale which is set down in the next chapter.

CHAPTER IV

Haraldsen

In the early years of the century the land north of the Limpopo River was now and then an exciting place to live in. We Rhodesians went on with our ordinary avocations, prospecting, mining, trying out new kinds of fruit and tobacco, pushing, many of us, into wilder country with our ventures. But the excitement did not all lie in front of us, for some of it came from behind. Up from the Rand and the Cape straggled odd customers whom the police had to keep an eye on, and England now and then sent us some high-coloured gentry. The country was still in many people's minds a no-man's-land, where the King's writ did not run, and in any case it was a jumping-off ground for all the wilds of the North. In my goings to and fro I used to strike queer little parties, often very ill- found, that had the air of hunted folk, and were not very keen to give any information about themselves. Heaven knows what became of them. Sometimes we had the job of feeding some starving tramp, and helping him to get back to civilization, but generally they disappeared into the unknown and we heard no more of them. Some may have gone native, and ended as poor whites in a dirty hut in a Kaffir kraal. Some may have died of fever or perished miserably of thirst or hunger, lost in the Rhodesian bush, which was not a thing to trifle with. In the jungles of the middle Zambezi and the glens of the

Scarp and the swamps of the Mazoe and the Ruenya there must have been many little heaps of bleached and forgotten bones.

I had come back from a trip to East Africa, and in Buluwayo to my delight I met Lombard, with whom I had made friends in the Rift valley. He had finished his work with his Commission, and was on the road home, taking a look at South Africa on the way. He had come by sea from Mombasa to Beira, and was putting up for a few days at Government House. When he met me he was eager to go on trek, for he had several weeks to spare and, since I was due for a trip up-country, he offered to go with me. My firm wanted me to have a look at some copper indications in Manicaland, north of the upper Pungwe in Makapan's country. Lombard wanted to see the fantastic land where the berg and the plateau break down into the Zambezi flats, and he hoped for a little shooting, for which he had had no leisure on his East African job. My trip promised to be a dull one, so I gladly welcomed his company, for to a plain fellow like me Lombard's talk was a constant opening out of new windows.

In the hotel at Salisbury we struck a strange outfit. It was a party of four, an elderly man, a youngish man, and two women. The older man looked a little over fifty, a heavily built fellow, with a square face and a cavalry moustache and a loud laugh. I should have taken him for a soldier but for the slouch of his shoulders, which suggested a sedentary life. He spoke like an educated

Englishman--a Londoner, I guessed, for he had that indefinable clipping and blurring of his words which is the mark of the true metropolitan. The younger man was an American from his accent, and at the first glance I disliked him. He was the faux bonhomme, if I knew the breed, always grinning and pawing the man he spoke to, but with cold, cunning grey eyes that never smiled. We were not a dressy lot in Rhodesia, and the clothes of these two cried out like a tuberose in a cottage window. They wore the most smartly cut flannels, and soft linen collars, which were then a novelty, and they had wonderful buckskin shoes. The cut of their jib was not exactly loud, but it was exotic, though no doubt it would have been all right at Bournemouth. Even Lombard, who was always neat in his dress, looked shabby by contrast.

The women were birds of Paradise. They were both young, and rather pretty, and they were heavily rouged and powdered, so that I wondered what their faces would be like if the African sun got at them. They wore garden-party clothes, and in the evening put themselves into wonderful fluffy tea-gowns. They seemed to belong to a lower class than their male escort, for they had high vulgar voices and brazen Cockney accents. The party, apparently, had money to burn. They made a great outcry about the food, which was the ordinary tinned stuff and trek-ox, but they had champagne to all their meals, and champagne was not a cheap beverage in Salisbury.

I had no talk with any of them except the young fellow. He was very civil and very full of questions, after he had mixed me a cocktail which he claimed was his own patent. He and his friends, he said, were out to cast an eye over the Rhodesian proposition and sort of size-up what kind of guy the late C. J. Rhodes had been. Just a short look-see, for he judged they must soon hurry home. He talked a ripe American, but I guessed that it was not his native wood-notes, and sure enough I learned that he was a Dane by birth, name of Albinus, who had been some years in the States. He mentioned Montana, and I tried to get him to talk about copper, but he showed no interest. But he appeared curiously well-informed about parts of Rhodesia, for he asked me questions about the little-known north-eastern corner, which showed that he had made some study of its topography.

Lombard had a talk with the elder man, but got nothing out of him, except that he was an Englishman on a holiday. 'Common vulgar trippers,' said Lombard. 'Probably won some big sweepstake or had a lucky flutter in stocks, and are now out for a frolic. Funny thing, but I fancy the old chap tries to make himself out a bigger bounder than God meant him to be. When he is off his guard he speaks almost like a gentleman. The women! Oh, the eternal type-- Gaiety girls--salaried compagnons de voyage. The whole crowd make an ugly splash of aniline dye on this sober landscape.'

We were to be off at dawn next morning. Before turning in I went into the bar for a drink, and there I met a policeman I knew--Jim Arcoll, who was a famous name anywhere north of the Vaal River. I didn't ask him what he was doing there, for that was the kind of question he never permitted, but I told him my own plans. He knew every corner of the country like his own name, and, when he learned where we were going, he nodded. 'You'll find old Haraldsen up there,' he said. 'He's fossicking somewhere near Mafudi's kraal. Give him my love if you see him, and tell him to keep me in touch with his movements. It's a rough world, and he might come by a mischief.'

Then he jerked his thumb to the ceiling.

'You've got a gay little push upstairs,' he said.

'I've only Lombard--the man you met in Buluwayo!' I replied.

'I didn't mean your lot. I mean the others. The two dudes with the pretty ladies. Do you know who the older man is? No less than the illustrious Aylmer Troth.'

People have long ago forgotten the Scimitar case, but a year before it had made a great stir in England. It was a big financial swindle, with an ugly episode in it which might have been suicide, or might have been murder. There was a famous trial at the Old Bailey, and five out of the twelve accused got heavy terms of penal servitude. One of the chief figures had been a well-known London solicitor called Troth, who was the mystery man of the whole business. He had got off after a brilliant defence by his counsel, but the judge had been pretty severe in his comments and a heavy mist of suspicion remained.

'Troth!' I said. 'What on earth is he doing here? I thought the chap upstairs looked too formidable for the ordinary globe- trotter.'

'He is certainly formidable. As for his purpose, ask me another. We've nothing against him. Left the court without a stain on his character and all that. All the same, he's a pretty mangy lad, and we have instructions to keep our eye on him till he gets on to the boat at Beira or Capetown. I don't fancy he's up to any special tricks this time. With his pretty love-birds he carries too heavy baggage for anything very desperate.'

Some days later, after a detour westward to pick up part of my outfit, we were on the hills between the Pungwe and the Ruenya. I thought that we had said good-bye to Troth and his garish crew, and had indeed forgotten all about them, when suddenly one noon, when we off-saddled at a water-hole, we struck them again. There were the four sitting round a fire having luncheon. The men had changed their rig, and wore breeches and leggings and khaki shirts, with open necks and sleeves rolled up, very different people from the exquisites of the hotel. Albinus looked a workmanlike fellow who had been at the game before, and even Troth made a presentable figure for the wilds. But the women were terrible. They too had got themselves up in breeches and putties and rough shirts, but they weren't the right shape for that garb, and they had a sad raddled look like toy terriers that had got mixed up in a dog-fight. The sun, as I had anticipated, was playing havoc with their complexions.

The four did not seem surprised to see us, as indeed why should they, for they were on the regular trail into Makapan's country, and a fair number of people passed that way. They were uncommonly forthcoming, and offered us drinks, of which they had plenty, and fancy foods, of which they had a remarkable assortment. They seemed to be in excellent spirits, and were very full of chat. Troth was enthusiastic about everything--the country and the climate, and the delight of living in the open, of which, he lamented, a busy man like himself had never before had a chance. Alas, they could only have a few days of this Paradise, and then they must make tracks for home. No, they were not hunting; they had shot nothing but a few guinea-fowl for the pot. He wished that he wasn't such a rotten bad naturalist, or that he had somebody with him to tell him about the beasts and birds. Altogether you couldn't have met a more innocent Bank Holiday tripper. The girls too spoke their piece very nicely, though I couldn't believe that they were really enjoying themselves. Albinus said little, but he was very assiduous in helping us to drinks.

I asked if we could do anything for them, but they said they were all right. They proposed to have a look at a place called Pinto's Kloof, which they had been told was a better view-point than the Matoppos, and then they must turn back. It seemed odd that a man with Troth's antecedents should be enjoying himself in this simple way, and Albinus didn't look as if he had any natural taste for the idyllic, nor the high-coloured ladies. But I must say they kept up the part well, and Troth's last word to me was that he wished he was twenty years younger and could have a life like mine. He said it as if he meant it.

When we had ridden on, Lombard observed that he thought that they were anxious to make themselves out to be greater novices and greenhorns than they really were. 'I caught a glimpse of their ironmongery,' he said, 'and there was more there than scatter-guns. I'll swear there were rifles--at least one Mauser and what looked like an express.'

I nodded.

'I noticed that too,' I said. 'And did you observe their boys? Two they may have hired in Salisbury, but there was a half-caste Portugoose whom I fancy I've seen before, and who didn't want to be recognized. He dodged behind a tree when he saw me. Arcoll is right to keep an eye on that lot. Not that I see what mischief they can do. This part of the world can't offer much to a shady London solicitor and an American crook.'

Three days later we were well into Makapan's country and I had started on my job, verifying the reports of our prospectors in a land of little broken kopjes right on the edge of the Scarp. I had with me a Cape half-caste called Hendrik, who was my general factotum, and who looked after the whole outfit. There was nothing he could not turn his hand to, hunting, transport-riding, horse- doctoring, or any job that turned up: he was a wonderful fellow with a mule team, too, and he was the best cook in Africa. We had four boys with us, Mashonas whom I had employed before. Lombard spent his time shooting, and, as it was a country where a man could not easily get lost if he had a compass, I let him go out alone. He didn't get much beyond a few klipspringer and bushbuck, but it was a good game area, and he lived in hopes of a kudu.

Well, one evening as we were sitting at dinner beside our fire, I looked up to see Peter Pienaar standing beside me. It was not the Peter that you knew in the War, but Peter ten years younger, with no grey in his beard, and as trim and light and hard as an Olympic athlete. But he had the same mild face, and the same gentle sleepy eyes that you remember, and the same uncanny quietness. Peter made no more noise in his appearances than the change from night to morning.

I had last heard of him in the Kalahari, which was a very good reason why I should expect to find him next on the other side of Africa. He ate all the food we could give him and drank two bottles of beer, which was his habit, for he used to stoke up like a camel, never being sure when he would eat or drink again. Then he filled a deep-bowled pipe with the old Transvaal arms on it, which a cousin had carved for him when a prisoner of war in Ceylon. I waited for him to explain himself, for I was fairly certain that this meeting was not accidental.

'I have hurried to find you, Dick,' he said, 'for I think there is going to be dirty work in Makapan's country.'

'There's sure to be dirty work when you're about, you old aasvogel,' I said. 'What is it this time?'

'I do not know what it is, but I think I know who it is. It is friends of yours, Dick--very nasty friends.'

'Hullo!' I said. 'Was it Arcoll who sent you? Are you after the trippers that we found on the road last week?'

'Ja! Captain Jim sent me. He said, "Peter, will you keep an eye on two gentlemen and two ladies who are taking a little holiday?" He did not tell me more, and he did not know more. Perhaps now he knows, for I have sent him a message. But I have found out very bad things which Captain Jim cannot stop, for they will happen quickly. That is why I have come to you.'

'But those four tourists can't do anything,' I said. 'One I know is a crook, and I think the other is, and they've got an ugly Portugoose with them that I swear

I've seen before. But that's only three, and they are cumbered with two women.'

'The vrows have gone back to the town,' said Peter solemnly. 'They will wait quietly there till the others return. They will make the whole thing seem innocent--naughty, perhaps, but innocent. But the three you speak of are not the only ones. By this time they have been joined by others, and these others are very great scoundrels. You say, how do I know? I will tell you. I am at home in Makapan's country and Makapan's people do what I ask them. They have brought me news which is surer and speedier than Captain Jim can get. There is very bad mischief brewing. Listen, and I will tell you.'

The gist of Peter's story was that after they had got rid of the women Troth and Albinus had moved down from the scarp into the bush-veld. The third, the Portugoose, Peter knew all about. His name was Dorando, and Peter had come across his tracks in many queer places; he had done time for I.D.B. and for selling illicit liquor, and was wanted in Mozambique on a variety of charges from highway robbery to cold-blooded murder. An odd travelling companion for two innocent sight-seeing tourists! Down in the flats the three had been joined by two other daisics, one an Australian who had been mixed up in the Kruger Treasure business, and one a man from the Diamond Fields called Stringer. I opened my eyes when I heard about the last, for Jim Stringer was an ill- omened name at that time in South Africa. He was the typical 'bad man,' daring and resourceful and reputed a dead shot. I was under the impression that he had been safely tucked away for his share in a big Johannesburg burglary.

'He came out of tronk last month,' said Peter, 'and your friends must have met him as they came up-country and arranged things. What do you say, Dick? Here are three skellums that I know well, and your two friends who are not good people. They have with them four boys, Shangaans whom I do not know, but they are Makinde's people, and Makinde's kraal is a dirty nest. What are they after, think you? They are not staying in the flats. They have already moved up into the Berg, and they are moving fast, and they are moving north. They are not looking for gold, and they are not hunting, and they are not admiring the scenery. Where are they going? I can tell you that, for I found it out before they joined Jim Stringer. The two English do not drink, or if they drink they do not babble. But Dorando drinks and babbles. One of Makapan's people, who is my friend, was their guide, and he heard Dorando talk when he was drunk. They are going to Mafudi's kraal. Now who is at Mafudi's kraal, Dick? They do not want to see old Mafudi in his red blanket. There is somebody else there.'

'Haraldsen!' I exclaimed.

'Ja! The Baas.' Peter always called Haraldsen the Baas, for he had often worked for him, as guide and transport-rider, and Haraldsen had more than once got him out of scrapes. Peter was a loyal soul, and if his allegiance was vowed to anyone alive it was to the old Dane.

'But what on earth can they have to do with Haraldsen?' I demanded.

'I do not know,' he said; 'but they have got it in for the Baas. Consider, Dick. He is not a young man, and he is up there alone, with his little band of Basutos and the Dutchman Malan, who is clever but not a fighter, for he has but the one arm. The Baas is very rich, and he is believed to know many secrets. These skellums have some business with him and it will not be clean business. Perhaps it is an old quarrel. Perhaps he has put it across your friends Troth and Albinus in old days. Or perhaps it is just plain robbery, and they mean to make him squeal. He cannot have much money with him, but they may force him to find them money. I do not know, but I am certain of one thing, that they mean to lay hands on the Baas--and he will not come happily out of their hands-- perhaps not alive.'

I was fairly flabbergasted by Peter's tale. At first I thought he was talking through his hat, for we were civilized folk in Rhodesia, and violence was more or less a thing of the past. But Peter never talked wildly, and the more I thought of it the less I liked it. Five desperadoes up in that lonely corner could do pretty much what they pleased with Haraldsen and his one-armed assistant. I remembered the old fellow's reputation for having hunted gold all his life and having struck it in a good many places. What more likely than that some hungry rogues should try to get him alone in the wilds and force out of him either money or knowledge?

'What do you mean to do?' I asked.

'I am going straight to Mafudi's,' said Peter. 'And I think you are coming with me, Dick.'

Of course I couldn't refuse, but I felt bound to go cautiously. Would it not be better to get Arcoll and the police? I didn't relish the notion of a private scrap with people who would certainly not stick at trifles. Besides, could we do any real good? Haraldsen and Malan might be ruled out as combatants, and we three would be up against five hefty scallywags.

Peter overruled all my objections in his quiet way. Arcoll was a hundred miles off. A native runner had been sent to him, but it was impossible for him to arrive at Mafudi's in time, for Troth and his little lot would be there by to-morrow morning. As for being outnumbered, we were five honest men against five rascals, and in all rascals he believed there was a yellow streak. 'I can shoot a little,' he said, 'and you can shoot a little, Dick.' He turned inquiringly to Lombard.

'I can loose off at any rate,' said Lombard. He was looking rather excited, for this adventure was a piece of luck he had not hoped for.

The upshot was that we had no rest that night. I sent off one of my boys with another message for Arcoll, giving him more details than Peter had given him, and suggesting a road in by the northwest which I feared he might not think of. I left Hendrik and the mules and the rest of the outfit to come on later--and I remember wondering what kind of situation they would find when they reached Mafudi's. The three of us took the road just after ten o'clock. Peter's boy accompanied us, a tough little Bechuana from Khama's country.

I had travelled the route several times before, and Peter knew it well, but in any case it was not hard to find, for it kept to the open ground near the edge of the scarp, bending inland only to avoid the deep-cut kloofs. There was a wonderful moon which made the whole landscape swim in warm light--an African moon, which is not the pale thing of the north, but as masterful as the sun itself. When it set we were on high ground, a plateau of long grass and thorns, with the great hollow of the lower veld making a gulf of darkness on our right. The road was easy enough to follow, and when dawn came with a rush of gold and crimson out of the east we were close to the three queer little peaks between which lay Mafudi's kraal.

We went straight to Haraldsen's camp, which was about half a mile from the kraal on one of the ridges. It was the ordinary prospector's camp of which at that time you could have found a score or two in Rhodesia, but more professional than most, for Haraldsen had the cash with which to do things properly. Gold is not my pidgin, but the heaps of quartz I passed looked healthy. He had struck an outcrop which he thought promising, and was busy tracing the run of the reef, having sunk two seventy-foot shafts about a quarter of a mile apart. But I wasn't concerned with old Haraldsen's operations, but with Haraldsen himself. We had been sighted by his boys, and he stood outside his tent awaiting us, a figure like a patriarch with the sun on his shaggy head.

While our breakfast coffee was being made I told him our story, for there was no time to lose, since Peter calculated that Troth and his lot, by the road they were coming, could not be more than five miles off. Haraldsen had a face so weathered and set in its lines that it didn't reveal much of his thoughts, and he had grey eyes as steady as a good dog's. But the mention of Troth woke him up and the name of Albinus didn't please him. He seemed to be more worried about them than about the other scallywags.

'Troth I know,' he said in his deep voice and his precise accent, for he always spoke English as if he had got it from old-fashioned books. 'He is a great scoundrel and my enemy. Once--long ago--he was my partner for a little. He does not like me, and he has a reason, for I most earnestly laboured to have him put in tronk. He comes now like a ghost out of the past, and he means evil.' Of Albinus, he would only say that his father had had a great devil in him, and that he did not think that the devil had been exorcized in the son.

He had not the smallest doubt that the gang were after him, but he didn't explain why. All he said was, 'They will try to make me do their will, and if I do not consent they will kill me. Unless, indeed, I first kill them.'

I tried as usual to put the common sense of it. 'If they find us with you,' I said, 'they won't dare to do anything. A quiet murder might be in their line, but they won't want to fight a battle.'

But Haraldsen shook his head. He knew Troth, he said, and he knew about Albinus. He must have laid these gentry out pretty flat some time or other for them to have such a murderous grudge against him, or else he knew the depth and desperation of their greed. But what impressed me most was Peter's view. He knew about Stringer and Dorando, and was clear that they would not go home without loot. They would not think of consequences, for they could leak away into the back-world of Africa.

I was never one for a fight except in the last resort, so I proposed that Haraldsen should take his best horse and make a bolt for it, leaving us to face the music, since there was nothing much to be got out of Peter and Lombard and myself. But Haraldsen wouldn't hear of this. 'If I flee,' he said, 'they will find me later and I shall live with a menace over my head. That I will not face. Better to meet them here and have done with it.'

That was all very well, but I wasn't keen on being mixed up in any Saga-battle. I asked him if his boys were any use. 'None,' he said. They are Mashonas and are timid as rabbits. Besides, I will not have them hurt.'

'What about Mafudi's men?' I asked.

It was Peter who answered. 'Mafudi is always drunk, and also very old. Once his people were warriors, but now they have no guns. They will not fight.'

'Well, then, it's the five of us--and one of us crippled--against the five of them.'

But it was worse than that, for it appeared that Malan had a bad go of fever and might be counted out. Also Haraldsen had run out of ammunition and had sent a boy off to get a fresh supply, and as his rifles were Mannlichers and ours Mausers we could do nothing to help him out. This seemed to me fairly to put the lid on it, but Peter did not lose his cheerfulness. 'We must make a plan,' he said--a great phrase of his; and he delicately scratched the tip of his left ear, which was always a sign that his mind was working hard.

'This is my plan,' he said at last. 'We must find a place where we can defend ourselves. Captain Arcoll will be here to-day--or perhaps to-night--at any rate not later than to-morrow. We cannot fight these skellums on fair terms in the open, but in a strong fort we may beat them off for perhaps twelve hours, perhaps more.'

'But where is your fort?' I asked. As I looked round the bright open place, the jumble of kopjes with the green of Mafudi's crops in the heart of it, I didn't see much hopes of a refuge we could hold. It was all open and bare, and we hadn't time to dig trenches or build a scherm.

'There is the Hill of the Blue Leopard,' said Peter, using a Mashona word. 'It is above the kraal--you can see the corner of it beyond that ridge. It is a very holy place where few go but the priests, and it has round it a five-foot hedge of thorns and a big fence of stakes. I do not know what is inside except a black stone which fell from heaven. It is there that the young men must watch during the Circumcision. If we get in there, Dick, I think we could laugh at your friends for a little--long enough to give Captain Arcoll time to get here. There is another thing. If the skellums were strong enough to break in, I think that Mafudi's men might be very angry. It is true that they have no guns, but very angry men can do much with knobkerries and axes.'

'But they'll never let us enter,' I protested.

'Perhaps they will. I will try. I have always been good friends with Mafudi's folk.' And without another word he strode off in the direction of the kraal.

I was doubtful about his success, for I knew how jealous the natives were of their sacred places, especially the Mashonas, who have always been in the hands of their priests. Still I knew that Peter had an amazing graft among the tribes, for he was not the kind of man who damned them all as niggers. People used to say that he was the only white man who had ever been present at the great Purification Dance of the Amatolas. It was a nervous business waiting for his return, for he took a long time about it. I made Haraldsen collect his valuables, and we prepared a sort of litter for Malan, who was at that stage of fever when a man is pretty well unconscious of his surroundings. Always I kept my eye on the corner of the kloof where any moment Troth and his gang might be expected to appear.

But they did not come, and at last Peter did. He had succeeded in persuading the elders of the tribe to let us inside the sacred enclosure. He did not tell me what arguments he had used, for that was never his way; he presented the world with results and left it to guess his methods. We bundled up our traps in a mighty hurry, for there was no time to lose, hoisted Malan into his litter, and told Haraldsen's boys to take the horses up into the berg and to lie low till we sent for them. In the kraal, in the open space in the centre of the kyas, we were met by most of Mafudi's people, all as silent as the tomb, which is not common among Kaffirs. We had to have water poured on our heads--what the books call a lustration--and to have little dabs of green paint stuck on our foreheads. Peter's Bechuana boy was not allowed to be of our party, only the white men. Then we were solemnly conducted up a narrow bush road to the Hill of the Blue Leopard, and as we started there was a great

'Ouch,' a sound like a sigh, from all the natives. There was a kind of cattle-gate in the wall of the scherm, which a priest ceremonially opened, and the four of us and Malan in his litter passed into the holy place.

At first sight it looked as if we had found a sanctuary. The hill was perhaps a hundred feet high, and most of it was covered with thick bush, except a bald cone at the top where the sacred stone lay. The bush was mostly waak-em-beetje thorn and quite impenetrable, but it was seamed and criss-crossed by dozens of little paths, worn smooth like a pebble by ages of ceremonial. One of the items in the Circumcision rite was a kind of demented hide- and-seek in this maze. Around the foot of the hill, as I have said, was a dense quickset scherm which it would have taken a regiment to hack through. The only danger-point was the gate, and I thought that in case of trouble two of us might manage to hold it, for I didn't envy the job of the men who tried to rush it in the face of concealed rifles. Anyhow, we could hold it long enough, I thought, to give Arcoll time to turn up. Indeed, I had hopes that Troth and his gang would miss us altogether. They would find Haraldsen's camp deserted and conclude that he had moved on.

In every bit of my forecast I was wrong. In the first place our enemies came round the edge of the kloof in time to see the movement of Mafudi's people toward the little hill, and if they didn't guess then what had happened, they knew all right when they got to Haraldsen's camp. For his boys had been too slow over the job of scattering into the woods. One of them they caught, and, since they meant business and were not fastidious in their methods, they soon made the poor devil blab what he knew or guessed. The consequence was that half an hour after we were inside the scherm the others were making hell in Mafudi's kraal. I had found a lair well up the hill where I could spy out the land, and I saw that Troth's party was bigger than I had supposed. I made out Troth and Albinus, their natty outfit a little the worse for wear, and the trim figure of Dorando, and Jim Stringer's long legs. They had left their natives behind, but they had four other white men with them, and I didn't like the cut of their jib. They were eight to our four, odds of two to one. I called Peter up beside me, and his eyes, sharp as a berghaan's, examined the reinforcements. He recognized the Australian and one other, a Lydenburg man whose name he mentioned and then spat. 'I think we must fight, Dick,' he said quietly. 'The greed of these men is so great that it will make them brave. And I know that Dorando and Stringer are bad, but not cowards.'

I thought the same, so I started out to make my dispositions, for I had learned some soldiering in the late war. Haraldsen I kept out of sight, for his life was the most valuable of the lot, and besides I meant to pretend that we knew nothing about him. Peter, who was far the best shot among us, I placed behind a rock where he had a good view of the approaches. I told him not to shoot unless they tried to rush the gate, and then to cripple if possible and not kill, for I didn't want bloodshed and a formal inquiry and screeds in the papers--that would do no good to either Haraldsen or me. Lombard and I took our stations near the gate, which was a solid thing of log and wattle jointed between two tree trunks. We had a rifle and a revolver apiece; but I would have preferred shot- guns. I could see that Lombard was twittering with excitement, but he kept a set face, though he was very white.

The affair was slow in beginning. It was after midday before Dorando and Stringer appeared on the track that led up from the kraal. They had a handkerchief tied to a rifle muzzle by way of a white flag. I halted them when they were six yards from the gate, and asked what they wanted.

Butter wouldn't have melted in their mouths. They had come to see Mr. Haraldsen, who was a friend of theirs--to see him on business. They understood that he was on the hill. Would he step out and come down to luncheon with them? They were kind enough to include me in the invitation.

I said that I knew nothing about Mr Haraldsen, but that I knew a good deal about them. I proposed another plan: let them leave their guns where they stood, and come inside the scherm and take a bite with us. They thanked me, and said they would be delighted, and moved to the gate, but they did not drop their rifles, and I saw the bulge of revolvers in their pockets. 'Stop,' I shouted. 'Down guns or stay where you are,' and Lombard and I showed our pistols.

'Is that a way to talk to gentlemen?' said Dorando with a very ugly look.

'It's the way to talk to you, my lads,' I said. 'I've known you too long. Strip yourselves and come inside. If not, I give you one minute to get out of here.'

Dorando was livid, but Stringer only smiled sleepily. He was the more dangerous of the two, for he was mighty quick on the draw and didn't miss. He had a long thin face, and few teeth, which made his mouth as prim as a lawyer's. I kept my eye on him, having whispered to Lombard to mark Dorando. But they didn't try to rush us, only said a word to each other and turned and went back. That was the end of the first bout.

All afternoon nothing happened. The heat was blistering, and as there was no water on the hill and we had nothing liquid but a flask of brandy, we suffered badly from thirst. Malan babbled in his fever, and Haraldsen, who was in the shade beside him, went to sleep. Old Haraldsen had been in so many tight places in his life that he was hard to rattle. Little green lizards came out and basked in the sun on the tracks, widow-birds flopped among the trees, and a great ugly aasvogel dropped out of the blue sky and had a look at us. The whole land lay baking and still, and down in the kraal there was not a sound. There was nobody in the space between the huts, not a child or a chicken stirred, and we might have been looking down at a graveyard.

Suddenly from one of the kyas there came a cry as of some one in deadly pain. In the hot silence it had a horrible eeriness, for it sounded like a child's scream, though I knew that a Kaffir in pain or terror often gives tongue like an infant. I saw Lombard's face whiten.

'Oughtn't we to do something?' he croaked, for his mouth was dry with thirst.

'We can't,' I told him. 'I don't know what these swine are up to, but it will soon be our turn. Our only hope is to sit tight.'

When the twilight began to fall Peter descended from his perch. Being higher up the hill he had had a better view and he brought news.

'The stad is quiet,' he told us. 'All Mafudi's people are indoors, for they have been told that they will be shot if they show their faces. Of the others, two are on guard and the rest have not been sleeping. They have been pulling down a kya to get the old straw from the roof, and they have been down at the byres where the hay is kept. As soon as it is dark they will be very busy.'

'Good God!' I cried, for I saw what this meant. 'They mean to burn us out.'

'Sure,' he said. 'They are clever men. The moon will not rise till nine o'clock. Soon it will be black night, and we cannot shoot in the dark. There are eight of them, and of us only four. At this time of year there is no sap in the thorns, so they will burn like dry tinder. The gate will no longer matter. They can fire this scherm at six places, and we cannot watch them all. We are in a bad fix, Dick.'

There was no doubt about that. At in-fighting those scallywags-- leaving out Troth and Albinus, whom I knew nothing about--were far more than our masters. If Peter was right, our sanctuary would very soon be a trap. I summoned Haraldsen, and the four of us had a solemn council. We couldn't hold the place against fire, and we couldn't escape, for the gaps made by the flames would all be watched, and likewise the gate.

'Have you any plan?' I asked Peter.

He shook his head, for even he was at the end of his resources.

'We can only trust in God,' he said simply, and his mild quizzical face was solemn. 'Perhaps Jim Arcoll may come in time.'

Haraldsen said nothing. He had no weapon, so I offered him my rifle. But he preferred to take an axe which Peter had insisted on bringing from the camp, and he swung it round his head, looking like some old

Viking. I apologized to Lombard for having got him into such a hole, but he told me not to worry. That cry from the kraal had stripped him of all nervousness or fear. He was thinking only of what mischief he could do to the eight devils at the foot of the hill.

The short mulberry gloaming faded out of the sky, and night came down on the world like a thick black shawl. I had sent Lombard and Peter up to the summit where they could get early news of what was happening, for I knew that an attempt would be made to fire the scherm in several places at once. I stayed at the gate, and Haraldsen for some reason of his own insisted on staying beside me. We moved the sick Malan out into the open, for I feared that the firing of the scherm might kindle all the bush on the hill.

I can't say that I enjoyed the hour we had to wait. I saw no chance for us, short of a miracle, and the best we could hope for was a good scrap and a quick death. You may ask why we didn't parley with our enemies to gain time. The answer is that we were convinced that they meant black murder if we gave them half a chance; at least they meant to do in Haraldsen, and we couldn't allow that. Haraldsen himself had wanted to be let out and to go down and face them alone, but Peter and I told him not to be a fool.

The crisis came, as such things do, when I wasn't expecting it. Suddenly I saw a red glow in the night, apparently on the other side of the hill. The glow spread, which must mean that other fires had been started. There was a rifle shot, which I assumed to be Peter's, and then Lombard stumbled down with the news that the scherm was burning in four places. The next thing I knew was that there was a big burst of flame about five yards from me, and at the same moment faces appeared in the gate. I fired at one, there was an answering crackle of shots, and I felt a raw pain in my left shoulder. Then I saw the gate in a sheet of flame, for the wattles had been fired.

After that there was a wild confusion. I found an ugly face close to me, fired at it, and saw it go blind. That was the man from Lydenburg, for we found the body later. I saw other figures in the gap, and then I saw an extraordinary sight. Haraldsen, looking like a giant in the hellish glow, had leaped forward and was swinging his axe and shouting like a madman. The spectacle must have confounded the attackers, for they made wild shooting. He had a bullet through one pocket and another through his hair, but he got none in his body. I saw him jump the blazing remnant of the gate and bring his axe down on somebody's head. And then he was through them and careering out into the dark.

I was pretty dazed and wild, and I decided that it was all up now, when suddenly the whole business took a new turn. Above the crackle and the roar of the flames I heard a sound which I had not heard since the Matabele Rising, the deep throaty howl of Kaffirs on the war-path. It rose to heaven like a great wind, and I clutched at my wits and realized what had happened. Mafudi's men were up. They had been like driven cattle all day, but this outrage on their sacred place had awakened their manhood. Once they had been a famous fighting clan and the old fury had revived. They were swarming like bees round the scherm, and making short work of our assailants. The Kaffir sees better in the dark than a white man, and a knobkerrie or an axe is a better weapon in a blind scrap than a gun. Also there were scores of them, the better part of a hundred lusty savages, mad with fury at the violation of their shrine.

There was nothing I could do except join Peter and Lombard on the top. But there was no sign of them there, for they had each made for one of the burning gaps to do what they could to hold the fort. As a matter of fact the fires at no place had gone far enough to make an opening, so none of our assailants had got inside the scherm. Pandemonium was in full blast around it, where some of Mafudi's men were rounding up Troth's lot and the rest were beating out the flames. This latter wasn't an easy job and the moon was up before it was over. I simply sat on the bald crest beside the sacred stone and waited. This was no work for me. Peter and Lombard were somewhere on the hill, but it was impossible to find them in that dark maze. The noise of native shouting soon died away, so I realized that they had finished their business. The fires were all mastered except one that kept breaking out afresh. Then over the rim of the horizon rose the moon, and the world was bright again. I was just starting out to look for the others when I heard the jingle of bridles and the clatter of hoofs and knew that Arcoll's police had arrived at last.

Arcoll made a fine bag of miscreants--five, to be accurate, who were firm in the grip of Mafudi's people. Three were dead--the man from Lydenburg whom I shot, one of the new fellows whose skull Haraldsen split with his axe, and, as the fates would have it, Troth himself. Peter had got Troth at the very start, when he showed up for a second in the gleam of the first fire. There he lay with his neat London outfit punctured by Peter's bullet, a home-bred hound among jackals, but the worst jackal of the pack.

'That's a pleasant yarn,' said Sandy. 'Old Haraldsen told me a good many of his adventures, but not that one. It had the right sort of ending.'

'That wasn't quite the end,' I said. 'Haraldsen had burst through the ring into the arms of Mafudi's men, who knew him well and recognized him and kept him out of danger. But as soon as Arcoll arrived and took charge the old man got busy. He had been berserk at the gate, and now he seemed to be 'fey.' He said there was something still to do, and he insisted on Peter and Lombard and me accompanying him to the top of the Hill of the Blue Leopard. There he made us a speech, looking more like an old Norseman than ever. He said that we were his blood-brothers, who had been ready to stand by him to the end. But the end hadn't come, though Troth was dead and the others would soon be in quod. There was a legacy of ill will that would follow him to his last day, and the dead Troth would leave it as a bequest to his successors. So he wanted the three of us to swear that if he called for us we would come to his aid wherever in the world we might be. More, we must be ready to come to his son's help, for he considered that this vendetta might not end with his own life, and we were to hand on the duty to our own sons. As none of us was married that didn't greatly worry us.

'It was like something out of one of his Sagas. There we stood above the silvered bush on rocks which were like snowdrifts in the strong moonlight. We took his right hand in turn in ours and put it to our foreheads, and then we raised our right arms and repeated a mad formula about dew and fire and running water. . . . Lord, how it all comes back--that white world, and the smell of charred bush, and the pain in my shoulder, and Lombard, who had had about as much as he could stand, whimpering like a scared dog!'

'Well, he's dead now,' said Sandy, 'and your oath is finished, for it's not likely that his son will trouble you. Heigh-ho! The old wild days have gone. Peter long ago entered Valhalla. What about the third--Lombard, I think you called him?'

'Curiously enough,' I said, 'I met him last autumn. He's not thinking about any Saga oath nowadays. He is bald and plump and something in big business.'

CHAPTER V

Haraldsen's Son

The Clanroydens went off to Laverlaw for a fortnight, Sandy to fish his Border burns, and Barbara to attend to her garden, and I was settling down to my farming, when I got a letter from Lombard. I had heard nothing of him since our meeting in the train the previous autumn. He had not invited me for a week-end as he had suggested--at which I rejoiced, for I would have had to invent some excuse for refusing; nor had he repeated his proposal to lunch together in London.

His letter began with apologies for this neglect; he had been very busy all winter and had had to make two trips abroad. But now he wanted to see me--wanted to see me urgently. Was there any chance of my being in town in the coming week, and if so, could we meet? He would keep any appointment, but he suggested luncheon and then going back to his office to talk. I couldn't imagine what he had to say to me, and I had an unpleasant suspicion that he wanted me for one of his financial ventures, but, as I had to go to London on other business, I had no grounds for declining. So I wired asking him to lunch at my own club, a quiet place with a smoking-room on the top floor which we could have to ourselves.

Lombard was looking worried, and he had also a heavy cold. His ruddy face had gone white, his eyes watered, and his voice was like a cracked tin-can. He had been drenched golfing, he told me, and the east wind had done the rest. But his bodily ailment was the least of his troubles, and I had the impression that this plump, four-square personage had been badly shaken. At luncheon I made him drink hot whisky-and-water, but he only picked at his food, and had very little conversation. There was something on his mind, and I was glad when I got him to the upper smoking-room, settled him in an armchair, and told him to get on with it.

His first question startled me.

'Do you remember a chap called Haraldsen?' he asked. 'Thirty years ago in Rhodesia? The time I went on trek with you when I was on my way home?'

'I do,' I said. 'Oddly enough I was talking about him last week.'

'Well, I've seen him.'

'Then you've seen a ghost,' I replied; 'for he is dead.'

He opened his rheumy eyes.

'I don't mean the old man--I mean his son. But how do you know that Haraldsen is dead? The young one doesn't know it.'

'Never mind,' I said. 'It's too long a story to tell you now, but it's a fact. What about the young one? I knew there was a son, but I never heard anything about him. What sort of age?'

'Over thirty. Perhaps nearer forty. He wrote to me and asked for an interview--found my name in the telephone-book--didn't say what he wanted. I thought he might have something to do with a Swedish wood-pulp proposition, for I've been doing a little in that line lately, so I agreed to see him, though I was very busy. I had completely forgotten the name, and it never suggested Rhodesia.'

He stopped, and then broke out quite fiercely. 'Why on earth should it? It's all more than thirty years ago, and I've long ago buried the callow boy who went vapouring about Africa. Hang it all, I've made a position for myself. Next year I hope to be a Director of the Bank of England. I've my reputation to consider. You see that, don't you?'

I didn't know what he was driving at, but it was plain that Lombard was no longer the sleek suburbanite. Something had jostled him out of his rut.

'But there was nothing in the old Haraldsen business to hurt your credit,' I said. 'So far as I remember, you behaved well. There's no skeleton in that cupboard.'

'Wait till you hear,' he replied dismally. 'This chap came to my office, and he told me a dashed silly story. Oh, a regular blood- and-thunder yarn of how he was in an awful mess, with a lot of crooks out gunning for him. I didn't follow him very clearly, for he was in a pitiable state of nerves, and now and then lost command of the English language altogether. But the gist of it was that he was in deadly danger, and that his enemies would get him unless he found the right kind of friends. I don't know how much was true, but I could see that he believed it all. There must be some truth in it, for he didn't look a fool, and I'll swear that he's honest.'

He stopped, and I waited, for I guessed what was coming.

'He asked me to help him,' Lombard continued, 'though God knows what he thought I could do. I'm not a Cabinet Minister or a Chief of Police. Did you ever hear anything more preposterous?'

'Never,' I said heartily--and waited.

'He had got it into his head that he had some claim on me. Said I once helped his father in a tight place, and that his father had sworn me to stand by him if called upon--or by his son. Apparently the old man had put it all down in writing, and this Haraldsen had the document.'

'Well, it's not the kind of thing you could sue on,' I said cheerfully.

'I know that. . . . But, I say, Hannay, do you remember the occasion?'

'Perfectly. We stood on the top of a kopje in the moonlight, and the old boy swore us by one of his Viking oaths. Oh, I remember it all right.'

'So do I,' said Lombard miserably. 'Well, what the devil is to be done about it?'

'Nothing,' I said stoutly. I had sized up Lombard, and I realized that to expect this sedentary middle-aged fellow to take a hand in a wild business was beyond all reason. My old liking for him had returned, and I didn't want him to have an uneasy conscience. But what puzzled me was why young Haraldsen had gone to him. 'There were three of us in it,' I said. 'You and I and Peter Pienaar. Peter is in a better world, but I'm still to the fore. Why didn't he tackle me? I had much more to do with his father than you had.'

'Perhaps he didn't think of you as a major-general with a title. He probably heard my name in the City. Anyhow, there we are, and an infernal worrying business it is.'

'My dear chap, you needn't worry,' I said. 'We have all been foolish in our young days, and we can't be expected to go on living up to our folly. If I had made a pact with a man when I was twenty-one to climb Everest, and he turned up to-day and wanted to hold me to it, I should tell him to go to blazes. But I should like to hear more of young Haraldsen's yarn.'

'I didn't get it quite straight,' he replied, 'for the fellow was too excited. Besides, I didn't try to, for I could think of nothing except that ridiculous performance in Rhodesia. But I jotted down one or two names he mentioned, the names of the people he was afraid of.' From his pocket he took a sheet of notepaper. 'Troth,' he read, 'Lancelot Troth. And a name which may be Albius or Albion--I didn't ask him to spell it. Oh, and Barralty--you know, the company-promoter that came down in the Lepcha goldfield business.'

This made me open my eyes. 'God bless my soul, but Troth is dead. You know that yourself, for you saw old Peter Pienaar account for him. Your second name is probably Albinus--you must remember him too. If he's still alive I can't think what the Devil is waiting for. Barralty I know nothing about. I tell you what, Lombard, this all sounds to me like sheer hallucination. Young Haraldsen has come on Troth and Albinus in his father's papers, and has let himself be hagridden by ghosts from the past. Most likely the man is crazy.'

He shook his head. 'He didn't impress me that way. Scared if you like, but quite sane. Anyhow, what do you advise me to do about it? He made an appeal to me--he was almost weeping--and I had to promise to give him an answer. My answer is due to-morrow.'

'I think you had better turn the thing over to me,' I said. 'I've had some news lately about old Haraldsen, and I'd like to meet his son. Have you got his address?'

'I know how to get on to him. He's desperately secretive, but he gave me a telephone number which I could ring up and leave a message for a Mr. Bosworth.'

'Well, send the message. I must go home to-morrow, but to-night I'm free. Tell him to dine with me here to-night at eight. Give him my name, and mention that I was deeper in the old business than you were. If the thing's genuine, he is bound to have some record of me. If it's bogus, he'll never turn up.'

'What will you do with him?' he asked.

'I'll cross-examine him and riddle out the business. I know enough about old Haraldsen to be able to cross-examine with some effect. I suspect that the whole thing is a lunatic's fancy, for there's a good deal of lunacy in the Northern races. In that case, you and I will be able to go to bed in peace.'

'But if it's serious?' he asked, and his face showed that he had not much doubt about that.

'Oh, if there's anything in it, I suppose I must take a hand. After all, I was a pretty close friend of his father, which you never were. You needn't worry about the Moonlight Sonata stuff, for I put nothing on that. That was only old Haraldsen's taste for melodrama. Consider yourself as clean out of the affair, like Peter Pienaar. You've been a responsible citizen for the better part of thirty years, with a big business to manage and a settled life and all the rest of it. No sane man would expect you to butt into a show of this kind. Besides, you'd be no sort of good at it. I've settled down, too, but I've led a different kind of life from you, and crime is a little bit more in my line. I've made several excursions into the under-world, and I know some of the ropes.'

There was an odd change in his face, which had hitherto registered only anxiety. I could have sworn that he was getting cross.

'If you were in my position, would you take that advice?' he asked in a flat voice.

'Most certainly I should,' I replied.

'You're a good fellow, Hannay,' he said, 'and you mean well. But you're a damned liar. If you were in my position, you'd do nothing of the kind, and you'd have the blood of anybody who advised you to. I can see what you take me for--I could see it in your eyes when we foregathered in the train. You believe I'm a fatted calf that has made a success in the City, and thinks only of his bank balance and his snug house, and his Saturday's golf. You believe that I'm the sort of herring-gutted creature that would take any insult lying down, or at the best run round to my solicitors. Well, you're wrong. I've had a soft life compared to you, but it hasn't been all fur-lined. I've had to take plenty of risks, and some of them mighty big ones. I had no wish to see you again after we met last autumn, for I saw that you despised me, and I didn't see how I could ever get you to change your mind. You're right in some ways. I'm a bit flabby and out of training in body and mind. But by God you're wrong about the main thing. I've never gone back on my word or funked a duty. And I'm not going to begin now. If there's anything in Haraldsen's story, my promise stands, and I'm in the business up to my neck, the same as you. If you don't agree to that, then you'll jolly well stand out, and I'll take it on myself.'

I felt the blood surging to my cheeks. Lombard had got up from his chair, and I had done the same, and we stood staring at each other across the hearth-rug. I saw in his face what I had missed altogether on the last occasion we met, a stubborn resolution and a shining honesty. In spite of his baldness and fleshiness and bleared eyes and snuffling, he looked twenty years younger. I recognized in him the boy I had known in Equatoria, and I felt as if I had suddenly recovered an old friend.

'Never mind what I thought,' I said. 'If I thought as you say I did I made a howling mistake and I grovel in apologies. We've picked up our friendship where we left it at Mafudi's kraal, and we'll see this thing through together.'

All the anger had gone out of his face.

'Mafudi,' he repeated. 'Yes, that's the name. I couldn't get to sleep last night for trying to remember it.'

I had two things to think about that evening. One was the revelation I had had of the true Lombard. That gave me extraordinary pleasure, for it seemed to remove the suspicion I had had all winter that I was myself old and stale and that all my youth had gone. If the fire still burned in this padded City magnate, it could not have died altogether in me. The second thing was Haraldsen, and I confess I felt solemn when I reflected that the week before Sandy Clanroyden had brought news of him out of the remotest East, news acquired by the wildest of chances. I had an eerie sense that this was all a sort of preparation engineered by Providence.

Lombard telephoned to me that 'Mr. Bosworth' would come to my club at eight o'clock. There was nobody in the smoking-room as I waited for my guest, and I remember trying to imagine what kind of fellow I should meet, and to reconstruct a younger version of old Haraldsen.

I got one of the shocks of my life when he appeared. For it was the man Smith, whom Peter John and I had met in the Rose and Crown at Hanham.

His surprise when he saw me was quite equal to mine.

'You!' he cried. 'Oh, thank God, I have found you. I never dreamed. . . .'

'You heard my name at Hanham,' I said.

'Ah, but I was looking for a South African engineer called Dick Hannay. In you I saw only an English general and a grandee. I took to you then--I do not know when I have so taken to a man, for I saw that you were wise and kind. But I did not imagine that you were my Dick Hannay.'

'Well, I am,' I said. 'I've seen Lombard, so two of your father's friends are with you. The third, the pick of the bunch, is dead.'

'You will stand beside me?' he stammered.

'Certainly,' I said. 'You may count us both in. Lombard told me that this afternoon.'

It was wonderful to see the effect these words had on him. As I have said, he was a very big fellow, but he slouched as if he were afraid of his size, and he had a shy, confused manner, like a large thing trying to hide behind something too small to cover it. He had cut an odd enough figure at Hanham, but in London he was clean out of the picture. When he entered the room my impression had been of a being altogether maladjusted to his environment, out of focus, so to speak, built on a wrong scale. But with his recovery of confidence he became almost normal, and I saw that the bucolic impression I had got of him was false. In his old-fashioned dinner-jacket he was more like a scholar than the farmer I had taken him for. His brow was broad and high, and his eyes had the unmistakable look of having peered a good deal over white paper.

At dinner he told me his story. He had not seen his father for eight years, or heard from him for three years, but it was clear that the old man was the dominant influence in his life. He had been brought up from childhood on a plan. While the elder Haraldsen was ranging the world the younger stayed in Europe, preparing himself for the task for which the former was laying up a fortune. He was to be the leader of the Northern peoples to a new destiny, and from a small boy he was put into the strictest training. First he was to be a master of all Northern learning, and imbibe its spirit. Then he was to know every corner of the North and every type of Northman. After that he was to have a first-class business education and learn how to handle big affairs. The old man's ambition for his son seemed to have been a kind of blend of Sir Walter Scott and Bismarck and Cecil Rhodes.

Of course, it didn't work--that kind of scheme never does. The young Valdemar (his Christian name was Valdemar) went stolidly through an immense curriculum, for he was clay in his father's hands, but the result was not the Admirable Crichton of the old man's dreams. He went to college in Denmark and Germany; he did two years in a Copenhagen bank; he travelled from Greenland in the west to the White Sea in the east, and even got as far as Spitzbergen, and there were not many places in Scandinavia and its islands on which he had not turned his unseeing eyes. But he did it all as a round of duty, for he had not a spark of his father's ardour. A scholar indeed he became, and a keen naturalist, but nothing more. He wanted a quiet life, and the future of the Northern races was no more to him than a half-forgotten fairy tale.

So at twenty-six there was Valdemar Haraldsen, sound in wind and limb, stuffed with much curious learning, but with no more ambition than a mole. I gathered that the old man had been disappointed, but had made the best of it. His son was young, so there was still hope, for there must be some fruit from so arduous a sowing. It seemed that his mother had come out of the Norland Isles, the daughter of a long line of what they called King's Yeomen there. She had inherited an island, and there the elder Haraldsen, on one of his longer sojourns in Europe, had built a house. He seemed to have made a minor hobby of it, for he had spent a good deal of money and filled it with Northern furniture and antiques. He agreed to Valdemar settling down there, after the boy had married with his consent, for no doubt he thought that the genius loci would have something to say to him. But the marriage had soon a tragic ending, for the young wife died with her first child.

I asked about the child.

'She lives and is well,' he said. 'She is now in her thirteenth year. She is at a school in England.'

He had stayed on in his lonely isle, and I gathered had become a good deal of a recluse, rarely coming south, and filling his time with his hobbies, which were principally natural history and an inquiry into the interaction of the old Norse and Celtic peoples.

'But I was happy,' he said in his gentle voice. 'I was indeed always anxious about my father, who did not come to me and would not permit me to go to him. But I had my girl Anna with me till she was of age for school, and I had my house and my books and my little kingdom. And I had good health and a quiet mind.'

'You're well off?' I asked.

A pained look came into his eyes, as if his mind had been engaged with pleasant things and now saw something hideous.

'I believe I am very rich,' he said slowly. 'I do not know how rich, for money has never interested me. There are bankers in Copenhagen who look after these things for me, and they tell me I need not stint myself.'

I thought what bad luck it was on old Haraldsen to go on piling up a fortune for a son who never wanted to hear how much it was.

'Well,' I said, 'I think I've got the lay-out. You've been squatting peacefully up in your island while your father has been gold-digging in the ends of the earth. What has happened now? What is the trouble?'

'The trouble,' he said slowly, and his eyes were full of pain again, 'is that I have lost my quiet mind.'

Then he told me, with long stops when he seemed to be hunting for words, the following story.

Two years before he had had a letter from a London firm of solicitors who said that they wrote on behalf of a client who had a claim on his father, and asked for his father's address. He replied that he did not know where his father was, and thought no more about it. Then came a second letter, asking whether the old man was alive or dead, and Haraldsen duly replied that he couldn't be sure, but hoped for the best. After that he was informed that an action at law would be begun, and that, if his father did not appear, an attempt would be made to have his death presumed, so that recourse might be had against his estate. I didn't quite get the hang of the argument, for Valdemar was not very clear himself. The correspondence was all perfectly civil in tone, but the last letter gave him a nasty shock, for the solicitors disclosed that their client was a Mr. Lancelot Troth.

Now Valdemar had a great quantity of his father's papers, which he had been at pains to read and arrange, and among them were records of his old days in Africa, and especially of his early work on the Rand. The name of Troth appeared in some of them. Troth had been the old man's partner at one time and had tried to swindle him. There had been a terrific row, and Troth had cleared out, but Haraldsen had been certain that he would come back again and make mischief. He took the trouble to write out a detailed statement of the case, and Valdemar said that it left the impression on him that while Troth was no doubt a rogue, he might have had some kind of a grievance, and that his father's conscience was not quite easy about the business.

Among the papers, too, was a full account of the affair at the Hill of the Blue Leopard, and of how he had sworn three men, Lombard, Peter Pienaar, and myself, to stand by him or his son, if there was any further trouble on that score. The funny thing was that he did not mention that Troth had been killed. He seemed to have the Saga notion that a vendetta went on from generation to generation, and that Troth's son, if he had one, might make things unpleasant for his own son. He mentioned Albinus too, who had apparently been a subordinate figure in the first row on the Rand, but a leader at Mafudi's.

So when Valdemar saw the name of Troth in the solicitors' letter he began to feel uncomfortable. I gathered that his father had been very solemn about the affair, and had gone out of his way to warn his son. Valdemar did his best to put the thing out of his head, but not with much success. And then he got a letter signed Lancelot Troth which had effectively scared him. The lawyers' correspondence had been, so to speak, only ranging shots, and now the guns started in earnest.

The writer said that his father had been grievously wronged by the old Haraldsen, and that he demanded restitution. If the old man was dead, or lost to the world, the son must pay, for he had ascertained that he was very rich. There need be no unpleasantness, if the writer were fairly treated, for he was convinced that his claim must be patent to any reasonable man. He suggested that a meeting should be arranged in Copenhagen or London, to which Valdemar could bring one adviser, while he, Troth, would bring his partner, Mr. Erick Albinus, who was a party to his claim. There was no talk now of any legal action. It was a straight personal demand to stand and deliver.

Valdemar was mightily put out, and, not being a man of the world, would in all likelihood have done something silly--seen Troth, agreed to his terms, and so put himself in his power for the rest of his life. But luckily he met an Englishman who came up that summer to fish in the Norlands, and in the course of conversation asked him some vague questions, in which he managed to mention Troth's name. The Englishman was a well-known barrister whose practice was largely at the Old Bailey, and he could tell him a good deal about Troth, though he had never heard of Albinus. Troth had succeeded to his father's business as a solicitor, and bore a pretty shady repute. The fisherman described him as one who didn't stick at trifles, but had so far been clever enough to keep on the sunny side of the law. He was believed to be at the moment in the environs of Queer Street, for he was mixed up with Barralty in the Lepcha Reef flotation, and that was beginning to look ugly. 'I hate the fellow,' said the Englishman, 'but I wouldn't go out of my way to cross him. He has an eye like a gunman's, and a jowl like a prizefighter.'

That talk opened Valdemar's eyes to the dangers of his position. He had sense enough to see that it was a case of large-sized blackmail, and that any sum he paid would only be a lever for further extortions till he was bled white. He went off his sleep, and worried himself into a fever, for he couldn't decide what his next step should be.

While he was still cogitating he got a second letter from Troth. Mr. Haraldsen need not trouble to come south, for the writer was about to pay a visit to the Norlands in his friend Mr. Barralty's yacht. He proposed a meeting in Hjalmarshavn some three weeks ahead.

This screwed Valdemar up to the point of action. Alone on his island he was at the mercy of any gang of miscreants that chose to visit him. His ignorance of the world made him imagine terrible things. He hungered for human society, for a crowd in which he could hide himself. So he buried his papers and some of the things he most valued, shut up his house, left the island to the care of his steward, and along with his daughter fled from the Norlands. He left an address in Copenhagen for forwarding letters, but he did not mean to go there, for he was known in Denmark and would be recognized. He determined to go to London, where he would be utterly obscure.

Troth and his friend duly arrived in the Norlands. They visited the Island of Sheep--this was the name of Valdemar's place--and, when they found it empty, pretty well ransacked the house, just like so many pirates from the sea. But they did no mischief, for they were playing a bigger game. Valdemar heard of this from his steward, his letter going first to his bank in Copenhagen, then to a friend in Sweden, and finally to his English address. He placed his child in an English school, and took to wandering about the country, calling himself Smith and other names, and never staying long in one place. He heard of the crash of the Lepcha Reef and Barralty's difficulties, and realized that this would make the gang keener than ever on his scent. He had letters from Troth--three I think--and the last fairly put the wind up. 'You have refused to meet me frankly,' said Troth, 'and you have run away, but don't imagine you can escape me. I will follow you till I track you down, though I have to give up my life to the job, and the price you will have to pay will double with each month I have to wait.' It was brigandage now, naked brigandage.

I am not sure that I believed all this tale, but there was one thing I couldn't doubt--Valdemar believed it, and was sweating with terror. That big man, who should have marched stoutly through life, had eyes like a hunted deer's.

'What an infernal nuisance for you!' I said. 'You can't go home, because of the threats of those scallywags! Well, anyhow, you're safe enough here, and can have an easy mind till we think out some plan.'

'I am not safe here,' he said solemnly. 'At first I thought that no one knew me in England. But I was wrong. They have had descriptions of me--photographs--from the Norlands and from Copenhagen. They have found people who can identify me. . . . One day in the street I saw a barber from Denmark who has often shaved me, and he recognized me, and tried to follow me. He is a poor man and would not have come here on his own account. He has been brought to London. The net is drawing in on me, and I know from many small things that they are very close on my trail. I change my dwelling often, but I feel that I cannot long escape them. So I am very desperate, and that is why I have sought out my father's friends.'

He sat huddled in his chair, his chin sunk on his breast, the image of impotence and despair. I realized that Lombard and I were going to have a difficult job with him. I had an uneasy suspicion, as I looked at him, that his story might be all moonshine, the hallucination of a lonely neurotic, and I wished I had never heard of him. Keeping a promise was one thing, but nursing a lunatic was quite another.

'It is not only for myself I fear,' he said in a leaden voice. 'There is my little daughter. I dare not visit her in case they follow me. They might kidnap her, and then I should assuredly go mad.'

To that I had nothing to say, for the mention of kidnapping always made me windy. I had had too much of it in the affair with Medina, which I have already written about.*

'There is my father, too,' he went on. 'He may at any moment go to the Norlands or come to England, and I cannot warn him.'

'You needn't worry about that,' I said gently. 'Your father died two years ago--at a place called Gutok, in Chinese Tibet.' And I repeated briefly what Sandy Clanroyden had told me.

You never saw such a change in a man. The news seemed to pull him together and put light into his eyes. To him, apparently, it was not a matter of grief, but of comfort.

'Thesauro feliciter invento,' he repeated. 'Then he succeeded--he has died happy. I cannot sorrow for him, for he has greatly ended a great life.'

He put his chin on his hand and brooded, and in that moment I was possessed by one of those queer irrational convictions which I have always made a habit of accepting, for I have never found them wrong. This Valdemar Haraldsen was as sane as myself, and he was in deadly peril. I believed implicitly every word of his tale, and my duty to help him was plain as a pikestaff. My first business must be to tuck him away comfortably somewhere out of the road.

I asked him where he was living and if he was sure he had not been followed here. He said that he had only moved into his new quarters two days before, and was pretty certain that he was safe for the moment. 'But not for long,' he added dismally.

'Well, you must clear out,' I said. 'Tomorrow you pack your kit. You are coming to stay with me for a little. I will go down by an earlier train, for we shouldn't be seen together. Put on your oldest clothes and travel third-class--I'll send my keeper to meet you, and he'll bring you up in the old Ford. Your name is still Bosworth.'

I fixed up a train, offered him a whisky-and-soda, which he declined, and saw him shamble off in the direction of his Bayswater lodgings. He looked like a store-farmer who had borrowed an ancient suit of his father's dress-clothes, and that was the rôle I wanted him to play. Then I rang up Macgillivray in his Mount Street rooms, found that he was at home, and went round to see him.

* In The Three Hostages.

CHAPTER VI

Sundry Doings at Fosse

I found Macgillivray reading Greek with his feet on the mantelpiece and the fire out. He was a bit of a scholar and kept up his classics. Of all my friends he was the one who had aged least. His lean, dark head and smooth, boyish face were just as I remembered them twenty years ago. I hadn't seen him for months, and he gave me a great welcome, rang for beer to which he knew I was partial, and settled me in his best armchair.

'Why this honour?' he asked. 'Is it friendship or business? A sudden craving for my company, or a mess you want to be helped out of?'

'Both,' I said. 'But business first.'

'A job for the Yard?'

'No-o. Not just yet, anyhow. I want some information. I've just got on the track of a rather ugly affair.'

He whistled. 'You have a high standard of ugliness. What is it?'

'Blackmail,' I said.

'Yourself? He must be a bold blackmailer to tackle you.'

'No, a friend. A pretty helpless sort of friend, who will go mad if he isn't backed up.'

'Well, let's have the story.'

'Not yet,' I said. 'It's a private affair which I would rather keep to myself for a little till I see how things shape. I only want an answer to a few questions.'

He laughed. 'That was always your way, Dick. You "keep your ain fish-guts for your ain sea-mews," as they say in Scotland. You never let in the Yard till the fruitiest episodes are over.'

'I've done a good deal for you in my time,' I said.

'True. And you may always count upon us to do our damnedest.'

Then he suddenly became serious.

'I'm going to talk to you like a grandfather, Dick. You're not ageing properly.'

'I'm ageing a dashed sight too fast,' I said.

'No, you're not. We're all getting old, of course, but you're not acquiring the virtues of age. There's still an ineradicable daftness about you. You've been lying pretty low lately, and I had hoped you had settled down for good. Consider. You're a married man with a growing son. You have made for yourself what I should call a happy life. I don't want to see you wreck it merely because you are feeling restless. So if it's only a craze for adventure that is taking you into this business, my advice to you as a friend is to keep out of it.'

He picked up the book he had been reading.

'Here's a text for you,' he said. 'It is Herodotus. This is the advice he makes Amasis give to his friend Polycrates. I'll translate. "I know that the Gods are jealous, for I cannot remember that I ever heard of any man who, having been constantly successful, did not at last utterly perish." That's worth thinking about. You've been amazingly lucky, but you mustn't press your luck too far. Remember, the Gods are jealous.'

'I'm not going into this affair for fun,' I replied. 'It's a solid obligation of honour.'

'Oh, in that case I have no more to say. Ask your questions.'

'Do you know anything about a fellow called Albinus, Erick Albinus? A man about my own age--a Dane by birth who has lived in America and, I should think, in many parts of the world? Dabbles in finance of a shady kind.' I gave the best description I could of how

Albinus had looked thirty years ago, and what his appearance to-day might be presumed to be.

Macgillivray shook his head. 'I can't place him. I'll have our records looked up, but to the best of my knowledge I don't know anybody like him. I certainly don't remember his name.'

'Well, then, what about a man called Lancelot Troth?'

'Now we're getting on familiar ground,' he said. 'I know a good deal about Troth. The solicitor, I suppose you mean? He belongs to a firm which has been going on for several generations and has never been quite respectable. The father was a bit of a rogue who died years ago somewhere in Africa. That was before my time, but in the last ten years we have had to keep an eye on the activities of the son. He operates on the borderland of rather dubious finance, but so far he has never quite crossed the frontier, though sometimes he has had to be shepherded back. Company promotion is his chief line, and he is uncommonly clever at taking advantage of every crack in our confused company law. I thought we had him the other day over the Lepcha business, but we were advised that a prosecution would fail. He has several side lines--does a good deal of work for Indian rajahs which may now and then be pretty shady--made a pot of money over greyhound-racing in its early days-- a mighty gambler, too, they tell me, and fairly successful. Rich! So-so. Flush one day and hard up the next--he leads the apolaustic life, and that's an expensive thing nowadays.'

I asked about his appearance and Macgillivray described him. A man in his early forties, strongly made, with the square, clean-shaven face of his profession. Like a cross between a Chancery barrister and a Newmarket trainer.

'He doesn't make a bad impression at first sight,' he added. 'He looks you in the face and he has rather pleasant eyes. On the occasions when I've met him I've rather liked him. A tough, no doubt, but with some of the merits of the breed. I can imagine him standing stiffly by his friends, and I have heard of him doing generous things. He's a bit of a sportsman too--keeps a six-ton cutter, and can be seen on a Friday evening departing in old clothes from his City office with his kit in a pillow-case. If your trouble is blackmail, Dick, and Troth is in it, it won't be the ordinary kind. The man might be a bandit, but he wouldn't be a sneak-thief.'

Then I spoke the name of Barralty, and when he heard it Macgillivray's attention visibly quickened. He whistled, and his face took on that absent-minded look which always means that his brain or his memory is busy.

'Barralty,' he repeated. 'Do you know, Dick, you've an uncommon knack of getting alongside interesting folk? Whenever you've consulted me it has always been in connection with gentry about whom I was pretty curious myself. Barralty--Joseph Bannatyne Barralty! It would take a cleverer man than me to expound that intricate gentleman. Did you ever see him?'

I said No--I had only heard of him for the first time that day.

'How shall I describe him? In some lights he looks like a half-pay colonel who inhabits the environs of Cheltenham. Tallish, lean, big-nose, high cheek-bones--dresses generally in well-cut flannels or tweeds--age anything round fifty. He has a moustache which has gone grey at the tips, and it gives him a queer look of innocence. That's one aspect--the English country gentleman. In another light he is simply Don Quixote--the same unfinished face, the same mild sad eyes and general air of being lost that one associates with the Don. That sounds rather attractive, doesn't it?--half adventurer, half squire? But there's a third light--for I have seen him look as ugly as sin. The pale eyes became mean and shallow and hard, the rudimentary features were something less than human, and the brindled moustache with its white points looked like the tusks of an obscene boar. . . . I dare say you've gathered that I don't much like Mr. Barralty.

'But I don't understand him,' he went on. 'First of all, let me say that we have nothing against him. He came down in the Lepcha business, but there was never any suggestion against his character. He behaved perfectly well, and will probably end by paying every creditor in full, for he is bound to come on top again. He has had his ups and downs, and, like everybody in the City, has had to mix with doubtful characters, but his own reputation is unblemished. He doesn't appear to care for money so much as for the game. Yet nobody likes him, and I doubt if many trust him, though every one admits his ability. Now if you find a man unpopular for no apparent reason, it is generally safe to assume some pretty rotten patch in him. I assume the patch all right in Barralty's case, but I'm hanged if I can put my finger on it, or find anything to justify my assumption except that now and then I've seen him look like the Devil.'

I asked about his profession.

'He's a stockbroker--a one-man firm which he founded himself. His interests? Not financial exclusively--indeed, he professes to despise the whole money-spinning business. Says he is in it only to get cash for the things he cares about. What are these? Well, yachting used to be one. In the days of his power he had the Thelma--six hundred tons odd--that might be the original link with Troth. Then he's a first-class, six-cylindered, copper-bottomed highbrow. A gentlemanly Communist. An intellectual who doesn't forget to shave. The patron of every new fad in painting and sculping and writing. Mighty condescending about all that ordinary chaps like you and me like, but liable to enthuse about monstrosities, provided that they're brand-new and for preference foreign. I should think it was a genuine taste, for he has that kind of rootless, marginal mind. He backs his fancy too. For years he has kept the ---- going (Macgillivray mentioned a peevishly superior weekly journal), and he imports at his own expense all kinds of exponents of the dernier cri. His line is that he despises capitalism, as he despises all orthodoxies, but that as long as the beastly thing lasts, he will try to make his bit out of it, and spend the proceeds in hastening its end. Quite reasonable. I blame nothing about him except his taste.'

'Isn't he popular with his progressive lot?' I asked.

Macgillivray shook his head. 'I should doubt it. They flatter him when necessary, and sponge on him, but I'm pretty certain they don't like him.'

I asked if all this intelligentsia business might not be a dodge to help Barralty's city interests. It made him a new type of financier, and simple folk might be inclined to trust a man who declared that his only object in getting money was to prevent anybody, including himself, piling it up in the future.

Macgillivray thought that there might be something in that.

'He's a cautious fellow. His name is always being appended to protests in the newspapers, but he keeps off anything too extreme. His line is not the fanatic, but the superior critic of human follies. He does nothing to scare the investor. . . . Well, I'll keep an eye on him, and see if I can find out more about his relations with Troth. And the other fellow--what's his name--Erick Albinus? You've given me an odd triangle.'

As I was leaving, Macgillivray said one last thing, which didn't make much impression at the time, but which I was to remember later.

'I should back you against the lot, Dick. They're not natural criminals, and their nerve might crack. The danger would be if they got into the hands of somebody quite different--some really desperate fellow--like yourself.'

I went down to Fosse next morning by the early train, and Haraldsen duly arrived at midday. He put up with my keeper Jack Godstow, who had a roomy cottage in which I reserved a couple of rooms for bachelor guns when Fosse was overcrowded during a big shoot. I hunted him up after tea, and we went for a walk on the Downs.

My impression of the day before was confirmed. Haraldsen was as sane as I was. Whatever his trouble was, it was real enough, and not a mental delusion. But he was in an appalling condition of nerves. He was inclined to talk to himself under his breath--you could see his lips moving, and he had a queer trick of grunting. When we sat down he kept twitching his hands and fussing with his legs, and he would suddenly go off into an abstraction. He admitted that he had been sleeping badly. I was distressed by his state, for he was a fifty per cent. sicker man than he had been at Hanham in January. I discovered that he had two terrors: one that something very bad might at any moment happen to himself or his daughter--especially his daughter. The other was that this miserable thing might simply drag on without anything happening, and that he would be shut off for ever from his beloved home in the north.

I did my best to minister to his tattered nerves. I told him that he was perfectly safe with me, and that I wouldn't let matters drag on--Lombard and I would take steps to clear them up. I encouraged him to talk about his Island of Sheep, for it did him good to have something pleasant to think about, and he described to me with tremendous feeling the delight of its greenery and peace, the summer days when it was never dark, the fresh, changing seas, the tardy, delicate springs, the roaring, windy autumns, the long, snug, firelit winters.

I impressed upon him that for the present he must lie low. He would have the run of the house and the library, and Mary and I would see a lot of him, but to the countryside he must be an invalid friend of a friend of mine, who had come to Fosse for quiet and mustn't be disturbed. Jack Godstow would take him out fishing and show him the lie of the land. I gathered that he had some belongings scattered up and down London which he would like to have beside him, and I said that I would arrange for Lombard to collect them quietly and send them on. But I chiefly told him to be quite assured that this persecution was going to be brought to an end, for I saw that it was only that hope which would soothe him.

I spoke confidently, but I hadn't a notion how it was to be done. Haraldsen's safety depended on his being hidden away--I was quite clear about that--so we couldn't draw the fire of his enemies so as to locate them. About these enemies I was wholly in the dark. An Americanized Dane, a shady sporting solicitor, a highbrow financier who looked like Don Quixote and had just crashed; it didn't sound a formidable combination. I had only met one of them, Albinus, and about him I only knew the episode at Mafudi's kraal; Macgillivray rather liked Troth, and Barralty sounded unpleasant but ineffective. Yet the three were engaged in something which had put the fear of death on a very decent citizen, and that had to be riddled out and stopped. There was nothing to do but to wait on developments. That night I wrote a long letter to Lombard, telling him the result of my talk with Macgillivray, asking him to keep his ears open for any news which would connect the three names, and warning him that I might summon him at any moment. As we went to bed I told Mary that I had not much to do for the next few weeks, and that I meant to devote them to getting Haraldsen back to an even keel.

But next day I had news which upset all my plans. Peter John at school was stricken with appendicitis, and was to be operated on that day. Mary and I raced off at once and took rooms near the nursing-home. The operation went off well, and after two days, which were purgatory to me and hell to Mary, he was pronounced to be out of danger. He made an excellent quick recovery, being as healthy as a trout, but it was a fortnight before he was allowed up, and three weeks before he left the home. Then, since the weather was hot, we took him to a seaside place on the East coast for a couple of weeks, so it was not till the beginning of June that we returned to Fosse.

Meanwhile I had heard nothing about Haraldsen. Lombard and Macgillivray had both been silent, and Jack Godstow had only reported weekly that the gentleman was doing nicely and was looking forward to the May-fly season. When I got back to Fosse I expected to find him rested and calmed and beginning to put on flesh, for all these weeks he had been deep in country peace and must have felt secure.

I found exactly the opposite. Haraldsen looked worse than when I had left him, leaner, paler, and his eyes had more of a hunted look than ever. He had little to say to me except to repeat his thanks for my kindness. No, he had not been disturbed; nothing had happened to alarm him; he was quite well and had got back a bit of his appetite, he thought; he wasn't sleeping so badly. But all the time his eyes were shifting about as if he expected any moment to see something mighty unpleasant, and he started at every noise. He was the very model of a nervous wreck.

I had a long talk about him with Jack Godstow. I won't attempt Jack's dialect, for no words could reproduce the odd Cotswold lilt and drawl, and the racy idiom of every sentence. The gist of his report was that Mr. Haraldsen was a difficult one to manage, since he never knew his own mind. He would make a plan to fish the evening rise, and then change it and start out at midnight when there was nothing doing. He didn't like the daylight no more than an owl, and he didn't like other folks neither, and would get scared if he saw a strange face. He was always asking about new folk in the neighbourhood, but Lord bless you, said Jack, new folk didn't come this way, except for an odd hiker or two, and the extra hands for the hay harvest, and the motor gentry on the Fosse Way. The gentleman needn't worry himself, and he had told him so, but it was no good speaking. I explained to Jack that my friend was a sick man, and that part of his sickness was a dread of strange faces. Jack understood that and grinned. 'Like that new 'awk of Master Peter John's,' he said.

The mention of Peter John gave me an idea. The boy was not going back to school that half, and was settling down to a blissful summer at Fosse before he went north to Sandy Clanroyden at Laverlaw. He had six little kestrels sitting all day on the lawn, and Morag on her perch in the Crow Wood, and a young badger called Broccoli that rootled about in the stable straw and gave him heart disease at night by getting down into the entrails of the greenhouses. He was still under a mild doctor's régime, but was picking up strength very fast. Haraldsen had taken to him at Hanham, and I thought that his company might be wholesome for him. So I asked him to take on the job of being a good deal with my guest, for everything about Peter John suggested calm nerves and solid reason. There was something else in my mind.

'Mr. Haraldsen is an invalid,' I said, 'and must keep quiet. He has been through rather a beastly experience, which I'll tell you about some day. It's just possible that the experience isn't over yet, and that some person or persons might turn up here who wouldn't be well disposed to him. I want you to keep your eyes very wide open and let me know at once if you see or hear anything suspicious. By suspicious I mean something outside the usual--I don't care how small it is. We can't afford to take any chances with Mr. Haraldsen.'

Peter John nodded and his face brightened. He asked no questions, but I knew that he had got something to think about.

Nothing happened for a week. The boy did Haraldsen good; Mary and I both noticed it, and Jack Godstow admitted as much. He took him to fish in the early mornings both in our little trout stream and in the Decoy ponds. He took him on the Downs in the afternoon to fly Morag. He took him into the woods after dinner to watch fox cubs at play, and try to intercept Broccoli's cousin on his way from his sett. Haraldsen began to get some colour into his face, and he confessed that he slept better. I don't know what the two talked about, but they must have found common subjects, for I could hear them conversing vigorously--Peter John's slow, grave voice, and Haraldsen's quicker, more staccato speech. If we were making no progress with Haraldsen's business we were at any rate mending his health.

Then one evening Peter John came to me with news.

They had been out hawking with Morag on the Sharway Downs, and on their way home had met a young man on horseback. At first Peter John had thought him one of the grooms from the Clipperstone Racing Stables exercising a horse, but as they passed he saw that the rider was not dressed like a groom. He wore white linen breeches, a smartly cut flannel coat, and an O.E. tie. He had taken a good look at the falconers, and the impression left by him on Peter John was of a florid young man with a small dark moustache and slightly projecting upper teeth. To their surprise they met him again, this time apparently in rather a hurry, for he was going at a quick trot, and again he scrutinized them sharply. Now, said my son, that meant that he had made a circuit by the track that led to Sharway Lodge Farm, and cut through the big Sharway Wood--not an easy road, and possible only for one who knew the country. Who was this young man? Did I know anybody like him, for he had never seen him before? Why was he so interested in the pair of them?

I said that he was no doubt a stranger who was intrigued by the sight of the falcon, and wanted to have another look at it.

'But he didn't look at Morag,' was the answer. 'It was Mr. Haraldsen that interested him--both times. You might have thought that he knew him and wanted to stop and speak.'

'Did Mr. Haraldsen recognize him?' I asked, and was told No. He didn't know him from Adam, and Peter John, not to alarm him, had pretended he was one of the racing-stable people.

Two days later I had to be at Gloucester for the Agricultural Show. When I was dressing for dinner in the evening Mary was full of the visitors she had had that afternoon at tea.

'The Marthews, no less!' she said. 'I can't think what brought them here, for Caythorp is thirty miles off and I scarcely know them. Claire Marthew was a god-daughter of one of my Wymondham aunts--I used to meet her here in the old days when she was Claire Serocold and a very silly affected girl. She hasn't improved much-- her face lacquered like a doll's, and her eyes like a Pekinese, and her voice so foolish it made one hot to hear it. She's by way of being uncommonly smart, and she babbled of grandees. But she was amiable enough, though I can't explain this sudden craving for my society. She brought her whole party with her--in several cars-- you never saw such a caravan. Mostly women who had to be shown the house and the garden--I wish I were a better show-woman, Dick, for I become paralysed with boredom when I have to expound our possessions. There was one extraordinarily pretty girl, a Miss Ludlow--a film actress, I believe, who was content to smile and look beautiful. There were a couple of young men, too, who didn't say much. I told Peter John to look after them, and I think he took them to see the hunters at grass, and Morag, and Broccoli. By the way, I haven't seen him since. I wonder what he's up to?'

Peter John was very late for dinner. In theory he should have been in bed by nine, but it was no good making rules for one whose habits, in summer at any rate, were largely nocturnal. At ten o'clock, when I was writing letters in the library, he appeared at my side.

'Did my mother tell you about the people who came to tea?' he asked. 'There was a flock of them, and one was the man that Mr. Haraldsen and I met on Tuesday--the chap on horseback who wanted to have another look at us.'

'What was his name?' I asked.

'They all called him Frankie. My mother thinks it was something like Warrender--but not Warrender. I took him to see the horses, and he asked a lot of questions.'

'Wasn't there another man?' I asked.

'Yes, but he didn't count. He was a sort of artist or antiquarian, and couldn't be got away from the tithe-barn. It was this Frankie chap that mattered. He made me take him all over the place, and he asked me all sorts of questions about who lived here, and what their jobs were, and who our friends were, and if many people came to stay with us. It would have been cheek in anybody else, but he did it quite nicely, as if he liked the place enormously and wanted to know all about it. But you told me to look out for anything suspicious, and I thought him a bit suspicious.

'And that isn't the end,' he went on. 'Frankie didn't go off with the rest. He started with them in a little sports car of his own, but he turned off at the lodge gate and tucked away his car in the track that leads to the old quarry. I was following him and saw him skirt the water-meadow and have a look at the back of Trimble's cottage. Then he moved on to Jack's, and lay up in the hazel clump behind it, where he could get a good view. I nipped in by the side door, and luckily caught Mr. Haraldsen, who was just starting out, and told him to stick indoors. Frankie was so long in the clump that I got tired of waiting and decided to flush him, so I made a circuit and barged in beside him, pretending I had lost Broccoli. He took it quite calmly, and said he was a keen botanist and had stayed behind to look for some plant that he had heard lived here. But he didn't want to stay any longer, so I saw him to his car, and he socked me two half-crowns, and then I went back to give the "All Clear" to Mr. Haraldsen.'

I told Peter John that he had done very well, and had better get off to bed. His story had disquieted me, for this Frankie man had clearly been interested in Haraldsen, and it looked as if he had spotted his lair. That wasn't difficult, for, if there was anybody at Fosse who was not staying in the house, Jack's cottage was the only one big enough for a guest. I cross-examined Mary about Frankie, but she could tell me little. He had seemed a very ordinary young man, with pleasant manners and a vacant face--she remembered his prominent teeth. But she had got his name--not Warrender, but Varrinder. 'He's probably the son of the snuffy old Irish peer--Clongelt?--Clongelly?--who was said to be a money- lender in Cork Street.'

It was, I think, three days later that Sandy Clanroyden came to visit us. He wired that he wanted exercise, and proposed that I should meet him at a distant railway station, send his kit back in the car, and walk with him the fifteen miles to Fosse. We had a gorgeous walk through the blue June weather, drank good ale at the little pubs, and dropped down from the uplands nearly opposite our lodge gates, where a wild field of stunted thorns formed the glacis of the hills. We had a clear view of a patch of highway, where two men were getting into a little sports car.

Sandy sank to the ground as if he had been shot. 'Down, Dick,' he commanded, and, after a long stare, fixed in his eye the little single glass which he used for watching birds. All I saw was two young men, who seemed to be in rather a hurry. One was hatless, and the other had his hat pulled far down on his head. At that distance I couldn't be sure, but I had the impression that both were a little the worse for wear, for their flannel suits didn't seem to hang quite right on them.

When they had gone, Sandy pocketed his glass and grunted. He didn't say one word till we reached the house and were being greeted by Mary. Instead of replying to her inquiries about Barbara, he asked, like a cross-examining counsel, if she had had any visitors at Fosse that afternoon.

'Oh yes,' she said. 'The Varrinder youth, who came with the Matthews, turned up again. I told you about him, Dick. He's a great botanist, and there is something very rare here, which he wanted to show to his friend. He said that on his last visit he had found the dwarf orchis.'

Sandy whistled. 'Not very clever,' he said. 'Ustulata is impossible on this soil. Who was his friend?'

'A Frenchman, a Monsieur Blanc. Mr. Varrinder called him Pierre.'

'Describe him.'

Mary wrinkled her brows. 'A man about thirty-five or forty, I should say. Very slim and elegant and beautifully dressed. A queerly shaped head that rose to a peak, rather like a faun's-- clean-shaven, and with the kind of colour that people get from living in hot climates. His chin was paler than the rest of his face, so I expect he once had a beard. They wouldn't stay to tea-- only wanted permission to explore the home woods.'

'Did Peter John see them?' I asked.

'I don't know. He has been out for the whole day, but he's back now, for I heard his bath running.'

As I was showing Sandy his room he said solemnly, 'We must have a long talk after dinner, Dick.'

'We must,' I said. 'I have a good deal I want to tell you.'

'And I have something rather startling to tell you,' he replied.

That night I brought Peter John into our conference, for I judged that he had better know everything. I began by going fully into the Haraldsen business, of which, of course, Sandy knew nothing. I told him of my talk with Lombard, and my talks with Haraldsen himself, and my conviction that the man was not dreaming, but was really in danger. I repeated what Macgillivray had told me about Troth and Barralty. I explained that I had thought it best to bring him down to Fosse, which seemed to me a safe hiding-place. Then I recounted what had happened since he came here, his growing restlessness and misery, which Peter John seemed to be in the way of curing, and finally the episode of young Varrinder. I said that I hadn't liked the business of that youth, for he appeared to have a morbid interest in Haraldsen, and I told of his lying up behind Jack's cottage, and I added that I liked less his coming here to- day with his tale of a bogus orchis. 'Do you know anything about him?' I asked.

'Not much,' said Sandy. 'I've heard of him. He's reputed to be something of a waster, gambles high at Dillon's, and so forth. But I can tell you a good deal about his friend Monsieur--Pierre-- Blanc.' Sandy repeated the name slowly as if each syllable had its flavour.

'Listen, Dick,' he said, 'and you, Peter John, though you'll have to get your father to explain a lot afterwards. I've told you pretty fully the story of what happened in Olifa two years ago.* You remember that the Gran Seco was a sort of port of missing ships, where all kinds of geniuses and desperadoes who had crashed their lives were inspanned in Castor's service. They were like the servants of the Old Man of the Mountain in the Crusades, and drugged themselves into competence and comfort. Well, you know what happened. The gang--they called themselves the Conquistadores--was cleaned out. Some were killed in our final scrap, and the rest were bound to die slowly when they were deprived of their dope. There was one of them, almost the boldest, called Jacques D'Ingraville, who had been in his day a famous French ace. He was as big a blackguard as the others, but more wholesome, for, though he doped, his work in the air kept his body from becoming quite so sodden. I was never very sure what became of him in the end. We had no certain news of his death in the fight at Veiro, but there was a strong probability that he had stopped a bullet there, and anyhow, I knew that his number was up, since the supply of astura was cut off. I pictured him creeping to some hole in South America or Europe to die.

* The tale of Lord Clanroyden's doings in Olifa will be found in The Courts of the Morning.

'Well, I was wrong,' he continued. 'Alone of those verminous Conquistadores--almost certainly alone--D'Ingraville lives. And I should say that he had recovered. He looked quite a fit man when I saw him this evening.'

Nobody spoke for a little. To me the whole affair suddenly began to wear a blacker complexion. It wasn't so much the appearance of D'Ingraville, for I had always suspected that Troth and Barralty and Albinus were not the whole of the gang. It was the fact that they had managed to trace Haraldsen here in spite of all our care. I reckoned that they must be far cleverer and more powerful than I had believed, and that my job of standing by Haraldsen was going to be a large-sized affair. I suddenly felt very feeble, and rather timid and old. But the sight of Sandy's face cheered me, for instead of being worried it was eager and merry.

'Who are in with you, Dick?' he asked. 'Only Lombard? Well, I think I must make a third. Partly because I've been funnily mixed up with Haraldsen, for Fate made me his father's legatee. The jade tablet was put in my hands for a purpose. Partly because of Monsieur le Capitaine Jacques D'Ingraville, alias Pierre Blanc. He's too dangerous a lad to be left at large. I haven't finished my Olifa job till I have settled with him. The time, I think, has come for me to take a hand.'

He got up and found himself a drink. I looked at him as he stood half in the dusk, with the light of a single lamp on his face--not much younger than me, but as taut as a strung bow and as active as a hunting leopard. I thought that Haraldsen's enemies had unloosed a force of pretty high velocity. Peter John must have thought the same. He had listened to our talk with his eyes popping out of his head, and that sullen set of his face which he always wore when he was strongly moved. But as he looked at Sandy his solemnity broke into a smile.

'I go up to town to-morrow,' said Sandy, 'and I must get busy. I want a good deal more information, and I have better means of getting it than Macgillivray. I wish I knew just how much time we have. The gang are on Haraldsen's track--that's clear--but the question is, have they located him? The Varrinder lad can't be sure, or he wouldn't have come back twice. . . . Of course they may have done the business to-day. I wonder how far they got this evening?'

Peter John spoke. 'They didn't get very far. They couldn't. You see, they both fell into the Mill pool.'

Sandy took his pipe from his mouth and beamed on the boy. 'They fell into the Mill pool? Explain yourself, my son.'

'I spotted them when they arrived,' said Peter John, 'and I knew they would be a little time in the house anyhow, so I nipped off and warned Mr. Haraldsen to keep cover. When they came out I trailed them. They went through the garden to the High Wood, but I was pretty certain that they meant to go to the hazel clump behind Jack's cottage. To get there they had to cross the Mill lead by the plank bridge just above the pool. The stone at the end of the bridge isn't safe unless the planks are pushed well up the bank. So I loosened it a bit more, and pulled down the planks so that they rested on it.'

'Well?' Sandy and I demanded in one breath.

'They both fell into the pool, and it's pretty deep. I helped to pull them out and asked them to come up to the house to change. They wouldn't, for they were very cross. But Mr. Varrinder socked me another five bob.'

CHAPTER VII

Lord Clanroyden Intervenes

Sandy departed next morning, and, as usual, was not communicative about his plans. I wanted him to see Haraldsen, but he said that there was no need, and that the sooner he was in London the better. He asked for Lombard's address and a line of introduction to him, and his only instruction was to keep Haraldsen safe for the next week. He suggested that to look after him might be made a whole- time job for Peter John.

Peter John took on the task joyfully, for here was something after his own heart. He worshipped Sandy, and to be employed by him thrilled him to the marrow. Besides, he had struck up with Haraldsen one of those friendships that a shy, self-contained boy very often makes with a shy man. Haraldsen came twice to dinner during the week after Sandy left, and there was no mistake about the change for the better in his condition. He spoke of his daughter at school without the flicker of fear in his eyes which had distressed me. He was full of questions about our small woodland birds, which were mostly new to him, and to which Peter John was introducing him. He was even willing to talk about his Island of Sheep without a face of blank desolation.

Then on the morning of Midsummer Day I got a shock on opening my Times. For on the leader page was a long letter from Sandy, and it was headed, 'The late M. E. Haraldsen.'

It told the story of the jade tablet and of how he had picked it up in a Peking junk-shop. He quoted the Latin in which Haraldsen had said good-bye to the world, but he didn't mention the place where the words had been written. The letter concluded as follows:

'Marius Haraldsen was known to many as one of the most successful prospectors and operators in the early days of the South African gold-fields. But his friends were aware that he was more than an ordinary gold-seeker. He had great dreams for his own Northern peoples, and his life was dedicated, as in the case of Cecil Rhodes, to building up a fortune for their benefit. He must have made great sums of money, but he always cherished the dream that before his death he would find a true Ophir which would enable him to realize fully his grandiose plans. I met him on this quest in the Middle East and others have met him elsewhere. He was no casual prospector, but, with ample means and the most scientific methods, was engaged in following up the trail of earlier adventurers.

'Now it would seem that before his death he had made good on the biggest scale. The jade tablet in my possession tells us that he had found his treasure. The inscription on the obverse no doubt contains the details, for Marius Haraldsen was above all things a practical man, and did not leave a task half finished. The writing is difficult, but when it is translated, as I hope it will shortly be, the world will know something of what may well prove an epoch- making discovery.

'Meantime, I thought that this interim report might give satisfaction to the surviving friends of a great man and an intrepid adventurer.'

The thing was signed 'Clanroyden,' and dated from Laverlaw, and the Times had as its fourth leader a pleasant little essay on the survival power of material objects and the ingenious ways of Providence.

I pondered long over that letter. The first thing that struck me was that it was not written in Sandy's usual fastidious style. It was frank journalism, and must be meant to appeal to a particular audience.

My second reflection was that I knew what that audience was. It was the gang who were persecuting Haraldsen's son. Sandy, in so many words, told them that the old man had brought off his great coup, and that the Haraldsen fortune was potentially far bigger than any of them had dreamed. Here was a new strong scent for the pack.

My last thought was that Sandy had now put himself into the centre of the hunt. Any one reading that letter must assume that he knew all about the Haraldsen family and its affairs. He wrote himself down as the possessor of what might be worth millions--he professed confidence about the meaning of the writing on the tablet and the certainty of its being translated. . . . His purpose was clear. It was to draw off the hounds.

I wired to him at once at his London club asking when I could see him, but I got no answer. Instead I had a telegram in the afternoon from Lombard requesting me to come at once to his country house. The telegram concluded: 'Lock up carefully behind you,' and that could only have one meaning. I brought up Haraldsen to stay at the Manor, with instructions to Mary and Peter John not to let him out of their sight, and by five o'clock I had started in the car for Surrey.

I reached Lombard's house about half-past seven. It was on the skirts of an old-fashioned village which had become almost a London suburb by the building of a ring of big villas round it. The house wasn't bad of its kind, a pseudo-Georgian edifice of red brick with stone facings, and its six acres or so of ground had been shaped into a most elaborate garden. There was a sample of everything-- miniature park, lily pond, water-garden, pergolas, arbours, yards of crazy paving; and he must have kept a largish staff of gardeners, for the place was blazing with flowers and manicured to the last perfection. Fosse was a shabby, old farm-house compared to it. It was the same indoors. Everything was shining white enamel, and polished wood, and glowing brass and copper. Some of the pictures looked to me good, but they were over-varnished and too pretentiously framed. There was overmuch glitter about the place, the masses of cut flowers were too opulent, the red lacquer was too fresh, there was no sober background to give the eye relief.

In the drawing-room I found the Lombards, and I recognized the inspiration which had created this glossiness. His wife, whom I had caught a glimpse of at the station in the preceding autumn, proved to be the most sumptuous of Lombard's possessions. She was dressed, I remember, in white and purple, and she had a wonderful cluster of orchids at her breast. As a girl she must have been lovely, and she was still a handsome woman of the heavy Madonna type--a slightly over-coloured Madonna. Being accustomed to slim people like Mary and Barbara Clanroyden and Janet Raden, I thought her a little too 'fair of flesh,' in the polite phrase of the ballads. I learned afterwards that she had been a tempestuous beauty, and well-dowered as well, for it was his marriage that first launched Lombard on his career.

'We are not to wait,' she told me. 'The fourth of our little party may be late. And we are not to use names, please, at table. Barton (that was the butler) is a confidential person, but it is not desirable that anybody else should know who is dining here. So you are to be Dick, please, and the fourth will be Sandy. These are Lord Clanroyden's own instructions.'

Dinner was announced, and I hadn't been seated five minutes at the table before I had Mrs. Lombard placed. She was a warm-hearted woman, without much brains, but with certain very definite tastes, and she dominated her environment. She was deeply in love with Lombard and he with her, and, since they had no children, each had grown into the other's ways. He had been swallowed up in the featherbed of her vast comfortableness, but she in turn had caught a spark from him, for she had a queer passion for romance, which I don't think she could have been born with. She amazed me by the range and variety of her not very intelligent reading, she had odd sensitive strains in her, and she sat in her suburban paradise expectant of marvels. Lombard had probably not told her very much about the present business, but he had told her enough to thrill her. I found her eyes looking at me sometimes just like an excited child, and I could see that she anticipated the coming of Sandy almost with awe. A few people no doubt knew my name, but half the world knew Sandy's.

He did not appear till the June twilight filled the big french windows, through which he slipped as if he had been a guest staying in the house. Barton and a footman were in the room at the time, and Mrs. Lombard behaved as if he were an old friend. 'So glad to see you at last, Sandy,' she said. 'I hope you had a pleasant journey.'

'Pleasant but longish,' he said. 'The air is the best route on a summer night. What a jolly place! I never smelt such roses.'

'Have you come from Laverlaw?' I asked when we were alone.

'No, only from London. But I didn't think it wise to come direct. I've been half round the southern counties, and I did the last stage on a bicycle--from Heston. You must give me a lift back there in your car, Dick.'

Sandy made an excellent meal and set himself to draw out Mrs. Lombard. I could see that he was asking himself the same question that I had asked, what part she played in her husband's life; and I think that he reached the same conclusion. She was not going to make any difficulties. Soon he had her talking about all her interests, the pleasantness of the neighbourhood, her brief season in London, her holiday plans--it was to be the Pyrenees, but her husband might not get away till later in the summer. He looked on her with favour, for her kindness and comeliness were manifest, and the embarrassment left her eyes as she spoke to him, not as a notable, but as a sympathetic human being. She had a delicious voice, and her prattle was the most soothing thing conceivable. It explained Lombard's smug contentment with his life, but it convinced me that in that life the lady was not an active force. She would neither spur nor impede him.

In the library after dinner I got my notion of Lombard further straightened out, for the room was a museum of the whole run of his interests. Sandy, who could never refrain from looking round any collection of books, bore me out. The walls on three sides were lined to the ceiling with books, which looked in the dim light like rich tapestry hangings. Lombard had kept his old school and college texts, and there was a big section on travel, and an immense amount of biography. He had also the latest works on finance, so he kept himself abreast of his profession. But the chief impression left on me was that it was the library of a man who did not want the memory of any part of his life to slip from him--a good augury for our present job.

'I've burned my boats, as you saw from the Times this morning,' said Sandy. 'I dare say you guessed the reason. The pace was becoming too hot--for Haraldsen.'

'How about yourself?' said Lombard.

'I have better wind and a better turn of speed,' was the answer. He filled his pipe, and sat himself crosswise in an armchair with his legs dangling over an arm.

'What do you make of Haraldsen, Dick?' he asked. 'Apart from his father and all that, is he worth taking trouble about?'

'Yes,' I said firmly. 'I have come to like him enormously. He is a high-strung being and has gone through a very fair imitation of hell, but there's no crack in his brain, and I'm positive there is none in his character.'

'Apart from the old man, and your promise, and one's general dislike of letting the Devil have the upper hand, you think he's worth saving?'

'Most certainly I do.'

'Good,' said Sandy. 'I asked, because this affair looks like being infernally troublesome, and it is as well to be sure about the principal personage. . . . Well, I haven't let the grass grow under my feet since I saw you last. I've seen Macgillivray, who didn't know much, but gave me some hints that were more useful than he imagined. Lombard here has been doing good work on the Barralty trail--by the way, the reason why I've been so melodramatic about coming here to-night is that Lombard must be kept free from suspicion as long as possible, or half his usefulness goes. I'm deeply suspect by this time; so are you, Dick; but Lombard has still a clean sheet. And I can assure you that the people we are up against are very active citizens. Chiefly, I've been busy with some of my old channels--very nearly silted up, some of them were, and one way and another I've convinced myself that Haraldsen is the quarry of a very dangerous and desperate gang. The most dangerous kind, for they range from stolid respectability down to the dirtiest type of criminal. They have every weapon in their armoury, and they are organized like an American football team.'

'Hold on,' I said, much impressed, for Sandy didn't use words like 'dangerous' or 'desperate' very readily. 'I don't quite see their purpose. I can understand a vulgar attempt to blackmail a simple Norlander. But isn't this organization you speak of a bit too elaborate, like using a steam-hammer to crack a nut?'

'No,' was the reply, 'for the possible reward is immense. Quite apart from what my jade tablet may have to contribute, old Haraldsen's fortune was very large. Those blackguards could milk his son to the tune of hundreds of thousands of pounds, if not millions. Lombard has been good enough to verify that.'

'It took some doing,' said Lombard; 'but I had a pull with the Scandinavian banks. Haraldsen holds the bulk of the preference stock in'--he mentioned some famous companies--'and he has ludicrous balances on current account.'

Sandy nodded. 'There's no doubt then about the bigness of the prize. And it should have been easy fruit. They had only to get hold of Haraldsen, a shy, unworldly recluse, to strip him bit by bit of his possessions--all by proper legal process. The man's a baby in these things. I can see him in Troth's hands assigning great blocks of his gilt-edged stuff--for consideration, of course, such as a holding in some of Barralty's shaky concerns. Then there would be a little peace for him, and then another cut at the joint. All very simple and pleasant, if ugly snags like us three hadn't got in the way. We won't be popular in certain quarters.'

'Have you a line on the gang?' I asked.

'So-so,' he said. 'I know a good deal about Troth, not all to his disadvantage. He has his enemies and plenty of critics, but he has also his friends. A sharp practitioner, of course, but there's more in his persecution of Haraldsen than mere greed. I haven't got the facts quite straight yet, but at the back there is some kind of family vendetta, which he inherited from his father. The elder Troth and the elder Haraldsen were once partners on the Rand, and I gather that they were together in a big venture which turned out well. Troth did something dirty, and Haraldsen kicked him out, as apparently he was justified in doing under their contract. But Troth thought that he had been badly treated and was entitled to his share in the profits of the big coup, and he was determined to make Haraldsen disgorge. That was the reason of the scrap on the Rhodesian hills you told me about. Troth believed that he was trying to get what belonged to him, and his son is on the same tack. Also, I suppose, Albinus.'

'Have you got in touch with Albinus?' I asked.

'Yes, and it wasn't hard. He's quite a prominent figure in his own line. Hc has lived for the last two years in a fashionable West- End hotel, and done himself pretty well. He seems to be comfortably off, for, though he does a little in the City, he spends most of his time amusing himself--races a bit and patronizes the drama, and entertains lavishly. Quite a popular citizen. I had him pointed out to me at Epsom--a fellow a little more than your own age, Dick, who has kept his figure as well as you have, but far better dressed than you could ever hope to be. His hair has gone grey, and he has the air of a retired cavalry colonel. I didn't care for his looks, for I don't like a face that is perpetually smiling while the eyes never change, but people don't seem to mind him. He's a member of ----.' And he mentioned a highly respectable club. 'They say his finances are dicky.'

Lombard nodded. 'I heard for a fact that his bank has pulled him up about his overdraft. He has been too thick with Barralty.'

'Ah! Barralty!' Sandy's face took on that look of intense absorption which meant that his interest was really awakened. 'There's the puzzler. I can place Troth and Albinus--they're types--but Barralty is his own species and genus. I've been collecting data about him and it's mighty interesting. It's going to take us a long time to get the measure of that lad. But I've managed to see him--from a distance, and I confess I was fascinated.'

Sandy laughed.

'I got a young friend to take me to a party--golly, such a party! I was a French artist in a black sweater, and I hadn't washed for a day or two. A surréaliste, who had little English but all the latest Paris studio argot. I sat in a corner and worshipped, while Barralty held the floor. It was the usual round-up of rootless intellectuals, and the talk was the kind of thing you expect-- terribly knowing and disillusioned and conscientiously indecent. I remember my grandfather had a phrase for the smattering of cocksure knowledge which was common in his day--the "culture of the Mechanics' Institute." I don't know what the modern equivalent would be--perhaps the "culture of the B.B.C." Our popular sciolism is different--it is a smattering not so much of facts as of points of view. But the youths and maidens at this party hadn't even that degree of certainty. They took nothing for granted except their own surpassing intelligence, and their minds were simply nebulae of atoms. Well, Barralty was a king among those callow anarchists. You could see that he was of a different breed from them, for he had a mind, however much he debased it. You could see too that he despised the whole racket.'

'What is he like?' I asked, for I had never had him properly described to me.

'Quite ordinary, except for his eyes. His pupils don't appear to be quite in the centre of the eyeballs, but rather high up, so he has always the air of looking over your head. And those pupils are intensely bright. An impressive face, but the more repellent the more you look at it. I have only begun my study of Mr. Barralty, but I have reached one firm conclusion. The man is inordinately, crazily ambitious. He has to assert himself even if it is only to be a Pope among the half-baked. I should say that he had about as much morals as a polecat, but he has what often does fairly well as a substitute, worldly wisdom. He is a cautious fellow, and up to now he has kept his feet on a very slippery floor, at least as far as repute goes. He wants to keep that repute, but he must have money, great quantities of money, so that he can prove to the world that a fastidious and cynical intellectual can beat the philistines at their own game. It's one version of the Grand Manner that our ancestors used to talk about. Do you follow me? Do you see how tempting the Haraldsen affair must be to him? Here is something quite secret and far away from the ordinary swim, which promises immense loot and not a word said. I think we can be certain that he is the brain in the enterprise and will get the biggest share. And that he won't stick at trifles. I can imagine Troth having scruples, but not Barralty.'

Sandy's tone was so grave that for a moment there was silence. Then I felt bound to put in a word of caution.

'You realize,' I said, 'that we are taking all this story of a plot on Haraldsen's word?'

'I do,' he said. 'That's why we must go slowly and wait on developments.'

'And the other two,' I said. 'We have nothing to link the young Varrinder and your Conquistador friend with the business except that they seem to have come sniffing round Haraldsen.'

'True,' was the answer. 'On that point we have no evidence, only suspicions. Therefore we must go very cannily. But not too cannily, or we may be caught. Who was it said that behind every doubt there lurked an immoral certainty? We must take suspicions for facts till they are disproved, for I don't think that in this affair we can afford to give away any weight. I'm coming in, partly because I don't like the Devil to score, and partly because I'm pretty certain that D'Ingraville is in it, and I have a rendezvous with D'Ingraville as long as he is above the sod. Therefore I'm going to follow my instinct and treat the thing seriously from the start. Our immediate duty is to safeguard Haraldsen.'

'Your Times letter to-day will help,' I said.

'It is a step in the right direction. But only a step. We must make it impossible for those blackguards to get at his money. So Lombard and I have made certain arrangements. To-morrow morning he goes back with you to Fosse with a bagful of papers which Haraldsen will sign. I assume that he'll agree, for it's the only way. We're making a trust of his possessions, with several most responsible trustees, and he must give Lombard his power of attorney. He will have enough free income for his modest needs, but till the trust is revoked he won't be able to touch the capital. That means that there can be no coercion on him to part with his fortune without considerable delays and a good many people knowing about it.'

'That sounds common sense,' I said. 'But will the gang that is after him ever discover it?'

'I shall take steps to see that they are informed,' he replied. 'I want to get them off his trail and gunning for me. My Times letter will have put them on my track. By the way, I propose presently to announce in the same admirable newspaper that I intend to present old Haraldsen's jade tablet to the British Museum.'

'Whatever for?' I asked.

Sandy grinned in his impish way. 'More ground bait. They won't believe it. They'll think it's a dodge to put them off the scent. They'll think too that something has happened to rattle me, which is what I intend. I don't want them to consider me too formidable. They'll fumble for a little and make one or two false casts, but soon I shall have the pack in full cry.'

It seemed to me that Sandy was going a little beyond the mark in his quixotry, and I told him so. His face was so lit up and eager that I thought it was simply another ebullition of the boy in him that could not die, and I reminded him he was a married man. That at once made him grave.

'I know, Dick,' he said. 'I've thought of that. But Barbara would be the first to agree. It isn't only saving Haraldsen, poor devil, though that is a work of necessity and mercy. It's putting a spoke in D'Ingraville's wheel, for if that sportsman is left on the loose there will be hell to pay for others than Haraldsen. You needn't worry about me, for as I've told you, they're bound to fumble at the start. They won't know what to make of me, and, if I may say it modestly, they may be a little worried. Presently, they'll pull themselves together, but not just yet. I must put in a week or two in London. I'll stay at the club, which I don't fancy they'll attempt to burgle. Violence won't be their line, at least not at the start. You see, I must get a line on D'Ingraville to make sure.'

I asked him how he proposed to get that, and he said 'Varrinder. I have found out a good deal about that lad, and I think I may make something of him. He's still only a novice in crime, and his nerve isn't steady. I fancy he may be turned into what the French police call an indicateur, half-apache and half-informer. We shall see. And meantime, Dick, I have a whole-time job for you. You are responsible for Haraldsen.'

He spoke the last sentence in the tone of a general giving orders to his staff. There was nothing boyish now about his face.

'Haraldsen,' he said, 'is the key of the whole business. I can't think how on earth he has escaped them so long. Probably his blundering simplicity. If he had been cleverer most likely they would have caught him. Well, we can't afford to let them catch him. God knows what might happen if they got a weak-nerved fellow into their clutches! Apart from what he might be made to suffer there's a good chance that they might win, for a trust can be revoked, and I can imagine a shattered Haraldsen giving them all the legal authority they want. He's our Achilles-heel, and we must guard him like a child. And there's the daughter, too, the little girl at school--I'm not easy about her if her father is left anywhere in the neighbourhood. It's a queer business to have as our weak point a neurotic Viking. All the same, I've a notion that in the last resort Haraldsen might surprise us--might go clean berserk and turn and rend them. I don't know him, but I remember the old man.'

'You mean that Fosse isn't safe?' I asked.

'Just that. It is almost certain that they have their eyes on it already, and even if they haven't they soon will have. It doesn't do to underrate the intelligence of that crowd. The place is not much more than seventy miles from London on a knuckle of upland accessible from every side--with a trunk road close to your gates, and hikers and tourists thick around it all summer. You're as defenceless as an old sow basking in the sun. Your own people are trusty, but your frontiers are too wide to watch. You must get yourself into a sanctuary, and there's one place only that fills the bill.'

I asked its name, but I had already guessed the answer.

'Laverlaw,' he said. 'I want you to shift your camp there at once-- you and Mary and Peter John and

Haraldsen. You'll only be antedating your yearly visit by a few weeks. There's nothing to keep you in the south, is there?'

'Nothing,' I said. 'But are you sure it's wise? They're still doubtful about Fosse, but now that you're in the business, they will be certain about Laverlaw.'

'I mean them to be,' he replied. 'The fight must come, and I want to choose my own ground for it. Fosse is hopeless--Laverlaw pretty well perfect. Not a soul can show his face in that long glen of mine without my people knowing it. Not a stray sheep can appear on my hills without my shepherds spotting it. Not the smallest unfamiliar thing can happen but it is at once reported. Haraldsen will be safe at Laverlaw till we see how things move. You remember in the Medina business that I advised you to get straight off to Machray? Well, Laverlaw is as good as any Highland deer forest-- better, for there are more of my own folk there. So, Dick, you've got to move to Laverlaw at once--as inconspicuously as possible, but at once. I've warned Babs, and she's expecting you.'

I saw the reason in Sandy's plan, but I wasn't quite happy. For I remembered what he seemed to have forgotten, that when I went to Machray to keep out of Medina's way I had had an uncommonly close shave for my life.

PART II. Laverlaw

CHAPTER VIII

Sanctuary

Laverlaw, Mary used to say, was her notion of the end of the world. It is eight miles from a railway station and the little village of Hangingshaw, and the road to it follows a shallow valley between benty uplands till the hills grow higher, and only the size of the stream shows that you have not reached the glen head. Then it passes between two steep hillsides, where there is room but for it and the burn, rounds a corner, and enters an amphitheatre a mile or two square, bounded by steep heather hills, with the Lammer Law heaving up its great shoulders at the far end. The amphitheatre is the park of the castle, mountain turf, diversified with patches of the old Ettrick Forest and a couple of reedy lakes. The house stands at the junction of four avenues of ancient beeches--the keep thirteenth century, most of it late sixteenth century, and nothing more modern than the Restoration wing built by Bruce of Kinross. There are lawns and pleasaunces and a wonderful walled garden, and then you are among heather again, for the moorlands lap it round as the sea laps a reef.

All the land for miles is Sandy's, and has been in his family for centuries, and though there is another property--Clenry Den, in Fife, from which, by an absurd eighteenth-century transformation, they take their title of Clanroyden--Laverlaw has always been their home. From Hangingshaw southward there are no dwellings but hill- farms and shepherds' cottages. Beyond the containing walls of the valley lie heathy uplands hiding an infinity of glens and burns, nameless except to herds and keepers and the large-scale Ordnance map. The highway stops short at the castle, and beyond it a drove road tracks the ultimate waters of the Laver, and makes its way, by a pass called the Raxed Thrapple, to the English Border. The place is so perfect that the first sight of it catches the breath, for it is like a dream of all that is habitable and gracious; but it is also as tonic as mid-ocean and as lonely as the African veld.

I took Haraldsen and Peter John from Fosse by road, while Mary with maid and baggage and Jack Godstow travelled by rail by way of London. I had always made a practice of taking my keeper Jack to Laverlaw on our annual visits, partly that he might act as my loader at grouse-drives, and partly to give him a holiday in a different sort of world. Also he made a wonderful gillie and companion for Peter John. Jack was a living disproof of the legend that the English countryman is not adaptable. He was in bone and fibre a Cotswold man, and yet wherever he went he met friends, and he had a knack of getting right inside whatever new life he was introduced to. There was something about him that attracted good will--his square face with little greying side whiskers, and his steadfast, merry, brown eyes.

So in the first days of July there was a very pleasant party at Laverlaw--Barbara Clanroyden and her daughter, Mary, Haraldsen, Peter John, and myself. But there was no Sandy. I gave him a lift to the aerodrome that night we met at Lombard's house, and since then I had seen nothing of him. I had an address in London, not a club but a bank, to which I wrote to report our arrival, but for days I had no word from him. He was publicly supposed to be at Laverlaw, for the press had announced his arrival there and his intention of staying for the rest of the summer. The Scotsman and the local papers chronicled his presence at local functions, like the Highland Show, the wedding of a neighbour's daughter, and a political fête at a house on the other side of the shire. But I was certain that he had never left London, and when I met his factor by chance and asked for information, I found that gentleman as sceptical as myself. 'If his lordship had come north I would have seen him,' he said, 'for there's some important bits of business to put through. These newspapers are oftener wrong than right.'

In a week the place had laid such a spell on us that Fosse was almost forgotten, and the quiet of the glen seemed to have been about us since the beginning of time. The post came late in the afternoons, bringing the papers, but my day-late Times was rarely opened, and I did my scanty correspondence by post cards and telegrams. It was still, bright weather with a light wind from the east, and all day we were out in the strong sunshine.

If we saw no strangers there was a perpetual interest in our little colony itself. There were the two keepers, Sim and Oliver, both long-legged Borderers whose forbears had been in the same glen since the days of Kinmont Willie, and who now and then in their speech would use phrases so vivid and memorable that I understood how the great ballads came to be written. There was the head shepherd Stoddart--Sandy kept one of the farms in his own hands--a man tough and gnarled as an oak-root, who belonged to an older dispensation. He had the long stride and the clear eye of his kind, and his talk was a perpetual joy to us, for in his soft, lilting voice he revealed a lost world of pastoral. Under his tuition I became quite learned about sheep, and I would accompany him when he 'looked the hill,' and thereby got the hang of a wide countryside. Also to my delight I found Geordie Hamilton, the Scots Fusilier who had been my batman in the War. He had been mixed up with Sandy in his South American adventure, and had been installed at Laverlaw as a sort of 'Laird's Jock,' a factotum who could put his hand to anything, and whose special business it was to attend his master out-of-doors, much what Tom Purdey was to Sir Walter Scott. Geordie had changed little; his stocky figure and his mahogany face and sullen blue eyes were the same as I remembered; but above the ears there was a slight grizzling of the shaggy dark hair.

The days passed in a delightful ease. We walked and rode over the hills, and picnicked by distant waters. The streams were low and the fishing was poor, though Peter

John did fairly well in the lochs, and got a three-pounder one evening in the park lake with the dry fly. It was only a month to the Twelfth, so Morag the falcon was not permitted on the moors, but he amused himself with flying her at pigeons and using her to scare the hoodies. The months at Laverlaw had made Barbara well again, and she and Mary, with their clan about them, were happy; even Sandy's absence was not much of a drawback, for his way was the wind's way, and any hour he might appear out of the void. It was lotus-eating weather in a land which might have been Tir-nan-Og, so remote it seemed from mundane troubles. When I gave a thought to my special problem it was only to remind myself that for the moment we were utterly secure. The pedlar who took the Laverlaw round from Hangingshaw had his coming advertised hours in advance; the baker's and butcher's carts had their fixed seasons and their familiar drivers; and any stranger would be noted and talked over by the whole glen; while, as for the boundary hills, the shepherds were intelligence- officers who missed nothing. All the same I thought it wise to warn the keepers and Stoddart and Geordie Hamilton that I had a private reason for wanting to be told in good time of the coming of any stranger, and I knew that the word would go round like a fiery cross.

We were all lapped in peace, but the most remarkable case was Haraldsen. It may have been the stronger air, for we were four hundred miles farther north, or the belief that here he was safe, but he lost his hunted look, he no longer started at a sudden sound, and he could talk without his eyes darting restlessly everywhere. He began to find an interest in life, and went fishing with Peter John and Jack, accompanied the keepers and Stoddart on their rounds, and more than once joined me in a long stride among the hills.

It was not only ease that he was gaining. The man's old interests were reviving. His Island of Sheep, which he had been shutting out of his thoughts, had returned to his mind while he was delighting in the possessions of another. Laverlaw was so completely a home, that this homeless man began to think of his own. I could see a longing in his eyes which was not mere craving for safety. As we walked together he would talk to me of the Norlands, and I could see how deep the love of them was in his bones. His mental trouble was being quieted by the renascence of an old affection. Once in the late afternoon we halted on the top of the Lammer Law to drink in the view--the glen of the Laver below us with the house and its demesne like jewels in a perfect setting, the far blue distances to the north, and all around us and behind us a world of grey-green or purple uplands. He drew a long breath. 'It is Paradise,' he said; 'but there is one thing wanting.' And when I asked what that was, he replied, 'The sea.'

Yet at the back of my head there was always a slight anxiety. It was not for the present but for the future. I did not see how our sanctuary could be attacked, but this spell of peace was no solution of the problem. We could not go on living in Laverlaw in a state of mild siege. I had no guess at what Sandy was after, except that he was unravelling the machinations of Haraldsen's enemies; that knowledge was no doubt essential, but it did not mean that we had defeated them. We were only postponing the real struggle. My one solid bit of comfort was that Haraldsen was rapidly getting back to normal. If he went on as he was going, he would soon be a possible combatant in any scrap, instead of an embarrassment.

Then one day that happened which woke all my fears. I had told Peter John that Haraldsen was in danger, and warned him to be very much on the watch for anything or anybody suspicious. This was meat and drink to him, for it gave him a job infinitely more attractive than the two hours which he was supposed to devote to his books every morning. I could see him cock his ears whenever Sim or Geordie had any piece of news. But till this particular day nothing came of his watchfulness.

It was the day of the sheep-clipping at the Mains of Laverlaw, the home farm. The two hill hirsels had been brought down to the valley the night before, and were penned in great folds beside the stream. Beyond was a narrow alley which admitted them in twos and threes to a smaller fold where the stools of the shearers were set up. At dawn the men had assembled--Stoddart and his young shepherd, whose name was Nickson, and the herds from the rest of the Laverlaw estate, many of whom had walked a dozen moorland miles. There were the herds of the Lanely Bield, and Clatteringshaws, and

Drygrain, and Upper and Nether Camhope, and the two Lammers, and a man from the remotest corner of Sandy's land, the Back Hill of the Cludden, who got his letters only once a fortnight, and did not see a neighbour for months. And there were dogs of every colour and age, from Stoddart's old patriarch Yarrow, who was the doyen of the tribe, to slim, slinking young collies, wild as hawks to a stranger, but exquisitely skilled in their trade and obedient to the slightest nod of their masters. On this occasion there was little for them to do; it was their holiday, and they dozed each in his owner's shadow, after a stormy morning of greetings with their kind.

We all attended the clipping. It was a very hot day, and the air in the fold was thick with the reek of sheep and the strong scent of the keel-pot, from which the shorn beasts were marked with a great L. I have seen a good deal of shearing in my time, but I have never seen it done better than by these Borderers, who wrought in perfect silence and apparently with effortless ease. The Australian sheep-hand may be quicker at the job, but he could not be a greater artist. There was never a gash or a shear-mark, the fleeces dropped plumply beside the stools, and the sheep, no longer dingy and weathered but a dazzling white, were as evenly trimmed as if they had been fine women in the hands of a coiffeur. It was too smelly a place for the women to sit in long, but twenty yards off was crisp turf beginning to be crimsoned with bell-heather, and the shingle-beds and crystal waters of the burn. We ended by camping on a little hillock, where we could look down upon the scene, and around to the hills shimmering in the heat, and up to the deep blue sky on which were etched two mewing buzzards.

We had our luncheon there, when the work stopped for the midday rest, and Haraldsen and I went down afterwards to smoke with the herds. The clipping meal at Laverlaw was established by ancient precedent. There was beer for all, but whisky only for the older men. There were crates of mutton-pies for which the Hangingshaw baker was famous, and baskets of buttered scones and oatcakes and skim-milk cheese. The company were mighty trenchermen, and I observed the herd of the Back Hill of the Cludden, to whom this was a memorable occasion, put away six pies and enough cakes and cheese to last me for a week.

After that we went home, but Peter John stayed behind, for he had decided to become a sheep-farmer and was already deep in the confidence of the herds. In the afternoon I took Haraldsen to visit the keep of Hardriding ten miles off, an ancient tooth of masonry on a crag by a burn. I remember thinking that I had never seen him in better spirits, for his morning at the clipping seemed to have cheered him by its spectacle of decent, kindly folk.

When we got back just before dinner I found Peter John waiting for me with a graver face than usual.

There had been visitors, it appeared, at the clipping that afternoon. One was Little, the auctioneer from

Laverkirk. That was to be expected, for 'Leittle,' as the countryside pronounced his name, was a famous figure in the shire, a little red-faced man with a gift of broad humour, whose jokes in the sale-ring were famous through the Lowlands. But he had also a rough side to his tongue, and this, with his profound knowledge of black-faced sheep, made him respected as well as liked. He was a regular guest at the Laverlaw clippings, and was a special friend of Stoddart's. But he had brought a friend with him whom nobody had met before. Peter John described him carefully. An average-sized man, quite young, with a small, well-trimmed moustache like a soldier. He wore riding breeches and cloth gaiters, and a check cap, and carried a shooting-stick. He was Scotch and spoke broadly, but not in the local fashion--Stoddart thought he must come from Dumfries way. His name was Harcus, and Little had introduced him as a rising dealer whom they would soon hear more of, and who was on holiday, taking a look at the Laver Water flocks. He seemed to know a lot about Cheviot sheep.

'Well, he sounds harmless enough,' I said, when I had heard his story. 'A dealer is the kind of fellow you'd expect at a clipping, and if Little brought him he must be all right.'

But I could see from the boy's face that he was not satisfied.

'I didn't much like him,' he said. 'He was too soft-spoken, and he wanted to know too much. Geordie

Hamilton said he would "speir the inside out of a whelk." He asked all about who was staying here, and if Lord Clanroyden was still here. He said a lot of nice things about Lord Clanroyden which Mr. Stoddart thought cheek. Mr. Stoddart thought he wanted something out of him.'

'There's nothing in that,' I said. 'That's the habit of dealers. He probably wants to buy the Mains hoggs before they're sent to Laverkirk. Was that the only thing that made you suspicious?'

'No-o,' he said slowly. 'There was another thing. He behaved rather queerly about me. I was sitting behind the keel-pot cutting a whistle, and I heard all his talk with Mr. Stoddart and Mr. Nickson. I saw that he had noticed me when he arrived. He pretended not to know we were staying in this house, and when Mr. Stoddart said that you were here he looked surprised, and asked was that the General Hannay that he had heard about in the War? And then he said suddenly, "Sir Richard's boy's here. I would like to have a crack wi' him," and Mr. Stoddart had to introduce us. That showed that he must have known all about us before, and that I was your son.'

'That was odd,' I admitted, rather impressed by Peter John's shrewdness. I asked what he had talked to him about, and he told me just ordinary things--what school he was at, what he thought of Scotland, what he was going to do when he grew up--and that he had laughed when he heard of the sheep-farming plan.

Stoddart had given the two visitors a drink, and after an hour's stay they had gone down the valley in Little's car.

I said that I didn't think there was any real cause to worry. But Peter John was obstinate, and then he added that which really alarmed me.

'I thought I had better do something about it,' he said, 'so I asked Mr. Sprot--he's the young shepherd at Nether Laver and lives nearest to Hangingshaw--to try to find out when he got home if this Mr. Harcus had been in the village before. Do you know what he told me? That he had been there for three days, and had been staying with Miss Newbigging at the post office. He said he had been to a lot of farms, and had bought the shorthorn bull at Windyways that got the second prize at the Highland Show.'

That word 'post office' alarmed me. It was the very place a man would choose for his lodgings if he wanted to make private inquiries. There was no inn in Hangingshaw, and the post office was the natural centre for a big countryside. Also Miss Newbigging, the postmistress, was a most notorious old gossip, and lived to gather and retail news.

'So I thought I'd better ask Geordie Hamilton to go down there' (in this case alone Peter John dropped his habit of 'mistering' everybody, for it was impossible to call Geordie otherwise than by his Christian name). 'He went off on his bicycle after tea. I thought he was the best man for the job, for he's a great friend of Miss Newbigging.'

'That was right,' I said. 'So far I give you good marks. I'll have a talk to Geordie in the morning.'

I dressed for dinner with a faint uneasiness at the back of my head. It was increased when, just as we were drinking our coffee, I was told that Geordie Hamilton wanted to see me urgently. I found him in the gun-room with a glowing face, as if he had made some speed on his bicycle from Hangingshaw in the warm evening.

'Yon man Haircus, sirr,' he began at once. 'Actin' under instructions from Maister Peter John I proceeded to Hangingshaw and had a word wi' Miss Newbiggin'. Sprot was speakin' the truth. Haircus is no there noo, for he gaed off in the car wi' Leittle the auctioneer, him and his pockmanty. But he's been bidin' there the last three days and--weel, sirr, I dinna like the look o' things. I didna like the look o' the man, for he was neither gentry nor plain folk. And gude kens what he's been up to.'

Geordie proceeded with his report, delivered in the staccato fashion of the old Scots Fusilier days. He had found Miss Newbigging alone and had had a friendly cup of tea with her. 'Yon's an awfu' ane to speak,' he said. 'She has a tongue on her like a pen-gun.' The post mistress had been full of her late lodger, and had described him as a 'fine, couthy, cracky body.' He was Galloway bred, but had been a lot in the north of

England, and his big market was Carlisle. He told her that he wanted to get in touch with the farmers in these parts, which he said were the pick of the Borders. 'He was aye rimin',' said Miss Newbigging, 'about this bonny countryside and the dacent folk that bode in it.' She had been glad to answer his questions, for he was bringing trade into the parish. When asked if he had been curious about Laverlaw, she had replied that he had, just as every one would be curious about the Big House. He seemed to know all about Lord Clanroyden and to have a great opinion of him. 'I telled him that his lordship was supposed to be in residence, but that I hadna clapped eyes on him for months. But says I, that's naethin new, for his lordship comes and gangs like a bog-blitter, though I whiles think that he should pay mair attention to his leddy wife, and her no that strong.' But Miss Newbigging had been positive that she had never given him the names of the party now at Laverlaw. 'Though he might have read them on the letters,' she had added.

On further examination Geordie discovered that Harcus had been what the postmistress called 'a usefu' man about the house.' He had helped her every day to sort out the mail, both the incoming and the outgoing. He had often been jocose about the former. 'Here's ane to Sundhope frae the Bank,' he would say. 'That'll be about the over-draft for the beasts he bocht at Kelso. And here is a bundle for her leddyship. It's bigger than I get mysel' after the back-end sales. But I see there's twa leddyships, Leddy Clanroyden and Leddy Hannay. There's walth o' rank the noo up the Laver Water.'

This had roused Geordie's interest. He asked if Harcus had made a point of looking at the outgoing letters. Miss Newbigging had replied: 'He did, now I come to think o't. I was aye tellin' him there was nae need, for the hale lot gangs to Laverkirk to be sorted. But he was a carefu' man, and he had time on his hands, and he would set them out in wee packs as if he was playin' at the cards. "That's for Embro", he would say, "an that's for the West country, and that heap's for England." He was aye awfu' interested in the English letters, comin' as he did frae Carlisle.'

Geordie, having learned all he wanted, had taken his departure after compliments. Now he sat before me with his shaggy brows drawn down. 'Ye telled me, sirr, to let naething gang by me, however sma,' and there's just a chance that there's mischief here. Haircus doesna ken wha's writin' to the folk in this house, but he kens a wheen o' the names that the folk here write to.'

That was precisely the point, and at first I thought that it did not matter. And then, when Geordie had gone, I suddenly remembered that though we were in a sanctuary our party was not complete. There was one absentee, one sheep outside the fold. Not Sandy--he could very well look after himself. It was Haraldsen's child, his daughter Anna.

I started out to look for Haraldsen, but he had gone off with Peter John to dap for trout in the park lake. It was nearly eleven o'clock before they returned, and, as they entered the lit hall from the purple gloom which is all the night that Laverlaw knows in early July, I thought what a miracle recent weeks had wrought in Haraldsen's appearance. He held his head up, and looked you straight in the face, and walked like a free man. When I called to him he was laughing like a care-free boy at the figure Peter John cut in Sandy's short waders. It struck me that it was just in this recovered confidence that our danger lay.

He had often told me about his daughter Anna. She was at a well- known boarding-school for girls in Northamptonshire, called Brewton Ashes, under the name of Smith, the name he had taken when he sought refuge in England. At first he had looked after her in her holidays, and taken her to dismal seaside resorts which he had heard well spoken of. But as his dread of pursuit grew he had dropped all this, and had not seen her for nearly a year. It had been arranged that one of the mistresses, to whom she was attached, should look after her in the holidays, and Haraldsen must have paid for pretty expensive trips for the two, since it was the only way he could make up to the child for his absence. He had always been very careful about letters, writing to her not direct, but through his bank, and he had never dared to show himself within twenty miles of Brewton Ashes.

I turned the conversation on to the girl, being careful not to alarm him, for I didn't want to spoil his convalescence. I pretended that Peter John wanted to write and tell her about Laverlaw, and asked how it was done. He told me that there was a choice of three banks, who all had their instructions.

'It seems a roundabout way,' I said; 'but I dare say you are wise. Do you stick to it rigidly?'

'Yes. It is better so. You never know. . . . Well, to be quite honest, I have broken the rule once, and I do not intend to break it again. That was last Monday. Anna's thirteenth birthday was yesterday, and I made a mistake about the dates, for I have been so busy here that I have grown careless. I could not bear to think that she would have no message from me on that day, so I wrote direct to her at Brewton Ashes.' His smile was a little embarrassed, and he looked at me as if he expected reproaches. 'I do not think that any harm is done. This place is so far away from everybody.'

'Oh, that's all right,' I said. 'You needn't worry about that, but I think you're wise all the same to stick to your rule. Now for bed. Lord, it's nearly midnight.'

But I thought it by no means all right. It was infernally bad luck that Haraldsen should have chosen to be indiscreet just at the time when the mysterious Harcus was in the neighbourhood. I told myself that the latter would make nothing of a letter addressed to a Miss Anna Smith at a country address in England. But I have never made the mistake of underrating the intelligence of the people I was up against. Anyhow, I was taking no chances. I routed out Geordie Hamilton from his room above the stables and warned him for duty. Then I wrote a letter to Sandy in London, telling him all that had happened and my doubts about Harcus. I left it to him to decide whether any steps should be taken to safeguard the girl. Geordie was instructed to set off at once to Laverkirk, twenty miles distant, and post it there, so that it might catch the London mail-- Laverkirk was on the main line to the south--and reach Sandy the following evening.

But I wasn't content with a letter. I also wrote out a telegram to Sandy in a simple cypher we had often used before--a longish telegram, for I had to explain how it was possible that the enemy might have got the girl's address. Geordie, when he had posted the letter, was to go to bed in the Station Hotel, be up betimes, and send the telegram as soon as the office was open. I had no fear of espionage in Laverkirk, which was a big bustling market-town with half a dozen post offices.

Then I went to bed with anxiety in my mind out of which I could not argue myself. The happy peace of Laverlaw had been flawed. I felt like the man in Treasure Island who was tipped the black spot.

CHAPTER IX

Lochinvar

Next day the heat-wave broke in a deluge, and by midday the Laver was coloured and by the evening in roaring spate. Peter John and I went out before dinner, and got a heavy basket with the worm in the pools above the park. The following morning it still drizzled, and we did well in the tributary burns with the fly known locally as the black spider. Burn-fishing has always had its charms for me, for no two casts are the same, and I love the changing scenery of each crook in the little glens. But after luncheon Peter John's soul aspired to higher things. There was a tarn six miles off in the hills called the Black Loch, a mossy hole half overgrown with yellow water-lilies and uncommonly difficult to fish. We had tried it before in a quiet gloaming and had had no luck, though we had seen big trout feeding. Sim had always declared that it only fished well after rain, when its sluggish inmates were stirred by the swollen runnels from the hills. So we set off with Oliver and Geordie Hamilton, warning Barbara that we might be late for dinner.

We did not return till half-past nine. The weather cleared, the sun came out, and the warm evening was a kind of carnival for the Black Loch trout. They took whatever we offered them, but for every five fish hooked four broke us or dropped off. We had to cast over an infernal belt of water-lilies and pond-weed, which meant a long line and a loose line. It was impossible to wade far out, for the bottom was treacherous, and once I went down to the waist. To land a fish we had to drag him by brute force through the water-weeds, and, as we were fishing far and fine, that usually meant disaster. There were two spits of gravel in the loch, and the only chance with a big one was to try to manoeuvre him towards one of these, not an easy job, since one had practically no purchase on him. Peter John, who was far the better performer, managed this successfully with two noble fellows, each nearly two pounds in weight, but he too had many failures. Nevertheless, between us we had two dozen and three fish, a total weight of just over twenty-seven pounds, the best basket that had been taken out of the Black Loch in Oliver's memory.

These two days' fishing had put everything else out of my mind, a trick fishing always has with me. As we tramped home over the dusky sweet-scented moors I had no thought except a bath and dinner. But as we approached the house I was suddenly recalled to my senses. Before the front door stood a big and very dirty car, from which a man in a raincoat had descended. He had no hat, he seemed to have a baldish head and a red face mottled with mud, and his whole air was of fatigue and dishevelment. He was in the act of helping another figure to alight, which looked like a girl. And then suddenly there was a noise in the house, and from it Haraldsen emerged, shouting like a lunatic. He plucked the girl from the car, and stood hugging and kissing her.

When we got nearer I saw that the man was Lombard, but very unlike the spruce city magnate with whom I had been lately connected. He looked tired and dirty but content, and somehow younger, more like the Lombard I remembered in Africa. 'Thank God we're here at last,' he said. 'It's been a roughish passage. . . . What do I want most? First a bath, and then food--a lot of it, for we've been living on biscuits. I've brought no kit, so you must lend me some clothes to change into.' As for Haraldsen, he went on behaving like a maniac, patting the girl's shoulder and holding her as if he thought that any moment she might disappear. 'My happiness is complete,' he kept declaring. This went on till Barbara and Mary appeared and swept the child off with them.

I provided Lombard with a suit of flannels, and we ate an enormous late supper--at least four of us did, while the other three, who had already dined, looked on. The girl Anna appeared in a pleated blue skirt and a white blouse, the uniform, I supposed, of her school. She was a tall child for her years, and ridiculously blonde, almost bleached. She had a crop of fair hair which looked white in certain lights, a pale face, and features almost too mature, for the full curve of her chin was that of a woman rather than a girl. There was no colour about her except in her eyes, and I thought that Haraldsen deserved something better than this plain, drab child. I had whispered that to Mary in the hall before supper, and she had laughed at me. 'You're a blind donkey,

Dick,' she had said. 'Some day she will be a raging beauty, with that ivory skin and those sea-blue eyes.'

When we had eaten, Haraldsen went off with the women to put Anna to bed and to look after her wardrobe, for she also was kit-less. Lombard had a couple of glasses of Sandy's famous port, and when we adjourned to the smoking-room, where a peat fire was burning, he stacked himself in an armchair with an air of great content. 'First score for our side,' he said. 'But it has been a close thing, I can tell you. Till about ten hours ago I wouldn't have given twopence for our chances. I'll have to do the devil of a lot of telegraphing tomorrow, but to-night, thank God! I can sleep in peace.'

Then he told his story, which I give in his own words.

Clanroyden (he said) had your telegram yesterday morning. There was a letter too, you tell me? Well, he hadn't had that when I left, but you seem to have explained things pretty fully in your wire. He got hold of me at once--luckily I was sleeping in town, having motored up the day before. There were one or two small matters I had to arrange before I took my holiday, and I had finished them and was going home after luncheon.

He said I must get busy--that the other side had probably got the address of Haraldsen's daughter and might be trusted to act at once. Possibly it was even now too late. I must go down to the school in Northamptonshire and fetch her back to town. He would arrange that she should stay with a great-aunt of his in Sussex Square till he made other plans. He would have gone himself, but he dared not, for he thought he was pretty closely marked, but I was still free from suspicion, and I was the only one to take on the job. He wrote me a chit to the headmistress, Miss Barlock, to say that he was Haraldsen's--Smith's, that is to say--greatest friend and managed his affairs, and that he had authority from him to bring his daughter to him in London for a few days in connection with some family business. He thought that would be enough, for the schoolmistress-woman was pretty certain to know his name, and my appearance, too, he said, was a warrant of respectability. I was to bring the girl straight to Sussex Square, where he would be waiting for me. He said he would expect me before four o'clock, but if there was any difficulty I was to wire at once, and he would send down one of the partners in the bank that paid the school fees.

I rather liked the job of saviour of youth, for I felt that I hadn't been quite pulling my weight in this business, so I started off in my car in good spirits. It was the big Bentley, which I always drive myself. I was at Brewton Ashes by eleven o'clock, a great, raw, red brick building in a fine park, which I believe was one of the seats that old Tomplin, the oil fellow, built for himself before he crashed. Well, I sent up my card to Miss Barlock, but by the mercy of God I didn't send up Clanroyden's chit with it. I was told that Miss Barlock was engaged for the moment, and was shown into a drawing-room full of school groups and prize water-colours and great bowls of fine roses. The room rather made me take to the place, for it showed that the people there knew how to grow flowers, and there's never much wrong with a keen gardener.

I waited for about ten minutes, and then Miss Barlock's door opened and three people came out. One was Anna, who looked flustered. The others were a man and a woman--a young man in a flannel suit with an O.E. tie, a pleasant-looking toothy chap with a high colour, and a middle-aged woman in a brown linen costume and big specs. A maid took the three downstairs, and I was ushered into the presence of Miss Barlock.

She was slim and grey-haired and bright-eyed, with that air of brisk competence which shy women often cultivate in self-defence. There was obviously nothing wrong with her, but I saw at a glance that she was a precisian and would be a stickler about rules. So some instinct warned me to go canny. Luckily I began by saying only that I was an old friend of Anna Smith's father, and that I had dropped in to see her and give her a message.

Miss Barlock smiled. 'It never rains but it pours,' she said. 'Dear Anna does not often have visits from friends. Her poor father, of course, has not been down for months. But this morning who should appear but Anna's cousins? They and Anna must have passed you as you came in. They brought a letter from Mr. Smith, who asked me to allow them to carry off Anna a week before the holidays begin. They propose, I think, a cruise to the Northern capitals. I readily consented, for the child has been rather wilting in the hot weather.'

At this I sat up and thought hard. It looked as if I was too late, and that the other side had got in first. I decided that it wasn't the slightest good my showing Clanroyden's chit. The others would have a water-tight case, a letter from Haraldsen himself in a good imitation of his handwriting, which perhaps Miss Barlock recognized, for she must have seen it in his early days in England. I thought how clever they had been in sending down an inconspicuous young man and a rather dowdy woman, instead of some smart female with scarlet lips and a distempered face whom the schoolmistress would have suspected. Those two were the very model of respectable country cousins. I couldn't discredit them, for if I told Miss Barlock the truth I would only discredit myself. Clanroyden's letter, even if she didn't think it a forgery, couldn't prevail against the ipsissima verba of Haraldsen. I realized I was in a cleft stick and must conduct myself discreetly. The first thing was to see Anna herself.

Miss Barlock glanced at the cards which lay on the writing table. 'Lady Bletso and her son--he is the young baronet--propose to give Anna luncheon in the Brewton Arms at one o'clock, and then to leave for London. The morning will be occupied in packing Anna's things.' I noted a baronetage on the table which had been moved from the stand of reference books. Miss Barlock was a cautious woman and had looked up her visitors before receiving them. I wondered who the true Bletsos were. I had heard of the name in Yorkshire.

I said cordially that I was glad that Anna's relations were carrying her off for a cruise. Excellent thing, I observed fatuously, to expand the mind of the young. But, having come so far, I would like to have a talk with the child, being her father's friend, and also I had a message to her from him which I had promised to deliver. I would have liked to give her lunch, but since she was engaged for that to her cousins, might we have a short walk in the park together?

Miss Barlock saw no objection. She rang a bell and bade a maid fetch Miss Margesson. Miss Margesson, she informed me, was the girl's chief friend among the mistresses, had been given special charge of her by her father, and had on more than one occasion accompanied her abroad on holidays. Presently Miss Margesson appeared, and the sight of her gave me my first glimmer of hope. For here was one who had none of the repressions and pedantries of the ordinary schoolmistress. She was a tall girl, with a kind mouth, and clever, merry blue eyes. At all costs I must make her an ally.

'Anna Smith's packing is being attended to, Miss Margesson?' her superior asked. 'It will be completed in an hour? Very good. A car will come for her at a quarter to one to take her down to the Brewton Arms, where she will meet her cousins. Meantime, this is a friend of Anna's father who has called to see her. Will you arrange that he has a short walk with Anna in the garden? Yes, now. It cannot be long, I fear, Mr. Lombard,' she added, turning to me, 'for Anna will no doubt desire to say good-bye to her mistresses and her friends.'

Miss Margesson took me downstairs and out into a very pretty terraced garden at the back of the house. She went indoors and presently returned with Anna. For the first time I had a proper look at the child, and what I saw rather impressed me. She's not much of a beauty, as you saw, but I thought that she had an uncommon sensible little face. I don't know much about children, having none of my own, but the girl's composure struck me as remarkable. She didn't look as if she had inherited her father's nerves. The sight of her was my second gleam of hope.

There was no time to waste, so I plunged at once into my story.

'Anna, my dear,' I said, 'we've never met before, but when I was young I knew your grandfather in South Africa and he made me and another man, whose name is General Hannay, promise to stand by your father if trouble came. Your father is in great danger--has been for a long time--and now it's worse than ever. That's why he hasn't been to see you for so long. That's why you're called Smith here, when your real name is Haraldsen. That's why his letters to you always come through a bank. Now YOU are also in danger. These people Bletso, who came this morning and say they're your cousins, are humbugs. Their letter from your father is a fake. They come from your father's enemies, and they want to get you into their power. Your friends discovered the danger and sent me down to bring you away. I'm only just in time. Will you trust me and do what I ask you?'

That extraordinary child's face did not change. She heard me with the same uncanny composure, her eyes never leaving mine. Then she turned to Miss Margesson and smiled. 'What a lark, Margie!' was all she said.

But Miss Margesson didn't take it that way. She looked scared and flustered.

'What a ridiculous story!' she said. 'Say it's nonsense, Anna. Your name's Smith, all right.'

'No, it isn't,' was the placid answer. 'It's Haraldsen. Sorry, Margie dear, but I couldn't tell that even to you.'

'But--but--' Miss Margesson stammered in her uneasiness. 'You know nothing about this man--you never saw him before. How do you know he's speaking the truth? Your cousins had a letter from your father, and Miss Barlock, who is very shrewd, saw nothing wrong with it. They looked most respectable people.'

'I didn't like them much,' said Anna, and again I had a gleam of hope. 'The woman had ugly eyes behind her specs. And I never heard of any English cousins.'

'But, darling, listen to me,' Miss Margesson cried. 'You never heard of this man either. How do you know he comes from your father? How do you know he is speaking the truth? If you have any doubt, let us go together to Miss Barlock and tell her that you don't want to go on any cruise, and want to stay here till the end of the term. In the meantime you can get in touch with your father.'

'That sounds good sense,' I said; 'but it won't do. Your father's enemies now know where you are. They are very clever people and quite unscrupulous. If you don't go away with the Bletsos, they'll find ways and means of carrying you off long before your father can interfere.'

'Rubbish,' said Miss Margesson rudely. 'Do you expect me to believe this melodrama? You look honest, but you may be half- witted. What's your profession?'

'Not one for the half-witted,' I said. 'I'm what they call a merchant-banker,' and I told her the name of my firm. That was a lucky shot, for Miss Margesson had a cousin in our employ, and I was able to tell her all about him. I think that convinced her of my bona fides.

'But what do you propose to do with Anna?' she demanded.

'Take her straight to her father.' That I had decided was the only plan. The girl would be in perpetual danger in London, now that our enemies had got on her trail.

'Do you know where he is?' she asked.

'Yes,' I said, 'and if we start at once I can get her there before midnight.'

Then it suddenly occurred to me that I had one convincing piece of evidence at my disposal.

'Anna,' I said, 'I can tell you something that must persuade you. You had a letter from your father on your birthday three days ago?'

She nodded.

'And it didn't come from London enclosed in a bank envelope. It came from Scotland.'

'Yes,' she said, 'it came from Scotland. He didn't put any address on it, but I noticed that it had a Scotch postmark. That excited me, for I have always wanted to go to Scotland.'

'Well, it was that letter of your father's that gave his enemies the clue. One of them spotted the address in a Scotch post office. Your father's friend, Lord Clanroyden, was worried, and he sent me here at once.

Doesn't that prove that I'm telling the truth?' I looked towards Miss Margesson.

Her scepticism was already shaken. 'I don't know what to think,' she cried. 'I can't take any responsibility--'

Then that astonishing child simply took charge.

'You needn't, Margie dear,' she said. 'Hop back into the house and carry on. I'm going with Mr. Lombard. I believe in him. I'm going to Scotland to my father.'

'But her things are not packed,' put in Miss Margesson. 'She can't leave like this--'

'I'm afraid we can't stand on the order of our going,' I said. 'It's now just twelve o'clock, and any moment the Bletsos may turn up and make trouble. We can send for Anna's things, and in two days everything will be explained to Miss Barlock. YOU must keep out of the business altogether. The last you saw of Anna and me was in the garden, and you know nothing of our further movements. But you might do me a great kindness and send this wire in the afternoon. It's to Lord Clanroyden--you've heard of him?--he's Anna's father's chief stand-by. He told me to bring Anna to London, but that's too dangerous now. I want him to know that we have gone to Scotland.' I scribbled a telegram on a leaf from my pocket-book.

Miss Margesson was a good girl, and she seemed to share Anna's conviction. She hugged and kissed the child. 'Write to me soon,' she said, 'for I shall be very anxious,' and ran into the house.

'Now for the road,' I said. 'My car is at the front door. I'll pick you up in the main avenue out of sight of the house. Can you get there without being seen? And bring some sort of coat. Pinch another girl's if you can't find your own. The thicker the better, for it will be chilly before we get to Laverlaw.'

I picked up Anna in the avenue all right, and we swung out of the lodge gates at precisely a quarter-past twelve. Then I saw something which I didn't much like. Just outside the gates a car was drawn up, a very powerful car of foreign make, coloured yellow and black. It looked to me like a Stutz. The only occupant was a chauffeur in uniform, who was reading a newspaper. He glanced sharply at me, and for a moment seemed about to challenge us. When we had passed I looked back and saw that he had started the car and was moving in the direction of the village. I guessed that this was the Bletsos' car, and that the man had gone to seek his master. He did not look quite like an ordinary chauffeur.

That was the start of our journey. My plan was to get into the Great North Road as soon as possible--Stamford seemed the best point to join it at--and then to let the Bentley rip on the best highway in England. I didn't see how we could be seriously pursued even if that confounded chauffeur had spotted our departure. But I was all in a dither to reach Laverlaw that night. This young Lochinvar business was rather out of my usual line, and I wanted to get it over.

Well, we got to Stamford without mishap, and after that we did a spell of over sixty to the hour. The morning had been hot and bright, but the wind had shifted, and I thought we might soon run into dirty weather. At first I had kept looking back to see if we were followed, but there was no sign of a black and yellow car, and after a little I forgot about it. Lunch was our next problem, and, as there was a lot of traffic on the road, I feared that if we looked for it in a good hotel we should be hung up. I consulted Anna, and she said that she didn't care what she ate as long as there was enough of it, for she was very hungry. So we drew up at a little place, half pub and half tea-house, at the foot of a long hill just short of Newark. While my petrol tank was being filled we had a scratch meal, beer and sandwiches for me, while Anna's fancy was coffee and buns, of which she accounted for a surprising quantity. I also bought two pounds of chocolates and a box of biscuits, which turned out to be a lucky step.

We were just starting when I happened to cast my eyes back up the hill. I have a good long-distance eyesight, and there at the top, about half a mile away, I saw a car which was unpleasantly like the Stutz I had seen at Brewton. A minute later I lost it, for some traffic got in the way, but I saw it again, not a quarter of a mile off. There could be no mistake about the wasp-like thing, and I didn't think it likely that another car of the same make and colour would be on the road that day.

If its occupants had glasses--and they were pretty certain to have-- they must have spotted us. I drove the Bentley as hard as I dared, and tried to think out our position. They knew of course what our destination was. They certainly had the pace of us, for I had heard wonderful stories of what a Stutz could do in that line--and this was probably super-charged--so it wasn't likely that we could shake them off. If we stopped for the night in any town we should be at the mercy of people whose cleverness Clanroyden had put very high, and somehow or other they would get the better of me. A halt of that kind I simply dared not risk. The road before us for the next hundred miles or so was through a populous country, and I didn't believe that they would try a hold-up on it. That would be too risky with so many cars on the road, and they would not want trouble with the police or awkward inquiries. But I had driven a good deal back and forward to Scotland, and I knew that to get to Laverlaw I must pass through some lonely country. Then would be their chance. I couldn't stand up against the toothy young man and the formidable-looking chauffeur. I would be left in a ditch with a broken head and Anna would be spirited away.

My chief feeling was a firm determination to go all out to get to Laverlaw. I couldn't outwit or outpace them, so I must trust to luck. Every mile was bringing us nearer safety, and if it was bringing us nearer the northern moorlands, I must shut down on the thought. At first I was afraid of scaring Anna, but, when I saw her face whipped into colour by the wind and her bright enjoying eyes, I considered that there was no danger of that.

'You remember the car we saw at the school gates?' I said. 'The black and yellow thing? I've a notion that it's behind us. You might keep an eye on it, for I want both of mine for this bus.'

'Oh, are we being chased?' she cried. 'What fun!' And after that she sat with her head half screwed round and issued regular bulletins.

Beyond Bawtry we got into the rain, a good steady north-country downpour. We also got into a tangle of road repairs, where we had to wait our turn at several single-track patches. At the last of these the Stutz was in the same queue and I managed to get a fairly good view of it. There was no mistake about it. I saw the chauffeur in his light-grey livery coat, the same fellow who had stared at us at Brewton. The others in the back of the car were of course invisible.

Beyond Pontefract the rain became a deluge, and it was clear from the swimming roads that a considerable weight of water had already fallen. It was now between four and five, and from constant hangups we were making poor speed. The Stutz had made no attempt to close on us, though it obviously had the greater pace, and I thought I knew the reason. Its occupants had argued as I had done. They didn't want any row in this populous countryside, but they knew I was making for Laverlaw, and they knew that to get there I must pass through some desolate places. Then their opportunity would come.

In a big village beyond Boroughbridge they changed their tactics. 'The Wasp is nearly up on us,' Anna informed me, and I suddenly heard a horn behind me, the kind of terrifying thing that they fix on French racing cars. The street was fairly broad, and it could easily pass. I saw their plan. They meant to get ahead of me, and wait for me. Soon several routes across the Border would branch off and they wanted to make certain that I did not escape them. I groaned, for the scheme I had been trying to frame was now knocked on the head.

And then we had a bit of unexpected luck. Down a side street came a tradesman's van, driven by one of those hatless youths whom every motorist wants to see hanged as an example, for they are the most dangerous things on the road. Without warning it clipped over the bows of the Stutz. I heard shouting and a grinding of brakes, but I had no time to look back and it was Anna who reported what happened. The Stutz swung to the left, mounted the pavement, and came to rest with its nose almost inside the door of a shop. The van-driver lost his head, skidded, hit a lamp-post, slewed round and crashed into the Stutz's off front wing. There was a very pretty mix-up.

'Glory be,' Anna cried, 'that has crippled the brute. Well done the butcher's boy!'

But she reported that so far as she could see the Stutz had not been damaged seriously. Only the van, which had lost a wheel. But there was a crowd, and a policeman with a note-book, and I thought that the whole business might mean a hold-up of a quarter of an hour. I had a start again, and I worked the Bentley up to a steady eighty on a beautiful stretch of road. My chief trouble was the weather, for the rain was driving so hard that the visibility was rotten, and I could see little in front of me and Anna little behind.

I had to make up my mind on the route, for Scotch Corner was getting near. If I followed the main North Road by Darlington and Durham I would be for the next hundred miles in a thickly settled country. But that would take me far from Laverlaw, and I would have the long Tweed valley before I got to it. If I turned left by Brough to Appleby, I should have to cross desolate moorlands, which would give the Stutz just the kind of country it wanted. I remembered a third road, which ran through mining villages where there would be plenty of people about. It was a perfectly good road, though the map marked most of it second-class. Besides, it was possible that the Stutz didn't know about it, and, if I had a sufficient start, might assume that I had gone by either

Darlington or Brough. Anyhow, unless it caught me up soon, it would be at fault. Clearly it was my best chance.

But Fate, in the shape of the butcher's boy, had not done its work thoroughly. The rain stopped, the weather cleared, there was a magnificent red sunset over Teesdale, and just as I was swinging into my chosen road with an easier mind, Anna reported that the Wasp was coming into view.

That, as they say, fairly tore it. I had not diverted the hounds and the next half-hour was a wild race, for I wanted to get out of empty country into the colliery part. I broke every rule of decent driving, but I managed to keep a mile or so ahead. The Stutz was handicapped by the softness of the surface after the rain, and by not knowing the road as I knew it. It was beginning to grow dark, and to the best of my knowledge what there was of a moon would not rise till the small hours. My only hope was that it might be possible somewhere in the Tyne valley to give the pursuers the slip. I had tramped a good deal there, in the days when I was keen about Hadrian's Wall, and knew the deviousness of the hill-roads.

I reached the mining country without mishap, and the lights of the villages and the distant glow of ironworks gave me a comforting sense of people about and therefore of protection. Beyond Consett the dark fell, and I reflected uneasily that we were now getting into a wild moorland patch which would last till we dropped down on the Tyne. Somehow I felt that the latter event would not happen unless I managed to create a diversion. I could see the great headlights of the Stutz a mile behind, but I was pretty certain that when it saw its chance it would accelerate and overhaul us. I realized desperately that in the next ten minutes I must find some refuge or be done in.

Just then we came to a big hill which shut off any view of us from behind. I saw a bright light in front, and a big car turned in from a side-road and took our road a little ahead of us. That seemed to give me a chance. On the left there was a little road, which looked as if it led to a farm-house, and which turned a corner of a fir-wood. If I turned up that, the Stutz, topping the hill behind us, would see the other car far down the hill and believe it to be ours. . . . There was no time to waste, so I switched off our lights and moved into the farm road, till we were in the lee of the firs. We had scarcely got there when, out of the corner of my eye, I saw the glow of the Stutz's lights over the crest, and I had scarcely shut off my engine when it went roaring down the hill fifty yards away.

'Golly,' said Anna, 'this is an adventure! Where is the chocolate, Mr. Lombard? We've had no tea, and I'm very hungry.'

While she munched chocolate I started the engine, and after passing two broken-hinged gates we came to a little farm. There was nobody about except an old woman, who explained to me that we were off the road, which was obvious enough, and gave us big glasses of milk warm from the cow. I had out the map (luckily I had a case of them in the car with me) and I saw that a thin red line, which meant some sort of road, continued beyond the farm and seemed to lead ultimately to the Tyne valley. I must chance its condition, for it offered some sort of a plan. I reasoned that the Stutz would continue down the hill and might go on for miles before it spotted that the other car was not ours. It would come back and fossick about to see which side-road we had taken, but there were several in the area, and it would take a little time to discover our tracks on the farm road. If it got thus far, the woman at the farm would report our coming, and say that we had gone back to the main road. I made a great pretence to her of being in a hurry to return to that road. But, when she had shut the door behind us, we crossed a tiny stack yard, found the continuation of the track trickling through a steep meadow, and, very carefully shutting every gate behind us, slipped down into a hollow where cattle started away from our lights and we had to avoid somnolent sheep.

The first part was vile, but in the end it was joined by another farm-track, and the combination of the two made a fair road, stony, but with a sound bottom. My great fear was of ditching in one of the moorland runnels. After a little it was possible to increase the speed, and, though I had often to stop and examine the map, in half an hour we had covered a dozen miles. We were in a lonely bit of country, with no sign of habitation except an occasional roadside cottage and the lights from a hillside farm, and we passed through many plantations of young firs. Here, I thought, was a place to get a little sleep, for Anna was nodding with drowsiness and I was feeling pretty well done up. So we halted at the back of a fir clump and I made a bed for Anna with the car rugs--not much of a bed, for, the weather in the south having been hot, I had only brought summer wraps. We both had some biscuits and chocolate, but the child went to sleep with her mouth full, snuggled against my side, and I wasn't long in following. I was so tired that I didn't want to smoke.

I woke about four. Every little pool left by the rain was flushed rose-pink with the reflection of the sky, and I knew that that meant dirty weather. I roused Anna, and we laved our faces in the burn, and had another go at the biscuits. The air was cold and raw, and we would have given pounds for hot coffee. The whole place was as quiet as a churchyard, not even a bird whistled or a sheep bleated, and both of us felt a bit eerie. But the sleep had done us good, and I was feeling pretty confident that we had puzzled the Stutz. It must have spent a restless night if it had been prospecting the farm roads in north Durham. My plan now was to make straight for Laverlaw and trust to luck.

We weren't long in getting to the Tyne valley near Hexham. The fine morning still held, but the mist was low on the hills, and I counted on a drizzle in an hour or two. Anna looked chilly, and I decided that we must have a better breakfast. We were on a good road now and I kept my eye lifting for an inconspicuous pub. Presently I found one a little off the road, and its smoking chimney showed us that the folk were out of bed. I turned into its yard, which was on the side away from the road, and Anna and I stumbled into the kitchen, for we were both as stiff as pokers. The landlord was a big, slow-spoken Northumbrian, and his wife was a motherly creature who gave us hot water to wash in and a comb for Anna's hair. She promised, too, bacon and eggs in a quarter of an hour, and in the meantime I bought some cans of petrol to fill up my tank. It was while the landlord was on this job that, to stretch my legs, I took a stroll around the inn to where I had a view of the highroad.

I got a nasty jar, for there was the sound of a big car, and the Stutz came racing past. I guessed what had happened. It had lost us right enough in the Durham moorlands, but its occupants had argued that we must be making for Laverlaw, and that, if we had tangled ourselves up in by-roads, we must have made poor speed during the night. They would therefore get ahead of us, and watch the road junctions for the North. There was one especially that I remembered well, where the road up the North Tyne forked from the main highway over the Cheviots by the Carter Bar. Both were possible, and there was no third by which a heavy car could make fair going. Their strategy was sound enough. If we hadn't turned into that pub for breakfast we should have been fairly caught, and if I hadn't seen them pass, in another hour we should have been at their mercy.

Yet after the first scare I didn't feel downhearted. I felt somehow that we had the game in our hands, and had got over the worst snags. I said nothing about the Stutz to Anna, and we peacefully ate an enormous breakfast. Then I had a word with the landlord about the countryside, and he told me a lot about the side-ways into the upper glens of Tyne. At eight o'clock we started again in a drizzle, and soon I turned off the main highway to the left by what I had learned was one of the old drove-roads.

All morning we threaded our way in a maze of what must be about the worst roads in Britain. I had my map and my directions from the inn, but often I had to stop and ask the route at the little moorland farms. Anna must have opened fifty gates, and there were times when I thought we were bogged for good. I can tell you it was a tricky business, but I was beginning to enjoy myself, for I felt that we had won, and Anna was in wild spirits. The sight of bent and heather intoxicated her, and she took to singing and reciting poems. The curlews especially she hailed as old friends, and shouted a Danish poem about them. . . .

Well, that's about the end of my story. We never met the Stutz again, and for all I know it is still patrolling the Carter Bar. But I was taking no risks, and when we got into the main road up the Tyne to Liddesdale, I didn't take the shortest way to Laverlaw, which would have been by Rule Water, or by Hermitage and the Slitrig. You see, I had a fear that the Stutz, if it found no sign of us on the Carter or Bellingham roads, might have the notion of keeping watch on the approaches nearer Laverlaw. So I decided to come in on you from the side where it wouldn't expect us. The sun came out after midday, and it was a glorious afternoon. Lord, I think we must have covered half the Border. We went down Liddel to Langholm, and up the Esk to Eskdalemuir, and so into Ettrick. For most of the way we saw nothing but sheep and an odd baker's van.

Lombard finished with a cavernous yawn. He grinned contentedly. 'Bed for me,' he said, 'and for Heaven's sake let that child have her sleep out. A queer business for a sedentary man getting on in years! I'm glad I did it, but I don't fancy doing it often.'

I asked one question. 'What was the chauffeur in the Stutz like?'

'I only got a glimpse of him,' he replied; 'but I think I should know him if I saw him again. An odd-looking chap. Tall and very thin. A long, brown face, a pointed chin, and eyes like a cat's. A foreigner, I should say, and a bit of a swine.'

I remembered the man who had come to Fosse with the youth Varrinder, and whom Sandy had recognized as Jacques D'Ingraville. We had not been quite certain if he was in the Haraldsen affair, and it had been Sandy's business to find that out. Now I knew, and the knowledge disquieted me, for of this man Sandy had spoken with a seriousness which was almost fear.

CHAPTER X

The Dog Samr

Anna Haraldsen's arrival made us tighten the precautions at Laverlaw. We were now all assembled there, except the laird, and he might be trusted to look after himself. Lombard showed no desire to leave. He had wound up his business affairs in anticipation of a holiday, and thought that he might as well take the first few days of it in Scotland. He wrote a long account to his wife of his journey, which he read to me with pride--certainly it was a vigorous bit of narrative; and at the end he put in something about staying on to watch events. 'That will please Beryl,' he said. 'She's very keen about this business, and will like to know that I'm doing my bit.' I asked him what events he expected, and he replied that he had a feel in his bones that things would begin to move. That was not my own view, for, short of bombs from an aeroplane, I didn't see what the other lot could do to harm us. Laverlaw was as well guarded as a royal palace.

I have mentioned that Haraldsen was becoming a cured man. Under Peter John's care he had lost nearly all his jumpiness, he ate and slept well, laughed now and then, and generally behaved like an ordinary mortal. You could see that he was homesick, for the sight of Sandy's possessions reminded him of his own. But he had altogether lost the hunted look. The coming of his daughter put the top stone on his recovery. It was as if a nomad had got together a home again. I expected him to be in a great state about the very real risk she had run; I knew that with Peter John it would have come between me and my sleep; but he never gave it a thought. Indeed, he scarcely listened when Lombard told him about it. He wrote to Miss Barlock and sent for Anna's kit, and then shut the lid on that chapter.

But it did one good to see him and the girl together. For a couple of years the two had not met each other. He talked a good deal to her of the Norlands, which she was beginning to forget, and he was always reminding her of things that had happened in the Island of Sheep. I noticed that he tried to appear interested in her stories about school, but on that subject she had better listeners in Mary and Barbara and me, and an infinitely better one in Lombard. He seemed to wish to forget all that had happened in England, as if it had been a bad dream. He reminded me one day with satisfaction that at Laverlaw we were half-way to the Norlands.

One thing was clear--for him that English chapter was closed. Haraldsen was not only a cured man, but a new man, or perhaps he had returned to what he had been before I met him. There was confidence in his voice, more vigour in his eyes, and he held himself and walked like a free man. That was all to the good, for he would be a combatant now, I hoped, instead of a piece of compromising baggage. He was beginning to assert himself, too, and I came to think that, if Lombard was right, and things started to move, Haraldsen himself might be the propelling force. He was becoming restless again, not from shaky nerves, but from some growing purpose. He and Anna had long serious palavers in Norland, and I guessed that he was trying to hammer out some line of action. He might soon take a hand in shaping his own destiny.

Peter John, his former comrade, was now wholly neglected, and Haraldsen and Anna made most of their expeditions together. I had asked myself how my son would get on with the girl, and I soon found an answer. They didn't get on at all. Peter John had never had much to do with women, except his mother, and to some small degree with Barbara Clanroyden and Janet Roylance, because they were the belongings of his friends. I did not believe that he would make friends with any kind of girl, and it soon became clear that, anyhow, Anna was not his kind. Never were there such obvious incompatibles. He talked little, and when you asked him a question it was like dropping a stone into a deep well--you had to wait for the answer. She babbled like a brook. He had a ridiculously formal style of speech--Johnsonian English, his house-master had called it whereas she revelled in every kind of slang--school slang out of novels, slang from film captions. I found her mannerisms often delightful, for she had not a complete command of English. For example, she would make unfamiliar positives from negative words, 'couth' (as the opposite of uncouth) was a favourite term of praise with her, and, contrary-wise, 'unbeautiful' a condemnation. Peter John thought them merely silly. Then she was always chaffing him, and it was about as much use chaffing Cleopatra's Needle for all the response she got. He treated her with elaborate politeness, and retired into his kennel, as an old house-dog will sometimes do when visitors bring a strange hound.

This went on for the better part of a week. Then suddenly Lombard's prophecy came true, and events quickened their pace to a run.

One afternoon all of us, except Barbara's infant, made an expedition to the shieling of Clatteringshaws, where the shepherd's only daughter--his name was Tarras--was being married to Nickson, the young herd on the home farm. It was a slack time in the pastoral year, before the autumn fairs began, and the whole Laverlaw estate turned out to the ceremony, for Nickson was popular and Tarras was one of the oldest hands on the place. The minister of Hangingshaw was to marry the couple at half-past two; after that there was to be high tea on the green beside the burn; then dancing was to follow till all hours in the big shed. Few of us had seen a Scots wedding, and, besides, Jean Tarras had been one of the Laverlaw maids, so we all set out on ponies to make an afternoon of it--except Peter John who, according to his custom, preferred to walk.

It was divine weather--just as well for the tea beside the burn-- and we made a cheerful party. Anna especially was in wild spirits, and I realized for the first time those good looks about which Mary had been so certain. Now that she was in prettier clothes than her school uniform, and had been out a good deal in the sun, she had become an altogether more vivid and coloured being. Her hair had gold glints in it. Her skin had flushed to a sort of golden ivory, and her lovely eyes had become deeper by contrast. She held herself well in the saddle, and her voice rang out over the heather as sweet and true as a bell. She was riding with Mary and Lombard, and I was behind with Barbara and Haraldsen, and I couldn't help telling her father that she was an uncommonly pretty child. The fact was so patent that he didn't trouble even to look pleased.

'Where does she get her name?' I asked. 'Her mother?'

'No, my mother. Anna is a common name in the Norlands. But it is not right for her. She is no Jewish prophetess. If I had the christening of her again, it should be Nanna, who was Balder's wife.'

I remembered vaguely that Balder was some sort of Norse god, and certainly the girl looked a goddess that afternoon. Haraldsen was getting very full of Northern lore these days, for he went on in his queer staccato way to explain that a goddess's name would not do for her either--that she was more like the maidens in the Edda, who had to live in the underworld in a house ringed with fire till a hero rescued them. He ran over a string of those ladies, of whom Brynhild was the only one I recognized.

'Poor Anna,' he said. 'Perhaps she will be like the women in the Sagas, ill-fated because her men are doomed. She may be as proud and sad as Bergthora, but she will never be treacherous like Halgerda.'

I wasn't quite sure what he was talking about. I had read one or two of the Sagas on Sandy's advice, and I observed that they were gloomy anecdotes.

'They are the Scriptures of my race,' said Haraldsen. 'And they have truths from which we cannot escape, though they are sad truths. They are true for me--and for you too, Hannay, and for Lord Clanroyden, and for our kind ladies, and for your son, who is striding yonder as if he were Thor on his travels. You Scots know it too, for you have it in your sayings. There is a weird which none can escape. Fenris-Wolf is waiting in Hell for Odin himself.'

'I should let Fenris-Wolf sleep in this weather,' I told him, and he laughed.

'True,' he said. 'It is not well to think of ultimate things. There is a Norland proverb which says that few can see farther forth than when Odin meets the wolf.'

He stopped and sniffed the scents, a wonderful mingling of thyme and peat and heather blown by a light west wind over miles of moorland. 'This place is like the Norlands,' he said with abstracted eyes. 'I have smelled this smell at midsummer there, when there was a wind from the hills.'

'It's my own calf-country,' I said, 'and I'm glad to think it reminds you of yours.'

'The reminder is not all pleasure. It makes me sad also. There is another of our proverbs--I seem to be quoting many to-day--that strongest is every man in his own house. I am in the house of a stranger--the kindest of strangers.'

'So am I,' I said; 'but I'm not complaining.'

'But you have your home--you can reach it in a day. Anna and I have a home, but it is shut to us. She is like the poor Princess in the tale--there is a ring of flame round her dwelling.'

'Oh, we're going to put those fires out,' I said cheerfully. 'It won't be long till you're as snug in your island as Sandy in Laverlaw and me at Fosse--a dashed sight more snug, for you haven't to pay income-tax. If the worst comes to the worst, I'll come up and join you.'

A sudden queer look came into his face. He had been talking dolefully in a brisk voice, and he had been half laughing. But now his eyes grew grave, just as his father's used to.

'I wonder if I shall ever find peace,' he said slowly. 'We Norlanders get tied up in a skein of fate from which there is no escape. Read in the Sagas, and you will see how relentless is the wheel. Hrut slays Hrap, and Atli slays Hrut, and Gisli slays Atli, and Kari slays Gisli. My father, God rest him, punishes the old Troth, and the younger Troth would punish me, and if he succeeds perhaps Anna or some child of Anna's will punish him.'

It was in a whirl of outlandish names and with Haraldsen looking as mysterious as a spae-wife that we plashed through the burn and off- saddled on the green of Clatteringshaws.

You could not imagine a pleasanter spectacle. A dozen shepherds had brought their womenfolk, and there was a big contingent of the Laverlaw servants, and an ancient horse-bus had conveyed a party from Hangingshaw village. The minister, an active young man who had got a Military Cross in the War, had come on a bicycle. Stoddart, the head-shepherd on the Mains, was the master of ceremonies, and he was busy with the preparations for tea, with Sim and Oliver as his lieutenants. Tarras welcomed us with that kindly composure which makes a Border shepherd the best gentleman on earth, for he is as sure of himself as any king. There must have been fully fifty guests. The older men were in their Sunday blacks, their regular garb for church, weddings, and funerals, but the younger wore the glen homespun, and the keepers were, of course, in knickerbockers. I noticed that every man had a black-

and-white checked necktie, a thing which Sandy always wore at home and which was the Laverlaw equivalent to a tartan. The women were in bright colours, except the bride, who wore white, and I thought how female clothes had been evened up since the War. Most of the girls were fully as well-dressed as Barbara or Janet.

The ceremony in Tarras's little parlour was a suffocating business, but happily it did not last long. Then the blushing Nickson and the very demure bride disappeared up a wooden ladder to shed some of their finery, and we examined the presents laid out in the kitchen. Tarras and his wife did hosts at the tea on the green, and I have never seen a company tuck in more resolutely to more substantial viands. There were hot mutton pies, and cold mutton hams, and all that marvellous variety of cakes and breads in which Scotland has no rival, and oceans of strong tea and rich cream, and beer for those who liked it, and whisky for the elderly. Old Tarras made a speech of Welcome, and Barbara replied almost in his own accent, for the American South, when it likes, has the same broad vowels as the Border. And then, after a deal of eating and drinking, all hands set to work to remove the tables, and the company split up into groups, while youth wandered off by itself. Presently dancing would begin in the wool-shed--the fiddlers were already tuning up--and there would be supper some time in the small hours.

The ladies started for home early, and, since I wanted exercise, I sent my pony back with Geordie

Hamilton. Lombard professed the same wish, and Haraldsen, who had been a silent figure at the feast, followed suit, so that Geordie departed like a horse-thief who had made a good haul. We were in no hurry, for it was less than an hour's walk home over hill turf, so we went round to the back of the cottage, where some of the older men were sitting on a rock above a small linn, smoking their pipes and talking their slow talk. I remember thinking that I had rarely had so profound an impression of peace. The light wind had dropped, and the honey- coloured bent and the blue of the sky were melting into the amethyst of twilight. In that cool, mellow, scented dusk, where the only sounds were the drift of distant human speech, and the tinkle of the burn, and the calling of wild birds, and the drowsy bleat of an old ewe, I seemed to have struck something as changeless as the hills.

The dogs were mostly congregated round Tarras's back-door, on the look-out for broken meats, and I had just taken a seat on a bank beside Stoddart when a most infernal racket started in their direction. It sounded like the father and mother of dog-fights. All of us got to our feet, but we were on the wrong side of the burn, and it took us some minutes to circumvent the linn, pass through the gates of the sheep-fold, and get to the back-door where bicycles and the Hangingshaw horse-bus were parked. For the last dozen yards we had the place in sight, where a considerable drama was going on.

The centre of it was Stoddart's dog, the patriarch Yarrow. He was about twelve years old, and in his day had been the pride of the countryside, for he had won twice at the big sheep-trials. I dare say he was an arrogant old fellow, and said nasty things to the young collies, for it isn't in dog nature to be a swell without showing it. But as Stoddart's dog he had a position of acknowledged pre-eminence, and at clippings and speanings and lamb sales he took precedence, and was given, so to speak, the first lick from the plate. But now he must have gone a bit too far. Every dog in the place had it in for him, and with bared teeth was intent on his massacre.

The old beast was something of a strategist. He had got into the corner where the peat-shed projected beyond the cottage wall, so that he couldn't be taken in flank or in rear, and there he was putting up a sturdy fight. He had a dozen enemies, but they had not much notion of a mass assault, for if they had come on in a wave they would have smothered him. What they did was to attack singly. A little black-and-tan dog would dart forward and leap for his neck, only to be hurled back by Yarrow's weight, for though his teeth were old and blunt, he was a heavy beast, and could have given pounds to anything else there. But some of his assailants must have got home, for he had an ear in tatters, and his neck and throat were blotched with blood.

His opponents' game was the old one of the pack, learned when their ancestors hunted on the plains of Asia. They meant to wear the old fellow down, and then rush in and finish him. Stoddart saw what they were after, and flung his stick at them, roaring abuse. I would have bet any sum that, but for us, in ten minutes the poor old beast would have been dead.

But I would have been wildly wrong, for suddenly Yarrow changed his plan, and the fight was transformed. Instead of standing on the defence he attacked. With lips snarling back over his gums, and every hair on his thick collar a-bristle, and with something between a bark, a bay, and a howl, he charged his enemies. He didn't snap--his teeth weren't good enough--he simply hurled his weight on them, using jaw and paws and every part of him as weapons of offence. Far more important, he let them see that he was out for blood. He didn't want to save his hide now, but to rend theirs. I have never seen such determination in any animal, except in African wild game. Yarrow's twelve years by Stoddart's fireside were forgotten. He was no more the household pet, the shepherd's working partner, the prize-winner at shows to be patted and stroked; he was a lightning-bolt, a tornado, a devouring fiend. . . . There was a cloud of dust and fur, and then the whole mob streaked into flight. One went between my legs, one tripped up Lombard, several felt the weight of their masters' crooks. As for old Yarrow, he had fixed his stumps in the hind-leg of a laggard, and it took Stoddart all his time to loose them.

I stopped to laugh, for it was one of the best finishes I had ever seen. Each shepherd was busy rounding up and correcting his own special miscreant, and Lombard, Haraldsen, and Peter John and I were left to ourselves. I got a glimpse of Haraldsen's face and gripped his arm, for I thought he was going to faint. He was white as paper, and shaking like a leaf. He looked just as he had done that morning on Hanham sands when the whitefront had escaped from Peter John's falcon.

Words came slowly from his pale lips. He was drawing a moral, but it was the opposite of the Hanham one. But the first words were the same.

'It is a message to me,' he croaked. 'That dog is like Samr, who died with Gunnar of Lithend. He reminds me of what I had forgotten.'

By now Stoddart had dragged Yarrow indoors to be washed and bandaged, and the other shepherds were busy with their own dogs. The gathering twilight showed that it was time for us to set out for home. Haraldsen followed us mechanically as we crossed the paddock where Tarras grew his potatoes, and the meadow where he cut his bog-hay, and breasted the long slopes which the westering sun had made as yellow as corn. He walked with great strides, keeping abreast of us, but a little to the right, as if he wished to be left alone to his gloomy Scandinavian meditations. But there was something new about him that caught my eye. He was wearing a suit of that russet colour called crotal, and it somehow enlarged his bulk. He kept his head down and poked forward, with his great shoulders hunched, and he had the look of a big brown bear out for action. There was fight and purpose in his air which before then had only been a lounging, loose-limbed acquiescence. Now there was something of old Yarrow when he had gathered himself up for the final rush.

At the watershed of the glen we stopped by consent, for the view there was worth looking at with its twenty miles of rounded hills huddling into the sunset. There was a little cairn on which Lombard and I seated ourselves, while Peter John as usual circled round us like a restless collie. Then Haraldsen spoke:

'I must leave you soon--Anna and I--at once,' he said. 'I have been too long a trespasser.'

'We're all trespassers on Sandy,' I said.

He didn't listen to me. He was in his proverbial mood, and quoted something from the Hava-mal (whatever that may be). It ran like this: 'Stay not in the same house long, but go; for love turns to loathing if a man stays long on another's floor.'

'Oh, nonsense!' I said. 'We're not here cadging hospitality. We're all in the same game, and this is part of it.'

'That is what I mean,' he answered. 'We are not playing it right. I, at any rate, have been a fool.'

We waited, for he was labouring with some thought for which he found it hard to get words. But it was only the words that were lacking, for every line of his face spoke of purpose.

He put his big hand on my shoulder.

'In January, do you remember, on the Norfolk shore? I saw the goose escape the hawk by flying low. I thought that I too might escape by being quiet and humble. . . . I was wrong, for humility drains manhood away, but does not give safety. To-day I have seen the virtue of boldness. I will no longer be passive, and try to elude my enemies. I will seek them out and fight them, like Samr the hound.'

All three of us sat up and took notice, for this was a Haraldsen we had not met before. Except for his shaven chin he might have been his father. He had identified old Yarrow with some Saga dog, and he seemed to have got himself into the skin of an ancestor. His great nose looked like the beak of a Viking galley, and his pale eyes had the ice-blue fanaticism of the North.

'I have been forgetting my race,' he went on. 'Always a weird followed us, and Fate was cruel to us. But we did not run from it or hide from it, but faced it and grappled with it, and sometimes we overthrew it. I have been a coward and I have seen the folly of cowardice. I have been sick too, but I am a whole man again. I will no longer avoid my danger, but go out to meet it, since it is the will of God. . . .'

'Quisque suos patimur Manes.' A voice spoke below us, but I did not know what the words meant. Lombard did, and perhaps Peter John, though I doubt it.

We turned to find Sandy. He had come quietly up the hill while we had been talking, and had been eavesdropping at our backs. He was wearing an old grey flannel suit, and looked pale, as if he had been too much indoors lately.

'How on earth did you get here?' I asked.

'Flew. Archie Roylance dropped me at Chryston, and that's only five miles off. I was just in time to kiss Jean Tarras and drink her health. . . . You were saying, when I interrupted?' and he turned to Haraldsen.

On Haraldsen's face there was no sign of surprise at Sandy's sudden appearance, for he was far too full of his own thoughts.

'I was saying,' he replied, 'that I will skulk no longer in a foreign country or in other men's houses. I will go home to my own land and there will fight my enemies.'

'Alone?' Sandy asked.

'If need be, alone. You have been true friends to me, but no friends can take from me the burden of my own duty.'

Sandy looked at him with that quick appraising glance of his which took in so much. I could see in his eyes that, like me, he had found something new in Haraldsen which he had not expected, and which mightily cheered him. His face broke into a smile.

'A very sound conclusion,' he said. 'It's the one I've been coming to myself. I've come up here to talk about it. . . . And now let us push on for dinner. Laverlaw air has given me the first appetite I've had for weeks.'

CHAPTER XI

We Shift our Base

That night after dinner we held a council of war, at which we all agreed that Peter John should be present. That was a comfort to him, for since Anna's coming he had been rather left out of things. Sandy, as was his habit at Laverlaw, wore the faded green coat of a Border dining club, but it didn't make him look, as it usually did, a Scots laird snug among his ancestral possessions. His face had got that special fining-down which I so well remembered, and his eyes that odd dancing light which meant that he was on the warpath again.

We had heard nothing of him for weeks, so I had a good many questions to ask.

'What have I been doing?' he said. 'Going to and fro on the earth. Trying to get a line on various gentry. My old passion for queer company has stood me in good stead, and by voluptuous curves I've been trying to get in on their flanks. One way and another I've learned most of what I wanted to know. Several of the unknown quantities I can now work out to four places of decimals. We're up against a formidable lot--no mistake about that.'

'More formidable than you thought?' asked Lombard.

'Ye-es,' he said slowly. 'But in a different way. That is my chief discovery.'

'What was your method' I asked. 'Have you been up to your old tricks?' I turned to Lombard. 'Perhaps you don't know that he's one of the best quick-change artists in the world.'

'Partly,' Sandy replied. 'I've had quite a lot of fun in the business. But I met some of them in my own name and person. We had better be clear about one thing--they know all about us. Dick they marked down long ago; and Lombard since he levanted with Miss Anna. They don't know our motive, but they realize that we are backing Haraldsen. If I've got a good deal of their dossiers, they've got plenty of ours. You'd be surprised, Dick, to know how zealously they have been searching into your tattered past, and I'm glad to think that what they found has made them fairly uncomfortable. They've been pumping, very cleverly and quietly, all your old pals like Artinswell and Julius Victor and Archie Roylance. They even got something out of Macgillivray, though he wasn't aware of it.'

'What do they make of YOU?'

Sandy laughed. 'Oh, I puzzle them horribly. I've got the jade tablet, so I'm in the thick of it, and they're gunning for me just as much as for Haraldsen. But I'm a troublesome proposition, for they understand quite well that I've taken the offensive, and they've an idea that when I fix my teeth in anything I'm apt to hang on. That's the worst of my confounded melodramatic reputation. It sounds immodest, but I've a notion that they've got the wind up badly about me, and if we had only the first lot to deal with I might make them cry off. . . . Only of course we haven't.'

'What's the new snag?' I asked.

'Patience,' he said. 'We'll go through the list one by one. First, Varrinder, the youth with the rabbit teeth. We can count him out, for he'll worry us no more. He was what I suspected--an indicateur, and at heart a funk. I laid myself out to scare Master Varrinder, and I succeeded. He was very useful to me, so far as his twittering nerves allowed him. Yesterday he sailed, under another name, for Canada, and he won't come back for a long, long time. Next, Dick.'

'Albinus,' I said.

'Right. He's the second least important. Well, I've seen a lot of Mr. Erick Albinus. I played bridge with him at Dillon's, which cost me twenty pounds. We went racing together, and I had a boring but illuminating day. I gave a little dinner for him, to which I made a point of asking one or two of his City friends about whom he is most nervous. He's a nasty piece of work, that lad, and it beats me how people tolerate him as they do, for he's the oily faux bonhomme if there ever was one. He's in the job for greed, for financially he's on the edge of Queer

Street, and also Troth has some kind of family pull on him. But I think I could scare him out of it, like Varrinder, if I wanted to. But I don't. I've decided that he's safer in than out, for he has a big yellow streak in him, and, though he's a clever devil, he'll be a drag on his friends in the long run. So I've remained on good terms with Mr. Albinus, and he flatters himself that he has thrown dust in my eyes, more power to him.

'Now we get to bigger business. Troth--Mr. Lancelot Troth. I've come to a clear decision about Troth. He's a ruffian, but I don't think he's altogether a rogue. A fine distinction, you say. Maybe, but it's important. First, he has his friends who genuinely like him, quite honest fellows, some of them. I got myself invited to the annual dinner of his Fusilier regiment, where he made a dashed good speech. I gathered that in the War he was a really good battalion officer, and very popular with the men. I did my best to follow his business tracks, and pretty tangled they are, but my impression is that he is more of a buccaneer than a swindler. He's a bold fellow who runs his head now and then against the law, because he likes taking risks. Did you ever read The Wrong Box? There's a touch of Michael Finsbury in Troth.'

'Did you meet him--I mean as yourself?' I asked.

'Indeed I did. Had quite a heart-to-heart talk with him. I went down to his office, sent in my card, and begged for a few minutes' conversation on private business. There was a fine commotion in that office, a client was cleared like a shot out of his private room, and he told his secretary that on no account must we be disturbed. I suppose he thought that I had come to offer terms. I was the guileless innocent--asked if he had read my letter to the Times--said I was very anxious to get all the information I could about old Haraldsen, and that I had heard that he had known him in South Africa. That puzzled him, and in self-defence he became very stiff and punctilious--said he had had nothing to do with Haraldsen, though his father might have met him. You see, he hadn't yet linked me up with you, Dick, and was playing for safety. Then I said that I was trying to get on the track of Haraldsen's family--believed he had a son somewhere, and could he help me to locate him? I had come to him solely as a matter of business, for I had heard good reports of his skill. I said I had got this jade tablet, which I couldn't possibly stick to, and that I proposed to present it to the British Museum unless I could find Haraldsen's heirs, in which case they should have it.

'That fetched him. He suggested luncheon, and took me to one of the few old City places remaining where you feed in a private box. He insisted on champagne, so I remembered a saying of my father's, that if a man gave you champagne at luncheon, you should suspect a catch. He was very civil and forthcoming, and began, quite cleverly, to dig things out of his memory which his father had told him about Haraldsen. He dared say that with a little trouble he could get some information for me about the people who had a claim to the equities in

Haraldsen's estate. We parted on excellent terms, after some highly technical talk about spring salmon in Caithness, and he promised to ring me up as soon as he had anything to tell me.'

'Did he?' Lombard asked eagerly. He was the one of us who knew most about Troth.

'No. For in the next day or two his scouts linked me up with Dick-- Laverlaw was enough for that--and he must have realized that I knew everything and had been playing with him. But I rang him up myself and got a very dusty answer. However, he agreed to see me again, and I made him lunch with me at Claridge's--planted him down in the middle of a crowded restaurant, where he couldn't make an exhibition of himself. For I meant to make him lose his temper, and if that had happened in his office the end would only have been a shindy. I managed it all right. I orated about old Haraldsen, that wonderful figure half-saint and half-adventurer, and the sacred trust that had been laid on me, and so forth. He listened with a squared jaw and ugly suspicious eyes while I strummed on the falsetto. Then he broke out. "See here, Lord Clanroyden," he said. "I've had enough of this stuff. You've been trying to fool me and I don't like it. I see what your game is, and I don't like it either. You take my advice and keep out of this business, or you'll get hurt, big swell as you are. Old Haraldsen was a scoundrel, and there's some of us who have a lot to get back from him and his precious son."

'I opened my eyes and started on another tack. I said that all this shocked me, and I'm hanged if I didn't get him to believe that I meant it. You see, I was the new-comer who might have heard any kind of story from the other side. He actually seemed to want to put himself right in my eyes, and he gave me his own version. What it was doesn't signify, except that he has a full-sized vendetta on his hands inherited from his father, and isn't going to forget it. I must say I respected his truculence. It was rather like the kind of family legacy you have among the Indian frontier tribes. I pretended to be surprised, and not altogether unsympathetic, and we parted on very fair terms. I had got the two things I wanted. I had kept the gang uncertain what part I meant to play, and I had taken the measure of Troth. A bit of a ruffian as I have said, but not altogether a rogue. If he were the only one in the show I think he might be squared. He wants what he considers to be his rights, not loot in the general way. But of course he's not alone, for there's a bigger and subtler mind behind him. Can you put a name to it?'

'Barralty,' said Lombard and I in unison.

'Yes, Barralty. He is the mind all right. I had to get a full view of Barralty, so I approached him from all kinds of angles. I've told you already about the Bloomsbury party, where he was a king among the half-baked. I followed up his trail in the City-- Lombard started me on that--and my conclusion is that the Lepcha business hasn't done him much harm. He has still plenty of money in the ordinary way, though not a hundredth part of what he wants, and his reputation is still high. I thought I'd have a peep at his political side, so I got Andrew Amos to arrange that I should attend a private conference between some of the intellectuals and the trade-union leaders--I was a boiler-maker from the Clyde and a fairly shaggy comrade. His performance there rather impressed me, for he managed to make himself a bridge between two utterly different worlds--put the idealistic stuff with a flavour of hard good sense, and the practical view with a touch of idealism. There's a considerable future for him in politics, if he decides that way.

'Then I thought that I'd better make his acquaintance. You know Charles Lamancha's taste for freak parties? Well, I got him to give a dinner at the club--himself, Christopher Stannix, an Under- Secretary, a couple of bankers, and Ned Leithen, and I had myself placed next to Barralty. Of course by this time he knew all about me, for the Laverlaw party had begun, and his friends had discovered the way we have tied up Haraldsen's fortune, so naturally I was considered the villain of the piece. He made no mistakes that night. He was very polite to me, and talked intelligently about my Far East Commission and foreign affairs generally, and even condescended to be enthusiastic about this Border country in which he said he often motored. He did not attempt to pump me, but behaved as if I were an ordinary guest of whom he had heard and whom he was quite glad to meet. There was some pretty good talk, for Stannix always manages to put life into a dinner table, and Barralty kept his end up. He had a wrangle with one of the bankers over some financial point, and I thought he put his case uncommonly well. So did the others, for he was listened to with respect. There's no doubt that he has a pretty solid footing in the world, and there's no mistake about his brains. He's as quick as lightning on a point, and I can see him spinning an immense web and keeping his eye on every thread in it.'

'I told you that weeks ago,' said Lombard. 'Barralty is as clever as the devil. But what about the rest of him--besides his mind?'

'I'm coming to that. That was the thing I most wanted to know about, and it wasn't easy to get cross-bearings. I had to dive into queer worlds and half-worlds and, as I've already said, I found that my unfortunate liking for low society came in useful. I found out most of what I wanted, but it has been a long job and not a particularly pleasant one. One piece of luck I had. There was bound to be a woman somewhere, and I scraped up acquaintance with Barralty's particular friend. She's a lovely creature, a red- haired Jewess, who just missed coming off as a film-star. Heaven knows what her real name is, but she calls herself Lydia Ludlow.'

'She came to tea at Fosse,' Peter John put in. 'I remember her name. My mother said she was an actress.'

'Dick,' said Sandy solemnly, 'I think Peter John should be in bed. But I won't enlarge upon Miss

Ludlow, except to say that she was hard to get to know, but that she repaid me for my trouble. I was an American film magnate, very well made up, and I don't think she is likely to recognize me again. I had a wonderful scheme for a super-film about Herod Agrippa, which would star her. So we had a number of confidential talks, in which Barralty's name cropped up as a friend who would take a share in the venture. You see, it was to be a great Anglo-American show, a sort of proof of the unity of art and the friendship of the Anglo-Saxon race. I learned from her a good deal about Barralty. He is her slave, it appears, but the fetters don't gall, for his success is to be her success. The two of them represent a pretty high-powered ambition, and Miss Ludlow won't let the pressure slacken.'

'What's your conclusion?' I asked. 'A first-class brain, but how much stuff behind it?'

'Not a great deal. I have collected all my evidence and carefully weighed it, and that is my verdict. Barralty has three spurs to prick him on--ambition, greed, which is part of his ambition, and his lady. But he has a lot of tethers to keep him still--fear of his reputation, fear of his skin, all sorts of funks. He's not the bold class of lad. Rather a sheep in wolf's clothing. If things were as they were a year ago, I believe we could settle the whole business out of hand.'

'You mean--what?' Haraldsen spoke for the first time.

'Well, we could do a deal with Troth, a reasonable deal, and I believe he would stick to it. I could scare Albinus as I have scared Varrinder. And in spite of Miss Ludlow I think I could scare Barralty. Only you see that is impossible now, for a fifth figure has appeared, who puts a darker complexion on the thing. Before, it was not much more than melodrama, but now the tragic actor is on the boards. For the real wolf has arrived.'

'We knew for certain that D'Ingraville was in it after Lombard's escapade,' I said.

I had to tell Sandy some of the details of Lombard's story, for he had not heard them.

'Yes,' he said reflectively. 'He must have been the man who drove the Stutz.' He referred to a pocket diary. 'There were three days when he slipped away from me, and now I know what he was doing. Otherwise I didn't let him often out of my sight. No, I never was in his sight, but there wasn't much he did in those weeks in London that I didn't know. You see, I was on my own ground and he was a stranger, so I had a pull on him. He tried a little contre- espionage, but it was clumsy. I've been sitting tight and watching him, and all I can say is, that if he was formidable in Olifa he's a dashed sight more formidable to-day.'

I whistled, for I had Sandy's Olifa doings clear in my head, and I remembered just how big a part D'Ingraville had played there.

'He's a beast of prey,' Sandy went on. 'But in Olifa he was a sick beast, living an unnatural life on drugs which must have weakened his nerve. Now he's the cured beast, stronger and much more dangerous than if he had never been sick. It's exactly what happens with a man who gets over infantile paralysis--the strength of will and mind and body required to recover from the disease give the patient a vitality and self-confidence that lasts him for the rest of his days. I don't know why God allowed it and by what magic he achieved it, but D'Ingraville to-day is as fit a man as any of us here, and with ten times our dæmonic power. . . . And he isn't alone. You remember, Dick, the collection of toughs that Castor called his Bodyguard. I thought that all of them had been gathered in, but I was mistaken. Two at least survive--the ones called Carreras and Martel, the Spaniard and the Belgian. At this moment they're with D'Ingraville in London, and you may bet they're in with him in this show.'

'But Martel was killed in your last scrap,' I put in. 'What was the name of the place? Veiro? You told me so. I don't remember about Carreras, but I'm positive about Martel.'

'So I thought,' said Sandy; 'but I was wrong. Carreras managed to leak out quite early, but I thought Martel was one of the bag at Veiro. But he's very much alive. I could take you any day into a certain Soho restaurant, and show you Martel in a neat blue suit and yellow boots having his apéritif. The same lithe, hard-trained brute, with the scar over his left eye that he got from Geordie Hamilton. We have the genuine beasts of prey on our trail this time, Dick, my lad. . . . And I'll tell you something more. We could have bought off, or scared off, the others, I think, but there's no scaring D'Ingraville's pack, and there's only one price to buy them with and that's every cent of Haraldsen's fortune and my jade tablet. D'Ingraville, I understand, is particularly keen on the jade tablet--naturally, for he's an imaginative blackguard.'

'But how will the old lot mix with the new?' I asked.

'They won't,' said Sandy grimly. 'But if I'm any judge of men, they'll have to do as they're told. None of them can stand up for a moment against D'Ingraville. Troth, the ordinary, not too scrupulous, sedentary attorney--Barralty, the timid intellectual-- what can they do against the real desperado? I could almost be sorry for them, for they're young rabbits in the fox's jaw. D'Ingraville is the leader now, and the rest must follow, whether they like it or not. He won't loosen his grip on either his opponents or his allies. He's the real enemy. My old great-great- great-grandfather at Dettingen led his regiment into action after telling them, "Ye see those lads on yon hill? Well, if ye dinna kill them, they'll kill you." That's what I say about D'Ingraville.'

'So much for the lay-out,' I said. 'What do you propose to do about it?'

'At first I was for peace,' Sandy answered. 'I thought that the gang could be squared or scared. I knew that D'Ingraville couldn't, but I fancied he might be dealt with in another way--he and his Bodyguard. I saw the Olifa Embassy people, but it's no good. There's not enough positive evidence against them to make extradition possible. Besides, even if there were, it wouldn't solve Haraldsen's problem. These hounds will stick to his track, and, unless they could be decently strung up, there's no lasting security for him. So I take it that things have come to a crisis. At any rate they're coming, and we must face it. It's no good our sheltering here any longer. I dare say we could stave them off for a bit, but it would be a rotten life for everybody, and some day they would get under our guard. We must fight them, and choose our own ground for it, and, since they are outside civilization, we must be outside it too.'

'I don't see the sense of that,' I said. 'This is a law-abiding country, and that will cramp D'Ingraville's style. If we go down into the jungle the jungle beasts will have the advantage.'

Sandy shook his head.

'First, you can't bring things to the point in a law-abiding land. Second, a move will cramp the style of Troth and Barralty worse than ever. Third, D'Ingraville is a product of civilization, and I'd be more afraid of him in a Paris street than on a desert island. So I agree with what I overheard Haraldsen say when I overtook you on the hill. We must fight the last round in the Island of Sheep.'

Then Haraldsen spoke.

'That is my resolution,' he said in his slow, quiet voice. He stood up and stretched his great form to its full height, much as I had seen his father do on that moonlit hill long ago. 'I will do as the old dog did this afternoon, and snap back at my tormentors.'

'Right,' said Sandy. We all felt the tension of the moment, and he wanted to keep the temperature down. 'I think that is common sense. I will arrange that the papers announce that you are going back to the Norlands. We had better divide up. I have a friend, a trawler skipper in Aberdeen, who will take you. By the way, what about your daughter?'

'Anna goes with me. I should be a wretched man if she were out of my sight. Also, it is right that she should share in my destiny.'

'I dare say that's wise. If you left her here, they might make a hostage of her. Dick, you can go by the monthly Iceland boat, which sails next week from Leith, and you'd better take Geordie Hamilton. I will come on later. You may be certain that the pack will be hot after us as soon as they learn our plans. Laverlaw and Fosse and Mary and Peter John and Barbara and the infant will be left in peace.'

There was a small groan from Peter John. He had been listening to our talk with eyes like saucers. 'Mayn't I come too?' he pled.

'No, my lad,' I said, though his piteous face went to my heart. 'You're too young, and there's no duty in it for you. We can't afford camp-followers.'

'But I will not permit it,' Haraldsen cried passionately. 'I go to meet my fate, whatever God may send, I and my daughter. But I will not have you endanger yourself for me. You have been most noble and generous; but your task is over, for you have restored me to myself and made me a man again. I go to my home to fight out the battle there with one or two of my own people. You, my friends, will remain in your homes, and thank God that He has given you peace.'

'Not I,' I said. 'I promised your father to stand by you, and I'm jolly well going to stick to that. Besides, I'm getting fat and slack, and I need fining down. I wouldn't be out of this for all your millions. What about you, Lombard?'

'I'm on,' was the answer. 'I swore the same oath as you, and I want some exercise to stir up my liver. I've tidied up my affairs for a month or two, for I meant, anyhow, to take a long holiday. Beryl won't object. She's as keen on this job as I am.'

I had spoken briskly, but my heart was in my boots. I was certain that Mary would raise no objections, as she had raised none in the 'Three Hostages' business, but I knew that she would be desperately anxious. I had no fears for her and Peter John, for the battle- ground would be moved a thousand miles off, but I saw a miserable time ahead for those that I loved best.

Haraldsen stared at us and his eyes filled with tears. He seized on Lombard, who was nearest him, and hugged him like a bear. I managed to avoid an embrace, but he wrung my hand.

'I did not know there was such honour in the world,' he said with his voice breaking. 'Now indeed I may be bold, for I have on either side of me a friend.'

Then he looked at Sandy, of whom he had hitherto been rather in awe.

'But of you, Lord Clanroyden, I can ask nothing. You have sworn no oath, and you are a great man who is valuable to his country. Also, you have a young wife and a little baby. I insist that you stay at home, for this enterprise of ours, I must tell you, will be very difficult. And I think it may be very dangerous.'

'Oh, I know that,' was the answer. 'Barbara knows it too, and she would be the first to tell me to go. I have a bigger interest in this than any of you. Give me some beer, Dick, and I'll tell you a story.'

I filled up his tankard and very deliberately he lit his pipe. His eyes rested on each of us in turn--Lombard a little flushed and excited, me rather solemnized by the line things were taking, Peter John who had suddenly gone pale, and Haraldsen towering above us like a Norse rover. In the end they caught Haraldsen's eyes, and some compelling force in them made him pull up a chair and sit down stiffly, like a schoolboy in the headmaster's room.

'Three days ago,' said Sandy, 'I had a little trip across the Channel. I flew to Geneva, and there got a car and motored deep into the Savoy glens. In the evening I came to a small, ancient chateau high up on the knees of the mountains. In the twilight I could see a white wedge poking up in the eastern sky, which I knew to be Mont Blanc. I spent the night there, and my host was D'Ingraville.'

We all exclaimed, for it sounded the maddest risk to take.

'There was no danger,' Sandy went on. 'I was perfectly certain about my man. He belongs to a family that goes back to the Crusades and has come badly down in the world. That little dwelling is all that is left to a man whose forbears once owned half Haute Savoie. There's a sentimental streak in D'Ingraville, and that hill-top of his is for him the dearest thing on earth. I had discovered that, never mind how, and I wasn't afraid of his putting poison in my coffee. He's a scoundrel, but on a big scale, and he has some rags of gentility left.

'Well, we had an interesting evening. I didn't try to bargain with him, but we exchanged salutes, so to speak, before battle. I wanted to find out the mood he was in, now that he was a cured man, and to discover just how far he meant to go. There's no doubt on that point. He is playing up to the limit. He is going to skin Haraldsen, and perhaps Troth and Barralty into the bargain. But there's more in it than greed. Once it might have been possible to buy him off with an immense sum--but not now, since he knows I'm in it. He has come to regard me as his eternal enemy. The main quarrel now is not between Haraldsen and the Pack, but between D'lngraville and me. He challenged me, and I accepted the challenge.'

He must have seen disapproval in my face, for he went on.

'There was no other way, Dick. It wasn't vanity. He might go about the world boasting that he had beaten me, and I would never give it a thought. I'm quite content that he should find his own way to Hell. But there's more to it than that. He's what is left over from my Olifa job, and till those remains are swept up, that job isn't finished. I can't leave the thing half done. I can't let that incarnate devil go loose in the world. If I shirked his challenge I should never sleep in my bed again.'

There had come into Sandy's face that look that I had seen once or twice before--on the little hill outside Erzerum, in Medina's library in Hill Street--and I knew that I might just as well argue with a whirlwind. He was smiling, but his eyes were solemn.

'He saw me off next morning in a wonderful mountain dawn. "It's good to be alive in such a world," he said. "Au revoir. It will not be long, I hope, till we meet again." Well, I'm going to hurry on that meeting. I'm going to join him on your island, and I think that one or the other of us won't leave it.'

PART III. The Island of Sheep

CHAPTER XII

Hulda's Folk

I had never before sailed in northern waters, and I had pictured them as eternally queasy and yeasty and wind-scourged. Very different was the reality in that blue August weather. When Lombard, Geordie Hamilton, and I embarked in the Iceland boat at Leith, there was a low mist over the Forth, but we ran into clear air after the May, and next morning, as we skirted the Orkneys, the sea was a level plain, with just enough of a breeze to crisp it delicately, and in the strong sunlight the distant islets stood out sharp and clear like the kopjes in a veld morning.

But the fine weather did nothing to raise my spirits. I had never started out on a job with less keenness or with drearier forebodings. Lombard put me to shame. This man, whom I thought to have grown soft and elderly, was now facing the unknown, not only composedly but cheerfully. He had a holiday air about him, and would have been glad to be in the business, I'm positive, even though he had never sworn that ancient oath. I began to think that the profession of high finance was a better training than the kind of life I had led myself. Part of his cheerfulness was due to the admiration he had acquired for Sandy, which made him follow as docilely as a small boy in the wake of a big brother. I yielded to no one in my belief in Sandy, but we had been through too many things together for me to think him infallible. That rotten Greek sentence that Macgillivray had quoted stuck in my mind. Both Sandy and I had had amazing luck in life, but luck always turned in the end.

My trouble was that I could not see how the affair could finish. We were to get to grips, in some remote island which was clean outside any law, with a gang that knew no law. That could only mean a stand-up fight in the old style. No doubt Haraldsen would have his own people, but the Norlanders were not a warlike folk, and, though we would have numbers on our side, I wasn't prepared to be cocksure about the result. If we beat them off, it might put the wind up Troth and Barralty for good and all, but it would have no effect on D'Ingraville. Not unless we killed him. If, on the other hand, we were beaten, God knows what would happen to Haraldsen and his daughter--and to the rest of us, and especially to Sandy. There could be no end to the business unless either D'Ingraville or Sandy perished. It looked like one of those crazy duels that the old Northmen used to fight, and I remembered that they always chose an island for the purpose. The more I considered the busincss, thc more crazy and melodramatic I thought it. Two sober citizens, Lombard and myself, were being dragged at the chariot wheels of two imaginative desperadoes, for Sandy had always a kind of high-strung daftness about him--

that was where his genius lay. And it looked as if Haraldsen had reverted to some wild ancestral type.

But most of all I was worried about those we had left behind. Mary I hoped did not realize the full danger, for I had always put the affair to her as a piece of common blackmail. We had gone to settle Haraldsen in his home, and see that he was comfortable, and the worst that could happen would be that we might have to read the Riot Act to some vulgar blackmailers. Sandy must have put it in the same way to Barbara--at least, I fervently hoped so. Neither knew anything about D'Ingraville. But Mary was an acute person who missed very little, and was extraordinarily sensitive to an atmosphere. She was greatly attached to the Haraldsens, and would never have hinted that I should back out of my duty towards them. But I was pretty certain that she understood that that duty was a more solemn thing than the light holiday task I had pretended. She had said nothing, and had bidden me good-bye as if we were off to Norway to catch salmon. Yet I had a notion that her calm was an enforced thing, for no woman had ever more self-control, and that her anxiety would never sleep till she saw me again. She would remember that August morning at Machray when I had gone out for an ordinary day's stalking, and had been found by her twenty hours later senseless on the top of a crag with Medina dead at the bottom.

With these thoughts in my head I got no good of the bright afternoon, as we skirted the northern butt of the Orkneys and approached the Roost through which our course lay. Suddenly I noticed that the ship was slowing down. The captain, a placid old Dane with whom I had made friends, joined me.

'We take another passenger, General,' he said. 'One who was too late for us at Leith. We were advised of him by wireless. He will have to pay the whole fare between Leith and Reykjavik, or there will be trouble with your British port authorities.'

I followed his eyes and saw approaching us from the land a small motor-boat, with a single figure in the stern.

'It is a man,' he said, handing me the glasses. 'Some Icelander who has tarried too long in Scotland, or some Scot who would come in for the last of the Iceland salmon.'

There seemed something familiar about the shape of the passenger, but I went below to fetch my tobacco pouch, and I did not see the motor-boat arrive. What was my amazement, when I came on deck again, to find Peter John! He was wearing one of my ulsters, and had his kit in a hold-all. Also, he had Morag the falcon on his wrist. There he stood, looking timid and sheepish like a very little boy. He said nothing, but held out a letter.

It was from Mary. She said simply that she couldn't bear the sight of her son's tragic face. 'He has been wandering about like a lost dog,' she wrote. 'I think some sea air would be good for him, for he has been rather limp in the heat lately. And if there is any trouble he might be useful, for he is pretty sensible. He has promised me to keep an eye on you, and I shall be happier in my mind if I know he is with you. Cable from Hjalmarshavn, please, to say he has arrived.'

That was all. Peter John stood very stiff, as if he expected a scolding, but I wasn't inclined to scold. It was a joy to have him with me, and that Mary should send him after me convinced me that she was not really anxious--though I doubt if that conclusion did justice to her stoicism. Then a thought struck me. The boy knew how dangerous our mission was, for he had heard Sandy expound it.

'Did you tell your mother that there was some risk in this business?' I asked.

'Yes. I thought that was only fair.'

'What did she say?'

'She said that she knew it already, and that she would feel easier if I were with you to take care of you.'

That was Mary all over. Another woman would have clutched at her boy to keep at least one of her belongings out of danger. Mary, knowing that a job had to be done, was ready to stake everything to have it well done.

Peter John's solemn face relaxed into a smile when he saw the change in mine.

'How did you get here?' I asked.

'I flew,' was the reply. 'I flew to Inverness and then to Kirkwall. The only difficult things were the motor-boat and the wireless message.'

At that I laughed.

'I don't know that you can take care of me. But there's no doubt you can take care of yourself.'

We came to the little port of Hjalmarshavn, the capital of the Norlands, in the same bright, west-wind weather. The green hills behind the black sea-cliffs, the blue tides creaming white on the little skerries, the wall of dimmer peaks to the north, all seemed to sleep in a peace like that of the Blessed Isles in the story. In Hjalmarshavn there was a gentle bustle, and about a thousand varieties of stinks, from rotting seaweed to decaying whale. The houses were painted in a dozen colours, and the little bay was full of many kinds of small craft--fishing smacks, whale boats, kayaks, and primitive motor-launches. The only big craft were the Grimsby trawlers, and a steamer flying the red and white Danish flag which had just come in from Iceland. Ours was the first passenger ship for a fortnight that had arrived from the south, so the other lot had not preceded us. I made inquiries and heard that the Aberdeen trawler had arrived three days before, and that Haraldsen had at once gone on to his island.

We hired a motor-boat, and that afternoon rounded the south end of the main island, skirted its west side, and threaded our way through an archipelago of skerries till we were abreast of Halder, the second biggest of the group. Its shore was marvellously corrugated, deep-cut glens running down from peaks about 3,000 feet in height and the said peaks sometimes ending in mighty precipices and sometimes falling away into moorish levels and broad shingly beaches. Presently on our port appeared a low coast-line, which from the map I saw was the Island of Sheep. It was separated from Halder by a channel perhaps two miles wide, but its character was wholly different from its neighbour. It reminded me of Colonsay, a low, green place cradled deep in the sea, where one would live as in a ship with the sound of waves always in one's ear.

Then I saw the House, built on high land above a little voe, half castle, half lighthouse it seemed, belonging both to land and water. There are no trees in the Norlands, but even from a distance I could see that some kind of demesne had been laid out, with stone terraces ending in little thatched pavilions. Below it, close to the shore, nestled a colony of small dwellings. What caught the eye was the amazing greenness. After the greys and browns of the Shetlands the place seemed to be as vividly green as an English meadow in May. The lower part of the House was rough stone, the upper part of a dark timber, but the roof was bright green turf, growing as lustily as in a field. When in the early twilight we put in to the little jetty, I seemed to be looking at a port outside the habitable world in some forgotten domain of peace.

As long as I live I shall remember my first step on land--the whiff of drying stockfish from the shore, the black basalt rocks, the clumps of broad-leaved arch-angelica, and the oyster-catchers piping along the shingle.

Haraldsen and Anna were awaiting us. Haraldsen was wearing the native Norland dress, coat and breeches of russet home-spun, with silver buttons at collar and knees, homespun stockings and silver- buckled shoes, and a queer conical cap of dark blue and red. He looked half squire and half pirate, but wholly in keeping with his surroundings. Anna had a navy-blue skirt and a red jumper, bare legs, and buckled raw-hide mocassins.

'You have brought the boy,' Haraldsen said after his first words of greeting. His eyes looked troubled.

'His mother sent him after us,' I said. 'He is supposed to take care of me.'

'He is very welcome,' was the answer, but his brow was furrowed. I could see that a second child in the party seemed to him to add heavily to his responsibilities. . . . Little did either of us guess that these two children were to be our salvation.

Very different was Anna's greeting. She seemed to have shed the English schoolgirl, and with that all her tricks of speech and manner which had annoyed my son. Hitherto, as I have said, she had treated him cavalierly, and driven him to a moody silence. Now she was a hostess in her own house, and she had the manner of a princess welcoming a friend to her kingdom. Amazingly handsome she looked, with her brilliant hair and eyes, and her ivory skin coloured by the sea-winds and lit by the sun. She took the boy's hand in both of hers.

'I am very glad to see you, Mr. Peter John,' she said. 'We shall have great fun together.'

I was not prepared for such a palace as the old Haraldsen had built. I had accepted the family fortune as a fact, but had seen no evidence in a hunted man and a rather shabby schoolgirl. Now I realized that there must be great wealth in the background. Above the low cliffs the land had been levelled, and there were wide lawns as fine as England could show, for in that moist climate the turf was perfect. There was some attempt at flowers too, roses and larkspur and simple annuals, but only in sunken hollows to avoid the winds, which in the Norlands can blow like the wrath of God. The House itself was of three storeys, sheltered on three sides by a half moon of hills, while the bulk of Halder across the channel was there to break the force of the eastern blasts. Following the old Norland fashion, the ground floor was mainly storerooms, as in a Border keep, with the living-rooms above them, and the bedrooms in the top storey.

It was all new except at one end, where stood a queer little stone cell or chapel, with walls about five feet thick. This, according to the tale, had been the home of an Irish hermit, who in the dark ages had found a refuge here till the heathen Northmen were the death of him.

The entrance was by a flight of steps which seemed to be hewn out of the living rock. First came a vast hall, at least a hundred feet long and the full height of the house. This had been constructed, I suppose, on the model of a Viking hall, and in it one seemed to cheat the ages. Where the old Haraldsen had got the timbers I do not know, but they were hoar-ancient, and the black-oak panelling was carved in wild grotesques. The furniture was ancient and immense; there was a long dining-table which would have accommodated fifty Vikings, and gigantic chairs which only Falstaff could have decently filled. For decorations there were some wonderful old pieces of tapestry, and a multitude of ship models of every age in silver and ivory and horn and teak, which must have been worth a ransom.

That was the state apartment, and a pretty comfortless one. But on either side of it were other rooms--a big drawing-room, expensively furnished, but as barren of human interest as a museum, and like a museum full of collector's pieces; a smoking-room, on the walls of which hung every kind of Norland implement from the Stone Age downward; a billiard room, with a collection of sporting trophies, including many of the old man's African heads; and above all a library. That library was the pleasantest room in the house, and it was clearly Haraldsen's favourite, for it had the air of a place cherished and lived in. Its builder had chosen to give it a fine plaster ceiling, with heraldic panels between mouldings of Norland symbols. It was lined everywhere with books, books which had the look of being used, and which consequently made that soft tapestry which no collection of august bindings can ever provide. Upstairs the bedrooms were large and airy, with bare oak floors, and not too much furniture, but with all modern comforts.

What struck me especially was that everything was of the best and probably of high value. It seemed queer to be contemplating a siege in a treasure house.

'The treasures were my father's,' said Haraldsen. 'Myself I do not want possessions. Only my books.'

The entertainment was as good as the lodging. There was an old steward called Arn Arnason, who wore the same clothes as his master and looked like Rumpelstiltzkin in the fairy-tale, and he had under him four elderly serving maids. I gathered from Haraldsen that it was his habit to send his motor-boat once a week to Hjalmarshavn for letters and such things as he imported. But the island itself produced most of his supplies. He had his own cows for milk, the mutton was about the best in the world, and he cured his own hams and bacon; he grew all the simpler vegetables, including superb potatoes: the sea yielded the fish he wanted, not to speak of lobsters, and there were sea-trout and brown trout to be had from the lochs. Indeed, I never ate better food in my life--simple food, but perfect basic material perfectly cooked. In two things only it deviated into luxury. There was a wonderful cellar in which the sherry and the madeira in particular were things to dream of, and following the Northern fashion, our meals began with a preposterous variety of hors d'oeuvre. Peter John, till he learned better, used to eat of so many small outlandish dishes that he had no room for solid food.

We went early to bed, but before turning in I had one word with Haraldsen about serious business.

'We are well in front,' I said. 'Any news of our friends?'

'None. We have a telephone to Hjalmarshavn, and I have arranged to get word of all strangers who arrive there. But I do not think they will come by Hjalmarshavn.'

'Any news of Lord Clanroyden?'

He shook his head. 'No doubt he will soon telegraph, and we will get the message by telephone. He said he would follow at once.'

I asked one other question, and got an answer which sent me to bed with an uneasy mind. 'What men have you on the island?'

He looked perturbed.

'There is Arn Arnason in the house,' he said. 'There are the three gardeners, Dahl and Holm and Evansen. Down at the harbour there is Jacob Gregarsen, who is in charge of the motor-boat. And there is also Absalon the fowler, who is bed-ridden. All these are old men, I fear.'

'Good God!' I cried. 'I thought you had a lot of hefty youths.'

'It is my blunder,' he said penitently. 'I had forgotten. There were a score of young men on the Island of Sheep, but now they are all abroad. Some have gone to Greenland and Iceland after cod, and some are at the halibut fishing. One, on whom I counted most, sailed last month for America.'

The clear blue weather ended that night. Next morning we were back in the typical Norlands, a south-west wind which brought scuds of rain, and mist over all the hills. Halder, as seen across the Channel, was only a grey wraith. The fashion of the household was for a skimpy petit déjeuner and then an elaborate midday meal. Haraldsen had some business of his own, so Lombard, Peter John, and I got into oilskins, and, escorted by Anna, started out to prospect the island.

Its main features were simple, and, since they are important to my story, I must make them clear. The place was about six miles long, and at the greatest two miles wide, and it lay roughly north and south. The House stood about two-thirds of the way up, and the highest ground, only five or six hundred feet in altitude, was just behind it. Towards the north end the land was broken moorland, with two or three small lochs full of trout, and the butt itself was a sheer cliff of at least four hundred feet, over which one of the lochs emptied in a fine waterfall. All that part of the coast was rugged and broken, little gullies descending from the uplands to a boulder-strewn shore.

Below the House, as I have said, was a small voe, with to the south a village close to the water. South of this again were stretches of sand, and, since the coast there ran out to a point, there was good shelter for boats in almost any wind. The southern part of the island was quite different in character. The ground fell to only a few feet above sea-level, and the shore was either sand or sprawling reefs. Inland there was a waste of bent and marsh, with several swampy lochs which looked as if they might furnish difficult fishing. Peter John's eyes brightened as we circumnavigated the place, for it was plainly a paradise for birds. A shout from him called my attention to a pair of purple sandpipers. In the Norlands no shooting is permitted on land, and only for a short season on the sea, so the islands are pretty well a sanctuary. It was absurd to see curlews almost running between our legs like tame pheasants, and so shy a bird as the golden plover coolly regarding us from a rock two yards off. That great bog must have been at least four square miles in extent, and it was alive with every kind of bird. It wasn't easy to get my son away from it.

Towards the south end the land rose slightly to hummocky downs, and the sea began to poke its fingers into it. There must have been a dozen little inlets, and a big voe a quarter of a mile wide into which one of the lochs discharged a stream. Seatrout were jumping merrily at the stream mouth. I wished to Heaven that I had come here for a holiday and not on a grim job, for I never saw a more promising fishing-ground. We walked to the mouth of the voe, where a swell was breaking under the wind, and looked out on low mists and a restless sea.

We had two days of dripping weather, and, since there was nothing I could do, I put in some hard thinking. Our total strength when Sandy arrived would be four reasonably active men, two children, three or four ancient servitors, and a batch of women. My picture had vanished of a lot of stalwart young Norlanders prepared to fight for their master. That was bad enough, but my real perplexity was what we should be called on to fight about. Sandy had been clear that we must come here to bring things to a head, but I hadn't a notion what that head would be.

I could see perfectly well the old game of Troth and Barralty. It would be easy enough to descend on a lonely island and terrify a nervous recluse into doing their will. It might not have been so difficult to lay their hands on him in England, a stranger in a strange land, and frighten him into compliance. But now he had formidable friends about him, and they knew it. Lombard was a figure in the City, Sandy was a famous man, and I had a reputation of sorts. Haraldsen's enemies were men of a certain position, and one at least was a man of devouring ambition; they couldn't afford to go brazenly outside the law when there were people like Sandy to advertise their trespasses. A raid even on the Island of Sheep would be too clumsy a piece of folly. Besides, it would be futile. Even if they had the bigger man-power, we could summon help. I understood that there were only half a dozen policemen in the Norlands and these not of much account, but a telephone message to Hjalmarshavn would certainly fetch volunteer support, and there was a Danish Government boat cruising somewhere about the fishing- grounds. A wireless message from Hjalmarshavn would bring it to the succour of law and order.

Gradually I argued myself into the conviction that the enemy would not come at all, that, like the wicked, we had fled with no man pursuing, and that the best thing Lombard and I could do was to make a fishing holiday of it. That of course couldn't last for ever. We couldn't roost indefinitely in these outlandish parts, for we had all a good deal to do at home. I decided that I would give the place a fortnight's trial, and then, if nothing happened, we would consider Haraldsen safe and go back to England.

But my decision did not greatly comfort me, for I could not get Sandy's words out of my head. He had been positive that a big climax was impending; and, besides knowing more of our enemies than the rest of us, his instinct wasn't often at fault. And then I remembered the words Macgillivray had spoken in the spring. I remembered the mysterious D'Ingraville, whom I had never seen. He was a different proposition from the others; he had no reputation to lose, no prestige to endanger; he was the outlaw at war with society who would stick at nothing to get his desire. Troth and Barralty were only the jackals that the lion forced to go hunting with him to find him game. Also he had a definite rendezvous with Sandy, and would not fail to keep it. With D'Ingraville in the affair there were no limits. He would bring things to a brute struggle, with death and treasure as the stakes. And we were not only feeble; with two children on our hands we were hopelessly vulnerable. By cunning or by force he would find out our weak points and play ruthlessly to win.

The upshot was that by the second afternoon I was as nervous as a hen; I longed for Sandy to cheer me, but there was no sign or word of him. The thick weather and the leaden prospect, only a rain- drummed sea and the ghost of Halder, and wet bogs and sweating black crags, did not raise my spirits. We could see the Channel fairly plain, and in those two days nothing passed up it except a drifter out of its course, and a little steamer flying the Danish flag which Arnason said was a Government ship sent out for the purpose of marine biology. It hustled north at a great pace, with a bone in its teeth, as seamen say. The fishing fleets were miles to the west, and the Iceland boats took the other side of Halder. I felt that the mist shut us into a dark world far away from the kindly race of men, a world into which at any moment terrible things might irrupt. Though I had Peter John at my side, an impression of deep loneliness settled on me. Also a horrid premonition of coming disaster, which I could not get rid of. A ridiculous sailor's rhyme haunted my memory:

'Take care, beware The Bight of Benin-- One comes out Though forty go in.'

But the third morning the wind shifted to the east, and we woke to steel-blue skies, Halder clear in every cranny, and calm sunlit seas. The tonic weather reminded me of South Africa, where in the Boer War I used often to go to bed supperless on the wet ground and wake whistling from pure light-heartedness. I simply could not keep up my reasoned gloom, and all the rest of us fell into the same cheerful mood. It was difficult to believe that this fresh shining place could ever harbour evil folk and dark deeds. Also there came a message from Sandy, telephoned on from Hjalmarshavn. It didn't say much--only, 'Delayed, but coming on. Expect me when you see me,' but it seemed to lighten my responsibility. The Hjalmarshavn office didn't give the date and the place from which it was sent, and it was too much to expect from it a written confirmation.

That day, and for the next day, we put care behind us. Haraldsen came out of his silent spell, and played the host manfully. He took us down to the village and showed us the life of the place-- the dry-houses for the fish, the queer old women spinning and weaving and making their native dyes of lichen and seaweed, wild geranium and clover. After the whale and the codfish the important animal was the sheep, which gave the island its name, funny little shaggy fellows with wonderful fleeces. 'Sheep's wool is Norland gold,' was a local proverb. It was a strange clachan, full of uncanny stinks, for the winter fodder for the cows was dried whale's flesh, and you could smell it a mile away. I had a great talk with old bed-ridden Absalon, the fowler, who was a 'king's bonder,' a yeoman whose family for generations had had a croft direct from the king. Haraldsen farmed his land for him, since his two sons had both perished at sea. He sat up in a bed made of ship's timbers, and told yarns, which Haraldsen translated, of seal hunts when there were still seals in the Norlands, and great walruses that had drifted down from the Arctic, and whale hunts when the waters of the voes were red with blood. His crooked old hands clawed at the blankets, and his voice was as wild as a solan's, but he had the benign face of an apostle.

I came out of his house a happier man, and my cheerfulness was increased by the sight of the Danish marine biology boat putting into the bay in Halder across the Channel. Gregarsen, the man in charge of our motor-boat, told me that her name was the Tjaldar, and that she had been trawling off the northern capes. 'This wind will last,' he said, 'for her men are cunning, and only choose that anchorage when it blows steady from the east.' Somehow I felt that the trim little ship kept us in touch with civilized things.

Haraldsen, as I have said, was a good host these days, but he was a queer one. At Laverlaw, when he had got over his nervous trouble, he was very like an ordinary Englishman, apart from a slight foreign trace in his speech. But on his native heath he was a Norlander, steeped in island lore, rejoicing in his home with the passion of a returned exile. He, who had been sparing of words, was now almost garrulous, as if he wanted to explain himself to us and let us into the secrets of his life. He used to recount the folk-tales as if he believed in them--how the seals were the souls of Pharaoh's soldiers who had been drowned in the Red Sea, and the wren who picked at the seams of the houses was the mouse's brother changed into a bird by the Trolls' enchantment. The Trolls by his way of it were the chief plague of the Norlands--with pixies and mermaids as runners-up. They were Hulda's Folk--Hulda being a sort of she-devil--and they were always on the watch to do mankind a mischief. They shipwrecked boats, and hag-rode the cattle, and sucked the blood of young lambs, and even kidnapped little girls-- and here his eye would turn anxiously to Anna.

Then he was full of the islands' history, from the famous old saga of Trond of Gate, which is the Norland epic, to the later days when Algerian pirates raided the coast and sent the people into the hills and the sea-caves. By and by I saw the meaning of his talk. He was reminding himself--and us--that in the Norlands life had always been on a razor's edge, and that what he had to expect in the near future was what all his kin had had to face in the past. Clearly it was a comfort to him that he was following a long tradition. He had none of my scepticism; he believed that Fate was waiting for us as certainly as that the sun would rise to-morrow.

He was unlike what he had been at Laverlaw in another sense, for his nerves were all tuned up again, but in a different way. He had become high-coloured in his talk, exalted, rhetorical, speaking often like somebody in a book, as if the words were not his own. There were times when he seemed almost 'fey,' his eye wild, his voice harsh and shrill, and his language like an Israelitish prophet. That was generally when he was telling us some legend, into which he flung himself as if it had been his own experience. One strange thing I noticed--he was always talking about fire, as if fire were the Norland weird. In that damp, salty place fire scarcely seemed the perilous element; one would have thought wind and wave the real enemies. But it was always through fire that his house marched to triumph, and by fire that the luckless ones perished. It was fire that Hulda's Folk employed to work their most evil deeds. It was fire that somehow at the back of his head he dreaded for himself and his belongings. 'Then fire came,' he would say, as if it was the natural conclusion to all things.

The happy people were Anna and Peter John. The old stiffness between the two had gone, and they had become like brother and sister. She was the mistress of the island, and she had a guest who was worthy of its treasures, for the boy had a whole new world to explore and was wildly excited. A good deal of the place was like Scotland, except that the heather was poor. There were pastures beside the burns, as bright with flowers as any English meadow. I never saw a better bloom of mint and meadow-sweet, ragged robin and cranesbill; flag-irises and a kind of marsh- marigold were everywhere, and the drier slopes were gay with ragwort. The hay was mostly tall clover. On the hills the tormentil grew as I have never seen it grow elsewhere, and the old women used to pound its roots in querns as a substitute for hops. The birds were mostly familiar, but the quantity of them was unbelievable--guillemots and razorbills, puffins as tame as sparrows, and gannets from a colony on the western cliffs. That was on the water, and on the land there was every moor bird known to Peter John except the grouse. There were no hawks, except one Iceland falcon which we got a fleeting glimpse of in the Channel. Peter flew Morag a good deal, and she brought in snipe and curlews for the pot; and she was nearly the end of one of the funny little blue Iceland cats at a cottage door.

I think that I have mentioned that my son was no horseman, but under Anna's coercion he got himself on one of the Norland ponies, and they quartered the island together. But the real passion of both was the sea, a novelty to Peter, who was inland bred. In the soft, bright weather they were hours in or on the water. Peter was a fair swimmer, but Anna was magnificent--old Arnason had a joke that she was web-footed, being descended from seals, which she refuted by displaying her shapely feet.

There was no great variety of craft to play about in--only the motor-boat which Jacob Gregarsen looked after, and which was never used except for an emergency trip to Hjalmarshavn for supplies and once a week to fetch the mail; and one or two ancient Norland boats, double-ended things with high sterns and stern posts, about twenty feet long and very broad in the beam. But there were a couple of kayaks in the houses, the Eskimo kind like a Rob Roy canoe, and these were taken down to the water and launched, and provided the children with their chief amusement. Anna could handle hers brilliantly, and make it turn over like a turtle and right itself, and Peter John was an apt pupil. The two of them racing about in the voe and adventuring out into the Channel were like nothing so much as a pair of diving ducks. The trouble was to get them home for meals, for those long-lighted days were deceptive, and, since neither had a watch, they would wander in about midnight, thinking they were in time for dinner. Anna's great hope was for a shoal of whales to come in and the whole Norlands to assemble for a whale hunt. She had only seen one in her life, but the memory of it was vivid. The whale was the small pilot-whale--what they call the 'ca'in whale' in Scotland--and I heard her discoursing to Peter John of the wild excitement of the chase, and its manifold perils. She spoke like a bloodthirsty young Viking, and was determined that they should join the hunt in their kayaks and be in at the death. I was determined in my own mind that there should be no such escapade.

Anna was wholly care-free, for Haraldsen had not told her the reason of his return to his island, and Peter John was under bond not to enlighten her. He, of course, knew the whole story, and since he was always on the move, I warned him to keep his eyes open for anything that seemed suspicious. He always carried his field glasses, and I was confident that nothing was likely to come to the island without his spotting it. It was well to have such a scout, for the place, except for the House and the village, was at the moment wholly unpeopled. He saw that I was anxious, and he did his best to live up to my instructions. The first day of the fine weather he had nothing to report. The second day he announced that in a voe on the other side of the island he had discovered signs of a visit from some petrol-driven craft. When I told Haraldsen this he paid no attention. 'Some trawler put in for water,' he said; 'many of them carry boats with out-board motors.'

But on the third day the boy came to me with a grave face.

'Gregarsen says that the motor-boat is out of order. Something has gone wrong with the engine--something bad--and he'll have to get a man from Hjalmarshavn to repair it.'

'How on earth did that happen?' I asked crossly, for the motor-boat was our only transport to the outer world. 'He has not had it out.'

'It happened in the night, he thinks. He says some fools have been monkeying with it.'

I went down to the harbour and had a look at it. Sure enough there was bad mischief. The sparking-plug had gone, and the main feed pipe had been cut through. Gregarsen was a stupid elderly fellow, with a game leg which he had got at the Greenland fishing, and he had only an elementary knowledge of mechanics.

'How did this happen?' I demanded, for he could speak a kind of American-English, having once been a hand on a Boston tramp. 'Have you been walking in your sleep?'

He shook his head. 'Hulda's Folk,' he said darkly.

The thing made me very uneasy, for the damage had been done by some one who had had tools for the purpose. There was nothing for it but to telephone to the little shipyard at Hjalmarshavn and get them to send up a man. I did not do this at once, for I was trysted with Haraldsen to walk to the north end of the island, and put it off till we returned to luncheon.

I did not enjoy that walk, for I kept puzzling over the motor-boat, and I could not shake off the feeling that something was beginning to flaw the peace of the island. The accident was utterly incomprehensible to me, except on the supposition that Gregarsen had been drunk, or had gone temporarily insane and had forgotten what he had done. It was a nuisance, for next day we should have been sending to Hjalmarshavn for letters, and I longed for some word from Sandy. I felt myself set down on a possible battlefield with no sign of the commander-in-chief. Haraldsen's conversation did not cheer me. He was as mysterious as a spae-wife, and his only answer to my complaint was, 'What must be, will be.' Also the weather suddenly began to change. By midday the blue of the sky had dulled, and the heavens seemed suddenly to drop lower. The clear outlines of the Halder hills had gone, and the Channel, instead of a shining crystal, became an opaque pebble. 'Ran is stoking his ovens,' was all Haraldsen said on the subject, and it did not comfort me to know that Ran was a sea-god.

Immediately after luncheon I rang up Hjalmarshavn, but could not get through. There was nothing wrong with the apparatus in the House, and the trouble was probably at the other end, but the motor-boat business had filled me with suspicions, and I set out alone in the afternoon to trace the telephone line. It ran on low posts by the back of the garden and then down a shallow cleft to the beach not a quarter of a mile south of the village. It was clearly all right as far as the water's edge. But then I had a shock. It entered the sea in a copper casing from a little concrete platform. There seemed something odd about the look of that take-off, and I ran my hand down the cable. I lifted up an end which had been neatly cut through.

That put the lid on my discomfort. The fog was thickening. While walking with Haraldsen I had been able to see the other side of the Channel and witness the Tjaldar, returning from one of her dredging expeditions, settling snugly into her little harbour. But now Halder was blotted out, and I could only see a few hundred yards of sea. I felt as if we were being shut into a macabre world where anything might happen. We and our enemies, for that our enemies were near I had no manner of doubt. They had cut our communications and had us at their mercy--three men, two children, and a batch of ancients. Where they were, how they had got here, I never troubled to think. I felt them in the fog around me--Hulda's Folk, who had their own ways of moving by land and sea.

I ran back to the House in what was pretty near a panic. Lombard and Haraldsen had gone for a walk, and to give myself something to do I overhauled our armoury. We had half a dozen rifles, four shotguns, and plenty of ammunition. There was a revolver for each of us, and a spare one which I had destined for Peter John.

At the thought of him all my anxiety was switched on to the children. If there were evil things afoot in the island they might be at their mercy. Haraldsen and Lombard returned for tea, but not Anna and Peter John. When he heard my story Haraldsen came out of his

Nordic dreams and became the distracted parent. The fog had drawn closer, and our search could only be blind, but we got together the garden staff and Gregarsen, and set out in different directions.

The dinner-hour came and there was no sign of them. In the dim, misty brume which was all the northern night, we stumbled about the island. Midnight came and we were still searching. In the small hours of the morning they had not returned.

CHAPTER XIII

Marine Biology

That morning Anna and Peter John had gone off for the day, with sandwiches in their pockets, to explore in kayaks the voes at the south end of the island. They ate their luncheon on a skerry which the tide had just uncovered, and which was their idiotic notion of comfort. The sea was like a pond, and the mist was slowly coming down, but Anna, after sniffing the air, said that it was only a summer darkening and would clear before evening. Then she proposed an adventure. The Tjaldar had returned to its home at Halder, and over the Channel came the sound of its dropping anchor.

'Let's pay a call on it,' said Anna. 'Perhaps they'll ask us to tea. Marine biologists are nice people. I've been to tea with them before, when the old Moe was here.'

Peter John demurred. No embargo had been laid on their crossing the Channel, but he dimly felt that the trip would be considered out of bounds.

'That doesn't matter,' Anna retorted. 'We haven't been forbidden to go. Besides, in this weather they won't see us from the shore. We'll be back long before dinner. There's not a capful of wind, and it's as safe as crossing a voe. We're not likely to get such a chance again.'

Peter John said something about currents, but Anna laughed him to scorn. 'There's a rip two miles north, but here there's nothing to trouble about. I've been across in the kayak often. You're a landlubber, you know, and I'm a seadog, and you ought to believe me. I believe you when it's about birds.'

Peter John felt this to be true. Children have a great respect for each other's expertise, and Anna had shown an uncanny knowledge of the ways of boats and tides and the whole salt-water world. She bore down his scruples with another argument. 'My father would send us across any time we wanted, but it would be with Gregarsen and the motor-boat, which wouldn't be any fun, or in the long-boat, which is as slow as a cow. In these wieldy little kayaks we'll slip over in no time. If you like, I'll give you five minutes' start and race you.'

No boy can resist a 'dare,' so Peter John acquiesced, and they got into their kayaks and headed for Halder, Morag the falcon sitting dejectedly on her master's knee.

The mist came down closer, but it was only a curtain of silk, through which Halder rose like a wraith. They did not race, but presently fell into an exciting conversation, so that the kayaks often rubbed shoulders. For Anna was telling of the whale-hunts, which she had held forth to Peter John as the chief glory of the Norlands. Only once in her memory had the Grind come to the Island of Sheep, for generally they took the wider channels beyond Halder. But that once was stamped for ever on her mind, though she had only been a little girl at the time. She told how the fiery cross was sent through the islands, by means of beacons on every headland; how every man at the signal tumbled into his boat and steered for the rendezvous; how the rendezvous could not be missed, for all the sea-ways were full of people, and the Grind only came in clear weather. She described how the boats guided the school of whales, as dogs headed sheep, trimming their edges and slowly forcing the leader into one of the voes. Once the leader entered the rest followed, and the voe would be churned white with blind and maddened monsters. Then came the killing, which Anna could only imagine, for her nurse had hurried her away from the scene; but all the same she described it as she had heard of it from others, and she made a barbaric tale of it. Peter John listened with interest, and at the end with disapproval.

'It sounds pretty beastly,' he said.

'Perhaps it is,' said the girl; 'but a lot of good things are beastly, like killing pigs and using live bait. Anyhow, it puts money in the pockets of our poor people, and gives them food and lighting for the long winter.'

'All the same, I'm sorry for the whales.'

'That's silly,' she replied. 'You're not sorry for haddocks and halibut and sea-trout. Fish are cold-blooded things and don't feel.'

'Whales aren't fish,' said the student of natural history, but he was overborne.

Their discussion had brought them across the still water into the shadow of Halder, and they looked up to see the Tjaldar above them. The kayak is a noiseless thing, and the fog had helped them to approach it unperceived. It sat at anchor very trim and comfortable, with a thin spire of smoke rising from the galley funnel, and a pleasant odour of food drifting from it. Some one was emptying ashes from the stokehold.

'Couth little craft,' said Anna appreciatively. 'I smell tea. Let's hail her. Tjaldar ahoy!'

The voice brought a face to the bulwark. It was the face of an elderly man, dark and aquiline and rather puffy. He wore a yachting-cap and a flannel suit, but he did not look any kind of sailor. He seemed puzzled and a little startled.

'That will be one of the Danish scientists,' Anna whispered. Then she raised her voice.

'You're the marine biologists, aren't you? We've come to call on you from the Island of Sheep across the Channel.'

She spoke in Danish, but the face showed no intelligence. Then she repeated her words in English, and the man seemed to understand.

'Wait. I will ask,' he said, and disappeared.

He was back in a minute accompanied by another man, a tall fellow with a sunburnt face, wearing an old Harris tweed jacket, and with a pipe in his teeth.

'Where did you youngsters spring from?' the second man asked.

'I'm Miss Haraldsen from the Island of Sheep--and this is my friend, Peter John. We're visitors. May we come aboard?'

'You certainly may,' said the man with the pipe, and he seemed to wink at his companion. The port ladder was lowered and the children tied up the kayaks to its bottom rung, and carefully transhipped themselves. It takes some skill to get out of a kayak.

When they reached the much-encumbered deck they found that three sailors had joined the party.

'Just wait here a second, my dears,' said the man with the pipe, and he and the others went forward, leaving Anna and Peter John with the three sailors. The boy saw nothing but a rather untidy deck, very different from the shipshape vessels of his fancy. There seemed to be uncommonly little free space, and what looked like a gigantic net was clumsily heaped abaft of a stumpy mast. The deck-hands were busy at the vessel's side. But the girl's experienced eyes darted about, and saw more.

'This is a funny place,' she whispered. 'I don't much like it, Peter John. These men aren't a trawler's crew--they've no sores on their hands. Trawlers' men are always getting stung and poisoned. They aren't Danes either--at least, they don't look like it. What are they doing with our kayaks?'

'They're getting them aboard.'

'Whatever for?' The girl's voice had suddenly a startled note in it. 'Look here, I don't like this. . . . Just look at the trawl. It's absurd. It has no otter-boards. . . . There's something wrong with this ship. Let's make them launch the kayaks again and get off.'

'We can't quite do that,' said Peter John. 'I think we must see it through now--wait, anyhow, till these men come back.' But Anna's suspicions had infected him, and he looked uneasily at the little kayaks as they were swung up on deck.

He turned in obedience to a smothered squawk from Anna. A woman was coming towards them--a woman in a white serge frock with a fur cape thrown over her shoulders. She was bare-headed and had wonderful red hair. It was now Peter John's turn to long for the kayaks, for he recognized some one he had seen before, the beautiful Miss Ludlow who, two months ago, had come to tea at Fosse.

The pretty lady advanced smiling. At the sight of her Morag the falcon showed the most lively displeasure. Had Peter John not tightened the lead she would have sought a perch with malevolent purpose on an exquisite red coiffure.

'What a wicked bird!' said the lady. 'You're sure you've got it safe. . . . How nice of you to come to see us! You must be ravenous for tea. Come along, my dears, but I think you'd better leave the bird here.'

So Morag's lead was fastened to a stanchion, and she was left in a very ill temper ruffling her wings on a spare yard. The children followed the lady to a deck-house, which was half chart-room and half cabin. It was a snug little place, and on an oilskin-covered table tea was set out, an ample meal for which their souls hungered. There were three men sitting there, the dark, sallow one to whom they had first spoken, the sunburnt one with the pipe, and another, a tall, slim man with a thin face, high cheek-bones and a moustache which was going grey at the tips. All three rose politely at their entrance and bowed to Anna.

'Here are our visitors,' said the lady; 'and I'm sure they are hungry. They have come over from the Island. The fog is getting thicker, and I don't think we can let them go till it clears. What do you think, Joe?'

'It wouldn't be safe,' said the tall man. 'We must wait anyhow till the Skipper returns. The dory should be back in an hour or so.'

A steward brought in hot water and a big plate of toasted scones. The lady made tea, and much conversation. The sallow man she called Erick, and the sunburnt man Lancie, but most of her remarks were addressed to the tall man called Joe. She prattled of the weather and the Norlands, of London, of Cowes, of ships, and the sea. It was very clear that this company was English, and had nothing to do with marine biology, and Anna's eyes showed her bewilderment.

When the tall man spoke it was to ask questions about the Island of Sheep. His manners were good, and he showed no intrusive curiosity, but it was plain from the others' faces that this was a topic that interested them. They talked much as a yacht's party might have talked who had come into strange latitudes and had suddenly got news of other fellow-countrymen.

'Your father is at home?' the man called Lancie asked. 'He has a wonderful place over there, hasn't he? We heard about it at Hjalmarshavn. Are you two brother and sister?'

'We're no relations. This is my friend, Peter John Hannay. He is English. He is staying with us.'

Four pairs of eyes seemed to open wider.

'Are you by any chance Sir Richard Hannay's son?' the man called Joe asked, with a sudden eagerness in his voice.

Peter John nodded. 'Yes, and Sir Richard is staying with us,' added Anna.

'We must return your call,' said the lady. 'I've always longed to meet Sir Richard--and your father too, my dear.'

Peter John's mind had been working furiously, ever since the sight of Miss Ludlow had opened for him the door on a dark world. Anna was bewildered, but only because the Tjaldar was so different from the old Moe, and she had had to revise her marine biology notions, but the boy knew enough to realize that they had blundered into the enemy's camp. He had heard Sandy's talk, and I had told him the whole story, and ever since his coming to the Island of Sheep his business had been to be on the watch. Behind all his escapades with Anna had been this serious preoccupation. The sight of Lydia Ludlow had awakened him, and now in this little cabin he was face to face with Haraldsen's enemies, the sallow Albinus, the stalwart Troth, the lean, restless Barralty. Only one was missing, the most formidable of them all. At any cost he and Anna must get off and carry the fateful news.

'We should be going,' he said as he got up, 'or our people will be anxious.'

'You can't go in this weather,' said Barralty. He too rose and opened the door, and sure enough a solid wall of vapour had built itself beyond the vessel's side.

'I've got a compass,' said Peter John, 'and we can't miss the way.'

'We daren't risk it,' said the man. 'We should never be able to face your father if anything went wrong.'

'They must wait till the Skipper comes back,' said Troth, and the others agreed.

Peter John was getting desperate. 'We're rather grubby,' he said. 'Could we wash our hands?'

'Certainly,' said the lady. 'Come down to my cabin, both of you.' She seemed to Peter John to look meaningly at the others and slightly nod her head. She took Anna's hand and led her out, and the boy followed. He lingered a little beyond the door, and he heard, or thought he heard, some one of the three exclaim: 'My God, we have got the trump card now. This will keep the Skipper in order.'

Miss Ludlow took them down a steep companion into a narrow alley lined with cabins. The big one at the end was hers, and she ushered the children into it with the utmost friendliness. 'You'll find everything you want there, my dears,' she said. 'Towels and hot water. The bathroom is next door. I'll come down presently to fetch you.'

But as she left them she drew behind her a sliding door at the end of the passage. Peter John darted after her and tried its handle. It was locked from the outside.

Anna proceeded to scrub her hands and use a pocket comb to tidy up her hair. 'This is a queer ship,' she said, 'and queer people. But they're kind, I think. They're ordinary yachting folk, but the Tjaldar isn't much of a yacht. Too much of a grubby trawler for their nice clothes.'

Peter John was looking out of the port-hole into the wall of fog. 'They aren't kind,' he said. 'They're our enemies--your father's and my father's. They're the people who tried to catch you at school. They're the people we were always on the look-out for at Laverlaw. I must tell you all I know, for we're in an awful hole.'

There and then in that dim cabin he told her the story as he knew it, told her many things which Haraldsen had jealously kept hidden from her, and gave point and shape to suspicions which had long lain at the back of her head. He may have told the story crudely, with a boy's instinct for drama, but Peter John was also a realist who made no mistake about the fundamentals. She sat quiet as a mouse, but at the end she gave a low cry.

'They're going to attack our island? And we've let ourselves be made prisoners? Oh, Peter John, it is all my fault! I dragged you on this silly expedition.'

'It is my fault, for I should have remembered. You see, I knew and you didn't.'

Two miserable children clung to each other, while the fog thickened without and the cabin darkened.

Meantime, in the deck-house they had left, there was a feverish council. From what I learned later I can reconstruct the scene as if I had been listening outside the door. In an hour's time the man called the Skipper would arrive, and three men and one woman had much to talk of before then. I can picture their rapid, confused speech, their alternations of eagerness and diffidence, their sudden confidence dashed by sudden fears. Always in the background there must have been this shadow of fear. For the absent Skipper had become to them no longer a colleague but a master. They were people whose plans lay well inside the pale of what we call civilization. They had reputations to lose, ambitions which demanded some respect for the conventions, comfortable lives which they were not inclined to sacrifice. But they had become yoked to one who cared for none of these things, a man from the outlands who had long ago discarded their world. They were like schoolboys playing at pirates who had suddenly found themselves enrolled under the authentic Blackbeard. Barralty, I fancy, was the worst scared. Albinus was the common rogue who had already known the shady side of the law. Troth was a robust fellow, a sportsman accustomed to risks who would not be greatly rattled till he knew the full extent of the trouble. But Barralty was the brittle intellectual, who found himself in a world where his old skill went for nothing, and with him was the woman who had worked with him, and who now saw all their careful schemes on the edge of a fulfilment more disastrous than failure.

Troth must have spoken first, for he had the coolest head.

'Things are brightening,' he said. 'This is a piece of luck for us, for we've got our hostages. Now we can deal.'

'You think so?' said Barralty, in a voice which he tried to keep calm.

'Well, we've got the girl, and she's what Haraldsen cares most for in the world. And we've got the boy, who's the apple of Hannay's eye. There's only Lombard left, and he doesn't count for much. There's no word of Clanroyden.'

'What has happened to Clanroyden?'

'God knows! Run out, perhaps. . . . No, he's not that kind of fellow. The Skipper must have put a spoke in his wheel, for he's devil enough for anything.'

'Have you got a line on the Skipper's plan?'

'Plain enough. Old-fashioned piracy. He'll descend on the Island like a marauding Viking and hold 'em up. If they show fight, as they're likely to, he'll kill. He'll get what he wants and he don't care a damn for bloodshed. When he has got it he'll disappear, he and his gang, into the outer darkness, as he has done before. I daresay he'll play fair with us--I don't know--but we'll have to disappear with him. Do any of you fancy spending the rest of your lives being hunted up and down the globe, even if your pockets are full? D'Ingraville won't mind it, for it's his profession, but what about you, Barralty? What about you, with your big ideas about public life? What about you, Lydia? You like your little comforts. What about you, Erick? No more race- meetings for you, my lad, and flutters at Monte?'

'My God!' Barralty groaned. 'Can't we bring the man to reason?'

'We can't, for all the reason, as he sees it, is on his side. He knows what he wants a little more clearly than we ever have, and he has the power behind him. We're only passengers--he's the fighting force. What can we do to stop him? He has his two infernal trusties from South America, Carreras and Martel--the very sight of them gives me the creeps. He has his crew of gunmen. He's going to implicate us all in his gangster business, so that we'll all hang together.'

'But he can't compel us if we object,' Albinus groaned.

'Can't he? I haven't got him fully taped, but he's the biggest size in desperado I've ever struck. I know what's in your mind, Erick. You think that we might make terms on our own account with the people on the Island. I've had the same idea myself, but I tell you it won't do. The Skipper knows that game too well. If we try to double-cross him he'll shoot.'

I can picture those four scared conspirators sitting for a moment dismally silent, till Troth's vigour woke them.

'But now things look better,' he said. 'We have got the materials for a civilized deal. Thank heaven for these blessed children! I don't much like using kids in this business--if you remember, I always stuck out against it before--but needs must when the devil drives. The Skipper can't be fool enough to neglect such a chance. It gives us a sitter, when the other way is an ugly gamble.'

'But do we want the same things?' Barralty asked. 'We want a good deal, but the Skipper may want everything. And remember that Haraldsen isn't alone. He has Hannay with him, and Hannay by all accounts is a tough customer.'

'That will be the moment for the double-crossing if the Skipper plays the fool,' said Troth grimly. 'Once we get to bargaining we put the lid on his bloody piracy, and that's what we most want.'

Then the Skipper arrived.

I picture his coming into the stuffy cabin, his face shining with fog crystals, and his pale eyes dazed by the sudden light.

'An hour till dinner,' he said, with a glance at the chronometer. 'There's time for a hot rum-and-milk, for it has been perishingly cold in the dory. But I've done my job. The reconnaissance is complete, gentlemen. To-morrow is The Day.'

Troth told him about Anna and Peter John. He listened with head lifted, rather like a stag at gaze, a smile wrinkling his lean cheeks.

'Fortune is kind to us,' he said. 'Now we can add point to our first cartel. For one kind of possession we can offer another--and a dearer.'

But there was that in his voice which made Barralty look up anxiously.

'Surely that alters our whole plan,' he said. 'Now we can treat, where before we could only coerce.'

'I do not think so, my friend.' D'Ingraville spoke lightly, as if the matter were not of great importance.

'They will not treat--not on our terms. You want much, no doubt, but I want all, you see, and men will fight for their all.'

'But--but--' Barralty stammered. 'Haraldsen cares for his daughter above everything, and Hannay for his son.'

'Maybe,' was the answer. 'But Haraldsen and Hannay are not all.'

'Lombard does not count.'

'I do not think of Lombard. I think of Lord Clanroyden.'

'But Clanroyden isn't there.'

'Not yet. But he will be there to-morrow.'

'How do you know? Have you any news?'

'I have no news. I have heard nothing of Clanroyden since we left London. But I know that he will be there, for I have an assignation with him, and he will not fail me. And Clanroyden will never yield.'

'But what do you mean to do, man?' Troth asked.

'I mean to follow the old way, the way of my Norman kinsfolk. Fate has been marvellously good to us. There is no man on the Island except those three--to-morrow they will be four--only dotards and old women.

The telephone is cut and they have no boat. The fog will lift, I think, by the morning, but the Island will be in a deeper fog which cuts it off from the world. We shall have peace and leisure to do our will. If they listen to us, so much the pleasanter for everybody. If they fight we shall fight too, and beyond doubt we shall win.'

'Win!' Barralty muttered. 'What do you mean by win?'

'Everything,' was the answer. 'I shall get my will, though I leave a house in ashes and an island of dead men.'

'And then?' It was Lydia's strained voice that spoke.

'Then we disappear, leaving a riddle in the Norlands which no man will ever expound. Trust me, I have made my plans--for you, my friends, and for you, my fair lady. You may have to face some little adjustments in your lives, but what of that? Le mouvement c'est la vie.'

He lifted his glass and looked towards Lydia, drinking the last mouthful as if it were a toast.

'And now,' he said, 'let me have a look at our hostages. Martel,' he cried to some one outside the door, 'fetch the babes.'

Peter John takes up the tale again. . . . The children had sat in a stupor of misery and fright, unable to think, deaf to all sounds except the thumping of their hearts. 'We must get away,' the boy had repeated at intervals, and the girl had replied, 'We must,'; but the words were only a kind of groan, so destitute were they of any hope. What Anna thought I do not know, but Peter John's mind was fuller of mortification than of fear. He had failed in his trust, and by his folly had given the enemy a crushing vantage.

They lost count of time, and it may have been an hour or two hours before the sliding panel in the alley opened and a face showed in the cabin door. A hand switched on the light. They saw a man slightly over the middle height, wearing sea-boots and a seaman's jersey--a man who did not look like a sailor, for he had a thin, shaven, pallid face, a scar on his forehead, and eyebrows that made a curious arch over weak, blinking eyes. When he spoke it was with a foreign accent in a hoarse, soft voice. 'You will come with me, please,' he said. 'M. le Capitaine would speak with you.'

The sight of the man sent a spasm of sharp fear through Peter John's dull misery. For he knew him--knew him at least by hearsay. Sandy at Laverlaw had taken some pains to describe to us the two members of the old Bodyguard of Olifa whom D'Ingraville had with him. This was the Belgian Martel--there could be no mistake about the scar and the horseshoe brows. At the door of the deck-house stood another man, a tall stooping fellow whose hatchet face and black beady eyes were plain in the glow from the cabin. This was beyond doubt the Spaniard Carreras. The wolf pack was complete.

'Don't answer anything,' the boy whispered to Anna. A stubborn silence was the one course left to them.

But there was no inquisition. Peter John had the impression of a company mighty ill at ease. The smooth geniality of tea-time had gone, and the four who had then entertained them seemed to have lost interest in their visitors and to be much concerned with their own thoughts. The pretty lady had become haggard and rather old, while Troth had lost his robustness and sucked his pipe nervously. Barralty had become a wisp of a man, and Albinus a furtive shadow. Only the newcomer radiated confidence and vitality. For a moment Peter John forgot his fear, and looked curiously at the tall man whom at Fosse he had assisted to put into the stream. He was so taut and straight that he had the look of an unsheathed sword. His pale eyes glittered like ice, and his smile had as much warmth in it as an Arctic sun. Magnificent, wonderful, terrible, inhuman, like some devastating force of nature. Yet, strangely enough, the boy feared the reality less than the picture he had made in his head. This was a wild thing, like Morag, and wild things could be tamed, curbed, or destroyed.

The Skipper bowed to Anna and nodded pleasantly to Peter John.

'You must be our guests for the night, I fear,' he said. 'We are not a very commodious ship, so you mustn't mind rather rough beds. You will want to turn in soon. What about supper?'

It was Anna who replied. 'We don't want any supper, thank you. But we'd like to turn in, for we're both very sleepy.'

'Right. Show the young lady and gentleman to their quarters, Martel. Mr. Hannay will berth forward, and Miss Haraldsen can have Miss Ludlow's couch. Good-night and pleasant dreams.'

That was all. The two followed Martel the way they had come, and Anna was left in the big cabin, where a bed had been made up for her on the couch. Martel did the expected thing, for he took the key from the inside of the cabin-door and pocketed it; then he pulled the sliding panel which automatically locked itself. The sight of Anna's desolate face was the last straw to Peter John's burden. He followed Martel on deck, feeling as if the end of all things had come.

Suddenly an angry squawk woke him to life. Morag, hungry and drenched with fog, sat on her perch in a bitter ill-temper.

'May I take my falcon with me?' he begged.

Martel laughed. 'I guess you may if you want company. Your ugly bird will be better below deck.'

Peter John found himself in a little cubby-hole of a cabin under the fore-deck. It was empty except for a hammock slung from the ceiling, and a heap of blankets which some one had tossed on the floor. There was a big port-hole which Martel examined carefully, trying the bolts and hinges. 'Don't go walking in your sleep and drowning yourself, sonny,' was his parting admonition. He did not clamp it down, but left it ajar.

Peter John's first act, when he found himself alone, was to open the port-hole wide. It was on the port side, looking west, and close to where they had embarked on the Tjaldar in the afternoon. The fog was thinning, and a full moon made of what remained a half- luminous, golden haze. The boy had a notion of getting out of the port-hole and trying to swim to the Island, but a moment's reflection drove it out of his head. He was not a strong swimmer, and he could never manage two miles in those cold Norland waters.

Then a squeak from Morag gave him another idea. There was no light in the cabin except what came from the moon, but he tore a leaf from a little writing-book which he kept for bird notes and printed on it a message. 'In Tjaldar, which is enemy ship,' he wrote. 'Expect immediate attack. Don't worry about us for we are all right.' He wrapped the paper in a bit of silk torn from his necktie, and tied it round Morag's leg. Then he slipped the leash, and cast the bird off through the port-hole. Like a stone from a catapult she shot up into the moonlit fog.

'An off-chance,' he told himself, 'but worth taking. She's savagely hungry, and if she doesn't kill soon she'll go back to the House. If she's seen there Mr. Haraldsen has a spare lure and knows how to use it. If he gets the message he'll at least be warned.'

The action he had taken had put sleep out of his head and had cheered him up for the moment. He could make nothing of the hammock, so he sat himself on the heap of blankets and tried to think. But his thoughts did him no good, for he could make no plans. His cabin door was locked and the key in Martel's pocket. Anna was similarly immured at the other end of the ship. They were prisoners, mere helpless baggage to be towed in the wake of the enemy. Oddly enough, the Skipper did not seem to him the most formidable thing. The boy thought of D'Ingraville as a dreadful impersonal force of nature, like a snow blizzard or an earthquake. His horror was reserved for Carreras and Martel, who were evil human beings. As he remembered Martel's horse-shoe brows and soft sneering voice he shivered in genuine horror. The one was the hungry lion, but the other was the implacable, cunning serpent.

How long he sat hunched on the blankets he does not know, but he thinks it must have been hours. Slowly sleep came over him, for body and mind and nerves were alike weary. . . . Then that happened which effectually woke him. The disc of light from the porthole was obscured by something passing over it, slowly and very quietly. He looked out, and saw to his amazement that one of the kayaks was now floating on the water beneath him, attached to a rope from above.

As he stared, a second object dropped past his eyes. It was the other kayak, which lightly shouldered the first and came to rest beside it.

His hand felt for one of the lowering ropes and he found it taut. Grasping it, he stuck his feet through the port-hole, wriggled his body through and slid down the rope. Almost before he knew he was sitting in a kayak, looking up at the dim bulk of the vessel.

Then came another miracle. A human figure was sliding down the rope from the Tjaldar's deck, and he saw that it was Anna, coming down hand over hand as lightly as a squirrel. She saw him, dropped into the second kayak, and reached for the paddle. All was done as noiselessly as in a dream. There was a helper on the deck above, for the taut rope was dropped after her and swished gently into the water.

Anna kissed her hand to the some one above, seized her paddle, and with a slow stealthy stroke sent her kayak out into the golden haze. As Peter John clumsily followed suit, she turned on him fiercely, 'Quiet, you donkey,' she whispered. 'Don't splash for your life. Hang on to me and I'll tow you.'

In half a dozen strokes the little craft were out of sight of the Tjaldar.

CHAPTER XIV

The Ways of the Pink-Foot

They had travelled a quarter of a mile before Peter John spoke. 'How did you manage that?' he asked excitedly.

Anna slackened pace and dropped into line with him.

'I didn't. It was the man--the one with the funny eyebrows--the one the Skipper called Martin or some name like that.'

Peter John emitted a groan of dismay.

'But he's Martel--the worst of them--my father told me. It's a plot, Anna. He didn't mean any good to us.'

'He's let us escape, anyway, and that's the good I want. I had dropped off to sleep on that beastly couch when he woke me up, and said I'd better be off, for this was no place for kids. He made me follow him up on deck, keeping in the shadow so that we shouldn't be seen. There was no one about anyhow, and not a light except the riding-light. He had already got the kayaks in the water, and he said you would notice them, for they were beside your port-hole, and if you didn't we'd go down and rouse you up. When he saw you sitting in a kayak, he said it was what he expected, for you were a bright citizen.'

'It's all a trick,' Peter John groaned. 'Martel's the worst devil of the lot. He wants us to escape so that we can be caught and brought back, and so give them an excuse to bully us.'

'That sounds to me silly,' said Anna. 'I they wanted to treat us rough there was nothing to prevent them anyhow. I think the man is friendly. He's a Norlander.'

'He isn't. He's a Belgian.'

'Well, he speaks Norland as well as my father. And he knows about the Islands. He was out in the dory this afternoon, and he says the Grind are coming. He says that they will rendezvous at the Stor Rock--the Grind always have a rendezvous. I don't know why he told me that, but he seemed to think it important, for he said it several times. Only a Norlander could know about such things.'

'He may know Norland, but he's a Belgian and the worst of the lot. My father told me. What else did he say?'

'He said that we must hurry like the devil, and we weren't to go straight to the House. If we could shape any kind of course we were to go to the south part of the Island, to the Birdmarsh. That looks as if he thought the

Skipper would be after us. I believe he meant well by us, Peter John, and anyway we're free again.'

'We won't be long free,' said the boy. He had his compass out, and halted for a moment to steady it. 'I don't trust him one bit, Anna. A course due west will bring us to the House, and that's where we steer for. If we can't make it, then we'll do the opposite of what Martel said and try for the north.'

'I don't care where we land,' said the girl, 'as long as it's on the Island.'

The boy held up his hand and listened.

'If they find out we're gone--or if Martel tells them--they can overhaul us in ten minutes with their outboard motor. Do you hear anything, Anna?'

The fog was breaking up into alleys and strips of moonlit sea, rayed round them like the points of a star. There was no sound, not even the ripple of water or a gull's cry.

'Come on,' Anna urged. 'We must be a quarter of the way across, and every moment counts. Take longer sweeps, Peter John, like me, and don't behave as if you were making butter-pats.'

Then for half an hour there was no further speech. The boy had not the girl's effortless skill, and put much needless strength into his strokes, so that his shoulders soon began to ache, and his breath to shorten. The fog was oddly intermittent. Now they would be in a circle of clear sea, now back in a haze so thick that Peter John had to keep his compass on his knee, and Anna closed in on him for guidance. On one such occasion she observed that Morag had been left behind, and that she wished well to the first hand that touched her.

'She hasn't,' was his answer. 'I flew her out of the port-hole, and tied a message to her varvel. If she doesn't kill, they may get her at the House.'

'What message?' Anna asked.

'Only that you and I were all right, but that they had better look out for squalls.'

Then, when they were in one of the patches of clear air, there fell on their ears the unmistakable sound of a motor behind them.

'Now we're for it,' said Anna. 'Heaven send the fog thickens. I was right about Martel. He told me not to go straight for the House, and that's what we've done, and they've naturally followed us. . . . Where are you heading for now?'

The compass had dropped to the bottom of the kayak and Peter John had altered course to the north-west.

'Martel said south,' said Anna.

'That's why we are going north,' was the answer.

Mid-channel in the small hours with an enemy close behind you is no place for argument. Anna followed obediently, the more as she saw that the new route was taking them into thicker weather. Presently on their port beam they heard the chug of a motor, but could see nothing when they screwed their heads round. Now they were back in dense fog, and the compass was brought into use again. Fear and the sense of pursuit had given both a fresh vigour, and the little craft slipped gallantly through the water. The moon was setting, and its golden light no longer transfused the sea-mist, which was becoming cold and grey. Soon it would be dawn.

Then suddenly they got a dreadful scare. The sound of a motor broke just ahead of them. They stopped and held their breath, living by their ears, for their eyes were useless in the brume. . . . The noise came nearer--soon it was not twenty yards ahead--but they saw nothing. Then slowly it died away towards the west.

'That was their second motor,' said Peter John. 'It had a different sound from the other.'

'Who was right?' said Anna triumphantly. 'I said we should trust that Martin man, but you wouldn't. We've disobeyed both the things he told us to do, and the result is we've been jolly nearly copped.'

After that there were no more alarms. The fog grew denser as they approached the Island, but it lifted slightly when the lap of the tide told them that they were close to shore. In this part the cliffs rose sheer from a narrow rock-strewn beach, but the children had visited the place before, and knew that a landing could be made in one of the tiny bays cut by descending streams. One such they found, where there was a half-moon of sand at the foot of a steep gully in the crags. They beached the kayaks and hid them in the cover of some big boulders. Then, taking hands, they proceeded to climb the ravine, which was stony and rough, but quite practicable. Near the top they found a recess of heath and bracken and there Anna resolutely sat down.

'Thank God for His mercies,' she said. 'If we had only some food I'd be happy. I'm going to sleep, and you'd better do the same, Peter John, for Heaven knows what sort of a day we have before us.'

They had no watch, and Peter John, who could usually tell the time by the sky, was out of his reckoning in those northern latitudes. They slept sound in the nook of rock, and it was only the sun on Anna's face that woke them. The time cannot have been much short of noon.

The mist had gone, and the day was bright and hot, but the visibility was poor. Halder, of which they had a full view, was a cone of dull blue with no details showing, and the Channel between might have been a bottomless chasm, for it had none of the sheen of water.

'It will be fine till three,' said Anna, who knew the Norland weather. 'Then I think it will blow again from the east, and blow hard.'

She stood up to stretch her arms, but Peter John caught her skirt and pulled her back. 'We mustn't show ourselves,' he enjoined. 'Remember, they're after us. Wait here while I reconnoiter.' He crawled out of the cleft, and lay prone on a knuckle of rock from which the view was open eastward. He was back in a few seconds. 'The Tjaldar has gone,' he whispered. 'No sign of her, and I could see twenty miles of water. It must be pretty late in the day, for I'm desperately hungry. Aren't you?'

'Perishing, but it's no good thinking about it. We'll get no food till we get home. How is that to be managed? I've been taking our bearings from Halder, and we should be about two miles north of the House. There's a track to it on the top of the cliffs, and it's mostly in sight of the Channel, but if the Tjaldar isn't there that won't matter. I expect she is somewhere on the west side of the island.'

'What lies between the House and the west side?' Peter John asked. It was about the only part they had not explored.

'There's the hill Snowfell. A little hill compared to the ones at Laverlaw. Then there's a boggy place which we call the Goose Flat, because the pink-foot breed there. Then there's the sea--a rather nasty bit of coast with only one decent landing. . . . Let's bustle and get home. If the brutes are going to attack to-day there's no reason why they shouldn't start early, for just now there's no darkness to wait for.'

They climbed to the top of the gully where it ran out on to the tussocky cliff-top. Peter John, upon whom unpleasant forebodings had descended, insisted on keeping close in cover and showing no part of themselves on the skyline. Presently they looked down on a small tarn, much overgrown with pond-weed, which they remembered as the only lochan which had no boat. The track to the House passed its eastern edge, and by this their road lay.

It was a terribly exposed track, and Peter John regarded it with disfavour.

'Hadn't we better hug the cliff-edge where there's a certain amount of cover?' he suggested.

'You may if you like, but I won't. The Skipper and his lot can't be near the place yet, and I want to be home soon. They'll all be mad with anxiety. I must loosen my bones, for I'm as stiff as a ramrod. I'll race you, Peter John.'

She shook her yellow locks, and before the boy could prevent her was off at a gallop along the track. There was nothing for it but to follow her. He found it hard to catch her up, and the effort put other things out of his head. When they topped the rise, which overlooked the hollow where the House lay a mile distant, they were abreast and going at their best speed.

Then the boy saw something which made him halt in his tracks, clutch at Anna's arm, and bring her slithering to the ground. . . . Behind a rocky knoll three hundred yards off a man was posted.

He had not heard them, for he continued to smoke and regard the House through binoculars. They had only a back view of him, but he was plainly a sailor from the Tjaldar by his blue jersey and baggy blue serge trousers. He had some notion of landscape, for he was so placed that he must command any access to the House from the north.

Peter, his hand on Anna's bowed head, lay for a little with his nose in a patch of lousewort. He was thinking hard and studying the environs of the House. Their only chance now was to reach it from the west or south. But west lay Snowfell, where there was scarcely cover for a tomtit. On the south the approaches were better, but to reach the south it was necessary to get to the back of Snowfell and fetch a wide circuit. One ugly thought struck him. If the Tjaldar had gone to the west of the island, might it not have all that side under observation? This watcher came from the Tjaldar. If the enemy had posted his vedettes up to the edges of the House, was he not likely to be holding the intermediate ground?

Nevertheless, it was their only chance. The two very cautiously wormed their way back over the ridge they had crossed, left the track, and made good speed across a marshy field which was the source of the stream that fed the lochan. They saw no sign of life except a group of Norland ponies, as tame as puppies, who came up to have their noses rubbed, and fell to grazing quietly as soon as they had passed. But, warned now, they made the final ascent of the spine of the island, a continuation of Snowfell, with immense care, pulling themselves up between two patches of bracken to look over the far side.

There was no sign of the Tjaldar. The hill fell steeply in screes and rocks to the water's edge. There seemed to be a bay there, the contours of which were concealed by the hump of the cliffs, with a spire of smoke ascending from it. South, the ground flattened out into a mantelpiece, where pools of water glimmered among rushes and peat. Beyond that a bulge of hill cut off further view. There was no sign of life except the white specks, which were birds down in the Goose Flat, a nimbus of screaming gulls over a dead porpoise on one of the reefs, and the column of smoke.

'That's all right,' said Anna with relief. 'They've been here this morning, and that smoke is the remains of a breakfast fire. They have landed that man to keep an eye on the House, and they have gone off in the Tjaldar on some other business. Probably they're back at Halder by now to mislead us. Their time is the evening. We can't go over Snowfell, for the picket would see us, but we can get round by the Goose Flat and reach the House by way of the reservoir. Come on, for I'm weak with starvation.'

Anna would have marched boldly down the hill, but Peter John had sense enough to make her keep cover. This was not so difficult as long as they were on the encumbered slopes, for any road had to be picked among secret tangles of rock and fern. But before they came to the Goose Flat they found themselves on short heather and screes and as conspicuous as rooks on a snow-field. Even Anna was sobered.

'Let's run this bit,' she whispered, 'and get it over.'

It was no doubt the best plan, but it failed. They had not covered ten yards before a whistle cleft the silence. A figure showed itself on the edge of the seaward cliff--and then another. To Peter John's horror, as he cast his eye in the opposite direction, a man appeared on the ridge of Snowfell.

'Three,' he groaned.

'Four,' Anna corrected. 'There's another behind us--we must have passed close to him.'

A rib descended from Snowfell, and Peter John saw that if they could get beyond that they would be for a moment out of sight of the watchers, even of him on the hill. The rib bisected the Goose Flat, making a kind of causeway across it. There was no real cover in the Flat, for to any one on the edge whatever tried to hide itself among the short rushes and shallow lagoons would be easily visible. But to gain even a minute or two was something. The children in full view raced beyond the rib, waded into the Goose Flat, and flung themselves behind exiguous tussocks.

'We're out of their sight,' Anna panted; 'but they'll be down here in a jiffy to nobble us. Let's get on. We might beat them and get first to the Bird Marsh. We could hide there.'

'No good,' said the boy. 'If we go south, we'll be in their view in twenty yards, and the man on the hill has only got to walk down to cut us off. The chap behind, too. We're done, Anna, unless they think we've broken back.'

'They can't. They saw us come here.'

'Then we're for it. We might as well have stayed on the Tjaldar.'

'Oh, Peter John, what a mess we've made of everything!' the girl wailed.

Suddenly the boy's eyes opened wide to a strange spectacle. Just in front of them the causeway made by the rib of hill was somewhat broken, and a glimpse could be got of the swamp farther to the north. In this gap appeared the foolish heads and poised necks of a little flock of pink-foot. They were young birds who, having been hatched out in the Goose Flat, had spent their early adolescence on the sea skerries, and had now, according to their ancestral habit, returned for a little to their birthplace. They were chattering among themselves, apparently alive to the presence of something novel in front, about which they desired to be better informed.

By the mercy of God Peter John remembered a piece of lore that he had learned from the wildfowlers at Hanham in January. The pink- foot is not a skeery bird. He has resolved that his duty is not to live but to know, and he is nearly the most inquisitive thing in creation. If you want to get in range of him, Samson Grose had said, show yourself, and the odds are that he will move nearer you to discover what sort of thing you are. With young pink-foot, that is; older birds have learned wisdom.

To Anna's amazement the boy got to his feet, while his right hand held her down. . . . She saw the echelon of geese stop and confide things to each other. Every eye of them was on to Peter John, and after a moment's hesitation they began to move forward. They seemed oddly self-conscious, for they did not keep looking in his direction. Some would stop for a second to feed, and all kept turning their heads every way. But the whole flock was steadily drifting south, as if there was some compulsion in their rear. In five minutes they had moved at least ten yards.

The pink-foot were in sight of the watchers, and Peter John was not. Would the watchers draw the inference desired? They must do it at once, for if the geese came too near, they would lose their heads, stream back, and all would be lost. To one who did not know their habits the conclusion must surely be clear. The children were behind them, and their presence there was making them move south. Therefore it was in the north part of the Goose Flat that they must be sought. They had been seen to disappear behind the rib of hill, but they must have crawled back and got in the rear of the geese.

Peter John's heart was in his mouth, as he stood staring at the bobbing heads and projected necks of these absurd pink-foot, who to him and Anna meant everything. At any moment he himself might come within sight of some watcher who had shifted ground. Two lots of human beings, invisible to each other, were regarding some foolish winged creatures with desperate intentness. It was a new way of taking the auspices.

Then on the boy's ear fell that which was like an answer to his prayers. A whistle was blown up on the hillside, and answered by another from the direction of the sea. The pink-foot had been correctly observed. . . . A second later he had confirmation, for something had come north of the geese to alarm them. They stopped their leisurely advance, and straggled to left and right. The watchers had appeared to hunt for the fugitives in the north end of the swamp.

There was no time to lose, for when they found their search fruitless they would undoubtedly cast south. Peter John dragged Anna out of the foot of mud where she sat like a nesting wild-duck, and the two scrambled out of the bog and raced for their lives along the harder skirts of the hill. They did not stop till they had rounded the flank of the massif of the Isle, and were looking down on the Bird Marsh and the rolling barrens beyond it. Only once had Peter John glanced back, and that was to see the pink- foot, shaken out of their comfortable ways, bunching for a seaward flight. Once they were in the deep of the Marsh, where Anna knew the paths, they felt reasonably secure, and dared to draw breath again. As Anna cast herself on a patch of heather she could not resist one word of reproach. 'I was right all along about the Martin man. If we had steered south as he told us we should have missed this heart-disease. We might even be home and having breakfast.'

When she had recovered her breath she spoke again.

'That was very clever of you, Peter John. I'll never laugh at you again for being silly about birds. I thought you had gone mad till I saw your plan. It was a miracle, and I feel happy now. We are going to win, never fear.'

'I wish I knew how,' said the boy dolefully. 'We have slipped through them, but we have still to get into the House. . . . I wonder if they've any notion there what's happening. . . . And after that? The brutes are three or four to our one, and they're desperate.'

'I don't care,' said Anna; 'we're going to win. There'll be another miracle, you'll see.' She raised herself and sniffed the air. From where they sat they had no view of the Channel, but the southern part of Halder was in sight. 'We can't see the Tjaldar's anchorage. I wonder if she has come back. Look at the sky over there, Peter John. I said the weather would change in the afternoon, and it's jolly well going to. There's the father and mother of a thunderstorm coming up over Halder, and after that it will blow like fury from the east. . . . Lordie, it's hot, and there's a plague of daddy-longlegs. That should mean that the Grind are coming. That was what the Martin man said. He may be a scoundrel, but we would have been better off if we had taken his advice this morning.'

Peter John was almost cross. There was no need to rub in the good intentions of Martel, which he knew to be moonshine, and less to babble about pilot whales, when the world was crashing about them. 'Let's start,' he said. 'We'll have our work cut out getting to the House even from this side.'

Anna let her head sink back on the moss.

'I feel dreadfully sleepy,' she said. 'Perhaps it's the storm coming. All the energy has gone out of me. . . . Martin said the Grind would rendezvous at the Stor Rock. That's only about seven miles from the south end of this island--half-way between it and Kalso.'

An exasperated Peter John got to his feet and regarded the girl as she lay with her eyes half-closed. She certainly looked very weary--and different, too, in other ways. She had become like her father--her skin had suddenly acquired his pallor, and her eyes, when she opened them, his light wildness. And her mind was still on her preposterous whales.

'You stay here and rest,' he said, 'and I'll go and prospect. There may be some difficult ground to cover, where one will be safer than two.'

'All right,' she said sleepily. 'Come back before the storm begins, for I hate being alone with thunder. . . . I didn't know there were so many daddy-longlegs in the world.'

Peter John, in a mood between irritation and depression, hopped over the tussocks of the Bird Marsh, struck the shore, and trotted northward on the edge of the shingle. Halder was beginning to veil itself in a gloom as purple as a ripe grape, but the Channel was clear, and there was no sign of the Tjaldar by the other shore. The air was oppressive and still, but he had the feeling that some fury of nature was banking up and would soon be released.

The road, which the other day had seemed but a step or two, was now interminable to his anxious mind. He came in view of the harbour and the cluster of cottages to the south of it; all was peaceful there. Then by way of the channel of a stream he climbed from the shore, and looked suddenly upon the shelf where the House stood.

There was peace there, too, but he saw various ominous things. There were pickets posted--one on the near edge of the main lawn, one on the hill behind, and one above the voe on the road up from the harbour. These pickets were armed. Their business was to see that none entered the House and that none left it. Even as he stared, the one nearest him detected some movement in the back parts and sent over a warning shot; he heard the bullet crack on the stone roof of an outhouse. These watchers were the terriers to guard the earth till the hunters arrived.

Peter John's first impulse was to dodge the cordon and get into the House. He believed that he could do it, for he must know the ground better than they did. But if he once got in he would not get out again, and Anna would be left deserted. If the House was to be entered it must be in Anna's company.

There was no time to lose, so he turned and made for the Bird Marsh again, no longer hugging the shore, but taking the short cut across the hill. His last glance back showed the Tjaldar rounding the cliffs north of the harbour. He felt miserably depressed and utterly feeble. The people in the House must know their danger now, but what good was that knowledge to them? There were three men there to face a dozen and more--the crew of the Tjaldar had seemed to him unduly large, and its members had not looked innocent. If Anna and he joined the defence they would only be two more non-combatants. . . . Where, oh where, was Lord Clanroyden? Peter John had come to regard Sandy as the sheet anchor in this affair, the man who had planned the whole strategy, the regular soldier among amateurs. His absence gave him a dreadful sense of confusion and impotence.

Before he reached the Bird Marsh the weather had changed with a vengeance. The purple cloud had crossed the Channel from Halder, and the afternoon had grown as dark as a winter's gloaming. There was no lightning, but the gloom suddenly burst in a tornado of hail. So violent was the fall that the boy was beaten to the ground, where he lay with his back humped, protecting every inch of exposed skin from that blistering bastinado.

This lasted for perhaps five minutes. But when the hail ceased the sky did not lighten. The ground was white like winter and a wind as icy as the hail blew out of the east. He threaded the Bird Marsh to where he had left Anna, listless in the heat of the summer afternoon. . . . The girl had gone. Peter John lifted up his voice and called her, but there was no answer.

She had not followed him, for in that case he would have met her. It was scarcely possible that the enemy could have arrived from the Goose Flat and captured her. East and west lay impassable lochs. She could only have gone south on to the low dunes which stretched to the butt of the island. The hail had obliterated her tracks in the heather, but a few yards on there was a deep scar in a peat- hagg as if some one had slipped. A little farther and there was another footmark in the peat. Peter John followed the trail till he was out of the swampy ground and on the thymy slopes.

Suddenly he became aware that there was another sound in his ears beside the whistle of the wind. It came from in front of him, a strange blend of excited shouting and what seemed like the dash of waves on a skerry. At first he thought it the screeching of gulls over a dead porpoise. And then there came a note in it which was human, which must be human--deep voices in the act of giving orders--a note which no animal can compass. He stumbled over the last ridge, and looked down on the big voe into which one of the lochs of the Bird Marsh discharged its waters, and the network of lesser voes which made up the south end of the Island.

The shores of the voe were dense with people, and its surface and that of the lesser voes black with a multitude of boats. But at the heads of each inlet was a spouting and quivering morass in which uncouth men laboured with bloody spears. It was a scene as macabre as any nightmare, but it was orderly too. There were men with papers on the shore pricking off figures. . . . For a second his mind wandered in utter confusion, and then he got the answer. Anna's tales had come true. The Grind had arrived.

At first he did not realize that this meant salvation. The strangeness of the spectacle lifted it clean out of his normal world. He only knew that Anna was down there, and that he must find her. But as he raced down the slopes the scene before him began to change. Men left their toil and moved to a post midway up the big voe. The boats from the lesser voes began to draw to the same place. The people with the papers in their hands did likewise--one of them was shouting what sounded like an order. Long before Peter John had reached the point at least three-fourths of the people had moved there. . . . Then as he came nearer he saw a group make a platform of their arms, and some one was hoisted on to it.

It was Anna, but an Anna whom he had not known before. Around her was bent and shingle grimed with blood--men with conical caps, and beards like trolls and wild eyes and blood-stained whale spears--a few women like mænads--and as a background a channel choked with animals dying or dead. She stood on a human platform, like a Viking girl in the Shield-ring, the wind plucking at her skirts and hair, her figure braced against it, her voice shrill and commanding. Something had been re-born in her out of the ages, some ancient power of domination; and something too had been re- born in her hearers, an ancestral response to her call.

She was speaking Norland, of which he understood not one word. What she said, as he learned afterwards, was that pirates were attacking her house and her father, and she summoned the men of the islands to their defence. She struck a note which reverberated through all their traditions, the note of peril from strangers-- Norse and Scots rovers, Algerian pirates, who had driven the folk to the caves of the hills. The Norlander is not a fighting man, but he has fighting strains in him if the right chord be touched. Moreover, these men had their blood hot and their spirit high from the Grind hunt. . . .

She saw Peter John, and she seemed to use him to point her appeal. An older man spoke and was answered with a frenzied shouting. Certain men were detailed to keep watch on the Grind--they drew themselves off from the rest as the speaker called their names. . . . Then suddenly Anna was no more on her platform. She had Peter John's hand in hers, and behind them, racing northward, was the better part of a hundred islanders babbling like hounds, and in each right hand a reddened whale-spear.

CHAPTER XV

Transformation by Fire

For sheer misery I give the night when the children were missing the top place in my experience. By dinner-time I was anxious; by midnight I was pretty well beside myself; but when morning came with no word of them, I had fallen into a kind of dull, aching torpor. Haraldsen, Lombard, and I were on our feet for ten hours, and we dragged the ancient servants after us till their legs gave out. My first thought was naturally for the kayaks, and we ascertained that they were not in the harbour. Gregarsen, the skipper of the now useless motor-boat, was positive that the children had been out in them in the morning, but he had a sort of notion that he had seen them return. The sea was like a mill-pond, so they could not have come to grief through ill weather. My special job was to range the coast, but nowhere on the east side of the island was there any sign of the kayaks, and I had to put the west side off till the next day. Lombard tried the fishing-lochs in case there had been a mishap there. As for Haraldsen I don't know what he did except to prowl about like a lost dog. He seemed almost demented, and hardly spoke a word.

When I returned to the House about 5.30, the riding lights of the Tjaldar across the Channel were just going out. I had a momentary idea that the children might have gone there, but I at once rejected it. Neither

Peter John nor Anna was the sort of person to condemn their belongings to a night of needless anxiety.

At the corner of the lawn, where a high trellis had been erected to shield a bowling green, I found Haraldsen looking a good deal the worse for wear. But he did not look maniacal, as I must have looked. It was rather as if his mind had withdrawn itself from the outer world altogether. His eyes were almost sightless, like those of an old dog which moons about the doors. He had been in a queer 'fey' mood, ever since we arrived on the Island, but Anna's disappearance seemed to have taken the pin out of his wits altogether.

He was staring owlishly at something which was making a commotion at the top of the trellis--staring helplessly and doing nothing about it. It was a bird which had somehow got tangled in the top wires, and was flapping wildly upside-down on the end of a string, and was obviously in a fair way to perish from apoplexy. I saw that it was Morag, caught by her lead.

It didn't take me long to extricate her, and get savagely bitten in the process. I saw the paper round her leg, and with some difficulty unwound it. My first feeling, as I read it, was a deep thankfulness. At any rate the children were still in the land of the living.

They were on the Tjaldar. I saw the little ship across the Channel. She had got up steam, and was moving away from her anchorage with her head to the north. But she would return. The message had said that she was our enemies' base, and that on that day they would attack us.

The news pulled me out of my stupefied misery into a fury of action. I shouted at Haraldsen as if he were deaf. 'They've got the children,' I cried. 'Out there on the Tjaldar! God knows how, but they've got 'em. They've cut the telephone and wrecked the motor-boat, and to-day they are coming for us. . . . D'you hear? The children are safe so far. But we must prepare to meet an attack. Don't look like a stuck pig, man. At any rate now we have something to bite on.'

I hustled him into the House, where we found a very gummy-eyed Lombard. I raked up some breakfast from a demoralized household, but I remember that none of us could eat much, though we swallowed a good many cups of tea. And all the time I was discussing our scanty defences, simply to keep my mind and those of the others from ugly speculations. . . . We had a pretty poor lay-out. None of the old servants could be trusted with a gun, for your Norlander knows little of fire-arms. The only man who might have been of any use was old Absalon the fowler down at the clachan, and he was bedridden. The fighting-men were Haraldsen, Lombard, myself, and Geordie Hamilton--all of us fair shots, and Haraldsen, as I had discovered, a bit of a marksman. Happily we had plenty of weapons and ammunition. But we had a big area to hold, and the House was ill-adapted for defence--it could be approached on too many sides. We were bound to be outnumbered, and we were badly handicapped by the fact that the enemy had the two children as hostages. From what Sandy had told me of D'Ingraville it was not likely that he would be too scrupulous in the use of them. . . .

Sandy! The memory of him was like a blow in the face. What in God's name had happened to him? Here were we up to our necks in a row of his devising, and no word of him! I pictured him held up by an accident somewhere on the road, and frantically trying to get a message through to an island which was now wholly cut off from the world.

I tried to think calmly and picture what an attack would be like. Our enemies were out for business, and their ways would not be gentle. What did they want? To occupy the House and ransack it at their leisure. Yes, but still more to get hold of Haraldsen. He was what really mattered. They must get their hands on him, and force him to do what they wanted. As for Lombard and me, they must silence us. Kill us, or hide us away somewhere for good. Or bribe us. The horrid thought struck me that they would try to bribe me with Peter John as the price.

I have never contemplated an uglier prospect, and the notion that the children were part of it made me sick at heart. No doubt the enemy would begin with overtures--Haraldsen and the House to be handed over--Lombard and myself to sign some kind of bond of conformity. When that was refused they would attack.

We might stall them off for a bit and do them a certain amount of damage, but in the end we must be overpowered. . . . Was there any hope? Only to protract the business as long as possible on the chance that something might turn up. I tried to make a picture of Sandy hurrying to our rescue, but got little comfort out of it. If he was going to do anything, he would have been here long ago.

The sole way of spinning out the affair was to keep Haraldsen away from their hands. So long as he was uncaptured they had not won. Therefore he must be got out of the House into hiding. Was there any place of concealment?

He was more reasonable than I expected. He forced his mind back from its wanderings, and his eyes became more like those of a rational being. He saw my point. I had been afraid that his bellicosity would make him refuse to keep out of the scrap, but Anna's loss seemed to have weakened the spirit in him. He agreed that our only chance was to delay his own capture as long as possible. . . . There was one hiding-place known only to Anna and himself. I have mentioned that to the north of the House, at the end of a kind of covered arcade used for pot-plants, stood the little stone cell of an Irish hermit who had brought Christianity to the Norlands and had been murdered by the sea-rovers. The elder Haraldsen had restored this, and had put a roof on it, not of living turf like the House, but of ordinary thatch. In the floor of the cell the workmen had discovered steps which led downward to the sea, ending in a cave in the cliffs at the north side of the harbour. The discovery had been kept secret--which was the only alternative to blocking the place up--and the entrance was through a trap carefully concealed by a heavy bench which old Haraldsen had had made of driftwood.

This seemed to be what we wanted. I told Haraldsen that he must get to it at once, taking with him a lantern and a packet of food. If the worst happened and we were all scuppered or kidnapped, the attack would still have failed if he remained at large. I told him not to try to get out at the sea end, for then he would be certainly taken, but to stay tight in the passage till the enemy had gone, and then to try what he could do in the way of getting help. The one thing that mattered was that he himself should keep out of their hands. Addled as his wits were, I think that he understood this. He looked at me with eyes like a willing, but stupid, dog's. Arn fitted him out with food and light, but the last thing he did was to go up to his bedroom and fetch a light sporting rifle and some clips of cartridges. 'I shall feel safer with this,' he said, and I saw no harm in his being armed. The enemy might find the passage, and the show conclude with a scrap in the bowels of the earth. I saw him into the cell, watched his lantern flickering down a stone staircase like a precipice, and pulled the bench back over the trap. There can have been no lack of ventilation in that passage, for a current of air drew up it like a tornado.

Then Lombard and I set ourselves to barricade the House. It wasn't a great deal that we could do, for the place was big and rambling, and had not been built for defence. We shuttered the windows, and stacked furniture at the doors, and at the back parts, where the entrance was simplest, made a kind of abattis of derelict machines like chaff-cutters and mangles and even an old weaver's loom. The ancient servants were no use except to watch certain entrances and give timely warning. To Geordie Hamilton, who was something of a shot, I gave the front of the House, his post being a little pavilion at the south end. He was to let nobody approach the main door, and challenge anybody who showed his face on the Terrace. Lombard I placed in command of the rear. He distrusted his prowess with a rifle, and preferred to trust to four double-barrelled shot- guns. There was not much of a field of fire in the back parts, owing to the rise of the hill, and any assault there was likely to be close-quarters fighting. For myself I chose the roof, which gave me a prospect of the whole terrain. I could see little of the Island, for the lift of the hill blocked the view to north and south and west, but I had the Channel clear before me, and that would give me early news of the Tjaldar.

So I sat down among the lush greenery of the roof, with a chimney- stack as cover, a revolver in my pocket, a couple of .240 magazine rifles beside me, and my spirits as low as I ever remembered them. The thought of Peter John made me sick at heart. The message on Morag's leg said they were both safe, but that was nothing; they were on the Tjaldar, and that meant in the enemy's power. D'Ingraville wasn't likely to fling away such a trump card. He would use these helpless children to the limit as bargaining counters, and if I refused to deal, he would not be scrupulous about the counters. . . . I remember wondering just how far his colleagues would approve of his methods--Troth and Barralty and the rest, who were probably more particular about the kind of crime in which they dabbled. But D'Ingraville would not pay much attention to the whimsies of sedentary folk who by this time must be putty in his hands. . . . I longed to see the Tjaldar appear, for, though that would mean the beginning of the end, it would also mean that I was within a mile or so of my son. I tried to concentrate my mind on a plan, but I simply could not think. I must wait and see how D'Ingraville opened the action.

It was a mild morning, growing closer as it neared midday. The visibility was only moderate, but the Channel was clear, and there was no Tjaldar in it. . . . Five minutes after twelve, just when I was thinking of taking a look round our defences, I saw the first sign of the enemy. Some one keeping well in cover came over the skirts of Snowfell, and took up position to the north of the House, about half a mile off. My glass showed me that he had a seaman's boots and jersey, and that he was armed. The timing must have been good, because five minutes later the sudden clamour of a flock of black-backed gulls to the south made me turn that way, and I saw a second man of the same type ensconce himself just behind the reservoir and rake the House and the gardens with his glasses. I knew now what was happening.

D'Ingraville was getting his vedettes placed, so as to prevent any movement out of the House. The earths were being stopped before the pack came up. . . . I turned my glass on Snowfell. There were two men squatting on its upper screes.

A thought struck me which gave me a moment of comfort. Why did he take these precautions? He must have thought, not only that we were helpless, but that we were unsuspecting. The breakdown of the telephone and the motor-boat might have alarmed us, but we had no cause to assume the near presence of the enemy. Or the Tjaldar as his base. But Anna and Peter John knew! Could they have escaped? Could D'Ingraville imagine that they were now in the House? . . . I rejected the vain hope. How could the children get out of the clutches of men who left nothing to chance? Or why should these men imagine that we could escape when we had nowhere to fly to? . . .

Nothing happened for an hour or two. I descended from my perch and made a tour of the House. Geordie Hamilton had seen nothing--he was too low down for any long views. Lombard too had not much of a prospect, and the watchmen on Snowfell were just beyond his radius of vision. I left Geordie lunching solidly off bread-and-cheese and beer, had a pow-wow with Lombard, and returned to my watch- tower. I noticed that the weather was changing. It was getting very dark to the east over Halder, the Channel was being flawed with odd little cat's-paws, and, though it was still close, I had the feeling of being in a hot room next to an ice box--as if something sharp and bitter were just round the corner.

Close on three o'clock there came a diversion. There was a shot behind me, and when I looked over the ridge of the roof I saw some stone splinters clattering off one of the byres. I hastened down to investigate, and found that it was Lombard who had drawn fire. He had remembered that Morag was immured in the cheese-house, and would probably be pretty thirsty. So he had set out to water her, and had been observed by a picket, who had fired a warning shot which sent him back to cover. The earth-stoppers were taking their job seriously.

A few minutes later we got our first news of the hounds. Round the seaward cliff north of the harbour came the bows of a ship. I had not seen the Tjaldar at close quarters before, and at first did not recognize her. As seen at her moorings under Halder she had looked a smaller craft. But with my glass I picked out her name. She was showing no colours, for the Danish flag was no longer at her masthead. . . .

I did not see her anchor and lower her boats. For she was no sooner off the mouth of the voe than the gloom which had been brooding over the Channel burst in the father and mother of a storm. I would have been beaten off my perch if I had not found some shelter from the chimney stack. In a minute or two the grass of the roof was white with hailstones the size of a sparrow's eggs.

The garden, the terrace, the hillside looked deep in snow. And with the hail came a wind that cut like a knife. It must have been the better part of half an hour before the tornado passed, and I could look seaward at anything but a blinding scurry.

There was the Tjaldar, white as a ship marooned in the Arctic ice, rocking in a sea which had suddenly become sullen and yeasty. Her starboard ladder was down, but there was no sign of boats. These must have landed. On her deck I thought I saw the flutter of a woman's dress. . . . And then I looked at the foreground, where a path from the harbour climbed on to the terrace. In the same second of time I saw heads appear above the terrace's edge, and heard Geordie Hamilton's challenge. The heads disappeared. I found a better stance in the corner of my chimney-stack and picked up one of the rifles. I considered that presently I might have to get busy.

The Tjaldar's party were no fools. Some of them must have gone south under the cliff to their picket stationed beside the reservoir, and learned from him how we had placed our men. I had hoped that Geordie had kept himself well in cover, but he must have shown himself to the sentry, who told the new-comers of his whereabouts. Anyhow, the next thing I heard was a roar like a bull's from Geordie's little pavilion, and I had a glimpse of a confused struggle there which ended in a sudden silence. The Scots Fusilier had been overpowered, and one of the three defenders put out of action. . . .

The next act followed fast. The terrace became suddenly populous, and the new-comers were unchallenged. D'Ingraville had not underrated his opponents, for to match our miserable trio he had brought at least twenty. I did not count the numbers beneath me, but there were at least a score, and there were also the pickets to be reckoned with. Clearly they knew all about us, for, now that Geordie Hamilton had been dealt with, they seemed at their ease. They were following a prearranged plan, based on exact knowledge of the place, for some made their way to the back parts, and some to the arcade which led to the hermit's cell, but more waited at the foot of the steps which led to the main door. They were grouped in two bodies with an alley between them, and seemed to be waiting for somebody.

Who that was soon appeared. Up the alley came three men. I had no doubt about who they were, for I remembered Sandy's descriptions. D'Ingraville was the tall fellow in the yachting cap and grey flannels--he had grown his beard again and looked like a naval officer, except that his light, springy stride was scarcely the walk of the quarter-deck. The dark, lean man, with the long face made in two planes, was Carreras the Spaniard. And beyond doubt the slim one, in the much-stained blue suit and the cap a little over one eye, was Martel, the Belgian.

Of the others I had only a vague general impression, as of something hard, tough, and ruthless, but well-disciplined. This might be a posse of gangsters, but they would obey orders like a Guards battalion. But the three leaders made the clearest and sharpest impact on my mind. They were perhaps three hundred yards away from me, but their personalities seemed as vivid as if they were in the same room. I had an overpowering impression of a burning vitality which was also evil, a glowing, incandescent evil. It cried out from the taut lines of D'Ingraville, from his poise like that of a waiting leopard. It clamoured from Carreras's white, pitiless face. Above all it seemed to me that it shouted from the Belgian Martel's mean, faun-like presence. It was the last one I hated worst. D'Ingraville was a fallen angel, Carreras a common desperado, but Martel seemed to be apache, sewer-rat, and sneak-thief all in one.

They had something to say to us. I moved out from the shelter of the chimney, was instantly seen, and covered by twenty guns. I dropped my own rifle and held up my hand.

'Will you gentlemen kindly tell me your business?' I shouted against the east wind.

It was D'Ingraville who replied. He bowed, and his two queer companions did the same.

'Sir Richard Hannay, isn't it?' he said, and his pleasant voice coming down wind was easily heard. 'We want a talk with Mr. Haraldsen. But it would perhaps save time--and trouble--if I could first have a word with Lord Clanroyden.'

'Sorry,' I shouted. 'Mr. Haraldsen is not at home. He has left the island.'

From where I stood I could see the smile on his face, repeated in those of his two companions. They knew very well that I was lying.

'How unfortunate!' he said. 'Well, what about Lord Clanroyden?'

Did they know that we were without Sandy? Or was this a fishing question? Or did they believe that he was in the House? Anyhow, it was not for me to enlighten them.

'If you have anything to say you can say it to me,' I said. 'Go ahead, for it's devilish cold waiting.'

'A roof-top is scarcely the place for a conference,' said D'Ingraville. 'Won't you come down, Sir Richard, from your eyrie? It's a cold day, as you justly observe, and we might talk indoors.'

'All right,' I said, 'I'll come down.' And then, as I looked at the three men, I had a sudden inspiration. I had meant to ask that D'Ingraville should be their envoy, when I observed the man Martel standing in an odd position, his left arm flung across his chest and clutching the biceps of his right. That was an attitude I had seen before, and it woke in me a wild surmise. It might be meant as a sign. My mind was pretty hopeless, for their desire to talk seemed to me certain proof that they wanted to make terms about the children, but it was just not sodden enough to miss this little thing.

'You can keep yourself for Lord Clanroyden,' I told D'Ingraville. 'I'll do my talking to that other chap--the one on your left. Send him forward, and I'll let him indoors.'

'If there's any dirty work,' said D'Ingraville, his voice suddenly becoming shrill, 'you'll pay for it bloodily. You understand that?'

'I do. I'll leave the door open so that you can keep your eye on me, and plug me if I try to be funny.'

I went downstairs with an ugly void at the bottom of my stomach. Old Arn was on guard at the main door, and had built up a perfect battlement of furniture, which it took some minutes to clear away. When I got the door opened and the east wind in my face, I saw that the three men had moved nearer--close to the foot of the steps. I beckoned to Martel.

'You two stay where you are,' I said. 'This man and I will be inside the hall out of the wind. We'll be well in sight.' I turned and re-entered the House. I heard footsteps on the stone and was conscious that Martel had joined me. My heart was in my mouth, for I was certain that his first word would be about the children and the price we were prepared to pay for them.

I swung round on him. 'Well?' I demanded. 'What do you want?'

But the words died away on my lips.

Said the man called Martel, 'Dick, my lad, we've made rather a hash of this business.'

God knows how he had managed it. There was no ordinary makeup about him, no false moustache or dyed hair or that sort of thing. But in some subtle way he had degraded himself--that is the only word for it. Everything about him--slanting eyebrows, furtive eyes, tricky mouth, slouching shoulders--was mean and sinister, because he chose that it should be so. But when he looked me in the face, with that familiar twinkle in his eyes and that impish pucker of the lips, he was the friend I knew best in the world.

There was just an instant when his eyes had the old insouciance. Then they became very grave.

'We must talk fast, for there isn't much time. I've made a deuce of a mess of things, and I thought I was being rather clever. First--to ease your mind. Peter John and the girl are safe--for the moment, at any rate.'

'Thank God!' I said fervently. Such a load was lifted from my heart that I felt almost confident. But Sandy's next words disillusioned me.

'I've done most of what I set out to do. I've got Barralty and his lot scared into fits. No more high-handed crimes for them! They're sitting in the Tjaldar sweating with terror. . . . I've collected enough evidence to keep them good for the rest of their lives, and incidentally to hang D'Ingraville and most of his crowd. Do you realize that up to now we had nothing against him that any court would listen to? . . . So I had to make him commit himself. You see that? He had to attack Haraldsen in his island, and have a show-down once and for all. Well, I thought I had got him taped. I was counting on Haraldsen doing as he promised to do, and having a hefty push of young islanders to defend him. I would know D'Ingraville's plans, being his chief staff-officer, and so could play into their hands. And lo and behold! when I get here, I find there's not a soul in the island but dotards, and the whole place is as unprotected as a stranded whale.' He stopped and sniffed, and then said a strange thing. 'Just the weather for the Grind,' he said. 'Gad, that would be a bit of luck.'

Then he demanded, 'Where's Haraldsen?' I told him and he nodded. 'I hope he'll stay in his earth. . . . See here, Dick. The layout as I planned it was that D'Ingraville should be encouraged to attack you and so commit himself. But before he had time to do any harm, your supports would arrive and hold him. Well, that's a wash-out, for there are no supports. I have got word to the Danish destroyer that patrols the fishing banks. She's on her way, but she's coming from the Westmanns, and can't be here much before midnight. That gives D'Ingraville time to do the deuce of a lot of damage. I tried to have the attack delayed, and I managed to have it put off till now--it was arranged for this morning--principally because I got them hunting for the children. But now we're for it. It's seven or eight hours till midnight, time enough for D'Ingraville to cut all our throats if he wants to. If he gets hold of Haraldsen there may be some ugly work. If it's only you and Lombard he'll be content perhaps with ransacking the House. How long can you stick it?'

'An hour maybe,' I said. 'We've no manpower to keep them out. They are old hands, and won't give us much of a chance of picking them off piecemeal.'

'They won't,' he said. 'If you can make it three hours we might do the trick. . . . I'll go back and report that you won't treat. I'll say you can agree to nothing without Haraldsen's consent, and that he isn't here, and that you'll do your damnedest to defend his property. I'll try to tangle up things at the other end. I'll have to come over to you some time, but I'll choose my own time for that--the moment when I can be of most use. If D'Ingraville finds that he has been diddled and gets his hands on me, then my number is up, and I won't be any use to you as a corpse.'

As Sandy spoke I had a vivid memory of a bush-crowned hillock in the African moonlight, when, to defend another Haraldsen, Lombard and I had imperilled our lives. I seemed to have done all this before, and to know what was coming next, and that foreknowledge gave me confidence. I must have smiled, for Sandy looked at me sharply.

'You're taking this calmly, Dick. You know it's a devilish tight fix, don't you? The one hope is midnight and the Danish boat. Spin things out till then without a tragedy and we have won. I must be off.' He waved his hand to D'Ingraville at the foot of the steps and turned to go. His last word was, 'Keep Haraldsen off the stage for Heaven's sake. He's our weakest point.' He went down the steps, and the next second I had clanged the great hall-door behind him and dropped the bolts. I left old Arn piling up the barricade again and skipped up to my post behind the chimney-stack, with the intention of doing some fancy shooting. I saw Sandy conferring with D'Ingraville and Carreras, looking once again the murderous scallywag.

Suddenly, in a pause of the wind, a voice rang out, a voice coming from the north, from the hermit's cell at the end of the arcade.

'Off the terrace,' it shouted. 'Back to your sties, you swine, or I shoot.'

It was Haraldsen--there could be no mistaking that voice--but it seemed to be raised to an unearthly pitch and compass, for it filled the place like the rumour of the sea in a voe. D'Ingraville's ruffians were accustomed to the need for cover, and suddenly the whole gang seemed to shrink in size, as it splayed out and crouched with an uneasy eye on the north. All but one--Carreras. I don't know what took the man. Perhaps he was looking for shelter in the lee of the steps and the House--at any rate, he moved forward instead of back. A shot cracked out, he flung up one arm, spun half-left, and dropped on his face.

In an instant every man of them was flat on the ground, worming his way back to the terrace wall which would give refuge from that deadly rifle. Then the voice spoke again, and what it said must have considerably surprised one at least of the crawlers.

'Clanroyden,' it shouted. 'Back to the House with you! Quick, man! Do as I tell you. I can't handle that scum if there's a friend mixed up in it.'

How on earth he saw who Martel was I cannot tell. But it was a foolish move, and it came very near being the end of Sandy. It was the words 'Back to the House' that did the mischief, for they enabled D'Ingraville to identify the man Martel, when otherwise it might have seemed a mere bluff. At any rate so Sandy thought, for to my horror I saw him scramble to his feet from behind a clump of Arctic willows. He knew his danger, for he twisted and side- slipped like a rabbit. I was choking with fright, for I couldn't get down to the main door in time, and there was Arn's barricade to get out of the way: the front of the House was bare of cover, and till he got round the corner of it he was in the centre of an easy field of fire. But only one shot followed him, and I'm pretty certain it did not come from D'Ingraville; he must have been confident of getting his revenge at leisure. The shot missed its mark--I believe that the reason was that the fugitive at the moment stumbled over the dead Carreras. In a few seconds he was out of my orbit of sight. He would be safe in the back parts for the time being, unless he fell in with a stray picket.

Presently he was out of my mind as well, for all my attention was fixed on D'Ingraville. He had got his main force under cover of the terrace wall--out of Haraldsen's danger, and it was plain enough what he proposed to do. It was child's play to take Haraldsen in flank and rear. The cell's door and window opened to the south, and its inmate could protect himself in that direction, but what could he do against an attack from above by way of the thatched roof? Three sturdy fellows with five minutes' work could uncover the badger's earth.

A figure squeezed in beside me behind the chimney-stack. 'A close call,' said Sandy. 'The bullet went through my pocket. If I hadn't tripped and turned side on, I'd be dead. . . . What's our friend up to? Oh, I see. Fire. They'll burn the thatch and smoke him out. This is our worst bit of luck. If only that damned fool had stuck in his burrow, instead of trying to be heroic. I dare say he's off his head. Did you hear his voice? Only a madman's could ring like that. And he gave me away, the blighter, though God knows how he spotted me! Another proof of lunacy! This show's turning out pretty badly, Dick. In about half an hour D'Ingraville will have got Haraldsen, and very soon he'll have got me, and he won't be nice to either of us.'

A kind of dusk had fallen owing to the cloud-wrack drifting up with the east wind, and the prospect from my roof-top was only of leaden skies and a black, fretful sea. The terrace was empty, but I could see what was happening beyond it, and I watched it with the fascinated eyes of a spectator at a cinema, held by what I saw, but subconsciously aware of the artifice of it all. My mind simply refused to take this mad world into which I had strayed as an actual thing, though my reason told me that it was a grim enough reality. I caught a glimpse of one figure after another among the stunted shrubberies and sunk plots which lay north and east of the hermit's cell. Then an exclamation from Sandy called my attention to the cell itself. There was a man on its roof pouring something out of a bucket. 'Petrol,' Sandy whispered. 'I guessed right. They'll burn him out.'

A tongue of flame shot up which an instant later became a globe of fire. A spasm of wind swept it upwards in a long golden curl. Directly beneath me I saw men appear again on the terrace. It was safe enough now--for Haraldsen could scarcely shoot from a fiery furnace.

D'Ingraville was looking up at us, for he had guessed where Sandy would have taken position.

'You have kept your promise, Lord Clanroyden,' he cried. 'I am glad of that, for this would have been a dull place without you.'

Sandy showed himself fully.

'Thank you,' he said. 'I like to keep my word.'

'You have won the first trick,' the pleasant voice continued. 'At least you have deceived me very prettily, and I am not easily deceived. I make you my compliments. But I don't think you will win the rubber. When we have secured that madman, I will give myself the pleasure of attending to you.'

I have called his voice pleasant, and for certain it was now curiously soft and gentle, though notably clear. But there was something feline in it, like the purring of a cat. There he stood with his wild crew about him, elegant, debonair, confident, and as pitiless as sin. The sight of him struck a chill in my heart. In a very little we should be at his mercy, and it was hours--hours-- before there was any hope of succour. I was not alarmed for myself, or even for Haraldsen, who seemed now to have got outside the pale of humanity; but I saw nothing before Sandy except destruction, for two men had wagered against each other their lives. . . . And the children!

Where and in what peril were they crouching in this accursed island? . . .

Suddenly there was a roar which defied the wind and made D'Ingraville's voice a twitter. It was such a thunder of furious exultation as might have carried a Viking chief into his last battle. Out from the cell came Haraldsen. His figure was lit up by the blazing roof and every detail was clear. He was wearing his queer Norland clothes, and his silver buckles and buttons caught the glint of fire. One part of his face was scorched black, the rest was of a ghostly pallor. His shaggy hair was like a coronet of leaves on a tall pine. He had no weapon and he held his hands before him as if he were blind and groping. Yet he moved like a boulder rushing down a mountain, and it seemed scarcely a second before he was below me on the terrace.

There was no mistaking his purpose. The man had gone berserk, and was prepared to face a host and rend them with his naked fingers. Had I been near enough to see his eyes, I knew that they would have been fixed and glassy. . . . Once in Beira I saw a Malay run amok with a great knife. The crowd he was in were almost all armed, but the queer thing was that not a shot was fired at the man, and he had cut a throat and split two skulls before he was tripped up and sat upon by a drunken sailor coming down a side street, who hadn't a notion what was afoot. That was what happened now. There were men behind him with guns, there were twenty men on the terrace with rifles and pistols, yet this tornado with death in its face was permitted to sweep down on them unhindered. A palsy seemed to have taken them, like what happens, I have been told, to mountaineers in the track of a descending avalanche.

What befell next must have taken many minutes, but to me it seemed to be a mere instant of time. I was not conscious till it was all over that Sandy beside me had grabbed my wrist in his excitement and dug his nails into my flesh. . . . D'Ingraville was standing in the front of a little group which seemed to close round him as the whirlwind approached. Haraldsen swept them aside like dead leaves, but whether the compulsion was physical or moral I cannot tell. He plucked D'Ingraville in his arms as I might have lifted a child of three. Then, and not till then, there was a shot. D'Ingraville had used his gun, but I know not what became of the bullet. It certainly did not touch Haraldsen.

Haraldsen held up his captive to the heavens like a priest offering a sacrifice. He had drawn himself to his full height, and in the brume to my scared eyes looked larger than human. D'Ingraville wriggled half out of his clutch, and seemed to be tossed in the air and re-caught in a fiercer grip. The next I knew was that Haraldsen had turned north again and was racing back towards the hermit's cell.

Then the shooting began. The men on the terrace aimed at his legs-- I saw rifle bullets kick up flurries of dust from the flower beds. But for some unknown reason they missed him. The men near the cell tried to stop him, but he simply trampled them underfoot. Only one of them fired a shot, and we found the mark of it later in a furrow through his hair. . . . He was past them, and at the blazing cell where the last rafter was now dropping into a fiery pit. For a moment I thought he was going to make a burnt-offering of D'Ingraville, who by this time must have had the life half squeezed out of him in that fierce embrace. But no. He avoided the cell, and swung half-right to the downland above the sea.

By this time he was out of sight of the terrace, but in full view of Sandy and me on the roof-top. We might write off D'Ingraville now, for he was beyond hope. Haraldsen's pace never slackened. He took great leaps among the haggs and boulders, and by some trick of light his figure seemed to increase instead of diminish with distance, so that when he came out on the cliff edge, and was silhouetted against the sky, it was gigantic.

Then I remembered one of his island tales which he had told us on our first arrival--told with a gusto and realism like that of an eyewitness. It was the story of one Hallward Skullsplitter who had descended a thousand years ago upon the Island of Sheep and cruelly ravaged it. But a storm had cut him off with two companions from his ships, and the islanders had risen, bound the Vikings hand and foot, and hurled them into the sea from the top of Foulness. . . . It was Foulness I was now looking at, where the land mouth of the harbour ran up to a sea-cliff of three hundred feet.

I had guessed right. At first I thought that Haraldsen meant to seek his own death also. But he steadied himself on the brink, swung D'Ingraville in his great arms, and sent him hurtling into the void. For a second he balanced himself on the edge and peered down after him into the depths. Then he turned and staggered back. I got my glasses on to him and saw that he had dropped on the turf like a dead man.

A tremendous drama is apt to leave one limp and dulled. D'Ingraville was gone, but his jackals remained, and now they would be more desperate than ever with no leader to think for them. Our lives were still on a razor's edge, and it was high time for a plan of campaign. But Sandy and I clutched each other limply like two men with vertigo.

'Poor devil!' said Sandy at last. 'He can't have known what was coming. Haraldsen must have hugged him senseless.'

'We're quit of a rascal,' I said; 'but we've got a maniac on our hands.'

'I don't think so. The fury is out of him. He returned to type for a little, and is now his sober commonplace self again.' He held out his watch. 'Not yet seven! Five hours to keep these wolves at bay. Hungry and leaderless wolves--a nasty proposition! . . . Great God! What is that?'

He was staring southward, and when I looked there I saw a sight which bankrupted me of breath. The murky gloaming was lit to the north by the last flames of the hermit's cell, but to the south there was a breach in the gloom and a lagoon of clear sky was spreading. Already the rim of the southern downs was outlined sharply against it. In that oasis of light I saw strange things happening. . . . At sea a flotilla of boats was nearing the harbour on a long tack, and one or two, driven by sweeps, were coming up the shore. Across the hill moved an army of men, not less than a hundred strong, sweeping past the reservoir, overflowing the sunk lawn, men shaggy and foul with blood, and each with a reeking spear.

The sight was clean beyond my comprehension, and I could only stare and gasp. It was as if a legion of trolls had suddenly sprung out of the earth, for these men were outside all my notions of humanity. They had the troll-like Norland dress, now stained beyond belief with mud and blood; their hair and eyes were like the wild things of the hills; the cries that came from their throats were not those of articulate-speaking men, and each had his shining, crimsoned lance. . . . Dimly I saw the boats enter the harbour and their occupants swarm into the Tjaldar like cannibal islanders attacking a trading ship. Dimly I saw D'Ingraville's men below me cast one look at the murderous invasion and then break wildly for the shore. I didn't blame them. The sight of that maniacal horde had frozen my very marrow.

Dimly I heard Sandy mutter, 'My God, the Grind has come.'

I didn't know what he meant, but something had come which I understood. In the forefront of the invaders were Anna and Peter John.

CHAPTER XVI

The Riddle of the Tablet

I have often wondered how we should define the courage of the ordinary rapscallion. A contempt, doubtless, for certain kinds of danger with which he is familiar and which for him have lost the terrors of the unknown. Not a settled habit of mind, for often he will be paralysed by the unexpected, and thrown into a panic by what is outside his experience. The first happened when Haraldsen went berserk and plucked D'Ingraville out of the heart of his gang; the second, when several score of ensanguined Norlanders turned the knees of the gang to water. Certainly it was the wildest spectacle I ever beheld, and he would have been a stout fellow who stood up against that nightmare army of bloodstained trolls. . . . As a matter of fact, two of the gang did put up some kind of resistance with their guns, and perished as if they had been pilot-whales. I doubt if the Norlanders knew what they were doing. Like Haraldsen they had gone back to type--they were their forebears of a thousand years ago making short work of a pirate crew.

The rest, who surrendered like sheep, were not maltreated, but were trussed up like bundles of hay with the home-made ropes that every Norlander carries with him. The detachment in the boats who had swarmed over the Tjaldar behaved with extreme circumspection. I fancy that the atmosphere of a modern steamer got them out of their atavistic dreams quicker than their kinsmen on the land. They were civil to Barralty and his friends, though they found it hard to find a common tongue, and, having brought the vessel round to a better anchorage and left everything shipshape about her, they came ashore soberly to take counsel with the rest of us.

For the madness did not take long to ebb. The case of Haraldsen was curious. As soon as I saw that there was no fear of resistance and that the Norlanders were ready to do whatever Anna told them, I started off with Peter John for the top of the cliffs, for Haraldsen seemed to be the one big problem left. I found him sitting up on the turf, with his huge fists stuck in his eyes like a sleepy child. I think it was the sight of Peter John, who had always been his close friend, that gave him a bridge back to the ordinary world.

'Anna's all right, sir,' said the boy. 'She's down there with all the Norland men behind her.'

'Good!' he said. 'They'll do what she tells them. Have the Grind come to my island?'

Peter John nodded.

'It is the first time for ten years,' said Haraldsen. 'I must go down and arrange about food and drink. The Grind are a hungry and thirsty job, and a dirty one.'

His wits were still wool-gathering, and I tried to steady them.

'You're safe,' I said, 'and the House, and Lord Clanroyden and all of us. You need never give another thought to this trouble.'

'I am glad of that,' he said dully. 'There was a lot of trouble. Where is the tall man with the beard?'

'Dead,' I said, 'in the sea.'

'He would be' was the odd answer. 'He came out of the sea, and he has returned to it.'

Then he yawned, his limbs relaxed, and before I could count five he was fast asleep. I knew better than to waken him. We got together a sort of litter, and had him carried down to the House, where he was put to bed and slept for thirty-two hours. He woke ravenous, had a bath and shaved, and then ate the better part of a ham and emptied three coffee-pots. He remembered not one solitary thing between his discovery that the children were lost and his waking in his own bed, and it wasn't for me to enlighten him. But one thing that berserk fit had done for him: it had drained him for good of timidity. He was now as steady-nerved and confident as his father had been, and a hundred per cent. more restful.

The fishery boat arrived an hour before midnight, by which time we had taken counsel, not only among ourselves, but with the folk on the Tjaldar and had settled on our story. It was no good having the true business broadcast to the world. Barralty and his people had gone yachting with D'Ingraville, who had picked his crew and had forced them into an attack on the Island of Sheep for his own purposes. They had refused to come on shore, and had seen nothing of the doings on land. The fortunate advent of the Grind had averted tragedy. The children had found the Islanders and had led them to the House, where we had been putting up a forlorn defence. Haraldsen had picked off one of the desperadoes, and had fought with D'Ingraville on the cliff-top to the latter's doom. (Sandy could provide a dossier of D'Ingraville which would prevent unavailing regrets about his end.) The coming of the Islanders had led to the general surrender of the invaders, two of the latter being the only casualties.

D'Ingraville's gang was a collection of blackguards of various races which it was left for the Copenhagen courts to sort out and deal with. Most of them were rather urgently wanted by their several countries. The Tjaldar, which had been chartered in Troth's name, had the rudiments of a regular crew who had not been mixed up in the piracy, and it was arranged that, under the convoy of the Danish destroyer, she should return to Aberdeen.

With the clearing away of our anxieties came a clearing of the skies. The Norlands seemed to swim into a zone of halcyon weather-- sunlit days, calm seas, and wonderful, long-lit, golden evenings. When I came there first I thought I was getting outside the world, and then presently I found that I was indeed outside the world in a nightmarish limbo. Now that the nightmare had gone, the Island seemed a happy place, where life could be worthily lived in the company of sea-tides, and friendly wild things, and roaring mornings, and blissful drowsy afternoons. To me it was Fosse, and to Sandy it was Laverlaw, but both, so to speak, set in a world of new dimensions. To Lombard, the man whom I had once thought of as degenerated into a sleek mediocrity, it was a revelation. It had brought back to him something of his youth and his youth's dreams.

I remember that he and I sat together on the highest point of Snowfell, looking across the empty Channel to Haldar, bright as a jewel in the sunshine. The Tjaldar and the fishery boat were at anchor below us; beside us curlew and plover kept up a gentle complaining; around us, except in the east, there was a great circle of glittering sea. The landscape was as delicate and unsubstantial as the country of a dream.

'I shall come back to the Norlands,' said Lombard, shaking out his pipe. 'It was good of you to let me into this show, Hannay; I hope I haven't misconducted myself.'

'You were the steadiest of the lot,' I said warmly. 'You never gave a cheep even when things looked ugliest.'

He laughed.

'I often wanted to. But I'm glad to find I haven't gone quite soft. I never really thought I had. But I've let myself get dull and flat. That's what this business has taught me. I want to get air and space round me, for I live in a dashed stuffy world. . . . So I'm coming back to the Norlands to make my soul.'

I suppose I must have looked at him in surprise, for he laughed again. 'You know well enough what I mean. The Norlands are a spiritual place which you won't find on any map. Every man must discover his own Island of Sheep. You and Clanroyden have found yours, and I'm going to find mine.'

My last recollection is of two meals in the great hall of the House. The first was the night of the coming of the Grind, or rather the small hours of the following morning. The Danish fishery boat had arrived; the malefactors were safely stowed away; and, while Haraldsen lay in his bed upstairs, in the hall were gathered the Norlanders who had saved us, both the boat parties and those who had come by land--the officers of the destroyer--Sandy, Lombard, and myself--and Anna and Peter John. The children seemed to have got their second wind, for, having been very tired and drowsy at first, they woke up before midnight to an astonishing vigour. The Danish officers, who knew the Norlands well and also Haraldsen, were the friendliest of souls. As for the Norlanders, to them the Island of Sheep was the home of legend and the Haraldsen family the centre of their mythology. At first they were shy and laggard, for your Norlander is an excellent giver but a poor taker. But they were very hungry, and Arn had provided a feast of fat things, and in twenty minutes they had squared their elbows to the job and were as merry as grigs.

I shall never forget that scene. Arn had supplemented the electric light by several score of candles, and the huge place was as bright as day. The tapestries, the carved grotesques, the many ships' models, the curious panelling--their minutest lines and their subtlest colours were displayed in that fierce radiance. And below sat a company which might have come out of a picture in a child's Grimm. Many of the islanders wore their cowls, for they were in doubt as to whether that vast hall should be reckoned a dwelling. And at the head of the long oaken table, in a chair like a galley's beak, sat Anna. I had never seen anything quite like her. She had changed from rough clothes into a white silk gown, and the coronel of lights under which she sat made her seem a creature of gold and ivory. She ruled the feast, too. It was she who gave the toasts; it was she who in musical Norland thanked our preservers. Here was the true fairy-tale princess, the Queen out of the North, and to that wild gathering she lent an air of high ceremonial. But she was a stony-hearted princess, for she insisted on toasting

Peter John. I don't know what she said about him, but it got the Norlanders out of their seats and he was hoisted--Morag angrily protesting--on a dozen shoulders. A speech was demanded, and his was of two sentences. 'Thank you all very much.--Anna, you beast, I'll pay you out for this.'

The second meal was the following day, when the Tjaldar was about to sail under the convoy of the Danish destroyer, and the islanders had returned to their homes. We had the Tjaldar party to dinner, and Haraldsen himself was the host. I have never been present on a more fantastic occasion. Sandy said we had to do it, to mark the close of hostilities, but it was a pretty cruel business for the ex-conspirators. Albinus was a dingy figure, still considerably rattled. Barralty was the frightened intellectual trying to recover his poise, but he was a long way short of getting back his self-esteem. The lady was the most composed. She wore a charming gown, and had the wit not to make any pretences. They had got themselves into an ugly show, and were now quit of it and correspondingly grateful. But they all looked at Sandy in some awe. I gathered that, as Martel, he had been chiefly responsible for scaring the life out of them.

I think I may say that we all behaved well. Lombard talked the City to Barralty and Troth, Sandy had some polite things to say about politics, a great deal of information was vouchsafed about the Norlands, some of Haraldsen's treasures were exhibited, and Miss Ludlow was caressingly sweet to Anna. I should add that old Arn excelled himself, that the food was perfection, and that the best of Haraldsen's cellar was forthcoming. This last point was especially appreciated by Troth, who soon relaxed into bonhomie. I found him a very friendly fellow, with sensible notions about the Essex creeks and tides.

It was he who, before they left, made an attempt at an apology.

'I hope, Mr. Haraldsen,' he said, 'that we're all going to forgive and forget.'

Haraldsen looked down on him from his great height.

'I ask for nothing better,' he said. 'I understand that you feel some grievance against me, Mr. Troth. On my father's account, I think, and for your own father's sake? Well, we are willing that some reparation should be made. Lord Clanroyden will tell you what.'

Sandy took from his pocket something in a chamois-leather wrapping.

'This belonged to the late Mr. Haraldsen,' he said. 'It came into my hands in rather an odd way, about which I wrote to the papers. I do not intend to hand it over to the British Museum. I propose, Mr. Troth, to give it to you in full settlement of any claims you may think you have against the late Mr. Haraldsen's estate.'

He took from a bag the tablet of emerald jade which he had shown us at Fosse.

Troth received it with a face in which surprise, greed, and a kind of shame were mingled. He turned the lovely thing over in his hands, made as if to read the inscription, and then looked at Sandy a little confusedly.

'D'you mean that, Lord Clanroyden?' he asked. 'It's extraordinarily good of you. Of course I give up any claims--I had already given them up. D'you mean me to act on what this tablet may tell me?'

'Certainly.'

'And to keep for myself whatever I may find?'

'Certainly. For yourself, and any friends you want to share with you.'

Troth peered at the inscription.

'One side's in Latin. The other side--the important side--I suppose I can get that translated?'

'It has been already translated,' said Sandy gravely. 'I have seen to that.'

'And you found?' The eternal treasure-hunter was in Troth's voice.

'We found a list of the Twelve Major Virtues and the Ninety-Nine Names of God!'

THE END

www.ingramcontent.com/pod-product-compliance
Lightning Source LLC
Chambersburg PA
CBHW020222110726
47898CB00004B/1114

* 9 7 8 1 4 7 3 3 1 7 6 9 7 *